THE LONGEST WALK

THE
LONGEST
WALK

An Odyssey of the Human Spirit

GEORGE MEEGAN

DODD, MEAD & COMPANY
NEW YORK

Published by Dodd, Mead & Company, Inc.
71 Fifth Avenue, New York, NY 10003
Manufactured in the United States of America.
First Edition

1 2 3 4 5 6 7 8 9 10

Library of Congress Cataloging-in-Publication Data

Meegan, George.
    The longest walk: an odyssey of the human spirit / George
Meegan—1st ed.
    p. cm.
    1. America—Description and travel—1981– 2. Meegan,
George—Journeys—America. 3. Walking—America. I. Title.
E27.5 M44 1987
917'.04537—dc19   87-32957
ISBN 0-396-08723-X

Yes, weekly from Southampton,
Great steamers white and gold,
Go rolling down to Rio.
(Roll down, roll down to Rio!)
And I'd like to roll to Rio
Some day before I'm old.

—Rudyard Kipling

Was that what travel meant?
An exploration of the desert of memory, rather
than those around me?

—Claude Lévi-Strauss
Tristes Tropiques

to Anthony Geoffrey Meegan,
brother and friend,

the late John Geoffrey Meegan,
father, who once raced
a little boy down our alley,

and

the late Mrs. Frieda Meegan,
Mum, the greatest mum of all

Contents

CONTENTS

ACKNOWLEDGMENTS

I would like to thank the following people who, along with of course so very many unnamed, made my odyssey and this book possible.

Anthony Geoffrey Meegan—Brother. At considerable personal sacrifice Anthony supported my mad schemes year after unrewarding year. He always saw to it that my family managed to get by, rescued me financially at various times, and most recently all but saved this book. All England can be proud of him, as I am, a true brother, a fine friend.

Dr. Hideo and Mrs. Toseko Matsumoto, my father- and mother-in-law. Their total and unflinching support of my family and dream made the long march possible. These are two truly gracious people.

Mr. Sebastian Snow, explorer, adventurer, and author, for his advice and encouragement. "It hasn't been done and ought to be done," he said.

To go back to near the beginning, Mr. Len Brown and Mr. Brian Fitzpatrick, leaders of the Fourth Gillingham (Rainham) Sea Scout troop, whose devotion to youth first struck the spark of adventure within me.

Mr. Assad Quayyum, F.C.S., and Captain Agustin Stebljaj, who financed much of my journey via the eccentric voyage of the *Omar* (1976).

Mr. Anthony Sharp of Berghaus, Newcastle, who kept my

ACKNOWLEDGMENTS

feet shod over several years in their Sella Boots and were totally alone in their sponsorship—I thank them for their exceptional faith.

Mr. Tommy Smithson of Brigham and Cowan Dry Dock on the River Tyne at South Shields, England, who built the Yoshikarts.

Mr. Tony Lack, F.R.G.S., for advice.

Lord Vestey, who granted me working passage to South America.

Mr. William S. Green of New York City, the brilliant general editor who reduced my bloated, partially handwritten manuscript (I brought it to his apartment in a milk crate) into this book. Bill constantly urged me to enroll in a handwriting course.

The late Mr. Allen Klots of Dodd, Mead, my courtly, kindly, and ever-gentle publisher.

Ms. Meredith Bernstein of New York City and Mr. Mark Hamilton of London, literary agents.

Mr. John Brooks, editor of the *South American Handbook*, who so splendidly corrected the Latin American sections and so stalwartly supported this book during its dark days of near-destruction.

Mr. John Muir, founder and director of the Prospect Park Environmental Center, Brooklyn, who is the virtual godfather of this book. John found not only my agent but also my general editor and offered superb criticisms throughout—a man of many parts.

Mr. John Walker, who on the strength of a five-minute chat found the publisher and encouraged me through a rough year.

Mr. George Greenfield of London, without whose name no adventure book is truly complete, for advice and a helping hand.

Typists Irene Hodgkinson, Rede Action Group; Yoshiko Meegan; Nita Camp; Cathreen Weaver; Stella Lucas; Laura Dennison Vargas; Nancy Sparrow; Betse and Nica Green. Next time I'll use a sharper pencil.

ACKNOWLEDGMENTS

Mr. Tim Jensen, Esq., of the Volunteer Lawyers for the Arts, New York City.

Rob Inglis, for his deep consideration of me and his inspirational songs based on my journey.

Peter Stallwood and Jim Goater, for their enthusiastic support.

Carol Wolf of Pennsylvania, the motel desk clerk who despite the ridicule of lesser souls tried to pay for my room herself when management refused me. She told me, "They don't understand your American dream." Miss Wolf, you *are* the American dream.

Mr. Bob Price and his wife Donna of Toad River, Alaska Highway, and Gayle Ferrar and her husband Al, of Williams Lake, British Columbia—for generous support.

Mr. Hank and Mrs. Karen Naisby, who said, "If we can ever help . . ." I rang them two years later, and overnight fifteen hundred dollars was sent to get my family down from Alaska to New York. (It was over four years before I could fully repay.)

Camille J. Brassard, for his unflagging enthusiastic support. He was the first to see the great dream.

The indefatigable Renée Donovan, Sister Luz, and all the other sisters at the Hogar Santa Catalina, Panama for their love and support.

David Walker of Texas, for his enthusiastic advice.

Scott Edwards, who, while I mixed in New York with the occasional millionaire, mailed me survival money, one hundred dollars—his life savings.

Chuck Lockman and Rafael Martinez, who looked after Yosh and me—thanks for sharing your homes.

The Cunard Line for taking my family home aboard the Queen Elizabeth II.

Air Alaska for flight tickets within Alaska.

Mr. Nick Nelson of DHL Courier Service, for Atlantic travel courtesies.

Daley Thompson, who gave me one of his own trophies.

Mr. Richard Wedemeyer of the Muppets, Mr. Tom

ACKNOWLEDGMENTS

McNeil, Mr. Bob Terry (artist), and Mr. Peter B. Kaplan, all of whom employed me during desperate postjourney days.

Messrs. Sheldon Zimet, George M. Williams, and Claude Lomden, and Mrs. Keiko Ueda, for their encouragement.

Professors Motoko Fujii and Shizuo Fukuta of the Japanese University of Social Welfare, for their faith in me, and Nobumasa Nishizawa, my mentor in Japan.

Richard Rapold of *Vision* magazine, for his advice and valuable assistance.

John van Eyssen, eminent film producer, for his great belief in the dream.

The late and gallant Mr. Marne Camp and his wife Nita of the Bronx, New York. Mrs. Camp invited me to stay for a few days. It turned into a year. No rent was asked or could be afforded. We shared our food. She may very well have saved this story. Thank you forever, Nita.

And of course to Yoshiko, my wife, the most wonderful of all women, whose journey this also is. Thank you, Kola-chan, for sharing my dream and once waking me to "come see the stars"—I love you so.

Last but not least, all the unnamed people, most of them poor, of South and North America who united to make this their dream come true.

Muchos gracias para todos—
To all, thank you.

Prologue

The afternoon of September 18, 1983, on the northern fringe of the Alaskan settlement of Prudhoe Bay, I took the final steps of a seven-year journey as I crossed a few yards of slimy tundra to the edge of the Arctic Ocean and dipped my hand into the cold, silvery waters. It was done. Exhausted physically and emotionally, I fell to my knees and wept.

This day was both the most longed-for and the saddest of my life. Finished was a walk of over 19,000 miles that had started in Tierra del Fuego, at the southernmost tip of South America, and ended here, on the shore of the Beaufort Sea, at the top of North America.

Now, at the very end, surrounded by family and the few reporters and oilmen who had gathered to witness the event, as the assembled flags of the fourteen nations I had traversed cracked desolately in the wind behind me and I continued to stare numbly at the seashells and slush at my feet, in my mind's eye I traveled the thread of my journey back to its beginning—down through the frozen Yukon and the southern tier of Canadian provinces with their endless prairies and golden wheatfields, back to New England and New York and the United States' eastern seaboard, down through the states of the Deep South where I had had the privilege to shake a president's hand, back through Mexico's torrid coastal plain, through Central America ripe with revolution and bursting with life, through the treacherous rain forest of the Darien Gap that links Panama and Colombia, through Ecuador and its soaring volcanoes, Peru's desert and steep mountain passes, Bolivia's altiplano—the great Andean plateau—and down through Chile and the Argentine pampas and so back to Tierra del Fuego, half a planet away, so long ago—seven long years, most of my adult life.

The journey had made history. Not only was it a walk of the entire Western Hemisphere—never done before—but it was also recognized as the longest unbroken walk of all time. It was, most importantly to me, the culmination of a dream come true. Why, then, the tears; why the heavy feeling in my heart? Because now I was forced to bid farewell to my good friend and harsh taskmaster, the constant and closest companion of ninety-odd months of walking: the road beneath my feet.

I was born in Hillingdon, Middlesex, and raised not far away in Rainham, in Kent, barely a mile down the hill from where the great explorer Sir Francis Drake himself grew up. When I was less than a year old, my mother died, and not long after that my father ran off, abandoning me to the care of relatives who proceeded to adopt me. All this was longer ago than I can remember, however; the clearest and most enduring memories of my boyhood are of carefree days as the son of the best mum and dad anyone could want.

Like many an English lad, from earliest childhood I cultivated a passionate admiration for the great travelers of history, whose accounts of journey and adventure never failed to enchant me. The idea for my own journey came to me when I was a raw merchant seaman, although at first it was little more than an idle fantasy. But once the idea seemed to be a real possibility, once I thought I *could* do it, I *had* to do it—for I knew that if I didn't, I would be haunted by the omission forever. The hardest thing to bear in life, I am sure, is never to have lived your dream. Having lived and survived this adventure, I can now say, with some sadness, that the second hardest thing to bear in life is already to have lived one's dream.

When I took the first, hopeful steps of the walk, in 1976, it was on the slimmest of budgets. I had only my savings of 5,000 guineas (about $11,500) and no backing except for a boot company who kept my feet shod across two continents. Preparations were minimal, and I had nothing to prove except that this thing could be done. On the plus side, I had the greatest expectations of adventure—and my girlfriend in tow.

I had met Yoshiko while on shore leave in Japan, and she kept up with me and my mad walk farther and longer than anyone could have predicted; she returned home, after our marriage in Argentina, only because she was pregnant with the first of our two children. From the trip's inception to its end—especially at the end, when she and the children accompanied me by car on the last leg north to the Arctic—I always considered the journey *our* journey, never mine alone. This knowledge, along with my intense love of home (surely paradoxical for one so long on the road), sustained me in my darkest and loneliest hours and gave me a reason to go on.

The initial gleam of an idea for the walk came to me when I was barely seventeen, during my first deep-sea voyage, aboard the tramp steamer *Trecarne*. The ship lay rolling at anchor one evening in the blistering heat of the Arabian Sea, and as I lay in my bunk, my gaze became fixed on a world map lazily swinging on the bulkhead opposite. This led me to thinking: If this old *Trecarne*, doing a mere ten knots (not so much faster than a jogger's pace) could round the world's capes and span such a wide area on that enticing map in just a few weeks, then surely, given time—and a healthy dash of recklessness—one could indeed contemplate a transplanetary journey on foot.

The dream lay fallow for the next two or three years, during which time I circled the globe both ways. I gained my second mate's ticket and eventually earned the money to finance the trek. I came to know the world's ports intimately and traveled its sea lanes from Cardiff to Calcutta, from Southampton to Zanzibar. But as much as I loved going to sea, I had discovered that what I truly longed for were the exotic lands that always beckoned beyond the horizon. In my country's tradition of grand adventure, I yearned to make my own effort, perhaps even make my own mark.

To circle the globe seemed "logical," but it had already been done and thus could not answer my need for geographical priority. Instead of going around the world, then, I would go straight up it! This became my plan, my all-absorbing dream. Being fearful of my own inflated scheme, I sought about for a companion among my shipmates and friends, but all saw better ways of ending a life. Some came straight to the point and told me I was a crackpot. My mum herself said that I was just going through yet another difficult phase, and my brother Anthony's only comment was, "Don't catch any diseases."

Just as I was about to resign myself to go it alone, I met Yoshiko. We hit it off from the start, and even though neither of us spoke the other's language, we "talked" for hours on end using gestures and struggling with a few standard phrases from her English-Japanese pocket dictionary.

Now, the idea had never occurred to me that a woman would be capable of such a journey or even want to attempt it; indeed, I didn't even mention the subject to Yoshiko in the early days of our friendship. When I finally made some casual reference to my outrageous plan, her enthusiastic nods seemed to reflect great interest—or was it just politeness? In any event, all this was still idle conversation (if one could call it conversation at all, under the circumstances).

After my ship left port, we struck up a passionate correspondence. By the time I returned to Japan a few months later, I had decided to conduct a "test." Without saying exactly why, I proposed we climb Mount Fuji together. The venture was a success—at least for Yoshiko, who had to help me to the top!

Over the following weeks, as we grew even closer, I sensed that it was time for me to make a final decision regarding a companion—or no companion—for the walk. One night as we sat sipping sodas in a dockside café, I came right out and asked this lovely girl with jet-black hair to accompany me. (My speech began, "Er, by the way . . .") She agreed! And so the matter was settled.

After some initial details were ironed out, again I returned to sea. When I had finally saved enough money for an initial stake, Yoshiko came to England to join in the final preparations. Shortly after she arrived in Rainham, however, it became clear that there had been a slight misunderstanding, due at least in part to an error in translation. Dear, sweet Yosh—she had thought all along that we would be going on a *bus* trip.

After the initial shock wore off, Yoshiko and I quickly adjusted to this new state of affairs—after all, we were in love . . . and Yoshiko had spirit . . . and as for myself, well, I was happy that she was willing to try at all.

Numerous decisions and preparations now had to be made, starting with where to begin. Should the walk start at the top and proceed from Alaska to Argentina, or the reverse? Argentina seemed the better starting point, for when my small initial stake should run out, I hoped to be in the richer northern lands. Here I also stood a better chance of recovering my health and strength after completing Latin America, which I expected to be the greater ordeal. This turned out to be not only a rational choice but a lucky one as well, for the alternative route would have placed me, an Englishman, smack dab in Argentina at the height of their war with Britain over the Falklands. A mere roll of the dice, it seems, can determine success or failure.

Neither Yoshiko nor I were able to carry provisions across Patagonia and beyond on our backs—she because such a weight would simply be too heavy, I because the skin on my back would erupt from such a burden. A solution occurred to me when my last ship to sea, the Pakistani merchantman *Omar*, lay at anchor on the River Tyne at South Shields. In exchange for a bottle of whiskey and a case of Newcastle Brown, the underemployed lads at the Brigham and Cowan Dry Dock were happy to knock out for me two shot-blasted-steel ruck-sack carriers, one red, one blue, each with an extended handle. They resembled oversize golf carts.

Camping gear was purchased, along with a few staples, and weeks were spent poring over maps and writing out an itinerary. (As it turned out, we ended up largely ignoring the itinerary, ultimately relying on maps picked up along the way.)

Finally, I was eager for the advice of the great English traveler, that fabulous Etonian Sebastian Snow, who at the time was the only man ever to have walked the length of South America, a journey he relates in one of his books, *The Rucksack Man*. Snow's walk had taken twenty months; toward the end it nearly killed him. By the time he had returned home, only a few short years before, he was a starved, half-mad wreck.

Snow agreed to see me, and I rushed to pay him a visit at his mother's flat in his native Devon. My best expectations were realized. This formidably tough traveler was brimming over with advice and information, all of it solid.

Halfway through our interview he turned his head toward the next room. "Mother, can I have another beer?" bellowed the great explorer, now fully recovered from his ordeal and as corpulent as a bank manager.

"Certainly not, Sebastian! And by the way . . . don't forget to take Lady Ponsonby's poodle for his evening constitutional."

"But Mother," Sebastian whined, half-rising out of his seat, "I'm forty-two years old!"

When there was no response, Snow settled back into his chair and finally glanced at the rucksack cart I had brought along for his inspection and approval—the cart which, I was certain, would be vital to the success of the venture. His judgment was brief and to the point: "Can you dump it?" he said.

THE LONGEST WALK

South America

Tierra del Fuego and Chile

Getting to the starting point of a 19,000-mile walk presented almost as many problems as planning the trip itself. While I had no trouble booking working passage to South America on the cargo liner *Brasilia Star*, for some obscure reason the line wouldn't allow Yoshiko on board. She would have to take an airflight—three weeks after my own departure from England, in order to coordinate our arrivals in Argentina. Meeting in Buenos Aires, we flew south to Río Grande, where yet another trip awaited us, one of a hundred miles by bus to our starting point, Ushuaia, the southernmost town on earth.

The jetliner south from Buenos Aires seemed to take forever, and each high-speed minute that streaked by underscored the great distances we would soon be attempting on foot. "Look!" I said to Yoshiko, pointing out the window at the landscape far below, a dull green flatland traversed by a thin brown line—a solitary dirt road.

The Argentine who sat across the aisle from us, overheard us talk of our plans, leaned over and haughtily predicted, "It will take you *four years* to get out of Tierra del Fuego." Yoshiko and I exchanged nervous glances. She paled; I felt my heart sink. What on earth had I gotten us into? Perhaps this was all a horrible mistake; perhaps this would all end up a nightmare.

3

Neither of us dared say anything for the remainder of the flight. On landing at Río Grande, it took a monumental effort simply to drag our gear through the airfield shed. Three hours later, after a cramped bus ride south along a winding, stony dirt road, we finally reached the end of the line.

The end of the line was the end of the earth—Ushuaia, on the main island of Tierra del Fuego, the group of offshore islands that on the map appear to be the severed tip of South America's tail. How strange it seemed, this ordinary little town: a few hundred low-slung, nondescript, wood-frame buildings along a grid of uncluttered streets, sitting on the small plain beside the Beagle Channel and surrounded by a breathtaking landscape. Directly inland, beyond the fields of coarse grass, stood rolling, thickly wooded hills, and beyond them, dwarfing both town and hills, a backdrop of snow-capped mountains.

We treated ourselves to a restaurant meal that evening with the anticipation that there were going to be few of these in the weeks and months to come, and by the time we finished dinner it was midnight—and still twilight so far south. In the dim light, we set up camp on a gentle slope near the stony shoreline. All our gear seemed so painfully new and exotic that first night; everything had the overpowering smell and feeling of brand-new leather and plastic, the tiny orange tent especially so. A half-hour after midnight, the sun at last dipped below the horizon, and soon after, the two of us, a little nervous but most of all exhausted, fell into a deep sleep.

January 26, 1977, the first day of the walk, was to be an eventful one. I woke just past dawn and, while Yoshiko continued to sleep, crawled out of the tent to get my first morning glimpse of southernmost America. Nearby the waves of the channel lapped gently against the shore, while in the distance I could see the black peaks of Lennox Island poking out of the mist. To the north, large snowcaps pressed close to the sea, crowding the village up to their foothills. And— for goodness' sake—here was ice on the tent's flysheet, and this in the Southern Hemisphere's midsummer!

I roused Yoshiko. After a light breakfast, we packed our

gear, loaded it onto the carts, and set out northward, Yoshiko staying a few paces behind me so that we could more easily negotiate the narrow dirt road. We had no sooner taken our first steps than the rain began to fall. We stopped to don our bright blue waterproofs, and then set out again, trudging over the first small hill beyond the campsite. By now everything was slick with mud. This starting and stopping and starting again had taken a full twenty minutes, and we hadn't gotten anywhere. Then it happened.

We were finally underway and had gone but a few hundred yards when I heard Yoshiko's small voice behind me. "George, I can't go on!"

I turned to see my trailmate burst into a flood of tears. Poor Yoshiko. She had accompanied me literally to the uttermost part of the earth for this bleak moment of truth. Some form of immediate consolation was clearly in order—for both of us—and so I did the only sensible thing I could under the circumstances. "Never mind, love," I said, "let's have a kiss."

Despite the pelting rain, we rolled under a dripping bush and began to cuddle. After hardly a minute of this, purely by chance I looked up. A man with a desperate, unshaven face was staring at us, barely six feet away. He had a gun.

"Yoshiko," I said in as calm a voice as I could muster, "there's a man pointing a pistol at us!"

"George, you so silly," she reprimanded. "You make joke, even now." Finally she, too, saw him, and then, to my amazement, without hesitation she scrambled to her feet and began to chant to the gunman the only Spanish she knew: "Sí . . . por favor . . . sí . . . por favor . . ." again and again. I could do nothing but sit there, hypnotized—as was the gunman.

The flustered mugger, finally giving up in apparent desperation of accomplishing anything, turned away and disappeared off into the woods. "You see, I tell him not to shoot us," exclaimed Yoshiko with a smile. Indeed, she had—and with just "yes" and "please"—which was exactly twice as much Spanish as I knew.

Such an inauspicious start called for at least a minor regrouping. We weren't overly worried about the desperado; in the end, he seemed more scared of us than we of him. (Although later we encountered two policemen and a posse of armed citizens who told us that they were hunting down a roving sex maniac—who knows, perhaps the same scoundrel.)

But then there was the matter of Yoshiko. I had anticipated that she would have difficulty with the cart, although not so soon and in so dramatic a fashion. I was even prepared for such a moment. While on board the *Brasilia Star*, I busied myself stitching up a canvas body harness—actually, two of them (I might want to use one also)—which could be directly attached to the carts, thus leaving the arms free and making the job of hauling that much easier. Judged solely by looks, the harnesses were ludicrous affairs, but there was no denying that, like the carts themselves, they were efficient. While we took shelter under a tree I dragged a harness out of the gear and demonstrated its use to a bemused Yoshiko; her spirits picked up immediately.

We were on our way again, Yosh less encumbered and both of us much happier. The road led us up and down short, steep hills and between heavily wooded slopes. Every so often, despite the noisy downpour we could hear the gurgle of a small waterfall somewhere beyond the trees. Perhaps every half hour a vehicle would pass us, but no one on foot this first, rainy day. At a small roadside shrine of a local saint, I rummaged around in the gear and found the huge Boots-the-Chemist candle that Mum gave us as a going-away present. We were planning to use it in the tent after dark, but instead we lit it here, together, in a little ceremony, and left it burning at the shrine to bring us luck on this, our great adventure.

We had no strict day-to-day schedule. Instead, the idea was every day to select a particular objective—a town or a bridge, say, or even a kilometer post (all distances in Latin America are posted in kilometers), or any other easily identifiable point on the map—and make that point our goal. There *was* a timetable tied to the seasons, however, and it was crucial that we keep to it: We had to clear Patagonia, the southern half of Argentina, before the snows cut us off, for otherwise the journey would come to a dead stop, probably for months.

The second day featured a difficult climb—actually, crawl was more like it—up the long Garibaldi Pass. At the top we paused to take in the spectacular sight of the blue-black waters of Lake Escondido before sliding and stumbling down through the mud, over fallen trees and past the collapsing sides of the hill, before reaching our day's goal, the Petrel, a *hostería*. *Hosterías*, which are found throughout Tierra del Fuego and mainland Argentina, are hybrid gas station-hotels. As modest as they are, dining at one would be an extravagance on our limited budget, but I felt that making this an occasion was only fair to Yoshiko after the numbing shock she received by realizing what the walk would really be like.

We pulled in at Petrel, which sat prettily overlooking a lake, and plunged heartily into a justly famous Argentine beefsteak dinner before setting up camp nearby. Afterward, we sat on the grass by the lakeshore for what seemed like hours in the waning late-night dusk, watching the crescent moon and its reflection on the lake's rippled surface. All the while, on the far shore the tall slender trees swayed in the slight breeze, and as it grew dark, from time to time we would spy the mysterious silhouette of a night bird. Such were the moments which pleased us most during these early days of our love.

Tierra del Fuego is a naturalists' delight, and we were constantly amazed at the variety of plants and animals, wild and domestic, that we encountered along the way. All during that first week we also kept running into foreigners, the few odd hardy types who are attracted to totally out-of-the-way places, and they all asked to take our pictures. Late one afternoon a small party of Belgian tourists stopped to chat—and of course photograph this unlikely pair, this slender blond chap and his Oriental companion lugging strange carts about the countryside. They were quite overcome to learn that we had walked the entire 60 km from Ushuaia. Afterward, we wondered what they would think if we ever managed 600 km or even 6,000.

Another day, while we were reorganizing our gear, a man left his car, strode up to us, bent stiffly over one of the ruck-sack carts, and began to tap it with his walking stick. "Very interesting . . . most practical," he said in clipped tones. His accent was unmistakably German. "Where are you going, my young man?"

I told him we intended to walk through Tierra del Fuego, for the moment choosing not to mention that the plan was to continue on to Bolivia (never mind, ultimately, Alaska—it seemed all too outrageous to admit).

His eyes lit up. "Ah! . . . you are *marchink*? Most com-mendable! When I was young I, too, marched."

"To such nice places as this?" asked Yoshiko.

"Eh, possibly . . . I vas marchink in *Russia*." The last word came out "Roose-ee-ah," and once he said it his eyes became fixed in the distance.

Yoshiko enthusiastically clapped her hands. "Ah—such a nice vacation!"

The man literally came to attention; he even clicked his heels. "Not exactly," he snarled, and marched off, frowning, to his Volkswagen. As soon as the man was out of earshot, I delicately explained to a perplexed Yoshiko something about the German troops' harrowing winter retreat from the steppes in World War II. Yoshiko reacted with wide-eyed embar-rassment, and then we both had a good laugh.

Reaching Lake Fagnano, we consulted the *South Amer-ican Handbook* (both this estimable volume and Sebastian Snow's *Rucksack Man* accompanied me throughout South America) to learn that it had been named after an eighteenth-century missionary to the Ona Indians, who were now all but extinct—there was supposedly one old lady left. In fact, the Onas, still limited to stone tools when the first Europeans arrived, built the ominous, ghostly campfires that Magellan had seen while sailing past this apparently uninhabited land-scape and that inspired him to name this land Tierra del Fuego, "Land of Fire."

Next day we hit an important objective, a small farm called Estancia Río Ewan. Yosh had suffered excruciating stomach pains all night, and at this farm, I had suggested, we might be able to rest, eat, and stay with a good Anglo-Argentine family. In his book, Sebastian Snow had mentioned stopping here four years before. My plan, I told Yoshiko, was to show these people Snow's reference to them and their generosity, hoping that this, together with his verbal introduction, might win their interest and perhaps even hospitality.

The main house of Estancia Río Ewan sat beside a brook crossed by a small, quaint wooden bridge. When we reached the bridge, which was as close as we ever got, a woman stuck her head out a window and yelled, "What do you want?"

"Good afternoon, I've been asked by Mr. Sebastian Snow, who stayed here two days back in seventy-three, to pop in and pay respects for him. You see, I'm also trying to walk the Americas."

"We don't wish to see any more tourists. We're fed up with them."

So much for that. "Miss, my girl has been ill all night. She has walked here from Ushuaia and needs a rest."

"Then go over to the Men's Club. It's not my business how you got here."

We slunk away, puzzled and pouting, and reluctantly found the way to the Men's Club, a large, smelly gaucho dormitory. Moses the cook was very kind, however, and gave us dinner on the house. And a decided bonus was getting to meet and speak for the first time with the gauchos, the legendary cowboys of Argentina whose life-style has changed little in the past hundred years. The diet of these men is amazing: two pounds or more of meat per day, strong coffee, wine, dark bread, and nothing else. They shun jam, milk, and other "niceties," and they refuse to eat vegetables altogether, which they regard strictly as feed for livestock. Everything in this place bore the taint of slaughtered sheep; in the months ahead we could never get used to this. (While the gauchos of the pampas, far to the north, mostly herd cattle, here and on the southern Argentine mainland the prevalent livestock are sheep.)

9

The bread, made with sheep lard, I found especially unpalatable. And where, I wondered, did they get their vitamins? One of them said from their *maté*, an infusion of the bitter leaves of the yerba plant which they suck through ornate silver tubes from gourds and which many Argentinians drink as incessantly as North Americans drink coffee or the English their tea.

We had been on the road for over a week now, mostly battling the wind and the rain. One evening the red tin roofs of Estancia Viamonte appeared on the horizon, a happy sight to us, for we had a solid introduction there, and within an hour we were knocking at the door. After the experience at Estancia Río Ewan we were subdued, but I was also excited because this was the home of Oliver Bridges, an Anglo-Argentine who was serving as the local British vice-consul and was the scion of the first European family to settle in Tierra del Fuego, back in the 1890's. Some people go bonkers over movie stars, rock singers, or football players for Leeds United. My special weakness is for historical figures—statesmen, generals, virtually anyone connected with history. These all command my fascination, and Bridges was close enough to qualify.

We spent two days at Viamonte hiding from the ferocious wind and enjoying its soft, cozy chairs and sparkling woodfire. Oliver Bridges was the very image of an English gentleman, and his home was like the set of a Noel Coward play. Tea was a grand affair with sterling and fine china. When Mrs. Bridges rang an antique bell, a white-coated butler entered with tea, cakes, and peaches.

From Viamonte we followed the open coast until Punta María, where much to Yoshiko's delight we found a tiny general store—a *boliche*—selling Coca-Cola, biscuits, and sheep dip. Everywhere on the walk, such shops held a greater fascination for Yoshiko than the ritziest fashion boutique.

Toward evening we crossed an open field and camped on the beach with the pounding Atlantic for company. On these flat sheep-grazing lands, in the clean air, the range of visibility was enormous—from the beach we could still see the small shop 16 km (10 miles) away. In the middle of the night, Yoshiko woke me with a start. "George, come look at the stars!" My first thought was: Is the woman bats? She knows how jealously I guard my sleep, yet here she is, waking me up to gaze at stars! At her insistence I poked my head outside the tent and was struck dumb by the sight of the miraculous hemisphere that seemed to float just over our heads—millions of twinkling lights spilling over a velvety black carpet. We stayed up another half hour, perhaps more, just to stare, while I rocked Yoshiko in my arms.

Another night, with the rain falling, we were given temporary shelter by a shepherd—a gaucho. His homestead was typical of others we stopped at: a simple hut made all of wood (some had tin roofs), nearby a rough stable where two horses were kept, and beside this a few raised wooden planks that served as shelter for the dogs. The man owned several of these tough, shaggy dogs which were always kept outside, and another, a toy breed he had named Perro (Dog!), which he kept inside as his special companion. Like almost all his *compañeros*, this gaucho was a professional bachelor.

The hut's interior was divided into two areas. In one stood the man's homemade leather-and-wood bed, under which he stored his few clothes; in the second area, a sort of dayroom, were a table and two stools in one corner, and in another a wood-burning stove—manufactured, according to the nameplate, in England in 1910, and equipped with a special side section for baking bread. By the full light of the oil lamp everything here had a rough, antique look, down to the yellowed newsprint pasted mosaic-fashion on the walls, from which hung a profusion of saddlery and harness worn to a dull sheen along with the man's *bolas* (the weighted slings gauchos use to catch livestock and rheas by entangling their legs), a lithograph of the Virgin Mary, and a photo of Carlos Monzon, the Argentine world champion prize fighter. Before we tented down for the night, the gaucho patiently taught us how to say "fork," "knife," and "spoon" in Spanish.

Midmorning the following day we turned a cliff to see,

just across the river, the town of Río Grande, where our plane had landed on the way south from Buenos Aires. The previous week, going in, we hadn't been much impressed by Río Grande; from the circling aircraft, this little town halfway up the island seemed to be not much more than a few dismal corrugated structures. Now, coming back on foot, we saw a roaring metropolis, El Dorado and Mecca combined, that held forth the glorious promise of food and a bed. When Yoshiko saw that we had reached our objective, she rushed to me and kissed me at the delight of it all. Then I had some hard explaining to do.

What Yoshiko didn't realize was that even though we stood only a few hundred yards across the river from Río Grande, ensuring the integrity of the walk required making a detour. One could cross the river by boat, but if there was *any* bridge across *any* body of water along the route, I had to walk over that bridge. There was in fact a bridge, and it was three hours away.

As the walk to the bridge bore on and we began to struggle against the increasingly powerful westerly headwinds, Yoshiko grew restless: "This journey is like coming never ending." Finally, on the bridge, she threw in the towel and stopped cold. "George, I can no go on never-ending forever. You must leave me."

"I cannot, love—I can't leave you. It's only six more kilometers to town," I lied (it was nine—and I had the map). "Please," I pleaded, "just one more effort."

"I don't want to ruin your journey—but I don't want to go on." By now she was sitting cross-legged on the stony road, petulant.

"Yosh, dear, you can't ruin the journey. It's going to go on for a long, long time yet. You—we—have to move sooner or later. Maybe you can't walk the whole Western Hemisphere, but think how wonderful it will be just to finish Tierra del Fuego."

"No, I don't wish to walk Tierra del Fuego. I want to sleep in beds, wear pretty dresses, and eat cream cakes." And so the revolt continued until she regained her energy and bravely (and angrily) limped into town for her longest day ever, 36 km.

To appease Yoshiko, the next morning I dipped into our small kitty for yet a third time and checked us into the corrugated-tin Hotel Argentina. I asked for the very best room in the house, which got us not only a bed but access to the hall bathroom. As soon as I finished taking a cold shower (the hot water had run out after Yoshiko took hers) we settled into the preliminary slow motions of lovemaking. Yoshiko became silly, we both fell victim to an attack of the gigglies, and soon the affair degenerated into a full-scale pillow fight. This riotous activity was just reaching a climax when the desk clerk, the same stern, arthritic woman who had assigned me the "suite," decided to burst into the room, hotel register in hand (I had neglected to sign it). She took one look and fled. In retrospect I couldn't blame her for her reaction, for eleven in the morning was admittedly a shade early for such goings-on, but I never did get around to signing that register.

Beyond Río Grande, past an oil-bearing plain with drilling rigs everywhere, stood one of the largest sheep farms on the island, Estancia Sara, with over a hundred thousand head. It was hard going that day against the terrific westerlies that tore up plants and set large stones rolling across the road. At one point we even hid in a ditch to escape the terrible roar and awful dust. A car stopped, and four Japanese men got out to talk to Yoshiko. She was very excited to meet them and happy to speak her own language for the first time in over three months. Yosh translated for me, and we learned that they were also having trouble with the wind, which had blown their car onto its side—with all four occupants!

By four o'clock Yoshiko had decided, as if on a whim, that it was time to camp, and so by herself, without a word, she set up the tent and then began to write a letter, which she deigned to translate for me: "Dear Honorable Father and Mother, George is very cruel and unkind to me. I wish to go home . . ." Indeed, I had pushed her. It was often necessary to move even when we were both very tired, for my fears for the winter were too real to allow slacking at this

13

stage. But now Yoshiko even refused my soup (possibly because I had burned it) and turned her back on me altogether. To escape this gloomy atmosphere I went for an unhappy stroll.

When I returned hours later Yoshie was smiling. "Sorry, George," she said in her sweet, girlish way.

"Sorry, love," I answered.

In mid-February, we crossed the frontier that runs straight down the middle of the island and crossed into the Chilean sector. This curious border dates back to the War of the Pacific in the previous century. All of Tierra del Fuego used to belong to Chile, but while Chile was busy sending its armies elsewhere—as far north as Lima, the capital of Peru—Argentina took advantage of the situation. (Another upshot of Chile's foray was that Bolivia, Peru's ally in the war, was deprived of its meager coastline and, with it, its only port, a situation that unfortunately holds to this day.)

Our road immediately deteriorated as soon as we passed the bent, rusty sign marking the beginning of Chile's Magallanes Province. After an hour we reached San Sebastián, where we found large, empty farm buildings, a jail under construction, and a partially destroyed estancia house, all depressing sights. We were only too glad to leave this decay and move on, but just beyond the town we had a problem: The question here was not whether we were on the correct road, but whether we were on a road at all.

The next night we were treated to dinner at the home of the family Cavarra, where we were introduced to a favorite Latin American phrase that seemed to characterize the roads we had recently traveled: *mas o menos* (more or less). "Does the bank open at nine?" "*Sí—mas o menos.*" Can you tell me the way to San Juan?" "*Mas o menos.*" "Does this road lead to town?" "*Sí—mas o menos.*" Every shortcoming, lapse, inaccuracy, and error was explained away by this phrase, accompanied by a despairing twist of the face and shrug of the shoulders.

By now, although on the road only a few weeks, we had

slept in so many different kinds of places, usually somewhere new and unknown every night, that it was only natural
we end up one night in a haunted house. On this particular
dusk we were being soaked under a constant drizzle and feeling miserable until we saw a sign reading "Estancia Natasha"
and a farmhouse dimly visible behind a low hill. Dinner, perhaps—or even a bed? When we reached the house our hearts
sank. The estancia was apparently deserted save for the several dogs howling forlornly outside. A cold mist hung over a
nearby lake. At the front door I pulled off my mitten and saw
that the dye had run, staining my hand red—blood red.
Yoshiko wasn't affected by any of this; hungry as usual, she
picked up a horseshoe, smashed in a convenient window,
reached in, and opened the door. Entering the house, we
were overwhelmed by a ghastly purple mural, dominating the
entranceway, that seemed to be a vision of hell.

We decided not to sleep here—actually, *I* decided. I was
scared. Instead we slept in the barn, where we spent a weird
night with whistling winds, rattling doors, and a candle that
flickered constantly and cast giant shadows. I'm glad to say
that nothing happened, and in the fresh light of day the world
looked such a different place. The house, on reinspection, was
charming, the dogs friendly, and the painting in the front room
a particularly refreshing landscape.

From Estancia Natasha we walked all of ten minutes before stopping at a charming cottage beside the Strait of Magellan, where a woman gave us a meal and we played with
her daughter, Mónica. Later the father returned on a handsome gray horse. What a fine, pure life this family leads, I
thought—the husband with his animals and the mother with
a pleasant home and quick-witted daughter, so content on their
green hill beside the blue waters. Could they possibly be aware
of their perfection under that midsummer sun?

We reached our first milestone at the Punta Espora Ferry
terminal, where we would embark on the voyage across the
straits to mainland Chile, mainland South America. We had

succeeded in walking the entire island, 451 km, which prompted me to ask Yoshiko, "Aren't you glad you didn't stop at the Río Grande bridge?"

Yoshiko pouted. "No, I wished to have stopped." Pure sham—really! She could hardly suppress a smirk that soon turned into a broad grin. To commemorate the occasion— Yosh was, as far as I could tell, the first woman ever to have crossed La Isla Grande de Tierra del Fuego on foot—I decided to name the carts in her honor: "I hereby christen thee 'Yoshikarts.'" In a fitting finish to this part of the journey, the commander of the ferry, a converted World War II landing craft, waived our fare. With the benefit of such friendly gestures and outpouring of goodwill, we had managed to cross the Chilean half of the island without spending any money at all.

On reaching the mainland, we were in high spirits. We had just put the first geographical barrier behind us and were now eager to reach the provincial capital of Punta Arenas far to the southwest, where I had arranged for the British consulate to hold our mail. Because the journey to Punta Arenas, far off our route, constituted a "side trip" and thus not part of the walk (we planned to hitchhike there), this required that I set my "mark." This requires a little explanation.

At any one time during the journey there were always two places that were meaningful to me: the farthest point in my journey (the point I had walked to) and the point where I stood at the moment. Most of the time these two points were the same place, but not always. If I left the route because I needed to seek water, or wanted to visit an ancient temple, or simply wished to post a letter, I would conscientiously mark my farthest point of advance, note my exact distance, run my errand, eventually return to the "mark," and start clocking my distance again. Setting my mark might involve circling a conspicuous tree two or three times, scoring the dirt in the shape of an arrow, or kicking a boulder. Also, whenever I entered a building for the first time, I was sure to leave by the same door I had come in. This was crucial: If I didn't take these precautions, the entire line of my steps

would be irreparably broken and the journey compromised—
and my peace of mind destroyed forever. Especially during
the trying days that lay far ahead, the traceable pattern of my
footsteps was a comforting image, a clean, neat thread that
imposed order on an otherwise confused landscape.

After the tiny towns and villages of Tierra del Fuego, Punta
Arenas was an impressive sight, an honest-to-goodness city
with well-laid-out plazas, sumptuous gardens, fine shops, and
impressive pre-World War II architecture, all spread out beside the Strait of Magellan, with the snowcapped peaks of the
southernmost Andes visible to the north. Punta Arenas had
in fact once been a major world port; its fortunes had declined only after the turn of the century, when international
shipping was diverted through the newly opened Panama
Canal. Even now the city managed to retain some of its former stature, thriving as a southern center of such local industries as meatpacking and wool.

While Yoshiko took in some of the sights, I went down
to the British consulate. Here I found Mr. King, the consul,
as one would expect, reclining in a highback chair reading
that good Tory newspaper the *Daily Telegraph.* Disappointed
to find that no mail had arrived for us here, I nevertheless
took the time to make a brief visit to the British Club, a great
mausoleum of a place which reeked of gaslight, creaky leather
chairs, and dusty Edwardian biographies with yellowing pages.
I almost expected Kitchener of Khartoum himself to step out
of the gloom.

Toward evening, still looking for somewhere to camp out,
Yosh and I found a modest house with a good view and gave
a brisk knock on the gate, over which hung the hand-painted
notice *"Entrada Prohibido."*

"What does that mean, Yoshiko?"

"Don't know."

A slow giant of a man resembling Oliver Hardy popped
out into the courtyard, and as quickly as it takes to read this
we were camped out in the living room of Juan Yaínez. We
ended up staying three full days at the home of this spontaneous and outgoing family. At our farewell dinner, Juan read

us some Chilean poems and then presented us with a history of Chile in two volumes. As a final gesture, he very deliberately took up a pencil and with a gentle *"Permiso?"* ("May I?") carefully emended my Argentine map, on which three tiny "Chilean" islands in the Beagle Channel had been labeled "Argentine." (Ironically, barely a year later, the dispute over these same, uninhabited islands very nearly escalated into a full-scale war, which was averted only by the eleventh-hour intervention of an emissary from John Paul II.)

After finding my mark and setting out on the road again, Yoshiko and I had a serious discussion. It was becoming clear that if we were to escape Patagonia's winter, we would have to move faster, and even Yoshiko's best walking pace was not fast enough. There were two alternatives—aside from her leaving off the walk and going home, which neither of us wanted: She could take buses, or she could hitchhike while I continued to walk. The buses so far south operate perhaps once a week, and so they weren't really an option. This left hitchhiking, and the prime consideration here was security. Judging by the people we had met so far, we concluded that hitchhiking would be far safer here than in, say, the United States, and so we worked out a routine: Yoshiko would hitchhike ahead each day and set up camp, while I walked. The ride, we figured, would never be a very long one—perhaps a half hour at most. The very next day, we gave it a trial run, and all went well. By the time I reached the campsite, Yosh was peacefully sleeping in the tent.

This now became our regular practice, and it had added benefits. One was that it relieved Yoshiko of much of the physical burden. It lightened my load as well: I continued to haul a cart, but now with only food, water, and emergency items like a sleeping bag. In fact, I had grown used to hauling the cart and by this time had established a comfortable, reassuring rhythm, swinging first one hand and then the other behind me to grab its handle in midair every few steps, all of which helped to keep my mind in repose.

The last day in Chile, however, I got carried away with walking. I went twelve hours virtually nonstop, including two wrong turns that cost me four hours. It was almost midnight by the time I neared the Monte Aymond border post, feeling absolutely shattered. I had covered 58 km that day, a distance I was never to exceed in my seven-year traverse.

As I approached camp, Yoshiko, who had been fearing for my safety, came out of the darkness and greeted me with relief and kisses. Then she led me to the tent, where she tended to my sore, aching body and began to speak excitedly of the prospect of reaching some town where we might buy sweet buns and shampoo. It was difficult for me to pay attention to anything she was saying, however. My mind that night was stuck on my damaged feet, while my spirit was already far ahead on the vast plains of Patagonia.

Patagonia

It was late February when we entered Santa Cruz Province in the southern part of Argentina called Patagonia. Crossing Tierra del Fuego and a small slice of southernmost Chile had taken less than a month, while traversing the enormous country we had now entered and which runs half the length of the continent was going to take almost a year. Santa Cruz Province alone has an area greater than the whole of Great Britain, although the population is only eighty thousand, half of the people living in the capital, Rio Gallegos. The huge distances involved, even from one solitary hut to the next, pose a problem for the walker, and carrying the necessary amounts of food becomes an overwhelming concern. Water is particularly critical in these arid flatlands, although fortunately with our "Yoshikarts" we could carry an enormous ten liters. There was much to be apprehensive about on the threshold of such emptiness.

At the Monte Aymond border post the police stamped us back in without incident and returned to hunching around their coal fires. After my last big day in Chile I could only limp 5 km, Yoshiko accompanying me for the occasion, before encamping at an estancia, where we dined with the gauchos who were in attendance—the standard bread, coffee, and two pounds of sheep meat apiece. (By the end of Patagonia we couldn't even look at mutton.)

We had no sooner established our new routine—Yoshiko hitchhiking ahead after I had begun walking—than problems arose. One early evening I reached our agreed-upon objective, a certain estancia, only to find that Yoshiko was not there. I anxiously dragged myself another 7 km to the next estancia, where indeed she was waiting; she had simply failed to see the first house from the car. Another day I had been walking a few hours when I was overtaken by the truck that had given Yoshiko a late lift; when they reached me, the driver spent a good ten minutes berating me for "abandoning the girl."

I couldn't really blame anyone who was baffled by our strange travel arrangements. Not everyone understood what we were doing even after I had given an explanation—and explaining our venture in a strange language was a complicated business. There had to be a better way, I thought. Yosh and I talked things over and revised the system.

We now began the walk together every day, Yoshiko looking to hitch a lift as we went. It might take five minutes or five hours before a car or truck stopped—no matter. I would tell the driver the destination, possibly just a number of kilometers, and then I would conspicuously write down the license plate number (to indicate that I could trace him, if necessary—a sort of deterrent against robbery, or even rape, God perish the thought). Later on, as an added precaution, I would even take a photo of the car and driver—even if there were no film in the camera. The illusion of an ounce of prevention, I reasoned, was bound to be better than none at all. If this seems to be overly cunning, one has to remember how vulnerable the foot traveler is. Our only "protection" against violence at the hands of the police or the military, we soon found out, was our foreign nationality; few of these people, we could only hope, wanted to risk provoking repercussions from Buenos Aires. As for the average citizens, we were totally at their mercy, whatever their whim or mood might be.

I reached the provincial capital, Río Gallegos, in the late afternoon to find Yosh waiting at the edge of town near some army barracks, where a sentry had been "detaining" her—apparently his idea of some fun. As soon as I arrived, he brushed Yoshiko aside, ordered her down the road, and bore down on me, gesturing and demanding something (probably money, my Spanish wasn't up to figuring out what). I simply shrugged and said, "*No comprendo.*" The soldier, running out of patience, allowed a twisted smile to cross his face as he carefully placed a clip of bullets in his rifle and crashed the bolt shut; the reluctant clip bounced out of the chamber and onto the ground. Being an obliging sort of chap and thinking the whole thing was just a ridiculous show, I picked the clip up off the ground and offered it back to him. The soldier furiously snatched it away from me and went through the whole process again, this time getting it right. Then he lifted the carbine, now with the bullets in, slowly brought its bayonet point to my temple, tilted his head to aim, and clicked the safety catch off! A strange electricity surged through me as I peered down along the barrel directly into his face—cold eyes, wicked smile, an ugly head in an ugly steel helmet.

Now, I knew it was unreasonable for him to blow my brains out for no reason at all, but I suddenly wondered whether *he* knew that. Again he pressed his demand for dollars—this all took place, mind you, in daylight in a public street with the town traffic passing blithely by. Annoyed no end with my "*No comprendo*'s," he finally settled for smashing me against the side of the concrete sentry box.

I rejoined Yosh down the road and told her what happened, adding by way of reassurance, "Don't worry, love, things will be fine. You'll see—we'll go to the British Club."

At the British Club, a bored, red-faced gin drinker bluntly informed us that no, we could not raise our tent around back. I asked why.

"Because it's never been done."

"Can we just leave our rucksacks here while we go eat?"

"No!"

"Why not?"

"Because there might be a bomb in there—*that's* why not!"

Yoshiko interrupted. "Please, sir . . . where to take bomb, please?"

"To the ACA—*that's* where."

At the local Automobile Club Argentina we erected our "bomb" on something resembling a rubbish heap and then went to sup at the cheapest café in town we could find. We knew it to be the cheapest because three people told us, "It's the cheapest café in town." Not only did we pay more here than we ever ended up paying for a meal in Argentina, but we ran out of money to boot. I had to put my watch in hock directly after dessert.

The following morning found us at the Bank of London, where I was informed that they had *not* received the money cablegram I was expecting from England—and that they could *not* cash my traveler's checks.

"Then where *can* I cash them?"

"Comodoro" came the bland reply—a town over 1,000 km away. That's like trying to cash a check in High Street, Rainham, and being told to go to Berlin. Eventually we found our way to the bank manager, a gray-suited, wide-tied strip of hysteria who spoke in rapid-fire English.

"I hate this place . . . I'm from Buenos Aires, you know . . . it's driving me crazy! . . . What do you want? . . . Is she Chinese? . . . No, I can't cash these checks . . . Oh, you got them in London from this bank? . . . Then I *can* cash them . . . A Jap, huh? . . . Fast trains in Japan." He then began imitating the frantic noise of a train. "Woo-oooh! Woo-oooh! Woo-oooh!" This frightened Yoshiko, who couldn't understand any of this high-speed nonsense.

"This is a personal favor, you know . . . I was once in London . . . what noise that underground train makes!" With this he stopped his ears and launched into another round of sound effects: "Rattle-tattle-a-rattle-tattle-a-rattle-tattle . . ." We left with our cash; the bank manager agreed to have the cable money forwarded.

After two days in Río Gallegos, we set out, passing through the poor quarter of town, where the kids grabbed our gear and helped haul it out to the National Route 3. The road was an impeccable tarmac leading to Buenos Aires, a couple of thousand kilometers to the north. To make myself conspicuous on this busy highway, I slung two brilliant yellow sleeping mats over the back of the Yoshikart every morning and always walked facing the traffic.

At Guer Aike we climbed onto the vast rise known as the Patagonian plateau, which stretches a thousand miles to the Río Colorado in the north and from the Atlantic west to the Andes. Progress along Route 3 was rapid, especially with the wind at my back, which swept me along like a kite, forcing me sometimes into barely stoppable runs. Half the *campo* (countryside) joined my flight in the form of great balls of grass, twigs, and grit.

One day the *"mas o menos"* syndrome hit us badly. Yoshiko had set up camp at a turnoff that the map indicated was 37 km from our starting point. I walked the 37 km, but found no tent. I wasn't unduly worried, because it's all a question of estimation based on time, there being few road-signs, and so I continued. Came nightfall and subfreezing temperature, things felt very different. In an increasing panic I shouted into the silent blackness, first with embarrassment and then in desperation, "Yooohhhh-sheeee-kooohhhh!" Finally, a tiny, shaking voice answered my cries. Yoshiko was in tears, having waited hour after uncertain hour. The Automobile Club map, normally excellent, had been 10 km in error.

As my fear subsided, my feet told me how much the pavement had smashed them. With difficulty, I limped the short distance to the tent and collapsed into the sleeping bag while Yoshiko stuffed my mouth with a jam sandwich, my only desire. After this experience we each carried a flashlight and a whistle.

The next walk produced only a short 18-km limp to Estancia Coy Aike, where we were greeted by the farm's manager, Alex Davidson. Alex and his sister Margaret spoke with a distinct Scots accent. Were they native-born Scots? No, their parents had come to Chile seventy years before, and neither Alex nor Margaret had ever seen the Highlands. Argentina's people are in fact an ethnic mélange almost as varied as the United States'. We met nearly as many Italians, Scots, Germans, Poles, Yugoslavs, and, farther to the north, Welshmen, as we did people of Spanish or Amerindian descent. In many cases, their grandparents and great-grandparents had come here from Europe to open the land in the boom years of the great in-migrations around the turn of the century.

In the estancia's big house, Margaret filled our rattling stomachs with her own baked bread, biscuits, and jam. Down here in windy isolation she grew or made everything they ate—except dairy products, as they had no cow. Indeed, it would be a thousand miles before Yosh and I were to see one. The estancia raised sheep; the poor land allows for little else. It was the same all over Patagonia, where the land is mostly scrubby semidesert with just a bit of farming in the valleys cut out of the plateau by slow rivers.

There's no mad rush about Patagonia; life is lived slowly, and people behave as though they had all the time in the world. One day after we had left the superhighway and were walking along a gravel road, a young man driving a battered truck pulled over out of curiosity and we began to chat. Before long Yosh and I and the driver, Mark Lewis—there were many families of English origin in these parts—were deep in conversation, sitting cross-legged in the most convenient location, the middle of the road. After a half-hour another truckdriver stopped, and without hesitation he joined our midmorning, middle-of-the-road tea party, which lasted yet another half hour.

I was particularly struck by the fact that Mark Lewis still spoke of distances in "leagues." I had grown up learning to measure distances in miles (Britain and the United States are the major holdouts clinging to this medieval unit of measure), whereas the distances on South American maps and roadsigns were all in kilometers. I quickly got the hang of thinking in these terms myself, and in fact they suited the journey perfectly. A mile is longer than a kilometer, and so I always felt a greater sense of accomplishment at the end of a day knowing I had bashed out a hefty 40 km instead of a puny 25 miles, its equivalent.

As an added fillip, a mile took sixteen minutes to walk,

whereas a kilometer took me a more conveniently reckoned ten minutes. For seven years I calculated the distances I marched by keeping track of the time. If, for example, my progress was interrupted by someone engaging me in conversation, or a roadside purchase, or stopping to bandage a foot—all normal daily occurrences—I would subtract a corresponding amount of time from my calculations. In populated regions I would sometimes lose an entire day's rest stops because of people curious to learn what I was about.

At Estancia La Julia, the manager (this one of Danish descent) allowed us to occupy a bungalow near the main house. This was our very first "home," and we stayed there five days, surrounded by sheep, trees, and gauchos. Yoshiko was especially fond of the swing in the garden and of the horses that tapped on the window with their noses for sugar. We even had our own sheep—"Billy," according to the red paint on his fleece—who thought nothing of entering the house by the front door. Every sundown at Estancia La Julia the sky behind the distant purple peaks became a fiery red wonder, a celestial epic that never ceased to delight and amaze us, and we would spend our evenings there sitting by the lake, watching the wild horses splashing and drinking, while overhead the constantly changing panorama of puffy clouds scudded across the dark blue sky, chased by the relentless Patagonian winds.

By late March, when we reached Estancia Ventana, we had covered 1,000 km. Estancia Ventana sits under Monte Ventana, a jagged tor of the sort one might see in a Disney cartoon and expect to harbor hordes of ghouls and goblins. The remarkable feature of Monte Ventana that gave it its name is the hole or "window" (*ventana*) that nature had carved through its peak. Especially at night, it was intriguing to look straight through this mountain, sitting in the great Patagonian emptiness, and see a small portion of the starry night as though from deep in a cave.

The estancia itself had gone completely to seed and was now given over to a few pigs and run by a Chilean Communist and another gentleman. The latter, "Drunken José," was lying on the floor when we arrived. Drunken José was famous throughout this corner of the province, having been at the estancia for upwards of thirty years, and no one could remember seeing or hearing of him sober during all that time. There had never been any work for José outside the estancia, and no one knew what his job was here, but all agreed that he would have lost it long ago had he ever been clearheaded enough to say what it was.

By a bad tactic we found ourselves drinking *vino* with Drunken José, and at four in the afternoon we rolled back to our gear, soused. Putting our tent up—inside out, as it happened—proved a drunken comedy. We fell into it, and then it fell into us, and there we lay giggling until we fell asleep. We didn't get up until evening. The Chilean had promised us pork for dinner, but José had been left to watch it, and so by the time we arrived it had been reduced to a cinder. "I think it needs turning," belched José.

Next day, the wind hit us so hard that it succeeded in blowing Yoshiko across the road and into a ditch before we were lucky enough to get her a lift. The prevailing winds here are westerlies that blow right around the world in a narrow band at these latitudes and are known appropriately as the Roaring Forties. In Patagonia, the Roaring Forties seemed to encounter no land obstruction but us. The difficulty of walking in this screaming misery was not limited to the physical hell of wading through treacle for hours on end; it extended to the mental buffeting we took with the flapping jacket hood constantly roaring in our ears. It was literally impossible to think about anything in this lot—except how much I despised the unremitting wind.

Yoshie met me some way out of the town of Gobernador Gregores with chocolate bars, my special yen at the time, and with one last push we walked in together. I slept better than a corpse that night, so much energy had the wind sucked out of me, and in the morning I made for the bank, where I picked up the cash that had been forwarded there by the hysterical bank manager in Río Gallegos.

27

While in a restaurant I showed off my Spanish by asking for a knife, fork, and spoon—but instead of asking for a knife (*cuchillo*), I said, *"Por favor, caballo"* ("A horse, please"). I got the strangest looks—but no horse. Much earlier, in one small café we had dined on soup, and when we finished the waitress addressed us (in Spanish). To be polite we both said (in Spanish), "Yes, please" (all we knew). We had four servings of soup that afternoon before cottoning on to the essence of this exchange. That night, Yoshiko admonished me, "As it is early, you must study the good book *Spanish in Three Months,* which your mother in much wisdom gave you." I spent a half hour on this bore before finally getting to page 3 and giving up.

Yoshiko and I had earlier discussed the desirability of buying a car for her use, and now I heard of one that was going for peanuts at a dealership in San Julián. Quickly we reorganized and took a lift in a freindly pickup to the town 150 km away. (It was here that Magellan said the first mass in Argentina—after hanging one of his crew.)

The car was an old Fiat. We took it out for a test drive—rather, Yosh did, for I have never driven. Yosh was excited and had soon worked out exactly where we would place all the gear: the water here, the bread there, the sleeping bag in the back, and so forth. When the moment of payment arrived, with everyone looking on I carefully ladled out ten million pesos onto the table and waited. (The country was suffering from something like 1,500 percent inflation at the time.)

"Where's the rest?" asked the salesman.

"That *is* the rest—ten million."

"That might buy a bicycle," he sneered. "The Fiat is going for one million *new* pesos, not ten million *old* pesos. Your ten million old pesos is worth only one hundred thousand new pesos. What we want is a *hundred* million old pesos. Is that clear?"

We left the showroom with our near-worthless money and were sitting in the plaza, dejected, when a car screeched to a halt and a friendly family got out to chat. Before we knew what had happened, they were taking us home to dinner. Over the next two hours we virtually cleaned them out; the wife even had to borrow from next door. This was no problem for them, however. In fact, they kept encouraging us to stuff ourselves just so long as we continued to talk into their tape recorder, for the family's hobby was "capturing" tourists and putting their voices on tape. One voice, spliced in among the others, with a staticky tango for the interludes, sounded familiar: "I vas marchink . . ." (It was *him!*)

The next day, we hitched a ride back to Gobernador Gregores in a truck. Seventy-mile-an-hour winds had turned the road into a strip of airborne dust so bad that we bought goggles for protection. Paradoxically, it was in these atrocious conditions that we got our first good view of the fabulous rhea, the South American version of the ostrich. As we rode in the truck, three of these comical birds thumped along beside us at a head-down speed of thirty miles an hour, their enormous feet kicking up plumes of dust like so many bursts of anti-aircraft fire.

Back in Gobernador Gregores, we met a Falkland Islander who insisted on taking us to an *asado*, one of those large and popular outdoor barbecues that Argentinians hold at the merest excuse. As it was fiesta time, among the day's exciting activities were horse races, drunken gauchos riding bareback over an impromptu course set up on the plain. The gauchos were out in their finery for the occasion—black wide-brimmed hats with short, flat crowns; brightly colored neckerchiefs; magnificent belts all studded with silver; huge, floppy trousers; and boots pleated like concertinas. All carried *cuchillos*, imposing silver-handled daggers imported from West Germany.

The *asado* itself might be better described as an ordeal by fire. First you are given a *cuchillo*, with which you get as close as possible to the red-hot fire and take a swing at the huge sheep carcass that is being roasted on a sort of spit stuck in the ground at an angle. If you're lucky, you'll get a piece not totally blackened by the fire, which will anyway drop into your hand and probably burn it. Assuming you have passed the stage of getting the black meat on a plate and finding something to sit on, the next point is to hunt round the district for bread, salt, *vino*, and so forth. After this exhibition, you shoo a cat away who has found the meat and taken the only edible piece off with him. At last all's ready. The meat goes on the bulletproof bread and then up to the mouth and . . . No, it's fallen right in the dirt, and one of the dogs has wolfed the lot. Now, that's the good news. The bad news is when it falls slap on your leg and then bounces to the dogs, having scorched you on the way by. Don't worry about clean trousers; they have already been saturated with black fat drippings during the earlier operations.

Ironically, once we got underway again, food, or rather lack of it, was becoming something of a problem. In Casa Riera, we passed a general store, and again one in Los Horquetas, each with perhaps a room or two to let out back, each grandly calling itself a "hotel." All they had to sell were a couple of eleven-year-old, grime-encrusted tins and some dusty boxes of biscuits mixed in among the saddles and harnesses. In one, Yoshiko perked up upon finding exactly three pairs of shoes for sale, in sizes ranging from enormous to middle-size to petite—as if the proprietor had stocked up against the day when the Three Bears should pop in. At least this was more encouraging than the "hotel" we passed, which was totally shut down due to the owner's passing—shot while caught in the act of stealing horses.

For days, we would go hungry most of the time. Nor could the infrequent estancias we now passed offer much relief, for their owners had all returned to Buenos Aires and other points north for the winter, leaving just a few gauchos behind. Once, when Yoshiko went by herself to seek water at one of these estancias, a gaucho accosted her. Yosh was terrified. We decided that from now on she should wait on the roadside until I arrived. As an added precaution, Yosh also carried pepper in her jacket, ready to throw it in anyone's face who put her in a tight spot.

We had been moving west and now could see the foothills of the Andes in the distance. Now we turned north and onto Route 40, which was to be our companion for the next 3,000 km. Instead of punching the fearsome westerly wind, now we could benefit from the wind to our left, like a broad port reach. Few vehicles passed. Sometimes we did not see even one for a day or more; airplanes passing overhead were more frequent. For days, it seemed as though we were the only humanity in hundreds of square miles. The land was silent and lonely, the straight road disappearing from one horizon to the next, the scrub brush apparently the same at the end of each day as at the beginning. It was as though we were on a treadmill. Soon we ran off the top margin of the first of five Automobile Club maps that covered our route through Argentina, and as the next map proved unobtainable, we had to consult one I had previously drawn up. Perhaps this was lucky, for I later saw the needed map and it is so blank and empty it certainly would have depressed us no end.

At Lago Posadas we mingled among the Araycana Indian women picking berries, our first real encounter with the Indians of Latin America. It was here that I initially gained the impression that, because Indians rarely if ever smiled, they were a naturally distrustful and sullen lot. I was eventually to learn otherwise. Granted, these people harbor a certain amount of mistrust of the white man—and with good reason. (The *South American Handbook* reports that the ancestors of these Araycanas were moved to take revenge against one particularly brutal colonial governor by pouring molten gold down his throat.) But none of this explains their facial expression. What seems to be wariness or hostility, I was later told by a student of the ways of these people, is more likely a deliberate pose handed down from their ancestors, who adopted it eons ago in order to avoid the attention of evil spirits. Indeed, I was to find out myself that behind this impassive mask there might be amusement or anger, generosity or sadness, contempt or pity, or any of the multitude of feelings and attitudes we all share.

We were aching from hunger when we arrived at Estancia Milanegro, where there was a gaucho with one leg and a cook who was nearly deaf. They offered us milk, but when we saw all the dead flies come pouring out the pitcher we excused ourselves. By morning, ravenous beyond belief, we had been reduced to gaping longingly at a huge cabbage growing in the kitchen garden. The sight of it was too much for Yoshiko, who took matters into her own hands by hacking it off. The one-legged gaucho, witnessing the caper, hopped to the scene—only a moment too late. We were already half-way up the hill, and the poor chap simply couldn't pursue us. He shouted to the cook, but the cook couldn't hear him, and so we made our getaway. We ate the cabbage raw, stalk and all. It was the most delicious cabbage we'd ever tasted.

After some bitterly cold nights—the water in our bottles even froze—we finally reached Perito Moreno, our objective for the past two weeks and our first town in all that time. As we rolled down the last hill together, holding hands, enormously pleased, the sun shining brightly, a pickup stopped and the driver stepped out to chat, and just like that, in no time at all, we were given an open invitation stay at his house.

During our three days with Sterio and María Faedo, Yoshiko and I were constantly entertained observing the frantic pace of their chaotic household. On a given afternoon, María might be stirring the soup with one hand while trying to read *The Congress of Tucumán* from the other and kicking a soccer ball out the back door to her daughter and telling us family gossip, all at the same time. Then the doorbell would ring and everything would stop as she welcomed in friends who had been invited to dinner and completely forgotten about. Desperately, like a juggler on ice skates, she would instantly reorganize. Off would come the soup (for the second time), on would go coffee (also to be forgotten about), a firm boot would put the soccer ball out the back door again, and *The Congress of Tucumán* would disappear with the dishes into the sink. Thus María coped—and always found time for us as well, somehow.

By contrast, Sterio was a calm, unflappable man who was totally unfazed by María's violent swings of activity. He managed his father-in-law's far-off estancia, commuting every few weeks, and when the roads were cut off by the winter snows he would fly his private plane there. Near the beginning of the century, the tough pioneers undertook such expeditions, which might last months, using huge wagons pulled by teams of oxen.

While with the Faedos in Perito Moreno, we renewed our acquaintance with the joys of unlimited food. Yoshiko especially, I observed, was becoming increasingly voracious, and so I mentioned to her before leaving that "it might be OK" to carry a can or so of food on our next leg. Back on the road, after the first few kilometers of pulling the Yoshikart, my arms feeling stretched out like an orangutan's, I opened the gear to see what in blazes she had packed. Sitting on top were a can of mixed vegetables and a tin of corned beef. Then I pulled the sleeping bag aside and found the following:

5 loaves of French bread
1 can of cream
1 can of condensed milk
1 half-kg bottle of caramel
1 tin of butter
1 one-kg can of milk powder
1 bottle of pickled carrots
1 half-kg bag of sugar
2 large Spanish onions
1 one-kg can of peaches
1 can of chocolate dessert
1 one-kg pot of strawberry jam
1 small bottle of mayonnaise
2 large salamis
2 cans of peas (green)
2 cans of peas (white)
1 one-kg bag of peanuts
5 bars of chocolate
1 one-kg sack of porridge
5 packets of soup

—and a small medicine bottle full of salt. That, with the ten liters of water, was about the extent of it, except for the thirty fruit "gobstoppers" (jawbreakers) that I later found hidden in

33

Yoshiko's jacket pocket—probably to compensate for the scraps of bread from the trail, my "gold," that I kept for myself in my own jacket pocket.

After passing the tin road sign at the Santa Cruz-Chubut provincial border, we went for two days before seeing another town and finally reached the village of Río Majo, for once not arriving famished. Farther north from here the land became less rugged; there were more villages, and the weather improved, although it was known to snow every winter as far north as Neuquén, still hundreds of miles away.

April 19, I bought Yosh colored ribbons for her beautiful black hair in celebration of her birthday. She reminded me gently that her birthday was April 16, and as for her much-admired "black hair," it was, she pointed out, actually "jet black": "In Japan, as we only have black hair, we make much difference from jet black through coal black, black black, and light black." I found this so typically affecting. Indeed, over the many shared miles, I had grown to love Yoshiko as no one else. For years we had been mysteries to one another, but now, as she became more conversant in English and our revelations to each other deepened, the veils were gradually lifted. One night in the tent she educated me about her family:

"My father's father was of samurai class, and as was custom then he wore hair only at sides of head and shaved bald the center. He had maybe four wives, sort of, one of whom happened to be my grandmother. I never met either one of them.

"Father had finished study in the Tokyo Institute of Technology, and while he was in Kyushu, the island of the south, he happen on my mother. My mother was much spoiled woman, being very pretty, and live in big house with sick father and servants. She had much talent for water and could swim under the sea for shellfish to eat—although, alas, poor me cannot swim. Father was with much passion for her and after negotiation with the family, marriage be complete.

"Then came terrible war, and Mother's only brother, just a boy, die in Burma. Father work in research and near end

34

go to Hokkaido, north island of snow, and with help of wife build such poor house—I know, for I returned with second brother to see what house I was born in. I was shocked to see such poor place, like only for horse!

"In Hokkaido Father was schoolteacher and in winter ski to school. The family are only people expect you to call me Yoshiko. For my friends it is Kola-chan, my special name, and for all others Matsumoto-san. I am youngest and most spoiled of family.

"Father was very strong on brothers because they are more important of course than such of as women. For many years Father would get up at five in morning and study—even study in bed until midnight. Eventually, he is made a doctor-scientist.

"Men are strong in Japan. In other age not long ago new wife need certificate with husband's agreeable comment on all woman duties—sewing, cooking, cleaning, management of money, and, yes, even 'it' in bed. If no such certificate signed, then no marriage certificate is issued. Girl must then return to family.

"This is all family history. I can remember no more. Please we go to sleep now, George."

At Los Tamariscos we found an excuse to celebrate—whereas at Estancia Ventana we had passed the thousand-kilometer mark, here we passed the thousand-*mile* mark. That same night, another celebrant decided to join us—a drunken gaucho who staggered up to our tent and started shouting from outside, "Señorita, I love you!" When I summoned up my deepest voice to warn him off, he wasn't the least perturbed: "Señor," he bellowed, "I love you, too!" (Now, this *was* worrying.) He even stuck his head inside the tent and seemed content to hold that pose all night until I shoved him back with a big push, and at long last he left, riding off into the night in his pickup.

I was becoming increasingly concerned for Yoshiko's safety. Pepper wasn't going to be enough. In the very next town, I bought her a large knife—basically as a deterrent—which from then on she wore hanging from a blue sleeping-bag drawstring around her neck.

Still, Yoshiko seldom gave me a hint of fearfulness; it was only long after the Roaring Forties that she related how the wailing wind had made her cry when she was alone in the tent. What a brave girl!—and a resourceful one, too, capable of remedying situations while I have stood by helpless. Once, on the road long after dark, a wheel rolled off one of the Yoshikarts. I was baffled over what to do, but Yoshie quickly discovered the trouble and fixed it, using some wire from a nearby fence while I held the flashlight.

Farther on, in the lively town of Gobernador Costa, Yoshiko insisted on some excitement and dragged me to a bar where she played a dice game called *cacho* without losing a single round. She then pulled off a minor coup after discovering a tailor selling chocolate at half the current price. Inflation was difficult to keep up with, and so in order not to arouse the tailor's suspicion she bought only a dozen bars at first, then returned with the excuse that she had eaten so many and that they were so good, she needed to buy more. Even then she stopped short of clearing out the man's stock. Next day at the shop the price had doubled.

In Gobernador Costa's post office, after waiting in line beneath a portrait of José de San Martín, the Great Liberator of the southern part of the continent, I bought a stamp with San Martín's portrait, paying for it with money similarly adorned. Out on the street—Avenida San Martín, of course— I walked to the plaza, where I was confronted by a bust of San Martín, while at a bakery the owner informed me that this town of Costa was bigger than nearby San Martín, which itself was bigger than San-Martín-of-the-Andes but smaller than Liberador San Martín in the north. After buying some San Martín biscuits I pondered on the great captain and liberator-general, whose face I now knew better than my brother Anthony's.

By early June we had reached the fabulously beautiful El Bolson valley. One day we camped near the small hamlet of Epugen, where a Mr. McWilliams introduced himself and educated us on the subject of Tschiffely's Ride: In the 1920's, the Argentine Aimé Tschiffely made a legendary journey with two horses from Buenos Aires to the U.S. capital, later recounting his adventures in a book considered to be one of the classics of travel literature. McWilliams, who was not only familiar with the book but had even met Tschiffely, was keenly interested in our trip, and especially in my idea of taking a roundabout route to Alaska (if indeed the impossible could be accomplished) that would bring me through Washington, D.C., thus emulating Tschiffely's Ride.

In fact, my itinerary, as I have hinted before, was influenced not so much by Tschiffely's journey—I hadn't even read his book—as by Snow's. Snow's original plan was not to stop after completing South America but to continue either straight up to Alaska *or* northeastward to Washington, D.C. My insane plan was to do both, thereby "completing" the Americas and, by virtue of the extra distance gained by the detour to the east coast, recording the longest unbroken walk of all time.

We entered our third Argentine province, breathtaking Río Negro, whose vivid green hills were dotted with Swiss-style chalets, all flanked by steep mountains and scored with numerous streams. This may be the most enchanting countryside in the Argentine; with so many streams and rivulets, we were rarely out of earshot of gushing water. Unlike the land to the south, where endlessly straight roads cut across the dreary scrublands, here every bend in the road would reveal a new and refreshing view—every so often even a lumbering cart pulled by yoked oxen. All this, along with the picturesque cottages and wooden bridges, made Río Negro seem a world Constable might have painted.

Now that we were traveling through more populated territory, Yoshiko was finding bread easy to buy and would gaily munch through an entire loaf while walking along with me. She put on weight; in fact, she was ballooning. As many of the roads were cut by streams, this presented a special problem for "fat" Yoshie, because now I couldn't carry her over them as before. The answer proved simple: She carried me across. (One night, after reading something I had written about her weight in my journal that she found offensive, she took issue with my remarks by boldly writing her own entry beneath mine, addressing some yet-unknown reader: "When George say fat, you must not imagine that I was fat—indeed not! I was strong-looking because I'm wider than average girl, and bigger-boned, too. I think you can understand this.")

Lacking any sort of introduction in San Carlos de Bariloche, Argentina's trendiest ski resort and a genuine tourist trap, we just kept knocking on doors until someone in fact consented to let us pitch our tent in his garden. There was even a watchdog thrown into the bargain, a Labrador retriever who took a great shine to us and enjoyed guarding— i.e., sleeping in—our tent while we were away.

This seemed an ideal town in which to drum up publicity—which, for lack of sponsorship or other sources of funds, we depended upon as a key element in the success of the entire venture. Things started off well enough when I succeeded in arranging an interview with a national newspaper, but the deal fell through when the correspondent simply forgot to show up. Then we were introduced to the publisher of the local rag. Here there was immediate keen interest, indeed excitement. No sooner did the publisher realize the import of the story sitting in front of him than he rushed out of his office and ran next door to borrow a camera from the butcher, hurried back, and herded Yoshiko and me and the entire newspaper staff outside the building, bunched us all up against the wall, and took his best shot.

I later had the opportunity to view this gem of photojournalism. Somewhere at the back of the throng you can even make out a smiling, half-hidden Yoshiko and George. It wasn't the staff's lucky day either, however, as their boss had been drunk and his aim understandably poor, and so the photo reveals only half the line-up, along with a huge, stunning display of pavement.

No, said the people at the local national bank in Bariloche, they had *not* received my two hundred dollars cabled to them from England a month before, but if and when they did, they would forward it to Neuquén.

After leaving Bariloche and reaching yet another province, Neuquén, our first priority was giving a name to the puppy sleeping quietly in Yoshiko's pocket. The puppy, a stray, was mostly black, with a motley face, one white paw, and more white on his breast, and had stubby legs and beady eyes—and we loved him. We at last decided that for an Argentine dog an Argentine Indian name would be apt. We knew only one Indian word, *putrochoique*, meaning "stomach of baby ostrich"—it was the name of a hamlet where we had camped out—and so the puppy became Choique ("choy-key"—baby ostrich). Everyone we met approved of this name.

On the second day from Bariloche it grew much colder, and before long the whole countryside took on the look of Christmastime, with snowflakes slowly falling and coating everything in sight. Pretty as it was, the snow represented risk to us, and so it was with much relief that by early evening we stumbled on a farmhouse. Soon we were in a cozy kitchen wolfing down hamburgers with our host Jorge. Jorge wore a full American cowboy's getup, including spurs, and was intent on living out some bizarre Wild West fantasy with his Winchester repeating rifle, Western-style saddle, and lazy American-type drawl. Indeed, he looked like a movie Western star.

As we talked, Jorge cleaned his Colt six-shooter. He pointed to one of his several cats. "Mouser, the black one there, he's a killer, all right—may even rough up that there mutt," he said, referring to Choique. In fact, tiny Choique soon had the terrible Mouser penned under the stove, and later slept very well in the cat's box. We were proud of our Choique—he was a special tiger, just like Yosh.

Jorge treated us very well and gave us a bedroom where we spent a romantic night listening to the hushed fall of snow, while all of Jorge's housepets slept on our sleeping bag, which we had laid out on the floor. Next morning, the snow had stopped, and we moved on, passing on our way out the bullet-riddled roadsign just beyond Jorge's "ranch." Despite the weather we ate only cold food in the *campo*—the countryside—and a hot meal only if we had reached a town. My Swedish gas stove, which I had brought out from England, had never been anything but trouble. Every evening produced the same foul language as the damned thing refused to light, ran out of fuel before cooking anything, or just covered everything in soot; no amount of tinkering, even Yosh's, ever cured it. Finally, one freezing night it not only cooked the porridge, it melted the pot into the mash, and then the whole shebang flamed up like a roman candle. With great satisfaction I booted the infernal contraption into the campo.

We now entered a national park that took three days to clear, and despite the downhill going my feet were giving me so much trouble that I could hardly notice the great splendor of the land through my watery eyes. The time was made lighter, however, by Yoshiko's recital of her life in Japan. One night after supper she told me: "At school I became very proficient in sewing and woman's duties. Can you believe I was top of grade in such things? But of English near bottom because I hated it, and history—which you love—I find bore. Imagine, I was once so skinny girl they call me 'Olive' from Popeye show off television, and my great height was biggest worry of me then as I was tallest girl in the class.

"My tallness helped me much in sport, and I played volleyball for and became sprinter of Nagoya City. But now I cannot run because of much greediness and fat legs.

"After high school I do not have idea of university. In Japan almost everybody can enter university. Instead I spend one year in special sewing school and take classes for tea ceremony that has not altered in more than one thousand years—and in Ikebana I learn the art of flowers."

By now Choique had grown too heavy for Yoshiko to carry in her jacket pocket, and so we transferred him to the top of the sleeping bag in the rucksack. Most of the time he would sleep there, but occasionally he would poke his puckish head out to see what was going on in the world. Few creatures can ever have shown such enthusiasm as did this little pooch for our tent. He would fight the sleeping bag, swing on the guyline, and chase his tail endlessly. Choique had a special job in life—he was to be a companion for my woman, and when he grew bigger he would be her guard. When one day a man came near her and the pup actually barked, Yoshiko was proud of little Choique. We started making him sleep outside to toughen him up, but he would inevitably sneak into the tent and end up in the sleeping bag. He had become part of the team. He drank the same milk we did, ate the same bread, and even slept on his back like us, with all four paws sticking up in the air.

Just outside Aguila we left the Roaring Forties behind, technically at least, and entered the more pacific latitudes of the thirties. In fact, never again would we awake in the morning thinking, before anything else, "What is the terrible wind doing today?" All the northern passes were blocked by snow, and therefore our only route through Neuquén Province led to the northeast, hugging the mighty Río Limay. The villages came thick and fast near the city of Neuquén, the largest so far on our itinerary, and the region steadily became more urbanized. Just before the city, I cleared 2,500 km— half of Argentina—and about this point the ghost of Sebastian Snow walking in 1973 passed me by: He had arrived in Neuquén a day earlier than I did. I had held off this formidable pacemaker far longer than I expected.

We spent three nights in the city, two of them writhing in luxury at the Hotel Inglés (translation: English Hotel, though it was run by a charming Polish family). The owner related his exploits in the Polish army while showing us faded photos of that history, including those of a fine-looking young man surrounded by horses and lancers, staring across the gulf of years. "I was a cavalry officer," he told us, "and in the great disaster we fought the Germans by day and the Russians by night. We were the last unit to surrender—I spent five years as a POW in Prussia." He also explained the medals on the wall—he had been decorated for stopping a German tank column.

Yosh wasn't thrilled by all this war talk, and later she again wrote in my journal: "In Neuquén hotel I was feeling low but George tried to make me happy by dance of striptease so funny with sexy whistle music. I laughed and thought how I love such a silly man."

No, the national bank in Neuquén had not got my two hundred dollars, but it would most certainly reach them eventually, and they would redirect it to San Rafael, our next large town.

Once across the busy bridge we were in another arm of the oddly shaped Río Negro Province. That night we camped in a fruit field, seemingly an innocent enough activity. But toward midnight, as we sat munching on jam sandwiches while Yoshiko animatedly discoursed on spaceships and the rest of the universe, the *policía* boldly approached, bellowing "Documento!"—their favorite word—and flashing bright lights. One of these clods blithely kicked the tent's main peg out, which then collapsed onto a lit candle. Fortunately no damage was done, but we had to pack everything up *rápido*, including our half-eaten dinner, and haul all this plus baby dog to the police station. There the farce concluded when the police returned our passports (choosing for some unfathomable reason to conduct this business by the latrine out back) and issued the admonition, "Don't do it again!" It took us an hour to walk back to where we had camped before, and there we resumed eating our jam sandwiches within a hundred yards of the fruit field.

At Bardia del Medio, we were finally on the verge of clearing the great Patagonian plateau. Here we were given a stiff warning to take lots of water along with us because just to the north lay a section of *pampa seca*—dry pampa. (The pampas are the prairies of Argentina.) We conscientiously filled our two five-liter bottles to capacity, just in case. I even considered the idea of strict rationing. Ironically, we had hardly cleared the town when down came the heavy rain, which soon turned to snow, and before we knew it we were in the midst of a blizzard. Fortunately, it looked like we would be able to reach the northern edge of the Patagonian plateau, a half-day's march away, just in the nick of time, but for the meanwhile we encamped in freezing whiteout conditions—visibility about three feet.

The wedge-shaped tent was only 7 by 4 by 4-1/2 feet high, and with an expanding Yoshiko, two large sets of gear, a dog, myself—and ten liters of water—this left about as much space as a pair of tight trousers. Gradually the weight of the snow reduced this to matchbox size, and eventually the snow-saturated tent developed freezing drips. Hugging our candle-flame, I passed the time by telling Yoshiko the tragic story of Captain Scott's expedition to the South Pole; Yoshiko cried at the sad ending. No one was going to get any sleep this night anyway—except Choique, who was sleeping on his back, paws in the air, on the only dry patch.

With morning's washed-out glow, we heard a truck struggling through the drifts. Digging my way out through the still-falling snow, I finally reached the road and casually asked the driver for a lift. All of us plus the gear—and ten liters of water—were bundled into the truck and taken to a bar back along the road we had walked the day before. There we spent a miserable day huddled in front of a few burning sticks (firewood is scarce on the *pampa seca*). This fire held us prisoner the entire day, for to move more than five feet away meant donning mittens (we already had our coats on). The family had built this bar themselves but for some reason had left a gaping hole above the window, and through this the snow was drifting in. In the evening they went ahead with their dinner while we sat in a corner eating our few tins of sardines. Then, for some obscure reason, we weren't allowed to sleep in the bar that night but had to pitch our sodden tent in a windswept shed, where the ground was iron-hard. We couldn't get a single peg in, and so all night the whole thing hung draped on our faces like a clothesline full of soaked wash. It didn't escape my attention that Yoshiko was not amused.

To our great relief, the snow had stopped by the following morning, allowing us at last to leave Cold Comfort Farm.

Farther on Yoshiko made the acquaintance of a family from Catriel who had given her a lift, and although Catriel was off my route, at her urging I agreed to go there for a friendly visit. The Mandones family were a wonderful bunch who cooked up a dinner for me as soon as I arrived despite the fact that it was midafternoon, let us use their shower, and gave us pretty much all we needed. Yosh put the filthy tent in a bucket of ice-cold water to wash it. It looked so grim, we weren't going to move that night. We ended up spending five days.

The first morning the youngest son took us to his school. What a staggering reception! Hundreds of kids were charging all over the place, classes were abandoned for the morning in favor of anarchy, and we were showered with bits of paper, textbooks, and math exercises—it didn't seem to matter so long as we signed our autographs. The staff were just the same. This mild hysteria grew with the arrival of a priest, Padre Luis Madinabeitia, who spoke to Yoshiko in perfect Japanese—he had spent four hours a day for seven years mastering this difficult language.

Later that day we were invited to yet another school, a commercial institute, where the teenage schoolgirls packed the aisles and even stood on their desks to get a glimpse of us. A question-and-answer session was held, with the principal, Mrs. Furmadavlos, serving as translator, and Yoshiko sang a Japanese song, to an enthusiastic reception. Most of the students' questions were very intelligent, concerning the good and bad sides of Argentina, England, Japan, and other countries we had visited. The question inevitably arose concerning the conflicting claims to the Islas Malvinas—the Falkland Islands. I said that no matter what Britain or Argentina thought, the ultimate question was: What did the people of the Malvinas/Falklands think? Most everyone agreed, a stance which in retrospect seems to have been most unpatriotic (or polite, or sensible, depending on one's point of view). At the end of this hectic session, the girls lunged forward toward Yoshiko, showering her with their rings, necklaces, and other bits of jewelry—indeed, anything to be considered a gift. At this point, our hostess, Mrs. Furmadavlos, turned to me and said, "You will never travel alone again, for you have these children's hearts with you always."

Northern Argentina

With our walk over the dam on the Río Colorado, we entered the temperate prairielands of La Pampa Province, at last freeing ourselves from Patagonia's snowy grip and thus overcoming the first great obstacle of South America's climate. With luck and proper timing, within one year, ten months, the walk would reach the Darien Gap, the slender neck of swamp and rainforest connecting the two American continents. Indeed, it had to, if I was going to beat the annual rains that would make passage impossible for months.

La Pampa is unremittingly flat, the air cool and dry. The resulting increase in visibility meant that at midday I would see, at a distance of perhaps twenty miles, a perfectly straight horizon that seemed to go on forever; and at nightfall I could detect the warm orange glow of the candlelit tent or the cold pinpoint of Yoshiko's flashlight hours before I ever reached camp. I never knew where she and the tent and the dog would be, only where they should be—just as I never definitely knew where I was myself in these lands. Choique would spot me first and come galloping out of the darkness, followed by Yoshiko with a hug and a huge smile. If I was in a bad condition, which was usual, Yoshiko would tend to my aches while humming songs of Mount Fuji, slow rivers, and lost love, and then we would have our dinner beneath the stars.

Because we were going across one of the province's short corners, it took less than a week to cross La Pampa. In the next province, Mendoza, we were surprised to learn that nearby there was a Japanese community in Colonia Los Andes, a three-day walk to the north. Yoshiko was excited at the prospect of staying among her people, speaking her language, and eating her native food, and so we agreed to split up temporarily so that Yosh could take a lift directly to the town. Once there, she could also take Choique to the veterinarian for an examination—he had not been his usual self since frisking around with a sick dog in Catriel.

Three days later I rejoined my family over a huge rice dinner at the home of the Makiguchi family. The change of environment had done Yoshiko a lot of good, while Choique, after his three injections, was subdued. Another evening was spent with the Kishimotos. The father ran a karate school and was one of the top-rated practitioners in Argentina. In fact, he considered himself better than his fourth-dan black-belt rating, although no one in South America was qualified to test him. Yosh and I were amused when this formidable man couldn't get the lid off a new jar of pickles, while his wife managed it fairly easily. "All a matter of technique," she said modestly.

The Japanese have a well-deserved reputation for being fastidious housekeepers—I had observed this myself in Japan—and so I wasn't prepared for the fantastic chaos in some of these people's houses. In one, junk and magazines were piled in great half-toppled towers, and important items were lost for days under the accumulated debris. The family promised to show us their special bathtub—when they could find it!

In mid-July we reached San Rafael. Yes, the local national bank had received my two hundred dollars—but they had sent it back to Neuquén because they didn't know who I was. They would write asking Neuquén to forward it to me in Mendoza.

The last pampa before Mendoza took longer than usual because of blisters brought on by my now-wrecked first pair of boots. With soles almost adrift and broken-down heels and gaping holes all around, my gait was reduced to a lopsided shuffle, more like scooping up the road with a dustpan and brush than walking. Each day, within an hour the accumulated dust and rubble would be packed hard into the boots' gaping mouths, the heels of my socks would be worn through, and I would have to wrap tape around my feet five or six times just to have a surface to tread on.

In this condition I was in no mood to be hauling extra baggage, no matter how slight. One day I happened to check the rucksack and discovered something new and unexpected. "What's *this*, Yoshiko?"

"Is nothing, George, just a little bottle of scent," she said, smiling sweetly and fluttering her eyelids in mock coyness.

"Little! That's half a liter without the glass bottle! Couldn't you have gotten a bigger size?"

"No, George," she answered truthfully, missing the point, "it is the biggest."

"How long have I been carting this dead-weight?"

"Only from Perito Moreno, George."

"But that's over a thousand miles! What's it for?" I asked stupidly.

It is to make me smell beautiful at night, George. All of women like to smell of pretty in their beds, you know." The perfume bottle remained. As the man said, women are downright unpredictable—you never know exactly how they will get their way.

On July 25, on the road exactly six months since leaving Ushuaia on that rainy morning, we arrived in Mendoza, a dynamic industrial city of a half-million, our largest so far. Having completed 3,469 km—roughly the distance from Paris to Istanbul—we had covered a third of the South American continent.

But we were not in a celebratory mood. Choique had been getting steadily thinner and sicklier despite periodic in-

jections from veterinarians along the way and the medicine
we had been steadily giving him. The most recent vet, here
in Mendoza, diagnosed his condition as distemper and gave
him a fifty-fifty chance of survival. That night, he lay listlessly
in a corner of the tent, all his past enthusiasm vanished. Then
he suddenly exploded out of the tent, barking and chasing
his tail in a comical way before collapsing in exhaustion, his
mouth foaming. Fearing rabies, which at the time was a serious threat in the Argentine, we kept our hands clear of his
mouth and took him back to the vet in the morning.

Slumped on the examination table, the gallant, pathetic
little bag of bones could no longer even stand. The vet said
the distemper had brought on epilepsy; chances of survival—
a hundred to one. Hearing this, Yoshiko let out a terrible
wail, her face contorted with pain, and she crumpled to the
floor, sobbing convulsively. I still remember the sight of
Yoshiko's twisted face and the crippled dog staring forlornly
through his sick eyes.

I refused to let him be put to sleep. If there was one
chance in a hundred, there was still hope; I wouldn't have
been attempting this trek if I didn't believe in long odds. We
returned Choique to the rucksack, and with yet more expensive, useless medicine and two broken hearts we left the vet's
office and found sunshine in a park nearby. Here we sat in
our misery while Choique averted his eyes from us, as though
we had let him down. We were too dispirited even to give
him more of the expensive drug. No doubt sensing his im-
pending death, he crawled away from us as best he could to
the shade of a tree.

Our misery gave way to exhaustion, and we dozed on the
grass. Late in the afternoon we awoke with a jolt. Choique
was gone. In the dying light we desperately searched every
corner of the now-freezing park, all in vain.

Choique had not been just another spoiled pet; he had
shared our food and bed, our home and our adventure. Above
all, he had kept Yoshiko company in the desperately empty
pampas. It was days before we recovered from our desolation
and sense of failure, but like most things the black turned to

gray and finally to near-white. We eventually found ourselves reminiscing about our lost trailmate and laughing at his foibles—about how he was going to become a Disney film star, or the time he chased a mouse into the tent and frightened Yoshiko, or the time I was in my usual late-morning hurry to hit the road and Choique had run off with the top of the water bottle and buried it somewhere out on the prairie.

But the lighthearted memories came only with time. That night Yoshiko looked at a yellow near-full moon and whispered sadly, "Do you think Choique on the moon, George?"

"Yes, love, I think he probably is."

The overall schedule permitted us to spend almost a month in Mendoza recuperating and taking in the sights. Near the vet's we had found a little shop where we regularly bought cheese and salami, our great rage at the time. After a while, we felt comfortable enough to ask the shopowners, a personable couple, if we could leave our gear there, which was handy since the shop was near the center of town. From this regular contact a friendship sprang up, and soon, at their invitation, we were camped out in the garage of their tiny home, at the back of the shop.

Germán Barboza (the first name is pronounced "hare-*mon*") was a tall man in his mid-twenties with a bushy beard and dark, burning eyes; the beard alone made him unusual, as I rarely saw one in Argentina, where it was generally regarded as the mark of a revolutionary. His raucous, humorous manner contrasted sharply with that of his wife, María, a slight blond girl of Spanish parentage who spoke some English. Rounding out the family was their son Germáncito, the prettiest baby imaginable.

As in most Argentine households we had seen, in the Barboza's disorder and chaos ruled supreme. Mealtimes were something of a mystery—we might eat dinner at midnight, or two dinners three hours apart around midday, or perhaps none at all. In many ways this was fortunate, as Yoshiko seldom emerged before the disgusting hour of one in the afternoon—I had risen with the larks and leapt out of the garage at twelve-thirty.

A typical mealtime might go something like this: María would be rocking Germáncito between forkfuls of cold macaroni and "la-la'ing" to a popular tango blasting out of the TV, while Germán would be waving his fork conducting the tango orchestra and reciting the "Alas, poor Yorick . . . " speech to the skull he had molded from garden clay. Meanwhile, Yoshiko had noticed that the milk had run over and the potatoes boiled dry. "No problem, Yoshika," María would happily shout. (Neither María nor most Latin Americans could bring themselves to say, "Yoshiko," as among Spanish speakers the -o ending is most common for male names.) They might run out of salt, sugar, or bread, even though bread was one of their shop's biggest items. "No problem, Yoshika. We'll just go to the shop next door and buy some." Meanwhile, Germán saw to it that they never ran out of his favorite sticky buns, which he would live on for days at a time.

Besides shelter and hot water and pretty much all we wanted, we had one thing at the Barbozas' we didn't want— a mad scientist. Every night about two in the morning, Little John—an erstwhile dental technician, we were told—would set down his bit of carpeting just outside the garage where we slept, lie down on it, and light up a cigarette. Then, propping up his head on his hand, he would launch into an extended harangue, roaring imprecations and ultimatums to the world in general and insults at the ruling military junta in particular, while periodically banging against "our" metal garage door with a slab of lumber. The first night this happened, before we had any idea of Little John's routine, Yoshiko and I clung to each other in terror; it sounded like two men were trying to kill each other, with the impact periodically buckling the garage door. The second night—after Germán had briefed us on the scenario—we dared a peep outside. While Little John raved and cursed at the world, all we could make out in the dim street light was a headful of long, disheveled gray hair frantically lashing the air.

We had been keeping a list of the Argentines with whom we had had more than a passing engagement, and while in Mendoza we wrote to many of them, over forty in all. Mum later asked for a copy of the list, and it was her special pleasure to send a postcard—one of the "Castles of Kent" or "Rainham, High Street" variety—to all those who had helped us, often lonely cowboys who might not get another letter in years. This was our way of saying thank you for all the hospitality we received; we were most careful on this.

One morning, I stopped in at the Bank of London and collected my first mail from home. Mum seemed to be in good spirits, although she noticed in a photo taken of me in Patagonia that I looked "a bit untidy" and hoped that I was combing my hair—she didn't want people "over there" thinking I had been "dragged up." (In fact, Yosh and I had neither a comb nor a brush at this time—we were using a dinner fork.)

At the post office I picked up my second, desperately needed pair of Berghaus boots, but not until some dim clerk had ripped the package to pieces and extorted twenty-five dollars in the name of customs duty. Later, at a newspaper office for an interview, when I complained bitterly about this robbery by bureaucratic estimation, I was told pointedly, "Keep quiet, or they will close us down." That's freedom of the press for you!

For some time now, we had been planning for a baby, in a quite active way. Not being married, not having a house, job, or much money—these weren't considered important. But Yoshiko's being twenty-seven was. To determine the proper timing, Yoshiko bought a thermometer and every evening took her temperature, which was always too high, and then thrust it in my mouth, often in midsentence, for comparison.

Then, during our stay at the Barbozas', Yoshiko ran seriously late on her monthly period. Sure that this signified something, she wanted to take a pregnancy test. "No problem, Yoshika," said María. "I have a home test kit right here in the shop—next to the sardines." And with that she tripped into the kitchen for hot water (Germán's tea water, as it happened) and like a medieval alchemist mixed Yoshiko's urine with all manner of potions. "No problem, Yoshika," announced María. "You're pregnant!"

When I heard this, my knees started quivering. What a shock . . . a surprise . . . no, a shock! Germán, who was still trying to locate his tea water, had to drop everything and help me to a chair. A concerned María offered to call a doctor, but I asked simply that my bed be prepared. All the while Yoshiko calmly carried on, oblivious to my dazed state, washing socks and humming merrily.

The next day, Yoshiko went to the hospital for proper confirmation, for if she were in fact pregnant, the nature of the journey would change drastically. Even before the results came in, however, we made the decision to get married and set the process in motion. After one or two frustrating preliminary rounds wrestling with the bureaucracy, we consulted a lawyer friend of the Barbozas, who mapped out the whole process for us. "You will need at least fifteen documents— birth certificate, passport, visa, medical history plus a medical examination . . ." she went on and on. And that wasn't the half of it.

First I rang up an English minister. "He's not in until October. Why not try the Methodist church? They have *two* ministers." I rang up the Methodist church: "One of the ministers is in Buenos Aires indefinitely and the other is in Europe. Why not try the Evangelist church?" We went to the Evangelist church: "Come back in two hours." Two hours later: "Come back in an hour." One hour later: "Wait." Eventually the minister came. "Can you marry us?" "Sorry—don't do weddings. Why not try the Schweitzer School?" The next day at the Schweitzer School, we found the minister in. "I would be delighted to marry you," said Pastor Ortega as we sighed with relief, "but of course this is impossible in Argentina unless you have been married in a civil ceremony first." Of course.

And so we proceeded to the Governor's Palace to apply for a marriage certificate. Wrong place. We were told to go to the local Registro Civil. We were up uncharacteristically early the next day and off to the local Registro Civil, which we were allowed to enter only after submitting to a thorough body search, as it sits atop the police station. The moment I spotted the office boss, an unpleasantly plump woman with the jaundiced look of an ex-con, I knew we were in for yet more harassment and delays. Dripping in gold jewelry and sporting owl-winged glasses, The Monster (not her real name) never looked directly at us but just snarled out her information through tight, sneering lips: "You must go to the Governor's Palace and get form 8.204/63."

Back at the Governor's Palace: "As you have no birth certificate, you must get a notarized translation of your passport—then you can have the 8.204/63." María quickly found us the necessary man, a public translator, or *traductore*. There are many of these *traductores* in Argentina; they are the ultimate middlemen, who owe much of their livelihood to the existence of obscure regulations. The noble *doctor,* as he styled himself, took our passports and our £5 and told us to come back in the morning.

We picked up our translation the next day and took it to the Registro Civil. The Monster examined the paper closely. "Jesús Cristo!" she cried. "Where are the father's names?" Where indeed! We rushed over to the *traductore doctor,* who reluctantly dropped everything to add the missing names, and then back across the city to the dreadful woman. "Take it to the Palace of Justice and get it notarized," she bellowed. She never once stopped her furious rubber-stamping activity to look at us directly.

At the Palace of Justice the clerk told us, "This document is useless; this *traductore* is registered to translate only Italian, not English." By this time María was constantly by our side, steering us through this lunatic maze. The next stop was another translator—a *profesor doctor traductore,* no less— who assured us that he was registered in English, and this time it would cost us only £7.

September 14 came the welcome news that we had passed

our medicals. At noon we collected our new *traducciones*. María gasped, "But where are the fathers' names?"

After an hour, the *doctor profesor* rectified this lapse, and we staggered to the Palace of Justice, where they legalized it with a whopping big stamp. We then made our way up the stairs for the clerk of the court to initial the whole mess. María was jubilant; we were just fed up.

But this was no time to rest. Now we had to rush over to the Governor's Palace to pick up the coveted 8.204/63 and then back across the city to The Monster, who wasn't overly keen on the green ink the *traductore* had used but with a resigned nod stuffed the nonsense into her files anyway.

September 15, Germán and María, who were to be our witnesses and hence by Argentina custom our godparents, came with us to the registry office to have their *documentos* checked while The Monster fingerprinted Yoshiko and me.

September 16, I sang, for the twentieth morning in a row, "I'm getting married in the morning . . ." and we all trooped down to the cop shop, where the police waved their automatic weapons to indicate we could enter the registry office and thus get married. Monster read some words to us, which María translated. (There was a *traductore* present, but of course he could only *read* English, not speak it.) In a bored, nasty voice, Monster told us to have patience and be considerate—and above all never to let the trivia of life interfere with our happiness. Finally, she shook our hands while managing to look the other way—I'm convinced she never did see us.

We were married! Legality satisfied, Yoshiko was already involved in the more important business of shopping for dinner; in fact, she had prudently brought along a shopping bag to our wedding.

But of course that was only our first wedding! For the religious ceremony we sent out invitations, and Germán and María even held a reception for us. Among the attendants were our friends Rolando and Florencia Pinto, who for the occasion had driven all the way from Piedra del Aguila, a thousand miles to the south in Patagonia, and who ended up being our witnesses—and thus our second pair of godparents. Everyone urged us to borrow "good" clothes for the religious ceremony, but we adamantly refused, for by now even Yosh wished to remain loyal to our serviceable road clothes. As a concession to propriety, we had them freshly cleaned, and for a special touch, Yoshiko had María plait red and white flowers through her black hair—she indeed looked so beautiful.

The service at the Albert Schweitzer School was read in lilting English by Pastor Ortega, who had gone out of his way to fulfill my request that the Book of Common Prayer be used and who did splendidly in his rendition of the difficult (and beautiful) phrases. Yoshiko spoke her responses very well, her English having improved dramatically, although afterward she asked me, "Who is this boy, Richard, in the line . . . 'for Richard or for poorer'?"

Florencia and Rolando drove us around the town in their Citroën, horn blaring, as is tradition, while we stood up and waved to everyone in sight through the open top. Eventually some univited guests turned up in the form of blue steel helmets and businesslike carbines, thus bringing an official close to our wedding celebration.

The second week of September we had received the wonderful news of Yoshiko's test: "Positivo!" The news made us both happy and sad, for it meant Yoshiko would now be leaving the journey; it would have been most impractical and probably even dangerous to continue a journey of this sort in her *embarazada* condition. Although we didn't articulate it as such, this had been our plan all the time. Indeed, I had always thought that Yoshiko would stay on until Mendoza, and that's exactly what happened.

Yoshiko's return home had to be arranged. As the Mendoza airport was closed for construction (it was being enlarged in preparation for the 1978 World Cup), she would be departing from San Juan, to the north. In order not to waste valuable time, I decided to walk ahead to San Juan and return at once to Mendoza by bus. Germán, stout fellow that he was, accompanied me for the first 6 km before turning around and limping back to town. I, too, was suffering on the hard *pavimento* road after such a long layoff.

I was soaked by the heat and turned immediately to a hot-weather routine, applying face cream in the morning and seeking shelter in the afternoon burnout. Sometimes the only protection was the desert scrub. After one agonizing morning haul through this all but lifeless country, I found the answer to a prayer. As I hobbled along exhausted, dizzily thinking of the famous Kentish brew, R. White's Lemonade, I stumbled upon an old bus without wheels. Inside was a bright young man and the provocative sight of a giant fridge, which actually worked. He not only gave me all the drinks I wanted free and freezing, but cooked me up a steak sandwich as well.

The man then led me to an abode hut, where the family let me lay out my sleeping bag on one of their beds. While I lay there quietly reflecting on solitary travel, a policeman from the nearby Mendoza-San Juan border post burst in and gave me an onion. "You tell him," he shouted, pointing to the owner of the hut, "that England is not in Africa as he thinks, but near Mexico, as I think." With this he drew a map in the sand covering the floor to compound everyone's confusion. The policeman was obviously correct because he shouted the loudest, and so I quickly agreed with him and thus was able to spend the rest of the afternoon in peace.

In the push to San Juan, although the asphalt burned my feet, one driving thought pushed me to do three 40-km days virtually on the trot—the thought of salvaging just a few more days or even hours with my love before she left me. I finished the 156 km to San Juan in three and a half days, despite one well-meaning man who warned me to give up before I was murdered on the roadside while I slept in the tent. What a hellish walk nevertheless! If this was spring, what on earth could summer be like? One thing for sure—I would need a damn good hat.

I took the bus back and rejoined my radiant Yoshiko long before she expected me. The cost of blisters, burned face, and five pounds off my frame was well worth hearing her sweet voice so soon again.

Come October, everyone bade us farewell at the railway station. Even Little John was on hand to say good-bye in one of his rare moments of lucidity. The train rattled along close to the mountains, and soon we had to shut the windows, as the desert sand was blowing through. I was reminded of the time I had arrived at Perito Moreno earlier than expected to find Yoshiko in the process of laboriously carving "I Love George" into the sandy hillside with a stick; I had reacted with surprise, she with girlish embarrassment. But now I was under a black shadow of melancholy. One more sunset together and then. . . .

"George," Yoshiko said, breaking the spell, "I must finish my story to you. Do you know I was once offered other husband? This happened because parents no understand my feelings, and so they make arrangement with matchmaker. It happen during our long being apart.

"My mother and I meet the thirty-three-years-old man in a lobby of large hotel in Nagoya. It was so strange experience. Eventually he take me for ride in car around park and we make small talk. Some days later Mother ask how I feel on matter, for she has intelligence that the man is willing to marry me, I being acceptable for him. Of course, I must decline, for our feelings were becoming stronger by this time and my desire to go on this journey with you. Mother was upset, and she imagine youngest daughter to be problematic burden forever.

"One evening with much courage I let about us be known to all my family together. George, I dare not mention about idea of South America because I think they must go like crazy! For whole of evening they all question me with much care and seriousness. They all disapprove with our reuniting in England except my new sister-in-law Yo-chan, who doesn't have sufficient bravery to express her view, being typical girl of Japan. Other sister-in-law think idea crazy because England people no eat fish.

"My elder brother say that it is only that I wish to travel and I don't really love you. Younger brother, who also has authority over me, think critically of me for not looking to what is near instead of what is far and anyway impossible. Mother is much worried that if I return to Japan unmarried no respectable Japanese man will want me for having been with foreigner. Father is concerned that if I live in England the local people will not accept me for it is known that the English look down on all us Asians. This is how my family think at this time.

"It took many months for me to gain the important permission from my parents; what persuade them was your many long letters and finally a letter from your mother.

"Mother and I travel to island of Kyushu for to consult with her family. I cause much embarrassment to Mother for not bowing low enough and for not using the very best form of address to betters. She has to apologize for such disrespectful daughter constantly.

"Finally all of everyone agree and I even gain the necessary permission from youngest brother, but he says, 'Just you see what happens to you, little sister.' All is fixed, and not even murder, two weeks before, of Japanese girl on Russian ferry ship *Baikal* can stop me now."

The train jolted to a stop; we had reached San Juan. At the airport, I gave Yoshiko a small going-away present to open on the plane and told her the story of the Laurel and Hardy movie where they are busy wrecking someone's house while the householder is wrecking their car in retaliation. In the end, everyone's unhappy because it was all a big mistake, and Laurel and Hardy give the householder a cigar as a consolation, but as they walk away the cigar explodes—and thus a sad ending is transformed into a funny one.

I finished the story just as we reached the final clearance desk. The clerk's "out" stamp thudded down on Yoshiko's passport like a guillotine severing me from a part of my life. I felt my insides shake. One last kiss, then one last glance, and she was gone. I watched through a veil of tears as the plane thundered down the runway, lifted off, dwindled to a dot, and then was all but a memory.

I felt I was choking, shattered like a broken bottle. When would I see her again? When would I see my child? If I could pull this off (and at the time it seemed a monumental "if"), it would take me a year and a half at the very least to reach Panama—if the Darien Gap didn't nail me. How would I manage in the meantime? I dragged myself to an empty corner of the airport compound, slumped down on the ground, and sobbed.

I wanted to be alone with my misery, but couldn't. One after another, people kept approaching me and striking up conversations. One chap ended up taking me to a local trade fair under construction, and this helped lift my spirits, but I certainly didn't need the company of the nasty young couple who next latched on to me. Learning of my immediate plans, they began lecturing me with the hauteur of those who pride themselves in successfully predicting the worst.

"Oh, you think *this* is hot? This heat is *nothing*," pronounced the husband. "In the desert to the north, it will be much worse for you—no shelter, *nothing*."

"Much, much hotter," the wife gleefully added.

"And there are those snakes, and out there are millions of deadly spiders," the man continued.

"They might kill you," beamed his sour-faced wife.

"Of course, then there's El Zonda, the hot wind—it will burn you up."

"Just like a dead rat," his echo obliged.

"Don't forget the Tucumán police," Mr. Misery thoughtfully concluded, "they'll shoot you for sure. They don't ask questions up there, you know."

A good night's sleep helped me put their dire warnings out of mind, and indeed, the next day, it was a relief to be moving again. For the first time I wore my giant sunhat, Yoshiko's present to me before departing. At first I felt embarrassed to wear it, but it quickly became my best friend, and eventually I would no sooner walk without it than without my trousers.

The first evening I camped out it took me forever to get

the tent up. I used to love the little orange wonder, but without warm Yoshiko and soft Choique I hated it. The tiny, trashy transistor radio I had purchased to help fight the loneliness had just the opposite effect: I could pick up only a Chilean station which announced its call letters every five minutes to the accompaniment of "I'm getting married in the morning . . ."

The next morning I was no sooner on the road than I was overtaken by blinding fatigue induced by the heat smashing down from the cloudless sky. I took to wearing a wet towel over my head, underneath the sunhat; but even then, the towel would be bone-dry and solid as a board within a bare fifteen minutes.

It took no time at all to realize that if I were going to survive such conditions, I would have to discipline myself, and toward this end I quickly developed certain routines. I would ration my five liters of water over a day and a half, two days if necessary, taking a swig every thirty minutes or so. In the very worst heat, in desperation, I would reduce this interval to fifteen minutes. By the fourteenth minute, I would begin involuntarily checking my watch every ten seconds. The last ten seconds would be a frenzied countdown, "ten . . . nine . . . eight . . ." and even then I cheated, "seven . . . four . . . one . . ." Frantically, I would rip the bottle free of the rucksack and ram it into my parched throat. At that, the sensation of drinking wasn't there. The liquid would be warm as bathwater, no different than the scorching air. As soon as the last drops had passed my lips I would think: I could do with a drink! And then it would take all my resolve to wait another quarter hour, another countdown.

Ordinarily I wouldn't stop walking on any account, be it a loose bootlace or a stone in my sock, until I had finished a set number of kilometers or hours or hit some other target. It was so important to keep a rhythm going, for if I broke it, I got nowhere. In fact, I wanted to stop and rest nearly all the time, sometimes desperately, and when things were tough going, the effort not to dump into an inviting ditch and lie down was enormous.

But now I had all but run out of water and was dizzy with dehydration. I stopped at an isolated mud house—a place barely fit for humans, I thought. When the occupants leaned a stump against the door to bar me, I walked over to their rusty water tank and filled my bottle after throwing a few handfuls over my face and taking a few gulps of the turgid gray liquid.

I began to realize that there was something wrong when I dropped the lid to the water bottle into the sand three times in a row while trying to screw it back on. I walked a few ragged kilometers, feeling very strange inside, desperately scanning the horizon for anything to provide shade. All I could see was the bubbling heat haze, scrub bushes, and more scrub bushes in the distance. At last I spied a cut in the roadside, perhaps four feet high, offering a tiny, two-foot strip of shade. I let the gear fall, and in the same motion I collapsed into the thin margin of shadow.

I came to. The shade was gone. I was lying on my back, splayed out, as though I had fallen from a high building. Three immediate objectives dominated my thoughts: Get out of the furnace-fire sun, get water, and find shade. I covered my head and reached for the water bottle. I no sooner took a swig than it retched back out of my mouth. Yet I drank on, always with the same result; no matter—I must drink.

Lacking the energy to stand, I crawled to a nearby bush and there constructed a cocoon using my sleeping bag, its plastic blazing hot to the touch, There I lay imprisoned for the remainder of the long afternoon, occasionally retching out the gray liquid that had attacked me despite all the water-treatment tablets I had thrown in. I wondered where on earth I would ever find the energy to move another half mile, let alone the ten I still had to go. It was only when I saw a hideous spider the size of a man's hand scuttling past my face that I discovered in a moment that I really was capable of moving at all.

Three hours short of my objective of Talocaster, Mr. Misery's "El Zonda," the hot, dry desert gale, sprang up from the north, further slowing my progress, removing the last vestige of perspiration, and drying my lips and tongue to the consistency of sandpaper. The sun, which had been smashing down on me the entire merciless day, at last dropped below the peaks of the Andes, which once again rose in the west.

For the last hundred yards before reaching a dimly lit bar, I had to stop three times to rest and take a swig of the gray filth. When I finally fell through the bar door, I was speechless with exhaustion and could only gesture toward the cola bottles. I remained silent for nearly half an hour, nursing one cold Coke after another, running my fingers over the sacred glass if it were one of the crown jewels. I must have downed two liters, all the while thinking: Heaven must be like this.

I bedded down in the bar's storehouse, a stick hut, grateful to escape the tent in that stifling heat, and lay near-motionless until the following afternoon. To prepare myself for the furnace outside, I drank and drank until I could drink no more, fully topped off like a rocket ready for the moon launch. I took two steps out the door . . . and the heat hit me like a hammer, forcing me back into the bar. "Another cola!" I yelled to the smirking proprietor.

In my walk through this region, if I were lucky, by midday I would reach one of the concrete bunkers that had been constructed as a refuge for roadworkers by the DNV—Direccion Nacional de Vialidad, the federal highway agency. The shelters were almost all filthy and swarming with flies, but I was in no mood to complain so long as they provided shade. Sometimes I even managed an hour's sleep. One night I bedded down in an abandoned railway station that was overrun with ants and bats.

In the village of Niquivil, I was quietly sleeping in someone's barn when a policeman burst in waving his revolver, dragged me to the local lockup, and after a rough search threw me in a cell (only one of scores of foolish run-ins with the police before the journey's end). The decor was hardly palatial—a broken bucket was about it—but at least the place was cool. I settled down on the earthen floor to a first-class sleep. No tunnels that night. In the morning they threw me out. I went on my way.

I reached San José de Jachal, 159 km from San Juan, and spent two nights sleeping again in the police station, but this time as a visitor. The *policía* were a quite pleasant if dim lot who never stopped asking daft questions and seemed to spend most of their time, when not interfering with the locals, gambling and tending to their *asado* out back. There were thirteen of them in this pleasant small town, where it was doubtful whether there was enough work for even one.

The next day's walking proved hard going. Something totally unexpected lay between me and my objective of Huaco: a mountain. In the day long effort to get over it, I must have lost two or three pounds, and was now down to 118. Still, luckily, I was feeling fit, and the panorama from the crest was worth all the work. A silver river snaked its way through a dead-flat sandy plain stretching to the north for over 100 km, all the way to the mountains of La Rioja.

The *pavimento* ended abruptly at Huaco, and while this helped my battered feet, hauling the Yoshikart became yet more difficult over the loose sand. As I passed a police post in Huaco, the men on duty, who had been radioed to expect me, offered a weak cheer before returning to their card game. Past Huaco, I entered La Rioja Province, which despite the gold and uranium in its hills was so poor that there was no sign announcing that the traveler had entered the province, only one stating that you had left San Juan. The shocking road eventually took me into the village of Santa María, where I was engulfed by a roaring swarm of flies; there must have been millions of them. I sought refuge in a bar-general store, and there I was treated to another terrific noise: A drunken gaucho, trying to cure the hiccups, had managed to get his head stuck in a tin bucket.

The way north alternated between a good dirt road and a dustbowl that buried my boots up to the ankles and made hauling the Yoshikart a gut-wrenching exercise in futility. Along the roadside, the sheep of Patagonia and cattle of La Pampa now gave way to the destructive goat, which alone seems able to survive in this rocky desert, eating the smallest roots and scraggliest shrubs. (Virtually every low tree for miles about was defoliated.) I also saw parrots several times a day and an occasional snake—and, in the evening, ugly toads, which I took great care not to step on. Huge ants habitually crossed the road in such large numbers and along such carefully worked-out paths that they had worn tracks in the loose dirt; watching their disciplined work and feats of strength fascinated me endlessly. One in particular caught my eye: He was staggering under the load of a giant leaf cutting—with another ant clamped to the top of it. The dung beetle was another creature that never ceased to amuse me, forever pushing his great ball of dung backward with his hind legs over obstacles three times his size.

At Los Tambillos I reached the foot of the mighty Miranda Pass. This is cactus country—not the miniatures I was used to seeing in British homes, but mighty, twenty-foot colossi, several with their own birds in residence. The road up the pass climbs thousands of feet via a series of over six hundred hairpin turns. (No, I didn't count them as I went; I read this in the *South American Handbook*.) The scenery in this region is among the most spectacular in Argentina. Whole mountains seemed to have been torn up, exposing various strata of red, brown, and white, the result, I am told, of the tremendous cataclysm that tore apart South America some ten thousand years ago.

I next reached Chilecito, a town now geared to agriculture even though its name (meaning "Little Chile") harks back to the turn of the century when gold was mined here by Chilean laborers. A Chilecito police detective hauled me in, grilled me for an hour and a half, and eventually typed out a report that dealt almost exclusively with the statistics of the *Brasilia Star*, the ship that had brought me south. The local Automobile Club Argentina (ACA) kindly allowed me to stow my gear on their premises and sleep in their meeting hall. Here, with a cool drink in my hand and a tough stretch of road behind, I should have been happy, but I was overtaken by great waves of loneliness; these moments of relaxation were what I most wished to share with Yoshiko.

In the evening, some children in the plaza playfully held me hostage in order to practice their English, and in no time almost a hundred of them had joined the general conversation, all excitedly asking questions. First they asked me to sing the songs I knew in Spanish. Then I asked the children what songs they knew in English, and they treated me to "My Bonnie Lies Over the Ocean"; and so a Scottish air filled the plaza of a South American desert town one magic night.

I next crossed into Catamarca, another poor desert province, and proceeded to Tinogasta, where the police went through my gear for what seemed like the five hundredth time. Then I lumbered on to Londres over a road even worse than the one in La Rioja. It was *"zona vados"* all the way—*vados* are large dips in the road caused by periodic streams that cut across the road, and the reason I found them so difficult to negotiate is that the gullies are filled with thick dust, and the constant uphills and downhills in quick succession quickly took their toll on me. It was monotonous going, my horizon limited simply to the next hill, and the next hill, and the next. . . .

In Londres ("London," so named by the conquistadors in honor of the marriage of Mary Tudor and Philip of Spain), I looked up some more people mentioned in Sebastian Snow's book. One, Arthur Bauer, an Englishman, had died only the previous year at the age of ninety-three—as a young man he survived the dreaded blackwater fever (odds—a thousand to one). I was sorry to have missed the opportunity to meet him, for he had been a World War I pilot and later an adventurer, a man after my own heart.

I next visited Alberto M. Saleme, a journalist whom Snow had mentioned, though not by name. Alberto M. Saleme expressed his annoyance at the fact that the "worthless Snow" had not seen fit to put his name in his book and had referred to him only as "a journalist for a leading Argentine newspaper." For Alberto M. Saleme, this was not good enough, and I was to tell this to the worthless Snow, with the recommendation that his name be added to any future edition of the worthless *Rucksack Man.*

"After all I *did* for him," Alberto M. Saleme added disgustedly. He then showed me a copy of "all he had done"— a single paragraph on Snow's trip in *La Prensa.* From various corners Alberto M. Saleme now brought out an armory of rubber stamps bearing his august name and with wild abandon pockmarked the pages of *The Rucksack Man*—my copy!— with no less than ten "Alberto M. Saleme's" plus one for luck, using a stamp with his wife's name. Elsa D. Romero de Saleme. "He won't forget me next time," he snarled. "And don't *you*—if ever you get around to writing anything." What especially galled Alberto M. Saleme was that Snow had devoted an entire page to the worthless Arthur Bauer, giving details of the man's extraordinary adventures.

The road grew even poorer as the land grew more rugged. From Santa María, I followed the road through a beautiful gorge cut by a winding river for most of the day until I reached tiny Tucumán Province, the smallest in the republic, notorious for its gun-toting extremists—the *policía.* My journal read:

November 8: Entered Tucumán Province.

November 8, evening: Left Tucumán Province. Saw not one copper, nor was shot at.

Later the same evening, I entered my third province of the day, Salta, a great horseshoe of land that borders not only on six other provinces but Chile, Bolivia, and Paraguay as well. Here the countryside again turned green. The first town I reached, Cafayate, sat so prettily in the mountains that it had become a great tourist attraction. My initial impression of the locals was that they were a spoiled bunch who had lost all respect for people and treated everyone with the shallow sincerity generally accorded tourists. Nor was my impression upgraded by the family running the ACA hotel, a sour-faced lot from Buenos Aires who recoiled from my untouristy, sweat-soaked appearance. When I had the temerity to request a glass for the bottled soda I had bought from them, I clearly overstepped the mark and was asked to remove myself. The ACA accommodations throughout the country had been consistently excellent, the management always friendly. The ACA Cafayate people were the only ones in the entire federal republic to give me the Order of the Boot.

The next day, I was going quickly and strongly when I was suddenly hit with diarrhea that left me spinning and weak. Not long after, a policeman beckoned me over to the roadside, not to offer help but to order me to check in at his headquarters 20 km up the road. Being so open and vulnerable in this landscape, I had no option but to comply. Hours later I literally staggered into the police station at La Viña, by then just thankful to find a place to sit down out of the sun. I was striken with fever. One moment I was sweating fiercely, the next shivering with my hood up over my head. All the while the *policía* were going through their ritual of shouting *"Documento?"* and nosing through my gear and demanding, "Where are your dollars?" I was sure they were stealing my money, but I was ill, and I had an undeclared belt of money to worry about as well. So I said nothing and settled for the dubious honor of staying the night in the stationhouse. In the morning, I staggered out, minus ten dollars, gradually recovered my strength, and walked till well after dark.

Farther on, the fields grew richer, with tall, swaying corn and large green cabbages while fat, white-faced Hereford cattle roamed occasional pastures, all beneath a stunning backdrop of snowcapped peaks. One evening, before El Carril, the wind suddenly picked up, great, bilious stormclouds blew over, and within moments the countryside was the setting for an epic display of lightning and rain and savage thunder. I reached the town soaked, though exhilarated by the natural fireworks. The next day, under a clear sky and a blazing sun, I reached the important goal of the city of Salta, the de facto capital of northern Argentina.

In late November I left Salta for Jujuy Province, where my more memorable experiences involved even further run-ins with the police. It is only with hindsight that I could characterize such incidents as clues to something bigger and uglier. It is now common knowledge that during these years, Argentina's military dictatorship routinely utilized death squads to keep its citizens in line. In 1977, however, the outside world (and I) were still largely unaware of the "silent war" and the horror stories concerning the *desparacidas* (the disappeared ones). The idea of such a reign of terror was simply incomprehensible to my naïve mind.

Nor were the victims necessarily dissidents; anyone who couldn't produce the proper identification was just as likely never to be heard from again. What I did see was that ordinary people were constantly and needlessly harassed. One man, a taxi driver, told me that he had been pulled in by the police eleven times in the past year simply because he had long hair. Another poor fellow told me that police had shot his dog for "target practice." The nephew of the president of the republic himself told me that the police frequently pulled him off the commuter bus on his way home. Why? Because he wore rimless "hippie" glasses.

In Mendoza, I had seen a pair of soldiers patrolling the main shopping mall, one with a shotgun and the other with an attack dog. What their orders were I couldn't imagine. Both were in full battle dress, including green steel helmets—perhaps in case an irate shopper were to lob a pot of jam at them. I also remember the time Yosh and I went to the movies in Bariloche. Before the feature came on, the audience was subjected to a public service film trumpeting the benefits of a police career. In the film, a civilian strolling innocently down the boulevard is being tailed by a slow-moving car. Suddenly three or four uniformed thugs pour out and slam the hapless fellow against a convenient wall. "You, too . . ." the voice-over intones as Juan Q. Public is dragged off to an unspecified fate, "can save the republic!"

In San Salvador de Jujuy, the police of course ran me in. After the brief detention, I nevertheless spent two nights skulking about town because I needed sustenance. I finally left for the north—perhaps fled is the better word—and on November 28, amid a horrendous and properly tropical thunderstorm, crossed the Tropic of Capricorn. Now that I was technically in the tropics, I wondered seriously whether I would ever live to leave them.

I reached the Great Andean Plateau, the *altiplano*, having gradually climbed to above ten thousand feet. This was a different world. Now, everywhere, instead of grazing mules, I saw gorgeous llamas, with their camel faces and powderpuff tails.

And I began seeing many more Indians on the road. In fact, I had entered "Indian South America," and as foreign as Argentina was to me, this was yet another world. The Indians here—and throughout Latin America, much of which is dominated by their presence—are an independently minded people who largely ignore the customs and styles of the surrounding "Europeanized" culture. From now on, these people were a common sight, and every day I would meet women on the road dressed in long, brilliantly colored skirts and bundled in striped blankets, all topped off by a gray homburg— Indians, both men and women, were proud of their hats— and often carrying their young on their backs. One of my first memories is of a woman so dressed and so burdened accompanied by a flock of goats being herded by her dogs; as she walked she was also spinning wool on a distaff.

The first week of December, I reached La Quiaca, my last town in Argentina. The roadsign read "Ushuaia, 5,121 km." Interminable Argentina was behind me: I had completed half of South America.

I took a long look across the bridge into "the promised land," Bolivia, and turned away. It was not yet time. Long before La Quiaca I had made the decision to rest a while before crossing into Bolivia, for two reasons. Food, I knew, was less plentiful there, and at this time of year, the wet season, I could look forward only to being soaked to the skin at ten-thousand-feet-plus by fierce winds while struggling through roads cut by rapid streams and awash with mud.

Moreover, crossing the Andes ony to face the Peruvian desert at its worst would also be folly. In planning the walk through South America, I knew that I would have to encounter at least one bad season. The trick was not to hit two. I had already taken northern Argentina's hot season on the chin. Rather than suffer more discomfort and risk my health, I decided to lay up in some quiet backwater, rest, and write down my recollections of the journey so far.

Luckily, I found the ideal place for hibernation right away. Pastor Long, a friend of Pastor Ortega, had converted a private house back in Salta into a mission church. The church therefore had running water, including a hot shower, a gas cooking range, and refrigerator. I had my own spacious room with writing table and a bed with two mattresses. A genial couple, Olga and Octavio Morales, the church caretakers, also lived there, and their peals of laughter were the only interruption of an otherwise tranquil atmosphere. Such calm is very difficult to find in Argentina because the people are such an excitable, fun-loving lot; for me it was absolutely necessary if I were to recover from the strain of a year's walking and do any writing. As a bonus, at dinnertime I would join the Moraleses, who, being Chilean, always prepared something extremely good. The Chileans have heard of vegetables.

As the holidays approached, I even had the whimsical notion of recreating an English Christmas dinner, and toward this end I bought cabbage, potatoes, apples for applesauce, and a huge slab of pork. As the church where I was staying was holding a pot-luck affair, my items became a reluctant contribution. On the big day, we all loaded into a truck, drove down to a nearby river, and kicked off an afternoon of avoiding the sun by hiding in the bushes and simultaneously trying to keep away the ants and flies. Everyone, except me, seemed to regard this as all very exciting; this, after all, was their traditional Argentine Christmas. Soon the cooking fires were roaring, and the inevitable *asado* materialized. Even though I had long since learned that roasted meat was totally alien to the Argentinians unless it was burnt, it was still with a mixture of horror and amazement that I watched my poor

71

slab of pork barbecued to the point of combustion. As for the apples, they had been rerouted to the dessert menu, and the cabbage . . . well, no one would want to eat this "fodder," and so it was chucked out to a stray cow.

I spent the next weeks waiting out the Bolivian rainy season. Even down here, on the plain, the windows rattled when it thundered, and the rain fell in torrents. I waited it all out, basically stoking up my stomach in preparation for the lean days ahead. Just before my departure from Salta, a university student introduced herself. Over tea, my new friend casually mentioned that she had decided not to finish her university course, and when I asked why, she told me it was out of fear—a number of her student friends had already "disappeared" while in police custody. She believed that the police had murdered them; she didn't elaborate. This was the first direct reference I had heard to the horrors under the military regime. In those days people spoke of such subjects only in whispers, and at that usually out of my (or any other foreigner's) hearing. Looking back, I can now see that anything was possible in Argentina in those days. But I didn't stick around: I was moving north.

Bolivia

After more than a year of walking Argentina, I was elated finally to have reached another nation. But I had been away from the road for over a month while waiting out the Bolivian wet season, and the inactivity had left me unprepared for the altiplano. Inching up the dusty main street of tiny Villazón, I was breathing as slowly and deliberately as a deep-sea diver. It would be days before I adjusted to the thin air at this altitude, where newcomers find the slightest exertion a monumental effort.

I found this out in dramatic fashion. My first approach to the altiplano, in the process of completing Argentina, had been a gradual ascent, by foot, and had taken weeks. Even after ten thousand feet, I felt fine and was congratulating myself for being impervious to high altitudes. My second approach, however, was after my stay in Salta, and the train had taken but a few hours. After disembarking at La Quiaca, just the other side of the Argentine border, I took exactly three steps up a slight hill before I felt like my head was spinning into orbit. I went down like an express elevator.

Early the next evening, now recovered, I walked out of Villazón and through gently rolling hills, with the sinking sun for a companion. This was the best walking road I had yet been on, its mud surface perfectly resilient, like firm sponge rubber. But once the sun was gone, it quickly grew cold. At this altitude the temperature plummets to freezing not long after sunset, and so I eagerly accepted the offer from the men at a customs control post to join them for dinner.

These control posts are frequent in Bolivia, at intervals of perhaps 30 km, and some are the vestiges of the old *postas,* government-run resting-houses where at the turn of the century travelers could still rent a mule and the services of an Indian guide. These days the occasional trucks that pass—there are very few private cars in Bolivia—are forced to stop at a great chain that is stretched across the road. The officials then perfunctorily rummage through the highly stacked load before sending the driver on his way.

Truck drivers throughout most of Latin America are a colorful, wild bunch, reckless hypermacho buccaneer types—*suicideros*—who regard their vehicles with both affection and reverence. Bolivians go a step further by bestowing names on their "babies"—and even hiring a priest to "christen" them. While walking the roads of Bolivia, I saw, emblazoned across various beat-up trucks, such names as "Romeo," "Che Guevara," and even "Kennedy."

In a similar vein, the day after leaving the customs post, I came across an adobe fort, straight out of *Beau Geste*, complete with guard towers and sentry boxes, whose wall bore the slogan, smeared in black paint, *"Bolivia Demanda Aceso al Mar!"* ("Bolivia demands access to the sea.") Poor Bolivia! For almost a century she has been without a seaport, ever since Chile annexed her entire coastline in the War of the Pacific. Lack of a seaport is a major reason Bolivia continues to be steeped in poverty, and it also helps explain why anti-Chilean sentiments still run deep in Bolivia. I was to encounter similar sentiments later on in Peru, Bolivia's ally in that disastrous war.

For two pleasant days in Tupiza, I was treated royally by the proprietors of a *residencia,* but the third ended with a soggy night in my tent when I was caught unprepared by a sudden torrent of freezing rain. My route next took me through a succession of unmarked villages, bleak, filthy places with pigs rutting through the dust and lying in mud pools in the middle of the road. Virtually every building had adobe walls and grass roofs, no windows, and ill-fitting double doors held shut with padlocks. An open door often signified a *boliche* ("shop"—really a hut), where I might find a few dusty bottles of sickly sweet soda, some cans of Peruvian anchovies, and perhaps an old Argentine meat tin. To one quickly passing by, an adobe hut could be a shop or just as possibly a pigsty or the town hall. You never could tell. Few outsiders ever get to these backwaters, and the sight of this strange traveler would bring the Indians to the door, adults as well as children, all staring out in silent mistrust. Bundled and ponchoed against the high-altitude cold, I would press on.

I spent one evening with a family, typical *campesinos*, residents of the countryside, who kindly offered to share their meal with me. The family owned two hundred goats, fifty sheep, an old horse, and three donkeys, and of course there was the usual batch of snarling dogs. Their hut, little more than a heap of scrub brush and cactus wood, was exclusively for sleeping. Built alongside was an open-air compound of similar construction that served as a kitchen. Here the daughter, encrusted with filth but otherwise resplendent in her brown bowler with the brim turned down, tended a small wood fire. The rest, including myself, sat on stumps, squinting through the smoke while slurping up the standard altiplano meal: a stew consisting of rice, corn, perhaps another vegetable, and one piddling chunk of goat meat per bowl. This insipid fare is almost without variation morning, noon, and night. Water hauled up from the river sat about the compound in none-too-clean oil drums. The largest drum was filled with *chicha*, a corn-based beer, almost fifty gallons of it, and all just for this one family. For a journey of this sort, I thought once again, one must have a very strong stomach.

A continual nuisance were the countless streams and small rivers that cut the road, frustrating, rhythm-breaking time wasters. Off would come boots and socks, as well as the plasters so carefully put on the blisters in the morning; then a quick splash and a stifled scream (the water was very cold), and out the other side. On the way to Cotagaita, I was fording yet another watercourse, a deep one this time, when the holding bolt on the Yoshikart snapped and my gear, including passport, tent, food—everything—gaily floated downriver. I allowed myself an involuntary curse before splashing after the "vessel" and catching it just as it was about to sink out of sight.

Cotagaita was the other side of the Río Cotagaita, which at this point was more than two hundred feet wide and in places over five feet deep, and as there was no bridge, I teamed up with a gang of heavily laden Indian women. We forded across in a bunch, clinging tenaciously to one another as the water swept by up to our chests, occasionally sweeping a boulder smack into our legs. I would certainly have been hurled down the waterway like a piece of straw had I not hung on like a limpet to the fattest woman of the party; she in turn, seemed delighted with my attentions.

Just before the village of Cotagaita, another large Indian woman, sitting by the road selling fruit, beckoned me over and asked the usual questions about me and my enterprise, to which I gave the usual answers—or at least most of the usual answers. I had learned to avoid one subject in this nation, for the few times I mentioned my merchant sailor background to Bolivians, a sadness crept over their faces; it was like showing baby photos to a couple who had lost their only child.

The woman was so amazed to hear about the walk that she dug deeply into her huge cleavage and gave me five pesos bolivianos on the spot—about twenty-five cents, almost enough for a day's food. I had noticed her scratching a rash on her leg, and so in return I gave her my skin cream. She smiled, tossed me a bunch of grapes, and then invited me to stay at her "hotel" in the village.

The woman was Señora Buena Aventura—a given name, of course, meaning literally, in Spanish, "good adventure." Like most Indians of southern Bolivia, La Señora was a Quechua and spoke the language that once graced the Inca court.

(Even today, about half of the entire Bolivian population of 5 million speak no Spanish, only Quechua or, in the north, Aymará.) Señora's style of dress was common among Bolivia's *cholitas*, as the Indian women here are called: several voluminous skirts in brilliant colors (which in this instance exaggerated an already bulky bottom to an extraordinary degree), a thin blouse draped by a number of multicolored wraps, all held fast by large blanket pins, and a striped blanket tied about the shoulders which often held fruit or a baby. Sandals are the customary footwear, but when the weather turns cold, out come blue or red knee-length socks and plimsolls. The entire affair is topped off by the famous bowler hat, always a half size too small, worn at a dashing angle over two pigtails tied at the bottom with black lace.

Señora showed me her two bowlers, one black and one brown, each bearing the label "Elegant Superior" on the red silk lining. Each of them, she told me, cost the equivalent of fifteen dollars—perhaps three months' wages for an average Indian worker. Such millinery is considered both fetching and chic, and when worn in the rain is conscientiously protected by a plastic bag even while the rest of one's outfit becomes soaking wet. A frequent, curious sight on rainy days was a hillside seemingly planted with plastic cabbages that were actually Indian women, their hats all covered, squatting while waiting out the downpour.

The men of the region are not so spectacularly attired. Their usual outfits consist of sackcloth tunics and trousers (although many now wear "modern" shirts and trousers), ponchos, and felt state-trooper hats; the Aymará to the north prefer multicolored woolen Punchinello caps, while some Indians wear both, one on top of the other. Add to this sandals cut from discarded automobile tires worn on feet that seem better suited to a mummy.

Thus it was that I reached Cotagaita with an invitation to bed down. This small village sits snugly in a protected valley, the dwellings clustered about an impressive if tumbledown church and plaza. An oil-fueled generator supplies the town electricity, while water is obtained at communal taps in the main street. An unavoidable observation is that garbage, rubbish, dirty water—everything—is tossed out directly into the streets. What most surprised me the first few times I encountered this mode of existence was not the fact itself but the idea that the villagers weren't much bothered about establishing a better system. In this and other respects, Cotagaita was a typical large village of the Bolivian altiplano.

Eventually I found La Señora's "hotel," a two-story hut with a medieval siege ladder leading up to a sleeping loft from the outside. About the only thing that set her dwelling apart from the surrounding buildings was the white rag hanging out front, which throughout the region signifies "*Chicha* sold here."

As soon as I marched through the broken front door, La Señora gave me a big bowl of soup, an ear of corn, and fruit juice. Half the village children now swarmed in to watch the "loco" eat. I missed a heartbeat halfway through the corn when a withered hag clamped her bony hand on my shoulder and growled in my ear, "We fruit sellers have heard about your sacrifice, and we know you are a loco, because all ingléses [Englishmen] are loco—we all know that. So we have made a collection for you—please accept these coins for food." I gazed in disbelief at the twenty-nine pesos strewn across the table in ones and halves.

I was originally to bed down in the loft, but La Señora thought better of this when she considered that her two girls were to be sleeping there, too, and "for safety" (i.e., my safety) recommended I sleep alongside her sons.

Everyone gathered to wave good-bye as I marched out of town the following afternoon. Game to the last, a boy roared up on his motorbike to give me a lift—"only up the first hill." My polite refusal drew gasps from the company, for they knew the first hill.

In the late afternoon, I began the ascent of a mountain pass. At one point, all the water in my three-liter bottle leaked away. An Indian watched with consternation as I grubbed about on my knees and filled my bottle with dirt from the road. Most certainly he thought me mad, but actually I was only seeking to restore my walking rhythm: The bottle, when full and hanging off the back of the Yoshikart, served as a perfect counterweight.

A whipping wind picked up, and for the better part of an hour I hid behind a low stone wall with a shepherd boy, who occasionally poked his head out and let go with his slingshot to bring his llamas under control. We shared my small tin of fish and some bread before I struggled on. It took three hours of savage work before, long after dark, I hit the crest, thousands of feet higher than where I had started. Next morning, I awoke late to find that an enormous slug was stuck to my coat (which I was using for a pillow) and that a regiment of ants had set up camp in my food bag. By now the tent was just a muddy, filthy rag. In the old smiling days with Yoshiko, if I so much as poked my head in the tent without taking my boots off, her eyes would narrow and she would have words for me: "How can I keep my house happy with such a one as you?"

One hot midday, having cracked off 20 km in just over three hours, I was hailed from an adobe hut—a bar, full of serious drinkers. While a few noisy chickens pecked about the dirt floor, an old pig slept undisturbed under the single, broken table. The arrival of a gringo in such an out-of-the-way location caused a mild stir, and very soon an ear of roasted corn and a soda were thrust upon me.

Don Fernando, a self-styled supermacho, took me into his confidence: "I have fifty wives and two hundred children and—"

"Are they all boys?" I interjected. (No Latin ever bragged of having daughters.)

"Why, of course—what else? It gets cold at night, and no man can live in the cold up here without a fat wife. Anyway, it's not macho to sleep alone." This sort of talk went on for a good half hour after I had finished downing the last of my colas. As I rose to go, protesting that I had to reach Potosí by next week, Don Fernando offered some parting advice: "And as for you—why don't you strap our bargirl onto your cart and wheel her to Potosí with you?" As I walked out

79

the door, the barmaid, all two hundred fifty pounds of her, giggled and beamed at me under her bowler hat.

I rolled into Vitichi, a small, well-kept, clean town—probably because the local pigs, hundreds of them, roamed the thoroughfares at will like so many streetcleaning machines. Here I was escorted by a small herd of children directly to two of Snow's old friends, Max and Margaret Rojas, who without any concern for my rough appearance immediately gave me a bed and dinner. Margaret had come to Bolivia from Canada twenty-five years before to work in a mission school. When she married Max, a colorful reformed drunk, she was forced to resign, but the couple, undaunted, continued evangelical work on their own.

Margaret is something of a local legend, and the house is always full of wool-spinning *cholitas* feeding their babies and patiently waiting for their medicine, injections, or next child. Max, for his part, is always joking in his fluent Quechua with the country visitors. A self-taught student of law, Max was mayor of Vitichi for a term, during which time he earned the voters' gratitude by bringing electricity and tapwater to the town.

The office of mayor was not the most secure or respected position in Vitichi. A mere six years before, one of Max's predecessors had been assassinated—shot down in the plaza. And the current officeholder, a priest (who, according to church law, should not have been holding public office), was strongly suspected of dipping his hand into the public till. The voters in fact tried to remove the priest from office, but their efforts came to naught when one of their meetings was broken up by the police—at the instigation, Max was positive, of a certain big-city *político:* the priest's son. (According to church law he wasn't allowed one of these either!)

After four recuperative days, I left the Rojases late in the afternoon, headed for Potosí along a road that followed the Río Vitichi. As there were no big hills, I was able to hammer out a quick 15 km before nightfall. But because I had set out on a full stomach—not best for walking—and didn't stop once to rest, I was so exhausted by the time I set up the tent that

I just crawled in and dozed off. I began dreaming of deserts and great heat—no real surprise, for I awoke only a few moments later to discover that I was on fire. I had rolled onto my lit candle and scorched a hole right through the sleeping bag and into me, and by the time I stopped thrashing about, the tent was a riot of duck feathers. I was sure the blackened, tattered bag was a goner—but I would still have it in Mexico two and a half years later!

I entered Potosí, a city with a rich and fascinating history, the evening of March 3. Reaching the downtown meant a hard slog around the perimeter of the mountain known as Cerro Rico (Rich Hill), which dominates the metropolitan area. All the while, I was haunted by thoughts of the mountain's grisly legacy. During the centuries of Spanish colonial oppression, hundreds of thousands of native workers had died in its bowels while mining its silver. On one occasion, twenty thousand people, including women and children, were marched in and never saw the sky again.

Potosí, at over thirteen thousand feet, is the highest city in the world, and it is inconceivable that anyone would ever bother to build, much less occupy, a city at such an altitude were it not for the fabulous riches of Cerro Rico. Indeed, at one time things were really humming here—French wines, Chinese silks, posh whores, etc.—Potosí's university was founded well before the Pilgrims ever thought to set sail, and in 1613 the population was a hundred twenty thousand, equal to London's.

When the lodes in Cerro Rico began to dwindle, however, and especially after the discovery of silver in Mexico, Potosí entered a period of decline, although recently it has enjoyed a minor renaissance thanks to the tourist trade. Potosí's major tourist attraction is the beautiful Casa de Moneda (House of Money—the imperial mint), where in colonial times the silver was pressed into strips, cut into coins, and then sent on the long journey to Madrid. The mint was in fact still in operation as recently as 1951, before Bolivia converted to paper currency and gave its business to a London concern.

Despite the cold, I liked Potosí and its narrow cobblestone streets, women in white "Pilgrim" hats with black hat-bands (or the reverse), and hairy dogs sprawled all over the pavement. I spent my nights in a pension that boasted hot water for fifteen minutes every noon; not bad for about a dollar a day. The place was run by a twelve-year-old boy who checked people in and out, did the maintenance work, and dealt with the ever-mysterious needs of the passing gringos. Other travelers told me that it's not uncommon in South America for a kid to run the show in place of the invisible adults, who are perpetually "under the weather." After four days and nights in town, including two trips to the movies and a Chinese dinner, I charged on.

One advantage of leaving the highest city in the world is that the only way onward is down. My spirits weren't even dulled by the huge rainstorm that began as soon as I was beyond the town, and I bowled along to the village of Yotala in fine form. The next morning, I was ambling along, singing "If I were a rich man . . ." when a van full of gringos stopped for me. The driver, a fellow named Bob from Miami, gave me the remains of a pot of honey. What luxury! On I loped, revitalized by my encounter, until midday, when I estimated that I was clear of my first Bolivian *departamento*. Unlike Argentina, Bolivia doesn't bother marking its internal borders. In fact, Bolivia has avoided error in her roadsigns by the simple measure of apparently not bothering to have any.

Past Ventilla, the cart's long-suffering wheel shattered and progress stopped dead. I dragged the wreckage over to a group of Indians and heavily laden mules who were waiting by the roadside in the hope of stopping a truck to transport their yearly crop of maize to Oruro's grand market. After a hot, boring two-hour wait, a government land cruiser stopped and whisked me off to a hole-in-the-wall shop in the nearest town, where the mechanic, much to my surprise and delight, deftly welded the wheel together. I was even lucky enough to find a truck that offered to give me a lift back to the exact spot where I had broken down.

In the back of the truck, I snuggled in among the cargo—alpacas. In my preoccupied state of mind, these gorgeous animals, with their huge dark eyes, long silken eyelashes, soft black hair, and powderpuff tails, appeared to be the loveliest young ladies I had ever seen. In fact, I was so distracted by my ride with the alpacas that when I disembarked, I failed to notice that I had left my water bottle on the truck. I managed to get hold of a castoff half-liter plastic bottle, and not long after, I got a nasty scare when I started to foam at the mouth. Rabies? "No," declared the drunk doctor propping up the bar at the local café, "it's quite common when you drink from a soap bottle."

I was halfway through Bolivia. From Challapata on, the land became sandy and the road was one long flat line disappearing to the horizon—an incredible sensation, to be on such flat land at ten thousand feet with not a mountain in sight. It was a relief to be clear of the mountains, but "what you gain on the swings you lose on the roundabouts," for the road was speckled with brick-size rocks, and every time a vehicle passed, the road was reduced to a dust-choked hell. Half the time it seemed as though I was wandering about in a London fog.

One night found me camping out on the road to Oruro, reading a book on the famous love affair between Townsend Harris, America's first consul general to Japan, and the geisha Okitchi. The descriptions of soft-speaking women, dazzling kimonos, and white mitten socks reduced me to a profound sadness as memories gushed back. Quite suddenly, a forceful wind hit the tent, flattening it. Over went the candle, which scorched a great hole in the groundsheet before the rain extinguished it with an ominous hiss. The thunder crashed with enormous violence; I could even hear the lightning sizzle. The rain fell virtually in a solid block.

To save my clothes, I took them off and crawled out into the freezing torrent in boots alone, my tears merging with the deluge. In anger and misery over half a year of love's loneliness, I picked up a huge stone and smashed the tent pegs with all my strength, battering one of them to junk, all the while thinking: Nothing is going to stop me from seeing my Yoshiko again, nothing, be it this tempest, one more year, or twelve thousand miles—nothing!

This was but one of the many nights when, sad and tearful and cursing the darkness, I would see myself only too well as the victim of a wandering heart. Some have envied my freedom, but few could see the prison I had created for myself.

After reaching Oruro, I was surprised to learn how many Mormons were living here. Or maybe they just stood out. They could probably be spotted from a high-flying jet, so conspicuous were they in their brown suits, wide ties, briefcases full of evangelical props, and close-cropped blond hair. I spent an hour and a half in the company of two of them, a pair of earnest, sincere, and intensely boring young men. While one with great solemnity sought to convert me, the other, standing a foot before my face, silently held a booklet with illustrations to accompany the lecture and periodically flipped the pages for my benefit. It was a hard-earned tea.

In a more sociable context, one night I attended a "Folkloric Evening," a presentation of native song and dance, accompanied by a new acquaintance, Tom Crumpacker, a friendly lawyer from Colorado. The evening's "folklore" turned out to be a variety of acts interspersed with breathtaking stage disasters and lengthy, yawn-producing speeches. Among the memorable turns were the pianist El Profesor, who played a souped-up version of "Chopsticks" punctuated by momentous pauses as he stopped to turn the pages of his music; a jovial nutter (all teeth) on the electric organ who just wouldn't stop; dancers who were left hanging in midair as the recorded music was switched off abruptly; theater lights that went on and off without reason; toppling scenery; and the very best of all, Lopy López, interrupted in the middle of her dance to *Scheherazade* when her bra abruptly rocketed off into the front row. I hadn't laughed so much in months.

After three nights in Oruro I left, headed for La Paz. Just as I cleared the city, a van stopped ahead of me, sped by in reverse, and came to a squealing halt—it was Bob from Miami again, who this time gave me a loaf of bread and still further encouragement. Two days before Oruro, near the end of a grinding afternoon, I had received a nice buckup when a company rep I had met back in Tupiza stopped on the road and warmly congratulated me on having come so far. Like these two, the regular traffic on any set run soon came to recognize me and would often stop to give me corn, bread, water, or just good wishes.

The road from Oruro to La Paz is over 200 km of flat, straight *pavimento,* good for traffic, hard on feet; I was nevertheless thankful for the absence of dust. The area about Oruro is rich with llamas and alpacas, thousands of them, who would raise high their long, graceful necks to stare as I swept by, only feet away. I never tired of staring back at these creatures, with their endless mixtures of black, brown, and white coats, like so many hairy camels with cottontails.

As I moved north over the altiplano, the land became more populated, the people richer, and the fincas larger. By contrast, in the scrublands of southern Bolivia there were wheatfields about the size of a rowhouse garden plot—smaller than a combine. To reap such a crop, one chap I had seen was cutting the stalks with a folded tin-can lid.

Some way before Villa Belén, I found a busy little market in progress under white sackcloth awnings. Entering a nearby general store, I discovered that I had been followed by a huge crowd of Indians, who had abandoned the market in favor of gaping at this traveler from the south. Packed into the entranceway in total silence, they intently watched me change the plasters on my pulverized feet. As a sharp-eyed girl asked me questions and translated my anwers into Aymará for the benefit of the majority, I could tell from the "oohs" and "aahs" that the general impression of my trip was one of horror— no doubt I had been touched by the sun. A vast, motherly woman, carrying on her back an equally fat baby slobbering on a carrot, pushed her way through the crowd, dug into her Grand Canyon cleavage, and pulled out two one-peso coins. *"Por refresco, señor"* (For a refreshment, sir), she said before fleeing in embarrassment with a charming ducklike waddle.

Four more bowler-hatted *cholitas* followed suit, each one repeating, *"Por refresco, señor."* Yet again, I was deeply touched by the good hearts and generosity of such poor people who would help a dirty, scruffy "loco inglés." I showed all of them photos of my family. Although the *cholitas*, especially the older ones, fear the loss of their souls in the "photo machine," they all love to see snapshots. Whenever I brought out the pictures of Yoshiko, it always caused great excitement, and they always asked if they could keep one as a souvenir—they were convinced she was an Indian.

After sundown, I reached an unlit village, where I made a desperate effort to obtain peanuts, my insatiable yen at the time. While I was squelching about the muddy streets, a gang of spirited Aymará kids trooped after me, copying my limping walk and mangled Spanish. Finding no peanuts and settling for a can of Argentine peaches, I marched out of the village, escorted by my entourage, who enthusiastically set up my tent for me in a dried riverbed, watched me tuck myself into my sleeping bag, and cheerily left me to gorge myself on the golden fruit.

Early next morning I reached the town of Sica Sica and went directly to the post office. "Sorry, we've run out of stamps," the clerk informed me. "Will the telephone do?" I plodded on to the little town of Patacamaya, some way off my route, where of course the post office was closed. Incidents like this were especially frustrating for me when I had to go out of my way, as now, for unlike the ordinary traveler, I was honor-bound to return to the place I left off to ensure the integrity of the journey.

I ate a kilogram of grapes in a café in Toki and afterward returned to the post office at Patacamaya. It was still shut tight. I began booting the door impatiently. Finally a broken window swung open and a young sweaty woman poked her head out and said, "The postmaster's not available today. He's studying for an examination." She then told me to come back *"pesado mañana"*—the day after tomorrow. On I marched, exasperated.

At the Hotel Porvenir in Calamarca, while the friendly

owner was plying me with chewing gum, biscuits, and bread, I noticed a wreck of a man, rotten drunk, slumped in the corner, and made the casual inquiry, "Who's he?" "Oh, that's Don Roberto, the postmaster," the hotelier answered in a singsong, as if the question were a familiar one. "He's often in here for 'tea.'" My letters would obviously have to wait until La Paz, fortunately now less than 40 km away.

On the last day before La Paz, I was astonished to see, once the clouds drifted open, a huge, beautiful snowcap to the east: Monte Illimani, covered with snow year-round, which, along with the lesser peaks of the cordillera, dominates the city. Just before the sprawling industrial area of Alto La Paz I arrived at a tollgate, where the police there were very interested in my Yoshikart. One even wanted to know where the license number was displayed. Before I left, the officer in charge pressed a twenty-peso note into my hand: *"Por refresco, señor."*

It was only 11 km to La Paz, but it proved an arduous morning's work. Initially, I galloped off, because of a misdirection, exactly 180 degrees the wrong way, but eventually even I, a former navigator, managed to find the large hole in which seven hundred thousand people were hiding. What an absolutely incredible and underrated panorama! There, just as I rounded a corner, sitting in a canyon a thousand feet below, lay the city, the highest capital in the world. For startling beauty, the sudden shock of La Paz seemed to me in the league of Rio de Janeiro and Hong Kong. It may be true that in La Paz the poorer you are the higher up you live, but what you lose in the amenities you certainly gain on the view.

I rolled down the long road into the canyon like a lost tennis ball and bowled straight into the central post office, only to be smashed out of court. "You can't post those letters here. Just look at those envelopes! You shouldn't carry them about so long, because they just get dirty—after all, in Bolivia we have well-staffed post offices in most villages."

I spent three restful weeks in La Paz, a city hell-bent on "modernizing" by building new Sheratons and Holiday Inns, those hallmarks of Las Vegas culture. What a contrast when, two days out, just past Tambillo, I paused at the crest of a hill to gaze at the miles of flatlands reaching toward the magnificent snowpeaks of the Cordillera Real that rose abruptly in the distance. To the west, in the failing light I could just make out a thin sliver of water: immense Lake Titicaca, at over twelve thousand feet the highest lake in the world. Starting at dawn the next day, I marched on with a great burst of energy to the lakeport of Guaqui and finally reached the sparkling, emerald-green waters.

My last day on the Bolivian road was spent walking beside the lake and the farms bordering it. Reaching the Río Desaguadero, I crossed the border bridge into Peru. I had completed my second nation—with a mixture of pride and poignancy, for Yoshiko had wanted to come this far. At the British Embassy in La Paz, I had picked up my long-awaited mail and tore open the letters from Yoshiko. One of them read:

> Dear my husband (and not some linda Indian's),
> I read from your letter you are very near to the lake Titicaca where I wanted to reach. Please take many, many photos there. Do you know what "Titicaca" means? It means "puma" or something like that. Anyway, this lake is shaped like such animal. But there is a riddle here. You know how big the lake is—so many years ago, how could people know the shape of the lake? Of course, they didn't have airplane. It was impossible to know to them what the lake was shaped at Titicaca (puma), but they somehow began to call it Titicaca. This was on TV film recently, and I myself believe UFO or space man. How about you?
> But enough of this. I want to meet you enormously! Are you all right on your alone journey? No, you're not. I know. But what can we do now? Let's have patience, both of us. We are in a great love!!
> I had dream of you more than usual, such as last night. You were somehow in my bed, and I realized it was you, George, as I was touching his stomach and around the pretty belly button. Come to me in my dream tonight again, even if I shall be sad tomorrow morning. "Dream"—this is the only way to touch you. The only way to be happy with you.

George, I love you so.

Today I went to the hospital for checkup. Everything is all right. I want our child to get golden hair as same as the daddy and brown skin as mine. About the time you get this letter, I wonder the baby is out or still in my belly as sleeping. Anyway, it is very soon. Very soon.

Love,
Yoshiko XXXX

Peru

The late April crossing into Peru brought me clear of *el Cono Sur*—the countries that lie entirely south of Brazil and thus form the continent's "southern cone"—and into one of the poorest countries in South America, as well as one of its most rugged and spectacular. As I entered the border town of Desaguadero, the sun was still reflecting sharply off the calm waters of nearby Lake Titicaca, the air was dazzlingly crisp and clean. The small, sandy town was a lively, colorful bustle of gaudily painted trucks laden with potatoes, grains, and wares and of Indians similarly laden, all bound for market.

Peru has no border control here; to get my passport stamped I had to find my own way to the local Immigration Office, marked by a torn and faded flag blowing in the wind. To avoid any possible trouble, earlier in the month I had secured from the British Embassy in La Paz, after some tooth pulling, a letter explaining the nature of my walk to any Peruvian "whom it may concern" in the event I was denied entry; the Peruvians, Our Man in La Paz had insisted, took umbrage at ragged gringos and the like roaming their countryside. Now was to be the test.

At the Immigration Office, there was a lone uniformed official, and he was slumped across his desk, fast asleep. "Señor, señor," I whispered while gently shaking his shoulder. The man awoke with a terrific start, looked around wide-eyed, then relaxed with a sigh as he gradually took in the situation.

He asked for my passport, and as he examined the document a whimsical leer crept into his features. Is this it? I thought. Is something wrong with my papers? No. Still staring downward through half-open eyes, the man began shaking his head and apologizing—he seemed to be addressing the desktop rather than me—and explained in a sleepy, half-smiling mutter that every night his wife was *muy dura* (very hard) on him. Then, with a gesture that seemed to last forever, he picked up his rubber stamp, took careful aim, and with a great heavy sweep let it fall onto a fresh page of my badly worn passport. Gravity had done most of the work; in midflight he had returned to his snoozing.

I gently lifted his arm holding the stamp, slid the passport free of the deadweight, and departed, shutting the door quietly behind me. I was in. It was the smoothest, most uneventful border crossing of the South American journey, thanks at least in part to some unknown *muy dura señora*.

Having no luck finding a map of Peru in the town, I packed up some biscuits, filled my water bottle, and marched out northward along a dusty road. The inhabitants of the region, predominantly the ubiquitous Quechuas, live in mud-and-reed huts that dot the picturesque countryside at regular intervals. More often than not, as I would pass one of these huts, a savage dog would bolt out at me, quickly followed, as if in a prearranged routine, by a string of children who would shout, "Gringo! . . . Gringo! . . ." and pelt me with stones and clods of earth. One youth caught up with me on his bike and spent a half hour riding alongside me and begging for money. (At times like these I had the uncomfortable feeling I was being hunted.) Before reaching Puno, I pitched my tent, and as soon as it was up I was bombarded by a heavy barrage of stones. Tired, hurt, and angry, I charged to the nearest hut and protested strongly—mostly with gestures, as these Indians spoke no Spanish and I not a word of Quechua. The salvos stopped.

Puno is a major tourist town catering to the sightseers

who flock to Titicaca, which has been the center of Indian life since before the Incas. I decided to see what all the fuss was about, and so after stowing my gear at a convenient tienda, I joined a group of tourists for the trip to visit the legendary Urhu Indians. The Urhus live on "floating" islands of matted reeds anchored in the middle of the lake. Their huts are built directly on the reeds, and they cook their meals over fires placed on large stones brought from the mainland. There is even a "floating schoolhouse" provided by the government. Some of the Urhus have never stood on dry land.

As soon as the tour launch approached the first of the islands the inhabitants madly scrambled to the waterline and began thrusting their hands forward asking for money, a posture they did not relinquish for a single moment until the boat had left. Everyone in the launch, myself included, was embarrassed to poke our clicking cameras into the faces and huts of these constantly begging people. The whole thing was a mutually demeaning experience.

As soon as I got back to Puno, I went to a movie to clear my thoughts and wash my soul. As I sat watching *Rocky*—for the second time—my thoughts kept drifting off to the first time, with Yoshiko. She was expecting any day now. Was she all right? Was I a father now? Of a boy? A girl? I wouldn't know until I could get to my mail or phone Japan. For that I would have to wait until Lima, at least three months away.

Beyond Puno and Lake Titicaca lies Juliaca. Here are alpaca goods to be purchased at the cheapest prices in the world. Even I could afford to buy a short, sleeveless pullover. It came in handy, for as hot as it was during the day, the instant the sun set at this great altitude all warmth seemed to disappear from the universe. For three nights I camped out in appalling cold. (Months later, I met a man who complained of the intense cold in his Juliaca hotel bed, despite four blankets.) Come nightfall, I would climb into the tent and wrap myself in two pairs of socks, two trousers, two shirts, two pullovers, and hooded coat plus gloves and woolen ski mask. Steeling myself for the long hours of darkness, I would blow out the candle and reach up toward the apex of the tent to catch the last updrafts of warmth in the palms of my hands. Soon the tent skin would stiffen with frost and I would wait out the night, intermittently shivering in my icy pyramidal tomb, waiting for the morning, waiting for the sun. Like the Incas, I became a sun worshiper. Sometimes it was only when the sun finally rose that I could get enough warmth for a couple of hours' sleep. No wonder the Peruvians called their money *soles* (suns).

This was a particularly miserable section of the journey. On the road the pavement smashed my blisters, and my knee was an ever-moaning trailmate. Then I was seized by intestinal cramps that were to attack me off and on for the next fourteen weeks. Hot by day, frozen by night, I was visibly weakening. In the villages, the Indians would say how sick I looked, and despite their poverty some would even offer me hot goat's milk. *"Que sacrificio!"* ("What a sacrifice!"), they would say.

One morning, while limping along, lost in thought, I was approached by a soldier on an immense three-wheeled bicycle—in these lands, it had the authority of a Sherman tank. The man began hectoring me and demanded my watch. I wearily told him to "piss off" and just kept going, whereupon he backed up the bike, smashed it into the Yoshikart, and dismounted. "What next?" I thought. He then spat at me and, in the most bizarre gesture of intimidation I have ever seen, rolled his eyes and stuck his tongue out before charging forward. In my weakened condition I would surely have fallen as he cannoned into me had he not clamped his hands around my throat. I was choking. My head was spinning. I was beginning to lose consciousness. At that instant, by rare grace a truck appeared and the driver jumped out and rushed to my defense.

The soldier let me drop to the ground like a kitbag and hurriedly began explaining himself to the driver, claiming by way of excuse that I was a *"Chileno millonario."* (This would have made me fair game, as Peruvians have never forgiven

Chile for occupying their capital during the War of the Pacific.)

Shaken, I waited out much of the afternoon in the shade of an adobe wall. Toward evening, I moved on in the hope the soldier wasn't waiting up the road for me. Had I been able to mark my position, I could have hitched to the nearest town, but the land was featureless, and I feared accidentally cheating a few yards of the walk more than the possibility of a bashing.

Again I was staggered by abdominal pains, and so together with two aspirin I took myself to a residencia in Ayaviri and lay there waiting for the latest attack to pass. This, as it turned out, was no treat, either. My rock-hard bed was near the plaza, and throughout the long afternoon and evening the music blasting from the radios there—1960's British pop music, of all things—added to my misery. It was too much. It was the last time I ever paid for a bed in South America.

I was eager, if not fit, to move on. At the next town, Santa Rosa, I went to the local café and was served the specialty of the house, a ghoulish sheep's skull. The evening's entertainment began as soon as the local drunk appeared for dinner and took up a seat opposite me. Immediately the man knocked a giant potato off his plate and onto the moderately clean floor. With great effort he retrieved the object and wiped it "clean" on his moderately filthy sleeve. For a second attempt he swung his spoon with such wild energy that not only did he drive the spud to the far wall, but in the process threw himself out of the chair, spoon and all, onto the ground, where he remained. Later he was booted out, and I took up his position on the floor for a night's sleep.

The following day, I pushed on to reach an animal research facility in La Roya, just beyond the continental divide, where I had an introduction of sorts. Surrounding the facility are several fenced-off ranges populated by hundreds of pure white alpaca (the result of selective breeding), a few llamas, and a small herd of vicuña, an endangered species resembling the guanaco. All these animals are relatives of the camel; indeed, the llamas are used extensively as pack animals in Peru and Bolivia. The station's director, Dr. Julio Sumar, was interested in the reference to him in *The Rucksack Man*, but was mystified by Snow's observation that he "laughed like an alpaca." "That's sheer nonsense!" said the good doctor, laughing like an alpaca.

Among the features of La Roya are thermal springs and, even more remarkable, the very source of the Amazon. Early one morning I was given a tough, leather-skinned guide named Félix, who led me cross-country to a tract of still water no more than eighty yards across. Here, by Laguna Verde, we sat in the long grass, resting in the sun. All was silent, save for the few birds on the lake and a tiny gush of water trickling down the slope. It was hard to imagine that this trickle would eventually connect with dozens of others to form the mightiest waterway in the world. Most of the Amazon, of course, flows through Brazil, which lay just over the eastern mountains. How sad, I thought, that the route of my journey meant I would miss this colossus entirely. The tragedy of travel is what you *don't* get to see, whatever it is that lies just beyond the horizon—and that means most everything except for the thin line of one's trail.

In the next departamento, Cuzco, people were generous to a fault. At San Jerónimo, they insisted I accept the village speciality, bread. I tottered away under the awkward burden of ten large loaves, waiting until I was out of sight to redistribute all but one of them to the group of passing Indian women resplendent in their blue-and-red woolen knee-highs.

I had trouble knowing exactly where I was going, however, owing to the incredible map I had recently acquired, something that might be found as a prize at the bottom of a box of cornflakes. It showed Peru beset with spaceships and dinosaurs. The exotic Quechua place names also presented a problem: As if my abominable Spanish were not handicap enough, I now had to ask people the way to Checapupe and Quiquijana.

During the few days preceding the city of Cuzco, I was puzzled to see no moving traffic whatsoever, while the otherwise decent road inexplicably became an obstacle course of boulders, assorted rubbish, even felled trees. Restless people milled about in groups. When I asked the grim-faced Indians for an explanation, the only answer was the one-word reply *"Huelga!"* Given my poor Spanish, and the fact that I depended on a glance at *Time* magazine every few months to keep me informed of current events, I was largely unaware of what was going on in the greater world about me. Soon enough, I learned that a general strike against the military government was now in progress, largely in response to runaway inflation; the price of numerous necessities like gasoline had more than doubled overnight. In the city, the only traffic seemed to be jeeps and army trucks, the latter with machine guns mounted atop the cabs. Heavily armed troops guarded every streetcorner.

To get off the streets quickly, I went straightaway to a family living in Barrio Tío—the Uncle District (!)—where I had an introduction from a family member I had met in La Paz. The Guevaras, ignoring my appearance (I was certainly by now an apparition), welcomed me festively, treating me like a long-lost relative. After washing off the road under an ice-cold shower, I was shivering so much that Don Guevara wrapped a floor rug around me. There was absolutely no room to put me up, but the redoubtable Don Guevara insisted I camp out behind the settee. In a small but significant gesture, my toothbrush was retrieved from the bathroom windowsill and tossed in the glass with all the family's toothbrushes.

I spent over a week with this big-hearted family and discovered a whole new world in and about the city. Cuzco, the capital of the Incan empire, is a fabulous place that fully deserves its reputation as a showcase for archaeological wonders. Although it is four centuries since it was put to the torch by Francisco Pizarro—at the climax of one of the most bizarre invasions in history, in which a handful of Spaniards with a few horses conquered an empire—all construction that has taken place since overlies the original stonework foundations, still visible almost everywhere.

Barrio Uncle was not an Inca ruin; had it been, it might have been more intelligently designed. The district was a modern urbanization project, then about ten years old. The small, boxy houses were adequate, I suppose, in most respects, but they all inexplicably lacked either a kitchen or any other room capable of serving as one: not part of the plan! And so the Guevaras, like their neighbors, had constructed a makeshift kitchen in the backyard out of a few planks, adobe, and tin sheeting. Cooking was all done on sticks, and water had to be carried through the house from the bathroom.

One evening Don Guevara proudly showed me a photo, which he always carried with him, of his only and beloved daughter Julia. Don Guevara never carried a photo of his three sons, which was not surprising, as one of them was the notorious Adolfo Guevara, a rowdy teenager known throughout the district as "Hitler." I hadn't been in the house five minutes before Adolfo clapped eyes on me and bummed fifty soles.

Adolfo is remembered here with a combination of fondness and dread. Once after leaving a movie I was met by Adolfo on his bike. He thought I might be hungry; he was "worried" about me. Under protest I let him guide me to a fine restaurant, a real tourist trap, where I refreshed myself with tea while Adolfo helped himself to a full chicken dinner—all of couse, on my account.

I rode back to the Guevaras on the crossbar of Adolfo's bike, heavy going as the youth zigzagged wildly across both lanes. It was dark, and naturally there were no lights on his bike, thus adding to the drama. Among his tricks was a high-speed "Look—no hands, Jorge!"

We were nearly upon an unmarked railroad crossing at the bottom of the hill leading into Barrio Tío, and as luck would have it a slow train was approaching.

"Adolfo, you're not thinking of racing that train . . . Adolfo! . . ." My words were cut off as he put on an extra spurt.

"You bloody nut . . . Hit-ler!!! . . ." I screamed as we practically flew across the bumpy crossing just slightly ahead of the diesel. Then, just before reaching home, we hit a curbstone head-on, nearly splitting my backbone as I bounced off the crossbar.

Don Guevara, as usual sitting in his favorite armchair reading the newspaper, glanced up at my crippled entrance. "Oh," he said, addressing Adolfo with a smile, "you've given Señor Jorge a lift . . . glad you're making yourself useful for once." Adolfo smirked.

Don Guevara was chief of transport of Petro Perú, the government oil company, and he, like almost everyone else in Cuzco, indeed Peru, was on strike. I might note that throughout Peru, unlike Bolivia, I saw not one picture of the president displayed in public, although his name appeared on many a wall, always coupled with an insult. The mood of the country was also reflected in the bookstore displays, which often featured the works of Marx, Lenin, and even Stalin.

One day I ventured to the center of town, around the Plaza de Armas, where there were gathered disorderly groups of disaffected people. One poor multiskirted Indian harangued the troops. "To double the price of gasoline is one thing," she cried, "but cooking oil, too?! God, how can we campesinos live?" Although the distraught lady insulted the soldiers fiercely, they acted with commendable restraint. No sooner had the soldiers ordered the group that I was with out of the area than tear-gas canisters began flying. While I was trying to make a teashop, one of the missiles clattered at my feet and forced me into an urgent run as tears poured down my cheeks, prompting the Peruvians in my vicinity to give me jolly thumbs-up signs. There's nothing like a gringo in distress to raise the local spirits.

Thursday, May 25, was Corpus Christi Day, the centerpiece of the grandest fiesta of the year, and the only time the gold pieces and other valuable objects leave the cathedral. The bulk of the outlying Indians flocked into Cuzco to eat and drink and to marvel at the huge statues carried in the procession around the main plaza. I counted twelve of these models, including one of Jesus dressed as a cavalier astride a white horse. A few weighed nearly a ton and require a small army of carriers, some of whom were doing penance.

Traveling solo, one hungers for familiar faces. By good fortune my great friend in Cuzco was Bob, the lad from Florida I had run into in Bolivia several times—and whose last name he would never give me. Bob had traveled in sixty countries, and was now picking up some spare change by conducting informal sight-seeing tours in his van (Cuzco is the de facto gringo capital of South America). As this enterprise was only marginally successful, Bob was often reduced to scrounging around the disreputable Hotel Bolivar trying to drum up business among the "freaks"—offbeat expatriates who were drawn in large numbers to Cuzco and its famous Inca ruins.

Over the course of a week, Bob introduced me to some of these characters. One was a Belgian who walked around barefoot in monastic garb and claimed to be the reincarnation of a medieval pope. His Holiness's constant companion was a hippie from Switzerland—known to all, naturally, as the Swiss Guard. (These two actually went on Bob's tour.)

But my favorite was Jim, an American pothead who vegetated in the Bolivar's cheapest room, knee-deep in debris, lost in blue smoke. Jim was actually a committed outdoorsman, after a fashion: He once paid a Peruvian, he told me, to climb a mountain, return, and tell him what it was like at the top.

There was so much to see in Cuzco. At Ollantaitambo stands an unfinished fortress where the Incas gained their only victory over the conquistadors. Huge, half-unfinished blocks litter the site, which consists of a spectacular series of stepped battlements threaded between two steep cliffs. The surrounding villages still make use of the Inca waterworks.

At the great fortress of Sacsahuaman, huge, asymmetrical fifty-ton blocks are fitted together, jigsaw fashion, so perfectly that not even the *Book of Modest Texan Achievements* could be slipped between them. No mortar was used in constructing this stonework, so that instead of cracking during earthquakes, the stones just settle, snuggling even closer together.

Inspired by these sights, I got up one morning at the ungodly hour of four in order to take the four-hour train ride to Machu Picchu, the fabled Lost City of the Incas, one of the wonders of the New World, whose ruins, undiscovered until this century, sit atop a sugarloaf mountain over seven thousand feet above the raging Río Urubamba. At day's end, I left the eerie calm, exalted, and returned late at night to Barrio Tío. My hosts were all fast asleep and unrousable. I was just about to leave to bed down at the police station, when I remembered the living-room window. It was broken, courtesy of Hitler, the broken sections now held together with adhesive tape. Some days earlier Hitler had been playing with a new slingshot and fired it at the harmless family dog who was sunning himself on the lawn. The stone bounced off the poor animal's head and crashed into the living room, where Don Guevara sat reading his newspaper. Mercifully, Hitler was out of circulation for a couple of days after this episode.

Before leaving Cuzco I was provided the opportunity to repay the Guevaras for their hospitality. Young Julia Guevara's American husband was to have taken a medical examination to obtain the one last document needed to make their marriage legal in Peru, but there was a problem: He was in Argentina on business, and the certificate had to be submitted before he could return. Don Guevara immediately nominated me for the role. "After all," he said, only half-joking, "one gringo is much the same as another."

I spent the entire evening memorizing my new identity. In the morning, alias Richard Horner, I went to the hospital, accompanied by the family, where we ran into another problem: The medical workers had gone on strike, too. Just as well. I almost certainly would have failed.

My first two days out from Cuzco featured drastic changes in accommodations. The first night I slept in a pigsty, and the next day, to escape the constant chilling drizzle, I took a long rest in a tiny chicken coop. While I was half-napping, a chicken bobbed over to me, let out a terrific cackle, and laid a large brown egg next to my hat. It was a gift from whomever the gods are that protect the traveler, and not to be turned down. Delighted, I broke the warm egg into a two-ounce can of condensed milk and whisked myself up a nourishing drink.

One of the towns I now passed through was Limatambo. The *tambo* in this and other local place names, I was told, means "rest house," referring to the posts established for Inca runners, messengers entrusted with the communiqués of the Inca (the Sun God—Emperor); their arrival was announced by the blare of a conch shell. These runners must have been magnificent, supertough specimens to run these distances, I thought, for the rest houses were customarily situated 40 km apart (perhaps not coincidentally precisely my perfect distance for a day's walk).

Next followed a series of disasters, as first one of the Yoshikart's wheels broke down (it had lasted an incredible 4,500 km when I had been expecting 300 or 400 at the most), and then its next two replacements collapsed as well. This set me about shuttling back and forth between towns—with gear, without gear, dragging the Yoshikart, *carrying* the Yoshikart.

At one point I hauled the wreckage to a few mud huts on the banks of the Río Apurímac, way down on the valley floor. What a ghastly place! The heat was a nightmare and the insects were sheer hell. Without feeling a thing, I happened to look down at my hands and to my amazement discovered numerous droplets of blood trickling off my fingers and onto the dust in the road. A dozen or so tiny black insects were responsible, which along with the durable flies were swarming about my face and neck. Trying to wipe the bastards out of my eyes, I nearly screamed in misery. There was no escaping them. I fled to a hut and found inside the most wretched people I've ever seen. All of them, including the baby, were wearing stocking masks to reduce the damage done by the insects.

With unspeakable relief I got a lift northward from a truck in order to dump the wrecked cart up ahead. In the back I discovered that my traveling companion was yet another freak who would have fit in perfectly with Bob's bunch: an Austrian who had relocated in the tropics and, although half-bald, hadn't washed or combed his remaining long hair in three years. Explanation? This was the practice of ancient Egyptians. He called himself Time. Like most other freaks, however, Time was an agreeable fellow. He shared his bread and cheese with me, and even gave me ointment for my horrendous insect bites, some of which were still irritated ten days later.

After a good night's sleep in a straw-filled barn next to a police station I hitched back to the torrid Río Apurímac and galloped full speed out again, chased by the same band of flying horrors I had encountered the previous day. Without trouble, they matched my best walking speed. Hour after hour and they pursued me until they eventually fell away with the rising altitude and dropping temperature.

When the cart's wheels—both of them—collapsed for the third time, I had reached a particularly desolate spot and it was near sundown. I finally found a group of Indian huts and approached one of them. One of its walls was simply a bank of earth, and the roof was thatched of yellow, untrimmed straw that sloped downward over the entrance, hiding it from the road. In fact, unless you were deliberately looking for human habitation, as I had been, it was the sort of place you would never notice at all.

I explained my situation to the occupants, mostly through gestures, and the family at last silently bade me enter. Inside it was dark, the interior blackened by the wood fire in the center of the packed-earth floor. There was no furniture to speak of, just a few wood blocks, and a boulder served to hold the door shut. Dinner consisted of potatoes boiled in their skins and coffee with sugar, after which the woman silently took to spinning coarse cloth on a loom that was certainly of ancient design. All during this time the couple never talked to me. After sundown, they prepared for sleep by wrapping themselves in ponchos of the same coarse weave and lay down on the floor next to the fire. The comforting glow of the fire was allowed to die quickly, as stick fuel is scarce in this region and is saved for cooking. All about me were asleep. Through a hole in the grass roof I could see the stars. It was barely seven-thirty, and in the cool darkness I felt absolutely alone in a world of long ago.

At first light everyone in the family got up, and for once

so did I. I carried the gear along the road for a half hour, and when a truck stopped for me I dumped in everything (except for my documents and valuables, such as they were) with instructions to leave it at a police station up ahead, outside Abancay.

Up hundreds of hairpin turns I moved strongly without gear. The Peruvian mountain roads are not very steep—the beat-up local transport (save pack teams) would not be able to negotiate much more than a shallow rise—but the resultant crisscrossing of slopes made for much longer distances, and the rarefied air makes it fairly tough going in any event.

I quickly crested the mountains and began one long 30-km slide down to the white cross that sits above most Andean towns and villages. It always looked tantalizingly close, but never seemed to grow any larger. Whereas walking uphill was usually tough on the muscles in my legs and trunk and on my wind, going downhill hour after hour like this was very tough on the knees. Also, the greater freedom of going downhill was always somewhat marred by the clear view of some distant mountain, which would be so enormous as to make whole towns look like ants' nests and which, I knew, I would eventually have to climb, perhaps two or three days hence. I therefore developed a curious outlook while walking in Peru: If I were going uphill I was relatively happy, since I would sooner or later be going downhill, whereas if I were going downhill I wasn't all that happy, because I knew I would eventually have to be going uphill.

In Abancay, things looked a little better when the mechanic put his son's kiddy cart wheels onto the Yoshikart—a *little* better, that is, because although they were stronger than the former ones, they were much harder to pull, being smaller and without tires. Soon after my latest set of wheels had been installed on the Yoshikart, I was ascending a gravel road strewn with boulders the size of human heads. The cart's wheels, being rubberless and therefore without friction, simply would not roll; they just slid across the surface like a sled. After an hour, I decided to deposit my gear at a roadside bar and walk on liberated of burden except for water, pullover, and coat.

As hot as it was now, I knew that toward evening it would be cold indeed.

The rest of the lonely day I climbed up and up, higher and higher. Always I could see a point I imagined to be the top, and as close as I would get on one hairpin curve, the road would violently swing away from the crest on another one. Whenever I could see clearly the next zigzag, I would leave the road and cross directly up, but this is not always as simple as it seems. Once I completely missed the next bend and had to descend to the road below again. Crosscuts also broke up my rhythm badly; I was often left panting on my back.

Toward the end of the day, with the sun weakening and the huge mountains sinking deeply into shadow, I began looking for shelter in case I couldn't get a lift back to my gear, but there was no shelter to be found. Then, just short of my objective—an arbitrary 40 km that I was now setting for myself—I found a parked truck taking on a load of potatoes that had been brought to the roadside by mules. The farmers were as exuberant and drunk as the mules were patient and quiet. The revelry gave me the chance to jog-trot the last few hundred yards to the 40-km post and back in time to catch the lorry just as it was honking away. I was lucky, for it was the last vehicle off the mountaintop that day.

After 55 km uphill, I eventually crested the mountain road the following day. Success! Two things, however, didn't go according to plan. First, when I reached the village on my map, there wasn't any village; second, I lost my coat. In the hot sun, before leaving off the Yoshikart, I had hung my coat on the rucksack, and it must have shaken loose as the cart vibrated over the bumpy road. The first problem was more than just annoying, as I had precious little water and no food at all. But the loss of the coat was catastrophic. Not only did it contain my gloves, diary, sunglasses, can opener, and money—all more or less important—but I desperately needed it to protect me from the cold.

I was frantic. Finding a beehive-shaped hut, I tossed my gear inside with the confused permission of the occupants and

The first days. January 1977.

The faithful Yoshikart.

Tierra del Fuego. Yoshiko cooking and camping.

A boy with a big dream. Chile.

Above: And we were wed. September 16, 1977. Mendoza, Argentina.

Happy birthday, Yoshiko. Patagonia.

Mr. and Mrs. Meegan. Mendoza, Argentina.

Right: I lose my new wife. San Juan, Argentina.

Below: South American topography. Toward Andean Argentina.

Desert country, North Argentina.

Right: The endless road north. North Argentina.

Below: I enter the tropics, wondering whether I will live to ever leave them. November 1977.

Halfway through a typical day.

Right: My home, Ecuador. November 1978.

Below: Before the assault on Darien. South American soldiers are often a menace. Colombia. February 1979.

Bolivians shared their food. Note poor childless woman carries her plastic baby.

Left: Sleeping in pot. Peru. July 1978.

Right: A reed canoe on Lake Titicaca, Peru.

Right: Berto whistled up a dugout. Darien. March 1979.

Chocos in the Darien.

The border mark, Darien.

With the Kunas in Darien.

Right: We reach Panama City, March 1979.

Below: Berto and I after the Darien crossing.

then began a race against the dark to retrieve the lost coat. I remembered last seeing it 10 km before. The sun was already low as I began to run—uphill, at eleven thousand feet.

Why waste your energy, George? I thought. Accept it. You've lost it. Anyway, that mule train you passed two hours ago must have found it. Give up!

After 4 km of hard running in the thin air, in the halflight I finally saw it: my filthy coat, now covered with hoofprints. What luck—what a miracle! All was intact except for cracked sunglasses. The mule train had walked right over it; they probably thought it was just a discarded rag. In any event, the coat would last two more years—until I got to Texas.

That night, back at the beehive hut, the family shared their baked potatoes with me and allowed me to spend the night in the corner, next to a colony of cooing guinea pigs. (These are raised by people throughout the region as food for special occasions, a sort of substitute for beef, as cattle fare badly at these altitudes.) I was freezing all night—despite the coat!

The owner of this particular hut left a firm image in my memory, because as I left the next day, cocooned in my all, he was swinging a pickax into virgin earth, breaking open a new potato field. He was clothed in nothing but a pair of trousers, sweat pouring off his back, and at intervals he would take up a digging fork and ram it into the iron-hard soil with his bare foot. Nor was he unique among these remarkable people. Sometimes I would see a mountain and wonder whether anyone had ever bothered to climb it. Then, near the top, I would spot a tiny field staked out by some sturdy campesino.

My immediate objective upon reaching the very next town, Andahuaylas, was to find food, a lot of it. I headed for the first restaurant. "Got any eggs?" I asked. *"No hay"* ("Ain't got it") came the customary bored response. "Bread and butter?" "No bread." "Potatoes—you must have potatoes." "All finished." "Meat?" *"No hay."* "Fish?" *"No hay."* "Spaghetti?" *"No hay."* "Soup?" *"Sí—hay."*

The soup was not just nasty, it was stone cold and nasty.

Incensed, I told the proprietor just what I thought of Peruvian food. The man was apparently so impressed by this display of "honesty" that he immediately put me up in his home and gave me my own room. It even had a radio!

Three days later found me in Departamento Ayacucho and easier going. What a territory Apurímac had been: almost 400 km of continuous up- and downhill slogging. I had crossed three mountain ranges. By contrast, from Ocros, where I now stood, to the departmental capital of Ayacucho there was practically nothing but a rolling, high plateau.

At one point, needing a rest, I paused under the lip of an embankment created by a cut of the road. Unseen, somewhere above my head, a Quechua lad on the grassy hillside calmed his sheep with a song. The beautiful melody was exceedingly haunting, sung in a voice as crisp as the high-altitude air. I was not at all surprised to learn, years later, that such a song had been literally sent by earth as an emissary to the rest of the universe. Aboard a *Voyager* spacecraft, which has since passed out of our solar system, are a variety of artifacts documenting our existence, among them a golden disk that carries the music of our planet: the cry of the whale, Mozart, and several other pieces, including a Peruvian shepherd's air.

From 40 km out, high above the valley, I could make out a forest of church spires—I counted thirty-three of them—that fill the town of Ayacucho. Just outside this "Capital of South American Liberation," Grand Marshal Sucre decimated the Spaniards in the last pitched battle of the War of Independence.

For me, Ayacucho was such a friendly town that to meet all the invitations to dinner I had to get up before midmorning. With all this hospitality it was a pity the food wasn't better. In fact, it's the worst in South America, especially in this region, where I saw more gold teeth than anywhere else. Bread in the campo is a small roll which, when cut open, reveals no center whatsoever—all crust and no bread! Rather than harp any further on the subject of Peruvian food, I'll just mention that the most popular condiment is cilantro, an acrid green leaf that overpowers everything it touches—and it touches everything.

Then what did I eat in the Peruvian Andes? Not much. I practically lived on small tins of salted fish, fried eggs, tomatoes, and biscuits. Peruvian chocolate and biscuits are the best in South America, and the local condensed milk, Leche Gloria, is better than any import. It was a real treat for me to mix sugar with a two-ounce tin for instant energy, instant luxury—very good for the morale.

The Yoshikart fell apart again near the village of Mayú, a dusty, rocky spot. I asked a villager where to get another wheel. I had asked the same question at virtually every village and town since Cuzco. The answer seldom varied: It was always "Lima" (hundreds of kilometers away) or "the village after this one." Peruvians naturally assume that gringos are always going to Cuzco or Lima and can't possibly have any interest in anywhere else.

I got similar answers when looking for a map. The one I had—still the one with the dinosaurs and UFOs—told me not so much where I was as where I wasn't. Once I asked an elderly woman on a donkey, "How far to the nearest place where I can buy a drink?" Our exchange was typical:

"The nearest place is Lima, señor."

"No, no, I just want a drink," I would say, making drinking gestures with my hands.

"Then Cuzco, señor," replied the ancient Quechua, trying to be helpful.

"No, no, that's the wrong way. The next village. What's the *next* village?"

"Village? But nobody, not even we Peruvians, go to that village. It is half dead."

"Is it near?"

"God, no. It's days away."

"Any tiendas before this village?"

"No, señor—nothing." The good lady then tilted her cap, struck her donkey on the bottom, and we parted.

As often as not, round the very next corner would be a perfect little shop with a few Inca-Colas—and the half-dead village would appear just over the horizon.

From Mayú I proceeded for two days, mostly uphill, finally reaching the hamlet of Chonta, which consisted of three huts and an evil-smelling restaurant. It was a bitterly cold spot, and near nightfall an Indian clad in nothing but a shirt, thin trousers, and automobile-tire sandals slowly approached me along the road. In his light clothes he looked like a block of ice. The only thing I had to keep him warm was my tent, which he wrapped about himself like a gift from the gods. I lay my sleeping bag in the only available place for shelter, a shallow concrete drain lined with straw—a ditch.

The next thing I remember is the strange sensation of squinting at the morning's strong sun blasting out of a steel-blue sky and everything being occasionally blotted out by large, swiftly passing shadows. As I lay there in the ditch, Indians were going about their business, the town's morning traffic striding over me, considerately ignoring my existence, the soles of their feet passing a few inches above my face.

I roused myself and drifted over to the restaurant—and pondered this odd perspective on another new day.

Late one afternoon, in the near-darkness, I began to hear the jingle of harness bells approaching. Soon I was overtaken, enveloped in the dust of a caravan: six or seven llamas marching single file. Each was laden with a single 20-kilo sack (the weight carried by llamas is limited by government regulation, strictly enforced), while a burro toting an even greater load brought up the rear (no regulation for poor burro). The entire train, animals and drivers, trotted by at a brisk canter. As they passed, without a second thought I fell in step with the noisy train, behind the burro, which was buried almost out of sight beneath an enormous load of fodder.

On we all swept, up and down the mountain roads, under the pale moonlight. There was no time nor reason for words, just a common aim: to get where we were going. After nearly two hours of this blistering pace—I had to jog occassionally to keep up—we exploded into the silent, still plaza of a small village, where everyone, including me, encamped.

Come morning, I awoke to find the plaza empty. Like a dream, they were gone, and I was alone again.

The land became increasingly green and cultivated as I marched into the Huancayo valley. Just south of Huancayo the axle of one wheel snapped in two. Nor was I the only one whose equipment was suffering from the rugged road. The previous night one of the four back wheels of a bus had fallen off, unnoticed, and the bus driver was now looking for it. He had hired a taxi and was now scouring the route up and down, shouting, "Anyone seen my back wheel?"

I was eager to reach Lima, where I could phone Yoshiko, but I still had to attend to the cart. It was one thing getting the axle welded back, but then I spent a full day hunting down a pair of wheels. The only ones I could find were iron, totally inadequate, and when they were mounted they rumbled along like coal carts—but it was Hobson's choice, and they would have to do.

The route continued through the first flatlands I had encountered in months, and then past wooded glades and black cliffs toward La Oroya. The tarmac, like a ruled margin, made the villages neater than before, and they were indeed more prosperous, some even boasting glass windows and a second story.

La Oroya was the dirtiest town on my route, in fact in all of South America. The great belching smokestacks, the highest in the world, dominated the bald hills on the horizon. The smelter factory to which they belonged employed over a thousand workers, who lived in tiny back-to-back concrete hutches slightly down the hill. The poisoned river, gray smoke, and frozen landscape looked like an etching of the English "Black Country" circa 1850. On the other hand, La Oroya is also modern: Of all the towns its size that I saw in South America, it was the only one without a plaza, just one long wretched street bursting with plastic wares and luxury consumer goods.

Out of La Oroya I took a sharp turn to the southwest and began a long climb that went on till dusk, when I reached the summit of the Ticlio Pass. At almost sixteen thousand feet, it was the pinnacle of my entire walk through the Americas. I had climbed my last great hill in Peru, the last for at least 1,300 km, when I would pick up the Andes again in Ecuador. At last I had broken out of my mountain stronghold. It was now downhill all the way to Lima and the Pacific Ocean.

But it wasn't all roses. On the descent in the darkness, a large truck approached, crossed the road toward me, but didn't stop. The driver tried to nudge me over a cliff, a lunatic action, incredibly dangerous for both of us in the deathly darkness. Luckily, except for the fright I escaped injury, and despite the incident, I bashed out an astonishing 51 km that day, continuing the next day into Departamento Lima.

On I walked for one of the most pleasant 40-km days I recall. Beside me the gurgling Rímac kept me company most of the way, and above the rocky outcrops dotted with patches of emerald green I would occasionally see a train running along the Callao-La Oroya railway.

This line is truly an engineering wonder. Built between 1870 and 1893 by the great American engineer Henry Meiggs, it is one of those turn-of-the-century structural feats, like the Panama Canal, made possible by the versatile steam engine (which still powers most supertankers). Just think of the proposition: Build a railway that can handle only a gradient of 4-1/2° from sea level to over 15,000 feet, all in the space of only 146 km. The result resembles an endless scribble. In addition to this the builders had to find a passage through the long, narrow, rocky gorge of Los Angeles. The result was sixty-six tunnels, fifty-nine bridges, and twenty-two switchbacks. Progress was by zigzag. The whole affair runs over your head in places, like a giant toy train. The trains thunder out of one rocky toehold only to disappear immediately into another improbable tunnel.

On the ground, my own iron wheels rumbled on with all the tranquility of a panzer division. "You need tires," shouted a roadside fruitstall man in clear English.

"Good English!" I shouted over the infernal din of my wheels. I ground to a halt beside his jam stall, and the jovial man introduced himself as Miguel González Rivero, age sixty-six, with the best wife in the world. "She is also the fattest," he beamed, in utter delight. Sure enough, when his wife appeared through a door at the back of the stall, she had to fit through sideways.

Miguel took me into his chaotic home at the back of his stand. His ten young children gave him a rousing welcome. Miguel was clearly a hero.

"Hide!" he shouted. The kids all disappeared behind boxes and assorted rubbish lying around the house. "Who does Daddy love the best?"

"Yo!" ("Me!") came the immediate reply from all corners of the room.

This vigorous, virile man sat down in the only chair, swept the remains of his dinner to the side, and opened a large, heavy Oxford dictionary, copyright 1919. Even at his age he had decided to learn English, and had been studying for only a few weeks.

I entered the suburbs of Lima after dark in a nightmare of traffic and immediately sought out an address recommended to me, but when it turned out to be an office, and hence closed, I ended up spending the night at a nearby police station. The entire next day was spent searching out my other introductions, all to no avail, until I came up trumps with a Methodist residencia. The normal fees were waived, and I was given a private room, painted pink and with a balcony. Very near total exhaustion, I lay in my bed and thanked God for my luck, and more particularly Pastor Ortega, whose introduction had opened this door. Another night of filth was more than I could stand.

My timing was excellent: Mum had been in Japan now just two days, and so I rang Yoshiko. For the last two and a half months, four questions had been constantly on my mind. Is Yoshiko OK? Am I a father? Have I a son? Have I a daughter?

"George, you are father! Beautiful daughter. Black hair, eyes black, and white skin, and such a round face, just like a volleyball. All stuff and things Japanese. Only your white skin, which means lucky."

We talked at length, reaffirming our love, and then I talked to Dr. Matsumoto, my father-in-law, and to Mum. Once I had rung off and was secure in the knowledge of success, I opened the letters I had picked up a few hours earlier, and out spilled dozens of photos of a roundfaced baby with almond eyes and white skin—tiny Ayumi. (Yoshiko had suggested the name, and we agreed on it before parting. It means "walk.")

My responsibility now was to see my wife and daughter—how deeply I missed them!—and this meant getting to Panama in nine months. It was a tall order, something that Sebastion Snow had accomplished only with monumental luck and guts.

Once I left Lima and was clear of the urban sprawl, traffic became manageable. The road now became a straight strip of pavement that would be unvarying for the next thousand or so kilometers as I entered the great desertlands of Peru.

The first town I encountered was Ancón, a seaside resort, but it was virtually empty, this being the off-season. North of Ancón was a fork in the road. I had reached the main wing of the famous Pan American Highway. In theory (and in the popular imagination), this "highway" spans all Latin America before connecting with the superb U.S. Interstate system. (In Central America it is called the Inter-American.) It is not so perfect. For instance, there is no route at all through the topographical hysteria of southern Chile, and of course the Darien swamps of Panama utterly defy the road builder. North of Lima, the Panamericana is a narrow tarmac strip encroached on by the relentless desert dunes. In other sections it is a highway in name only, and in some cases it is little more than a rubble-strewn track through the mountain.

Here I had a choice: climb over a 20-km-long sand dune along the Panamericana or take a smaller coastal road. I chose the latter, and it proved to be strangely evocative of other places and times. I heard the cries of seabirds overhead, the Pacific rollers crashing nearby. The smell reminded me of my days as a cadet on H.M.S. *Worcester* moored on the Thames. For some reason, there were constantly echoing in my ears the commercial jingles I had heard in childhood—lyrics like "This is a carpet you can afford . . . by Cyril Lord"—while all about me the desolate sounds and ancient landscape of sea and sand made me feel sad, impermanent, and very much alone.

After I rejoined the Panamericana north of Chancay, the view never changed: a black strip of road and immense golden sand dunes, which in places would creep across the road, forcing me to the center—and place me in considerable jeopardy should I let my thoughts wander, for the cars moved at great speed across this route, and no driver expects to encounter a walker in this bleak wilderness. Except for the occasional oasis every hundred or so kilometers, no outcrops or foliage deviated the contours of the dunes, which are shaped by the unvarying southeasterlies. These winds were most welcome in August, making it cool enough even at ten degrees below the equator to require a coat most of the day.

In Huacho, as I whiled away the time in a seedy fishermen's bar, a well-dressed chap sporting a diamond ring sidled over to me and in heavily accented English introduced himself, mentioning that he was a "collector." We then proceeded to have the following remarkable conversation:

"I learn you inglés have smaller penis than ten years ago."

"Well, I wouldn't really know about that . . . I . . ."

"*Have* you a big one, or a small one?" He clarified: "I mean, on you now?"

"Well, that's a difficult thing to . . ."

"If you do, could you show it to me?"

"Well, I don't really know . . ."

"I would very much like to see one," he pressed on, excitedly. "Even a small one."

"Well, I daresay you would, but . . ."

"*I* have a big one in my pocket." He reached into his

113

pants pocket. "Here, I've got my hand on it now . . . I will show it to you."

"Well, I'd rather you . . ." And then he produced it—or rather them—two large English pennies: George VI, 1947.

We spent the rest of the afternoon amiably chatting. Among the man's memorable observations was that "women are like anchovies" (anchovies are a major part of Peru's fishing industry): "They are there for two years, and then for no apparent reason disappear."

On the approach to Puerto Supe I attained another milestone, completing 8,000 km, and by the time I reached town I was famished.

"Got any food?" I shouted up the single step of a waterfront hut, a makeshift restaurant.

"No. Have *you*?" came the reply from inside.

"Well, actually . . . yes. I have a coconut and a tomato."

"Fantástico!" And with that I was ushered inside, the great nut was cracked open with the help of a hammer, and all the family reached in. To the accompaniment of squeals of astonishment I then fried the tomato; for these people, it was like frying an orange. I assured them that all Britons do the same, which elicited further gasps. And thus the patron fed the restaurant.

The average restaurant I passed in the desert can only be described as ghastly. To keep things on the up and up, the floors are given a daily washdown with gasoline. A common story in these parts is that some hapless traveler once stubbed his cigarette out on one of these floors and everyone was lucky to escape with his life from the ensuing fire.

Café children were kept busy separating the good grains of rice from pebbles and other rubbish that comes in the same sack—time-wasting work that makes car washing interesting by comparison.

Many people had told me that there was nothing between the towns, some of which were hundreds of kilometers apart. This is not strictly true, for every day I spent in the desert I came across at least one wayside café or hut that could furnish water. Just north of the town of Huarmey I got a drink from a hut partially hidden behind a dune. It was built of the only available material: rubbish from the town dump.

Motorists would nevertheless pull up beside me and plead on my behalf: "Gringo, there is *nothing* for hundreds of kilometers. Please, for your own safety, please take a lift." Especially as I neared the equator, the drivers themselves looked terrible—covered in sweat, a wet towel draped about their necks. Considering the sedative effect of the long, featureless stretches between towns and the desperate heat, it didn't surprise me that most drivers failed to notice the rare roadside hut.

In this respect, it was always a big moment for me when I could just make out the disjointed corners of a building somewhere ahead. Such a solitary structure by the roadside usually meant a café, and thus the possibility of—who knows?— even a cool drink. With mounting excitement I would paddle through the heat haze. A half-corroded Lulu-Cola sign was the only proof I needed.

God, the joy! The undiluted happiness of a cold, gaseous mini-explosion at the back of the throat . . . all the dust and thick, dry muck disintegrating in a torrent of sweet soda. These great, speechless moments, with the syrupy liquid dribbling over my open shirt, I count among the happiest of my life. Family, Yorkshire pudding, World Cup matches—all took a back seat. As often as not, the soda was just-warm, and then the second chug from the bottle would prove marginally cooler as the mouth came into contact with the liquid farthest from the glass sides. In the stupefying heat, one is acutely aware of such distinctions.

Early morning, back on the road, I could clearly see a large, modern cargo vessel steaming close in. As I peered at it through my steamy, cracked sunglasses, the sweat trickling off my forehead and into my eyes, I imagined the third officer, still rubbing his eyes, relieving the chief officer, and I felt a great nostalgia for the ship's breakfast, which surely included bacon—it was so near yet . . . I had not eaten bacon for twenty months, toast only once, cornflakes not at all.

From Chimbote to Trujillo is 130 km of practically nothing; therefore I camped out. Putting the tent up in soft sand is a surprisingly difficult and frustrating business: One sneeze and the whole lot would be away.

Trujillo turned out to be a tourist town, for on the outskirts stands Chan Chan, capital of the ancient Chimús. The ruins, consisting of enormous adobe brickwork, are only slowly crumbling. The reason such mud-brick walls have survived the ravages of seven or eight hundred years is of course that this section of the Peruvian desert is the most arid place on earth—one light shower every fifty years. Many of the locals have never seen rain in their lives. Another by-product of the climate is a unique feature of some houses in and around Trujillo: The living rooms are left roofless, open to the elements—which, of course, no one minds because here there are no elements.

Beyond Trujillo, the desert started affecting my state of mind. Because of a gross error in my map, I missed my objective and was left with only a single onion to eat. I had sufficient water, true, but what did it all matter? I didn't care if I ate or not, nor whether or not I went past my objective. I would walk until I hurt all over, to ease my inner pain. I was alone and missing Yoshiko and missing home. Sometimes I wandered along the road in tears. Perhaps I was sailing too close to the wind—cracking up. Everything seemed so distant. I would bash out a 40-km day only to find more sand, and so I would walk on under the Milky Way until exhausted. Whether I walked or stopped seemed to be the same to me.

What luck! I found a solitary bamboo hut with a single bottle of soda for sale. After making my purchase, I went through the ticklish business of putting up my tent, opened the soda (with difficulty, as I had no opener), and crawled into my weatherbeaten home, pursued by hideous insects. As I climbed in, the bottle toppled over in the sand. I just man-

aged to see the last drops disappear into the earth. I screamed
with anger.

Morning brought an unpleasant child's shaved head poking into the tent: I could even see his fleas leaping into my
kit. And so began another day on the road.

The day before Chiclayo, the departmental capital, proved
a scorcher, and this was the first day during which I felt compelled to wait out the afternoon heat entirely. I had done
very well and very soon covered 743 km of desert without
suffering too badly. Poor Snow had hit the Peruvian desert
in January, when the whole coast is a furnace. He, poor man,
shouldered a fifty-eight-pound backpack, wore a heavy coat
that was too bulky to carry—and even toted a briefcase!

Piura appeared like a mirage far off, a green oasis adrift
in a sea of sand. The shimmering specter grew as the hours
reduced the distance, and I eventually galloped into town
sweating and puffing like a horse. The next day the Ecuadorian consul in town gave me an entry visa and, surprisingly, a map—on the promise of a post card from Panama.
Eagerly I left Piura, capital of the last department before Ecuador, my immediate goal.

Upon reaching Sullana I had a choice of route. I could
continue along the Panamericana Norte or I could take a
shortcut to La Tina on the Ecuadorian frontier. Ecuador filled
my thoughts, and so I took the shortcut, as Snow had done
years before. This was a mistake: The road was absolutely beyond anything I had thus far met, nothing but a grossly un-
dulating strip of sand. At one point I went through the surface up to my thighs and had to crawl out on my stomach.
I walked on through country like this all day under a powerful sun, surrounded by the maddening buzz of a million
flies.

After following an empty, sand-filled canal built by the
Yugoslavs as part of a huge irrigation scheme, I switched onto
a series of countless tenth-rate roads to Las Lomas. In Las
Lomas I was told that there were *two* roads from Sullana to

Las Lomas. To my astonishment, I hadn't walked on either of them.

A sandstorm arose and battered me with Patagonian violence as I inched toward Ecuador. Sand poured in through a hole in my boot; blisters had me limping, and I stopped every ten minutes for a long rest. At one point I stumbled across a geologist surveying the countryside—his employers were uranium prospectors—and gratefully accepted his cool water, good directions, and the chance to glance at his excellent map.

Tired, gaunt, and burned brown, I reached La Tina on the Río Macará, which marks the international border. Here a German passed me fleeing south, stopping only long enough to relate how he had been robbed in Colombia—twice.

"You're late," drawled the yawning Peruvian border officer, all the while rhythmically tapping a pencil on his desk. "Your visa expired yesterday, the nineteenth. Today is the twentieth."

"October," I said brusquely, knowing myself to be on firm ground.

"Pardon?"

"October. The visa expires nineteenth *October*. We are now in *September:* September the twentieth."

He immediately became apologetic. "Oh, well, I never did like this job," the man murmured, and with that he stamped my passport and, like his colleague at the Bolivian border, settled back into his nap.

I have no reason to complain about the Peruvian bureaucracy, however, for they were generally excellent in their dealings with me. Even the madhouse ministry in Lima where I got my three-month extension had hired students to guide people to the right desks in the correct order. The process only took ten minutes. Most notably, in my five months in Peru I was never once asked for *"documento."*

Ecuador

Leaving Peru and entering Ecuador at the Macará crossing was like turning the page of a picture book. Behind me lay the fierce desert waste of northern Peru, a scene straight out of a Mexican bandit movie, while spread out before me was a lush tropical vista—hills abounding with palm and banana trees, a winding river, tidy whitewashed houses with red-tile roofs. The contrast was so vivid that neither a thousand miles nor a million years could have produced a greater transformation. According to the map, I had been in the tropics since northern Argentina, but only now did the landscape match the tropics of my childhood imagination.

Ecuador soon proved different from Peru in style as well as substance. The casual inefficiency of the Peru control had left me calm and unprepared for the Ecuadorian border officials. No sooner had I walked the bridge across the muddy, lazy Río Macará than a small detachment of soldiers in spotless, pressed khakis took me in tow to a crowded office where a similarly uniformed agent was sitting bolt upright behind a large metal desk.

"Pasaporte!" barked the desk man, whose nameplate identified him as Corporal Schmitt. Corporal Schmitt was a withered man in his fifties with an ultrathin mustache. We took an instant dislike to each other.

When I produced my passport he ignored it and demanded, "Show your money—you need a thousand dollars for a three-month visa." I showed him two hundred dollars' worth of bank drafts. Schmitt contemptuously swept these aside. "I want to see *money*, not worthless paper!" Reluctantly, in full view of several Peruvian day laborers and a ragged assortment of hangers-on, I hauled out two hundred in cash from my money belt.

"So, you think that we Ecuadorians are all robbers, like the Peruvians?" Without waiting for a response, he bellowed, "Only two hundred dollars equals only a ten-day visa. Next!"

Ten days! Not nearly enough time for me to reach the next immigration office at Guayaquil without drastically altering my itinerary. Now twenty months' worth of frustration in dealing with South American bureaucrats suddenly exploded. Spluttering like a broken teakettle, I snatched back my documents from the desk—in the process inadvertently grabbing the several papers that had been lying underneath them as well—and furiously slammed the whole package down so hard that my precious passport shot straight to the other side and struck the seated Schmitt smack in the chest, just beneath his medal ribbons, with an audible *thwack*.

This harebrained gesture immensely delighted the Peruvians, who had been watching with keen interest while awaiting their turn. Corporal Schmitt, not so amused, slowly rose from his chair as his face reddened, removed his dark glasses the better to glare at me, and growled, "You have insulted the uniform of an official of the Republic of Ecuador—I order you returned to Peru!"

The tension in the room was palpable. A soldier standing near the door unslung his carbine—and nearly fired it when a donkey farted outside the window. Schmitt fumbled with his pistol. With horror I realized what an awful mistake I had made. This nonsense had gone too far, and now this arrogant functionary was capable of ending my marathon on the spot. Unnerved, I squirmed and apologized at great length in my crippled Spanish; I even dragged out my South American newspaper clippings in an effort to establish some credibility.

The latter seemed to do the trick. Things eventually cooled down, and Schmitt even relented by giving me a thirty-day stamp.

The corporal was nevertheless determined to score the last point. *"Contrabando!"* he shouted, pointing at something in my gear, which by now had been strewn all over the room. My heart sank—and then I saw the object of his gesturing— a coconut an old Peruvian woman had given me. *"Es prohibido,"* he said, adding, "For reclamation you need a customs permit in quintuplicate from Quito." I thanked him for the information, quickly assembled all my things, and left— minus my coconut. An odd thought struck me as I walked the short distance to the town of Macará: If Ecuador had not allowed me entry and Peru refused me reentry, would I have had to spend the rest of my life on the frontier bridge? In South America, this seemed perfectly possible, even logical.

Macará was so much brighter than its Peruvian counterparts, with people swinging happily from hammocks in the gardens of well-maintained, brightly painted houses. Prosperity was in the air, down to the town market, where I saw hundreds of Quechua women in heavy woolen cloaks all colors of the rainbow, heavily laden mules, and great towers of baled fabrics and produce.

There was excitement in the air as well, for tomorrow would be "Macará Day," the beginning of one of those three-day fiestas that are held all the time in Latin America—or perhaps it only seemed that way to me because I was always being locked out of a bank, post office, or bureau on their account. In the central plaza a platform had been erected, and a crowd had gathered in anticipation of speeches from the town dignitaries. I stayed just long enough to watch a self-conscious boy of eight or nine being pushed to the rostrum; he was to recite the town anthem. After two or three minutes of silence, *el niño* finally provided some entertainment: He removed the chewing gum from his mouth and stuck it onto the microphone. Slight applause. A further delay brought a flapping mother onto the stage. More applause. She gently

121

tried to coax the illustrious words from her son, and then in frustration bounced the microphone on his head. All failed. Finally a triumphant, mute *niño* returned to the audience to a rousing cheer. No one wanted to hear the anthem anyway.

After one night I left Macará and headed for the departmental capital, Loja, along some 180 km of mountain road, where again I was impressed with the standard of living of the average Ecuadorian. One Indian family, woodcutters, took *my* picture with their Polaroid! New cars belted along well-maintained tarmac roads. Indians selling their wares at town markets did their recordkeeping with pocket calculators. Shops were well stocked, and even roadside cafés carried varied menus. New wealth was pouring into Ecuador, now an OPEC nation: The old banana economy was being supplanted in reaction to recent discoveries of oil.

Halfway to Loja, I reached the town of Catacocha, exhausted; I had just negotiated the steepest hill I was ever to climb in South America. A friendly family gave me a bed, but I had little rest. Numberless kids asked numberless questions about the Queen, the Beatles, and London. Throughout Latin America the people seemed to be particularly pleased to learn that I was British and not American. Most of them had never met a native Englishman before—nor probably an American for that matter, although anti-Americanism was a well-established tradition.

Snow had told me that Ecuador is "a joy to walk through," and indeed it was a pleasure to gaze at the wonders of the countryside while my mind ranged over a whole galaxy of topics: I might be musing on the decline of Britain or replaying a movie in my head or feeling sad for not being with Yoshiko and our baby or with Mum in Rainham. Certainly, while walking I was never bored. True loneliness only struck when I was waiting out the long evening in a poor village or, worse, a large city. The most comforting thought during this period was that I would soon be reaching the equator. Not that I wanted to be *at* the equator; rather I looked forward to being *beyond* it, in the Northern Hemisphere.

When I reached Loja, I immediately took note of the

"cat's-eyes"—reflectors imbedded in the roadbed that demarcate lanes—and a municipal garbage truck, compactor-type. Neither was remarkable in itself, but it was the only time I saw either in South America. During my first few hours in Loja, I had the good fortune to run into two young Mormon missionaries who let me sleep one night in their room and three further nights at their temple. My four days in Loja were somber ones, however, not so much because of the Mormons, who didn't try to convert me (at least not very strenuously), but because of the constant rain.

When the weather finally cleared I set out, entering mountainous country once again. At the very moment I cleared the suburbs of Loja, rain simply poured down, as if by higher authority. The savage downpour went on and on, soaking me. At nightfall I reached a mudslide that flooded the entire road. Under the feeble beam of my penlight I virtually floated the Yoshikart across the viscous mud; my boots were nearly sucked off in the process.

I finally found the unlit hamlet of Los Juanos that I was aiming for. Drenched and shivering, I entered a trading post and told the locals how I had nearly lost my boots in the mudslide. They said I was lucky not to have lost my life. Had I stepped off the narrow road, they explained, which was all too easy in the pitch-black, I'd certainly have disappeared into a bog hole and drowned. I was the only creature to have crossed the morass since the rains had begun fifteen hours before.

The morning brought great peals of thunder and not a pause in the engulfing gush. The trading post was filled with people seeking shelter, many of them grave-faced Indians in black capes, black hats, black shirts, black cutoffs, and black rubber boots. Shouting to make myself heard above the torrent, I asked one fellow, who had just come in, "When's the dry season?" Rain dripping off his nose, he looked at me as if I were mad before answering, *"This* is the dry season."

Venturing out into the nasty weather, I immediately got my only set of clothes soaked again. It rained for the next thirty-six hours. I had to keep walking, because every time

I stopped I began shivering uncontrollably in the mountain cold. Only days before I had been reeling in Peru's desert heat; now it was barely a memory.

It was still raining when I reached Saraguro and entered a general store for some bandages for my feet. Among the more prominent items for sale there were potatoes, chocolate—and coffins. I was still pondering this odd combination later in the day when I took shelter with the local carpenter, and so I asked him about it. "Coffins? They're my bread and butter," he said cheerily. "People are dropping off like flies— I can hardly keep pace." The wind and rain were rattling the door and windows in a melancholy way as I ventured to ask him how much he charged. "For you, señor, as you are going to Colombia and will shortly be in need, a bargain price: four hundred sucres."

As I continued north I considered again all the gruesome stories I had been hearing about Colombia ever since Argentina, and I briefly shuddered to think that I would soon be there. But my mind settled on other matters. I was now October 4, exactly one year since Yoshiko's departure. I wondered how she was faring—and Ayumi-chan, too. Did a baby of five-and-a-half months have teeth, or walk? I hadn't the slightest idea.

At nightfall I reached a collection of mud huts the map labeled "La Paz," and I was surprised to discover, in one of these humble dwellings, several bakers who worked two nights a week to churn out thousands of loaves of bread. The bread was so good that it was famous for miles around. I sat on a stump in the corner and was given a loaf straight from the oven. The bread was so hot that I had to hold it with my coat cuffs. My nose was filled with the smell; my stomach, recovering from the day's march, rattled like an empty bucket in the wind. Spreading butter all over the loaf's golden surface, I tore at the heaven-sent wonder and stuffed chunk after chunk into my mouth like a rabid dog. In all my life, before or since, I've never tasted its equal. I munched through four loaves before succumbing to bloated exhaustion and blissful sleep.

Cuenca, Ecuador's third largest city after Quito and Guayaquil, sits in a valley of manicured lawns and pastureland laced with whitewashed fences. As I approached the city, people came over to shake hands. This was happening more frequently as I proceeded north, for news of my walk, both published and word-of-mouth, had preceded me.

Past Cuenca, after a casual 14 km, I realized with an awful shock that three days earlier I just might not have actually walked the four blocks between the movie theater and the central plaza. Was there a gap in the journey? As I mulled this over, an inner voice made a strong argument for going on: "Look, you must have covered that stretch in all that walking about the town you did. Anyway, you're not going back all that way for a miserable few hundred meters."

"No, of course not," I muttered to myself. "I'm not such a fool."

"So what's bothering you?" said the voice.

"I can't be absolutely positive I covered it."

"Look, nobody will know the difference, dum-dum."

I walked on slowly, when yet another voice seemed to offer an opinion: "George, say they put you on a lie detector, you'd fail!"

That did it. I immediately took a lift back to Cuenca, walked the miserable four blocks, and returned to my walk a much happier man.

To live a lie is extraordinarily stressful, I have imagined, especially in this sort of enterprise, which so much depends on one's word and thus one's honor. The Englishman Donald Crowhurst made phony entries in the log he kept as proof of a record-making round-the-world sail, went mad under the strain, and ended up killing himself.

After Azogues the route slid downhill for two days. When I asked directions from an Ecuadorian pot smoker riding a motorcycle, he cheerfully gave me his farm address and insisted I drop by. When I reached the farm after dark, the young man was standing at the gate considerately holding a beacon to guide me in—another marijuana cigarette.

Lujo ("Lucho") Gonzalez went to great lengths to make me comfortable in his farmhouse and then promptly passed out. In the morning we drove his pickup to Guayaquil on the coast, where he had business to conduct with Fat Gonzalez (no relation) and where I wanted to get my visa restamped and poke around the port, perhaps even find a British merchantman and recapture some sense of home. During the two-hour drive, Lujo, speaking in English, kept me entertained with stories of his own travels. He had left home at sixteen, bound for nowhere in particular, and ended up spending a year touring South America. "I learned all kinds of new things," Lujo told me. "For instance, all my life I had believed the Brazilian interior to be all jungle, very hot and humid. But when I entered it from Uruguay not only was it wilderness, but it was freezing. I had to walk sixty kilometers before I found a road—and when I did, nobody would pick me up. Every time I put my thumb up for a lift, the passing Brasileros put up their thumb up, too, but they never stopped. Later I discovered that in Brazil the thumb-up sign means 'Keep going'!"

When we reached Guayaquil, the largest banana port in the world, it proved to be a hot, nasty, unpleasant place dominated by industry and full of whores, drifters, and other ne'er-do-wells. Getting my visa fixed with Immigration was easy, for once, but trying to find a place to stay for the night wasn't. First I tried to arrange something with the help of the British consulate, but was met with only condescending rebuffs, perhaps an omen of what was to come. The night was finally spent on the floor of a fire station, where the mosquitoes attacked with such fury that they bit me through my trousers.

Next day early I went to get a pass to enter the port. The shipping office told me it was flat impossible. I persisted elsewhere and found it a cinch: Down the hallway I encountered no less than an Ecuadorian rear admiral, who signed the necessary paper without even looking up.

Full of confidence, I marched up the gangway of the British motor vessel *Ortega*. I was looking forward to English newspapers and a chat with the lads, but when I entered the officers' smoking room, a subdued group looked at me indifferently. Finally a second engineer flashed me a hostile look, and said, "What do you want? . . . This is not a very hospitable ship, you know." In a few words I described my sea experience and explained the present trip. There was utter silence from the officers, and then a "sparky" (wireless operator) spoke up as if for all: "We're not interested in what you were, who you are, or what you're doing . . . so kindly fuck off." I stood there in disbelief, and the sparky repeated, "Fuck off." As I walked to the door, he followed as if to hit me, but settled for slamming the door on my back.

I suppose from that time I have really lost a piece of my faith in Britain. Up to then, I had thought I was doing this journey, whatever it meant, in some abstract way for Britain—a Britain I knew and loved. But what now? Of all the people I met in South America, my fellow citizens came out clear winners in arrogance and hostility, not to mention lack of understanding. Never again would I see my nation in quite the same light. It was a sad moment.

After Guayaquil I was more than content to be back with Lujo, this beaming young Ecuadorian who had become a successful farmer with a wife and two children. We shared the common bond of those who have foregone a hot dinner and soft bed to find something else in life, something beyond the horizon.

At the moment, however, Lujo was having in-law troubles. "Last month my father-in-law tells me he bought a tractor with money from selling his car. I asked him, 'How will you manage without a car?' 'Easy,' he says, 'I will borrow yours!'

"My mother-in-law has not spoken to me in three weeks because of the sugar. I raise sugarcane on a small plot, and in exchange for my crop the sugar factory gives me a huge sack each month, which I share with the whole family. Every time I see my mother-in-law she says, 'Lujo, don't forget the sugar!' Now I *never* forget the sugar but always she must remind me. Well, three weeks ago I got the damn sugar and gave her the complete sack and said, 'Look, this is a big bag—do you not think you might share it with other members of the family?' And she says, 'Don't be bad, Lujo!'—and never a word since."

That night Lujo's sister-in-law and her husband came to spend the night. Immediately, to Lujo's irritation, the sister-in-law picked up a cooking pot and asked how much it cost. Lujo shouted to his wife, "Your family are always robbing me. How do I know how much the silly pot costs? Why not take it?" He then addressed his in-laws: "Why not take it? Here, take my dog, take my children, my wife, my home, my farm . . ."

"Don't be bad, Lujo!" the couple chanted in unison.

I left Lujo's farm two days later. Before parting, Lujo offered me a piece of his land if I ever wanted to build a house there, while I promised him a copy of my book if I ever got to write one. As I walked away from his farm I shouted back, "Don't be bad, Lujo—*and don't forget the sugar!*" Lujo, in turn, gave me the Brasileros' thumb-up sign.

The coastal region through which I was now walking was utterly different from the mountains. Here the houses were of bamboo and sat on stilts to raise them above the periodically ravaging floodplain. There were fewer Indians, the population being mostly blacks and Creoles. Towns roared to a thumping music—an Afro-Hispanic mélange, like the people—and were decidedly unkempt, the tin roofs of shacks and warehouses poking up rudely from a field of litter and rubbish.

In one small village I was finally treated to a meal of fried guinea pig, the creature I had bedded down with in Peru. It tasted rather like chicken—as so many bizarre delicacies do—and was rather good at that. Pork is also popular in Ecuador, more so than in the rest of South America. Along the Ecuadorian roadside, I would sometimes come across a pig carcass charred to a black cinder atop a wood fire.

On the way to Quito I was struck by the rich variety of Indians living in Ecuador: Saraguros, Jíbaros, Runas, and others as well as the Quechuas that mainly inhabit Peru, each of them wearing a distinctive style of dress. Even the men's attire was occasionally eye-catching. I saw one chap wearing a Napoleon hat, which contrasted nicely with his Wellington boots. He would have been a star turn at Waterloo—probably shot at by both sides.

In contrast to the very tall, handsome Saraguro men in their long ponytails and black capes, the Saraguro women, who seemed a short, worn-out bunch (they do all the hard work), wore black or white hats almost two feet in diameter resembling flying saucers and huge piles of silver jewelry— the family savings. (I counted fourteen such necklaces on one woman.)

One evening on the road toward day's end, there appeared a group of Indian women in long black or royal-blue gowns, with long, two-inch-wide multicolored braided strips wound round their waists and tying up their ponytails. These spectacularly dressed women were the most remarkable porters. Lost under huge loads of wood or water, they would speed past me employing an extraordinary style of moving, a sort of shuffling jog trot which carried them along like so many speeding birds at between 7 and 9 km an hour. (My normal pace was 6 km per hour.) It was an odd experience for me to be overtaken by what in some cases must have been very old women. On one occasion, in the light just before sundown that turns the green slopes of the distant volcanoes a glowing gold, a gang of perhaps twenty of these women trotted up behind me and, perhaps distrusting me or perhaps just to avoid me, detoured clear across the road en masse. Then, like so many geese, they recrossed ahead of me before they finally disappeared below the crest of the next hill.

Slowly (and thankfully) I climbed out of the hot and humid coastal plain and back into the Andes. Little by little, I was making progress, and by October 22 I had reached Cajabamba. The capital of the province in colonial times, the town was rocked by an earthquake in 1797, after which the Spaniards moved the capital to nearby Riobamba, and Cajabamba has been a village ever since. In fact, it was so poor when I arrived that I had the greatest difficulty in securing my daily fix of an onion. The village did boast two radio stations, however. In remote areas like this, where the majority are illiterate, radios are far more important than newspapers for disseminating information.

From Cajabamba to Riobamba was a manageable 18 km, but from Riobamba to Quito was almost 200. Both Snow and the nineteenth-century mountaineer Edward Whymper (of Matterhorn fame) had walked the latter distance in a mere three days, Snow dashing the last 103 km in 18 hours 10 minutes with his monstrous pack and puffing up and down roads at an average altitude of ten thousand feet. It took me ten days.

I was headed in the direction of Quito along a stretch known as the Avenue of Volcanos. Chimborazo, the world's highest at over twenty thousand feet, sits along this route, as does Cotopaxi, the world's highest *active* volcano (defined as having erupted within historical times). In fact, when Europeans first attempted to scale Chimborazo, near the turn of the century, it was thought to be the highest mountain on earth.

By the time I reached the NASA satellite-tracking station on the slopes of Cotopaxi, it was a cold and moonless night, and the enormous radar disk looked like a prop from *Star Wars*. (How strange a world, I thought, where flocks of barefoot Indians scamper about beneath man's electronic communion with outer space.)

On my entire walk through South America I never lost a complete day due to sickness, which I take to be great testimony to the resiliency of the human body (even mine). Once in a while, if I were under the weather I would take off a half day, or even most of a day, in a town—at least there I felt secure, perhaps sometimes even "allowing" myself to become ill. In fact, I was fitter on the road than anywhere else before or since, save at sea. On the day I reached the outskirts of Quito, however, I developed a sore throat. The reason, I suspect, was that I was now encountering more cars on the road than at any other time in South America. All of

Quito seemed to be sweeping by in a bilious cloud of carbon monoxide. The immediate explanation is that it was November 2, El Día de los Muertos (Day of the Dead, or All Souls' Day), when everyone goes to pay respects at the graves of family and relatives and takes off from work (not necessarily in that order of priority). They might also have tossed a wreath over me for the dozens of times I was all but crushed on the narrow road.

I entered Quito in the pouring rain, hardly able to speak through my raw throat. As I dragged my gear slowly up the steep, cobblestone streets, a door opened, and from the courtyard within a black object was flung out and landed at my feet—a drowned cat. Welcome to Quito!

Having only recently survived a national holiday, I read in the newspaper the next day: "Today, the eyes of the nation look to Cuenca." Lord! It was yet another fiesta, Cuenca Day (followed by a long weekend). When I entered Macará the town was shut up for Macará Day. When I entered Cuenca, the town was shut up for Guayaquil Day. Now Quito would be shut up for Cuenca Day. What a country! What a continent! Boxing Day or August Bank Holiday—now, these were *sensible* holidays!

I went to pick up my mail from Yoshiko, and read:

Dear George,
At last I got your letters! I was really worried a lot of you, thought you might be eaten by some greedy people, but just seems it was fiestas that hold up mail.

Anthony wrote, "If something goes wrong on George, I'll look after you and Ayumi." Such a brother!

Congratulations upon your daughter, she really is so pretty, although I cannot imagine you as a father until I see you holding her. She is already creeping at 4-1/2 months (average is 8).

Are you really getting bald? Dear, dear, I must buy you Alain Delon wig. You are getting the same as Mr. Snow.

I hope Mum had a good time here, despite most hotness in 60 years. Everybody really loves her so much—I think you can imagine.

131

Goodnight, George. I love you so. I <u>don't</u> mind even if you are a silly clown.

There was a second letter, actually written before this one, when Mum was still in Japan, and its message came as a shock:

Dear George, Dad,
Yes, I know how terrible is the thing I'm going to tell you. But I must.
George, come back!!
Everybody is worried on you, knowing you are in danger. Especially such poor Mum! Of course, she understands your character and journey. To call success to walk from Ushuaia to 1 km past Panama, past Mr. Snow's walk, is enough, although not sufficient to your idea. But it's still too much because you still have most danger place to go, Darien.
You are already missing seeing Ayumi's pretty acts. This is utter pity to me. Also, don't make a widow and child having no father.
We all agree on this. (Actually, Father never say "Come back" because he tell us he is also a man as you are—he just wants you to decide.)
Yes, I can imagine your shock and terrible feeling now. But can you imagine my terrible feeling to ask you to give up your dream? The more I understand your desirous achievement, the more I've had to be in agony to say to you, "Come back."
I'm the exactly same Yosh who you know. Am still a bit crazy and love my also crazy husband. I'm still watching if you are hiding bread from greedy wife.
I'll write again in a few days.

I Love You, George
Yoshiko-Ayumi XXXX

This was indeed a shock. I wrote to Yoshiko immediately: I had replied the only way I knew how, and trusted the rest to the strength of our love.

Dearest my wife Yosh,

"Come home," you say. Never a day passes without my thoughts reaching that objective. Yoshiko, I do understand the many, many reasons why I could come home, but to force me into a decision I'm not ready to make would be disaster. Yosh, to give up now would mean I'm not the man you married. You may take a man's money, his home, or even his reputation, but never, ever take his dream. When the time to give up arrives, only I will know it.

Kola-chan, I am a prisoner of my own dream. I cannot escape. I am in the biggest open prison in the world, and I cannot escape.

Thank you, love, for putting up with me for so long.

Love
George

My hosts in Quito, on the recommendation of Pastor Ortega (who had presided at Yoshiko's and my wedding in Argentina), were a Canadian Anglican priest, the Reverend Duncan McLean, and his wife Beverly. The blessed reverend is a man of many talents, and in honor of my coming he played the bagpipes for me. This skill, he told me, had come in especially useful some months before when his next door neighbor had thrown a loud party that had run well into the wee hours. The next morning, in retaliation, Duncan had risen at dawn and held his daily practice on the front lawn—two solid hours of "Scotland the Brave." From then on, the neighbor always invited Duncan and Beverly to his shindigs.

I left Quito after a recuperative week and a half, and on November 14 reached the equator and simultaneously broke into five figures: 10,000 km done. As I neared the frontier at Lago San Pablo I entered Otavalo Indian territory. These people are the most splendidly dressed in all South America, the women in ground-sweeping blue velvet dresses, embroidered white blouses one expects to see on a Rumanian peasant, numerous bead bracelets, and dozens of colored-bead necklaces that hide the neck entirely—all topped off, not by a hat, but by a blue or black folded cloth balanced on the head. Footwear was optional, and most often consisted of tartan bedroom slippers.

The men wore canvas sandals, held about the ankle by no more than a thread, and short duck trousers of dazzling white, always spotlessly clean—when the wearers were sober. Sad to say, almost as if a perverse God had ordered it, men wearing such sparkling attire would be a group of supersonic drunks who litter the roads, fields, and ditches with their inebriate bodies. Seeing one chap asleep in a mud puddle, his white trousers barely showing through the mire, I dragged him to the roadside, where he offered me drowsy acknowledgment: "Thanks, gringo, I've been thinking of moving for some time."

By far my strongest impression of Ecuadorian Indians, however, is that they are a generous, hospitable people, always offering a friendly gesture. Not a single day of my two-month march through their country passed without them giving me something; once a ten-sucre note wrapped in a screwed-up piece of paper was tossed at me by an Indian from a passing bus. Nor did I ever have to use the tent in Ecuador: Someone was always taking me in. It was easy for me to see why Ecuador is the gringo's favorite South American republic. The only drawback for me was that, once through Ecuador, I had to cross into dreaded Colombia. If the tales I had heard were true, real peril lay ahead.

Colombia

"How many Ecuadorians did you sleep with?" asked the Ecuadorian border official at Tulcán half-jokingly. When I wearily replied, "None," he broke into roaring laughter. I could still hear his moronic guffawing echo through the night air as I crossed the border bridge to Colombia.

It was a nervous walk. Colombia requires incoming visitors to show an exit ticket, which of course I lacked. While in Quito, I had requested the British consulate to issue a letter of some sort explaining my case and asking the Colombians to forego their formality. But it soon became apparent that the vice-consul was more interested in giving me flak, and when she insisted that I pay a staggering eleven-pound fee for this piece of paper, I straightaway dropped the matter. My host in Quito, the Reverend McLean, was so incensed when I told him about this that he vowed never again to favor any consulate function with his bagpipe playing.

Could I get around the return-ticket nonsense without the vice-consul's letter? And how would the border guards react to the poor sight I presented these days? My trousers were tattered up to the knees, my blue seaman's shirt was held together by safety pins—and all this was topped off by a scarecrow hat.

"Welcome to Colombia," beamed the smart official. He

then offered me a chair. A *chair*, I thought. For *me!* Very soon not one but two Postabon Colas were brought to me, plus a three-month visa. They not only waived the ten-dollar-a-day and return-ticket rules but even thrust a chocolate bar into my unsearched bag. "You are a hero, gringo, to walk through Ecuador," one of them said as I left their post. "They're all homosexuals over there, you know!"

I walked the thirty minutes to Ipiales. Thirty minutes in Colombia and I haven't been shot yet, I thought. Gosh, things are looking up.

Without too much trouble, I found the town's fire station, where I was allowed to stow my gear while I wandered off to the local cinema to see *The Good, the Bad, and the Ugly.* Strolling back to the station after the movie, I met some real bad and uglies in a back street—soldiers searching for draft dodgers. Suddenly guns were pushed into my guts, and to the accompaniment of shouts of *"Documento!"* I was booted and shoved by the louts against a wall: "Hands up, feet apart!" Luckily, for once I had my faded passport on me and not in my gear. I had seen enough of the streets of Ipiales, I decided, and so after a night's sleep at the fire station, I set off first thing next day for the next town on the road north, Pasto.

The road out of Ipiales, the usual worn gray *pavimento*, passed through a glorious, rolling landscape: sloping meadows bordered by thick woods, an occasional open pasture, everything a sparkling green that reminded me of Ireland—except that the small houses had whitewashed adobe walls and red-tiled roofs. Many of the houses boasted add-ons that emphasized their ramshackle appearance, which was deceptive, for on closer look they were almost all serviceable, well-organized dwellings.

The hot sun was now burning my head, which had been hatless since my run-in the previous night with the militia in Ipiales. Late in the day I sighted an old Indian woman with her equally decrepit burro approaching me on the road. I stopped her with a wave, and for a few pence she sold me her burro's hat.

By the end of the day, in spite of the increasingly rugged

terrain, I found myself walking after dusk so as to be within striking distance of Pasto in the morning. Nineteen kilometers from my goal, too tired to climb over yet another long hill that lay just ahead, I pulled off the road and into a dingy hut, alongside which the señor granted me permission to camp. As I was struggling to set up the tent, never easy in total darkness, I just happened to notice one of the family removing my camera from my gear. When I demanded it back I was confronted by the entire household, the adults having armed themselves with machetes while the children laid on a barrage of rocks. Despite my exhaustion I beat a retreat, climbed that long hill after all, and camped on top. Write off camera number two.

Upon reaching Pasto in the morning, I went straight to the local police and began pestering them over my camera. The man in charge filled out some forms and shrugged, as if to say, "Nothing's to be done." And in fact they did absolutely nothing.

I stomped out of the police station disgusted yet resigned—after all, I rationalized, this *was* Colombia—and set off to find lodging in the fire station. The brigade were a fine bunch who were genuinely mortified upon hearing about my bad luck of the previous night. I still didn't know what to think of Colombia—*everyone* to whom I related the incident (except the police) seemed distressed.

Pasto was so comfortable that I regretted having to leave, but I desperately wanted to reach Medellín, over 700 km away, in time to pick up my Christmas mail. From the cool highlands, I rolled down into the heat of the Patia Valley, where the population changed from predominantly Creole and mestizo to pure black. Again it occurred to me, with a tinge of sadness, that the blacks of South America nearly always seemed to live on the poorest land in the hottest climate.

The heat of the lowlands shook me. I did a large 43-km day into Patia and was so thoroughly exhausted that I stumbled and fell in the plaza, like a bull keeling over after the matador's final pass. Two passing black men assisted me to their bare room, where I gratefully drank and slept. That day

I drank ten small bottles of cola, another two one-liter bottles of cola, and about a liter of the hot, filthy water I had been carrying.

I finally left the boiling valley and climbed into cooler lands once again before reaching Popayán, a town girded all about by sugar plantations. The narrow cobblestone streets were lined with ornate lampposts in place of the usual mercury-vapor streetlights; there were practically no cars. The smartly uniformed policemen wore sheathed swords. All these features were reminders of the fact that it was here the Spanish colonists had chosen to erect their haciendas while the less fortunate blacks toiled in the heat of the lowland.

I was hungry, and so after reaching the center of town, I spent a frustrating hour trying to get an onion. Of all the passions and food cravings I had in South America, the humble onion remained the king. For me a raw onion with salt on bread made a meal and provided a good vehicle for salt, which, after water, was my greatest need and desire in hot climates. Over the course of the journey my body had adapted to my new life-style, and foods that had once inspired dreams became objects of total disinterest. For example, I'd hardly touched chocolate or condensed milk since the Peruvian Andes, and after Argentina I had not tasted jam at all.

Colombian food was no more appetizing than Peruvian fare. It wasn't hard for me to see why two-thirds of all Colombian children, according to one account in a national newspaper, suffered from malnutrition. The populace seemed to live on beans, cold coffee, hard rice, fried bananas, and, as a special treat, corn *arepas,* hard pancakes that resemble Styrofoam but don't taste as good. Occasionally they would toss in a bit of salad or rubbery meat, or maybe a cold fried egg. In my three months in Colombia, I never saw a single Colombian eat a green vegetable, not even a pea.

Failing to find an onion in downtown Popayán, I settled for a hunk of bread and a bruised tomato, and then moved on. Just outside Santander I experienced one of those special moments that are forever etched in my memory. A friendly family had given me a popsicle and even hauled out a great armchair for me to sit in. From this vantage point, I watched a pretty Creole girl dance half the night away with an old, fingerless Negro, a strange sight beneath the pale glow of a waxing moon. (Later I was told that the man had lost his fingers engaging in the highly dangerous, and illegal, practice of dynamiting fish in a nearby river.)

Cali, the third largest city in Colombia (after Bogotá and Medellín), appeared wealthy and expanding, with new construction popping up all along the *calles*. The city even boasted an extensive nightlife. My first night there I donned some fresher clothes, ambled out to see the town, and soon ran into Mr. Fat Julian of Bogotá, stinking of rum, and his equally inebriate wife, Isabel, who took me for a hair-raising drive in their chauffeured Land Rover. We ended up at an Argentine steakhouse and toward late evening Fat Julian, all three hundred pounds of him, decided to sleep on the floor, where he took on the look of a beached whale. Ignoring the fact that I wasn't drinking, he had nevertheless been trying to drink me under the table, where his wife had been residing for some time. Finally, their driver, with the help of about half the restaurant, managed to haul my patrons to the car and thus put a finish to the evening.

The fire brigade wouldn't take me in, and so I camped out in an inconspicuous corner of the police station courtyard—I was trying to avoid the stretch of ground where they had rounded up all the town's transvestites, who at that moment were being noisily caned. The accommodations were adequate so long as I ignored the roving police searchlights, peering eyes, and high-pitched screams of the unfortunate señores in skirts. Then, promptly at 6:00 A.M., the guards turned me out. Stilled dazed, I spent the morning tracking down an American teacher from the Pan-American Institute I had met the night before. John very sportingly let me lay down my sleeping gear under the table in his spare room, where I slept most of the day.

Despite the allure of the city life, I was in a rush to leave Cali, still pursuing my Christmas mail in Medellín before the big fiestas closed everything down. Just before leaving, I stopped by the British Consulate to scan the British news-papers. Mr. A. E. B. Lawrence, sporting a splendid handle-bar mustache, introduced himself as the consul. "Hello, old man. I read your enormous piece in the local rag. Why not pop in for drinkies Christmas morning at eleven-thirty." He scrawled "11:30 A.M." on a bit of paper and handed it to me. "In case you don't know what eleven-thirty means, old man, down here it means one o'clock." Agreeing to return, I marched off to my next destination, Palmira.

John, my host in Cali, had warned me about Palmira, relating how his landlady's nephew had been murdered there only the previous month. Feeling my way through the dark-ness, still some 5 km short of the town, I thought myself a goner, when I practically walked into a compact, well-built man relieving himself on the wheel of a Land Rover beside the road. "Hey, what the fuck we got here?" he growled. The man, who was very drunk, introduced himself as Camille Brassard and made me give my story. "Hey, you can't *walk* into Palmira at night. Only last night at my nightclub, two people got themselves killed. And the night before that, my friend's father got his skull crushed in by a sledgehammer—they took his watch."

Camille wanted to help, and so I took his address and phone number. "Hey, remember—phone up from the out-skirts," he shouted after me as I retreated into the darkness. "We'll pick you up. A man can get killed in Palmira."

In Palmira, I asked a rifle-carrying vigilante protecting a gas pump for the way to Brassard's. He told me, adding that if I went direct, I'd get may face slashed open. I settled for a roundabout route.

Camille welcomed me at his front door like a long-lost brother. "See," he said to no one in particular, "I told you he wouldn't phone!" He then hustled me into his den, where we sat into the small hours talking and thumbing through his tremendous stock of well-worn girlie magazines. My remark-able host told me that he was born in France and raised in Quebec province. Camille spoke English with a gravelly French lilt and referred to himself as "French Canadian," never the trendy "Québecois." An Olympic skier as a teenager, he later emigrated to the States, where he started out as a construction worker and ended up a wealthy contractor. After being robbed blind by his partner, he settled in Palmira with his third wife.

Still rushing along, I left Camille with my promise to return. In Buga La Grande and the towns beyond, some of the locals had read about my trip in the papers, and everyone seemed to want to give me things. All this interest in me, however, could have its drawbacks. Entering the small town of La Victoria, I had the idea to find a quiet café and write a few letters when through the encroaching darkness a pack of kids spotted me. A shout went up: "Look, it's the gringo walker!" I was terrified; I thought they were going to kill me. In Bogotá, Camille had told me, the windows in the tourist buses were locked to prevent the street urchins from breaking in, ransacking the bus, and in the process possibly strangling a few blue-rinse maids with their own Bermuda shorts. Fortunately the kids now following me had apparently eaten that day, as all they did was take the Yoshikart and wheel us both into the central plaza. As a gesture of friendship, I took the hand of one of them—the one who seemed to be the least fortunate, a retarded boy—and we all marched round the plaza in a long Pied Piper procession, the kids shouting to the sidewalk café patrons, "Look, the walking gringo!" Some of the patrons even waved, and so like a presidential candidate I waved back. We ended up at a restaurant, where I was given a free dinner and allowed to sleep on the floor.

By this time, my fears about Colombia had been tempered by the frequent experience of being treated well by all manner of people far beyond any reasonable expectation. Most Colombians I met were sensitive about their country's reputation, and some seemed subdued, even embarrassed, when discussing it. A few even said, "Yes, we know there are many bad things going on here . . ." It was common knowledge, for example, that illegal drugs were the country's largest export, exceeding even coffee. My firsthand experience of this particular aspect of Colombia was limited to one: In a certain room in a certain city, I witnessed a half-dozen people busily stuffing cocaine into surfboards for quick and profitable export to the United States. When I was offered a sample, it was with the warning that I would lose a night's sleep. As I regard that as something too precious to waste, I decided to forego the "treat."

Despite their country's terrible reputation—or perhaps because of it—Colombians were often kindness personified. Here are two typical days from my diary:

18. Dec. 78. 44km. Campo restaurant. 11,048kms.
Up at 08.00, given breakfast of corn cakes and beans. Have to wait until 09.00 until Flora the cow is milked. They [an Indian family who ran a poor bar] cannot let me go until I taste Flora's milk. Go. Walk 100 yards. The daughter runs after me to give me potatoes for the day's march. Ten minutes later a car stops and gives 100 pesos ($3). Midday reach the town of Supia. In café refused service. (My appearance, I guess?) Indignant Colombian lady, Margaret, steps in, buys me my dinner, four colas, and gives me 50 pesos. One hour later Margaret passes on route for Medellín. Given another 50 pesos and biscuits. Late afternoon a Colombian youth walks two hours with me. I give him a drink. Heavy rain, I share my waterproofs and we are both soaked. Reach a campo café, given food. Sleep under the eaves of a hut, lie in mud.

19. Dec. 78. 38km. La Pintada. 11,086kms.
Away at 09.00, cafe gives bread, eggs, chocolate plus 50 pesos. Heavy rain all morning, soaked. Foot blisters due to rotten holed socks. Truck topples over 50 yds ahead. Few more seconds and I'd have been crushed. Midday cafe. Family speak, buy my meal and give 50 pesos. La Pintada for night. I buy my meal and sleep in prison cell.

I reached Medellín on December 21, after a rapid 448 km in eleven days. Between Cali and Medellín, eleven shirts, two pairs of trousers, and one pair of ladies' knickers had all come my way. No, I don't know why I was given the knickers; all I know is that the occupant had long since abandoned them.

Delighted to have reached Medellín just in time to pick up my mail before the holiday fiesta, I confidently swung down to the British consulate, but at the address listed in the *South American Handbook* I found an interior decorator's office, where the secretary informed me, "The consulate shut three years ago. No, I haven't any idea where your letters might be. Please leave."

Upstairs from the decorator's, the American consul, speaking to me from behind a bulletproof Plexiglas partition, was no more help: "We have no connection with the British citizens. No, you can't use our address. Good day."

Deflated, I wandered off to the post office, where the clerk claimed to have returned all my letters—despite the note on all the envelopes indicating "To be collected by 25 December, 1978." Eventually I got a fixed mailing address at the local Banco de Londres, thanks to Mr. William Russell Pennington, who soon became a friend.

Medellín, which now became my base of operations for nearly two months, would eventually be my last contact with the twentieth century before pushing north to El Tigre, where I could celebrate the completion of my South American walk. Beyond El Tigre loomed El Tapón del Darién, the Darien Gap, a 300-km stretch of coast-to-coast jungle swampland extending from just this side of the Colombian border to well inside Panama. Darien's climate, with an eight-month rainy season, ranks among the vilest in the world. According to the locals, the place is impenetrable; Snow had barely made it through, and Tschiffely had bypassed it altogether (he and his horses took a boat). Its climate, its topography, and various rumored horrors had long thwarted construction of the final link of the Pan American Highway.

Just as I was about to catch the bus back to Cali and the

143

consul's Christmas party, my new friends at the fire station where I had bedded down grabbed hold of me and insisted I accompany them on their rounds of the city.

We stopped at a nondescript building and walked in. Noticing a crucifix and a series of large washing stands, I concluded we were in a sports locker room—until I spotted a contorted body lying motionless on a slab. We were in the city morgue. Suddenly a revolting character in a short, filthy striped poncho appeared from nowhere and, hopping about with glee, treated us to an exhibition of the day's arrivals in the monstrous Japanese fridge. First out was an old tramp with an open box of Marlboros still in his shirt pocket. Next was a businessman, victim of a heart attack, his chest hacked open and inexpertly stitched together again.

The star exhibit, and the one that seemed to bring our ghoulish friend the most joy, was the victim of a motorcycle accident, in which the top of his head had been sliced off. His dead, lifeless eyes seemed to stare straight into mine, his twisted grin mocking me. Our guide, who had been told of my plan to cross the Gap, remarked, "Pretty—eh, gringo? You'll look the same in the Darien. Only this monster will be buried. Nobody will bury you!" I tried to brush his words aside—surely by now I was inured to such scare talk—but in this atmosphere they were definitely unsettling. Did my smiling friend in the refrigerator know something I didn't?

The bus ride back to Cali was the usual Latin affair: an eighteen-hour nightmare of blowouts, vomiting children, and bottles of urine rolling about with the debris on the floor. By comparison, walking a scorching road seemed heaven. In Cali I once again found refuge under the table in John's casa and learned with dismay that Sandro, a prospective guide through the Darien and a potentially valuable man, had left town for a job elsewhere.

Christmas morning I sauntered down with good cheer to the British honorary consul's residence. "Now, who are you?" questioned a surprised Mr. Lawrence, wearing a rather dashing cravat. "Oh, the chap walking—yes, of course. I invited you for drinkies—or was it dinner?" I hesitated. "Must have been dinner," he said. "Come in. Sorry, no servants yet. You're the first. It's only eleven-thirty, you know, old man," he gently admonished.

The consul's home was a magnificent bit of England buried away in the heat of Colombia. On the wall hung the Order of the British Empire certificate, and on a bookcase I immediately noticed a bust of Field Marshal Montgomery. "Yes," said Lawrence. "Had dinner only last week with his son. Great friend."

Soon people started drifting in and servants in black bow ties began doling out drinks. I hadn't anticipated all this; just a Coke or two and out is what I thought. Now I found myself involved in an entirely new experience—a full-fledged cocktail party. I was hardly dressed for such an occasion, although much more smartly than usual, in a newly ironed fire brigade shirt. What let me down were the muddy boots and torn trousers with the busted zipper. I felt like a freak from the start.

The house quickly filled up with pale-skinned men in business suits and women in floor-length gowns. Everyone minced about with one arm permanently crooked, the better to hold the obligatory gin and tonic. Why don't they ever put the drink *down?* I thought.

The next rule seemed to be: Never sit down in one of the numerous chairs. We must mill about, and we can't manage that sitting down, now can we?

For one long, uncomfortable moment I was totally alone in a Gobi Desert, everyone having retreated into groups. In the midst of all this humanity I felt even more lonely than at any time on the road. The Honorary Mr. Lawrence—"Wop," to his friends—cruised over, and I took the opportunity to apologize for my shameful appearance. "Nonsense, old man, you're a star," he said, escorting me into the breach in one of the circulating formations, and the show went on.

At the chime of a small bell, tiny sausages and English mustard circulated. Great! I chomped through three in quick succession. While looking around for my plastic bag to catch

145

any leftovers, I noticed a few severe glances being shot my way. Then it dawned on me: When offered a second sausage I must say no, as everyone else was doing.

After an hour or so, some of the guests began drifting out. I found my plastic bag, now nearly full, and joined them. The honorary consul quickly retrieved me from the rabble: "No, no, no—you're for *dinner*, old man," he said cheerfully, and led me by the elbow to the dining room, where the main course was just being carved up. And so I stayed.

After dinner, I was introduced to Her Britannic Majesty's ambassador to Colombia, Mr. K. Uffin, C.M.G. Having heard that he had spent time in Russia during the Stalin era, I mentioned that I had read Solzhenitsyn's *Gulag Archipelago*.

"What did you think of it?" he asked.

"Magnificent history," I said.

He made no comment. As the conversation had already touched on mass murder and communism, in all innocence I asked, "Why doesn't somebody do something about the millions being murdered in Cambodia?"

Uffin quickly turned away, put his glass down very heavily, and then swung round, bristling with anger, and spat out, "Because, dear boy, of *sovereignty*. Do you know what *that* is?"

I fumbled through a weak response, while thinking, When it comes down to having your family murdered in front of you versus loss of some high-sounding concept like "sovereignty," which would *you* choose?

He continued. "Who, pray tell me, tells us in Britian what to do?"

The International Monetary Fund, for certain, I thought. But I said, "Nobody," adding a belated "sir," realizing I had already said too much.

"How long have you been in Colombia?"

"Three weeks, sir."

He could barely control his contempt. "Who *are* you, anyway?" His eyes lowered and focused on the safety pin holding my fly closed. I was saved the misery of explaining who I was by the timely arrival of Lawrence the honorary consul. Unaware of my diplomatic contretemps, he jollily slid in with "Oh, Mr. Ambassador, you've met George, our South American walker."

The great man visibly calmed himself. "So then *you're* the chap . . ." he said, and, turning to Lawrence, "Thank you . . . Wop." For the next ten minutes Uffin questioned me closely on my journey, and I no longer had the temerity to ask any more out-of-court questions.

I was last to leave "Wop's," and by then my dignity was barely intact. With some relief I returned to the solitary comfort of staring at the underside of John's table.

Sleeping quarters once again became a problem when John left on holiday. Anticipating this, I had told everyone at the cocktail party, when they asked, that I was sleeping under a table, but no one took the bait. I was only too glad to move on to Palmira for New Year's Eve and a reunion with Camille Brassard.

New Year's in Colombia is a time for fireworks, and fireworks caused Fat Ivan, Camille's brother-in-law, some distress this particular year. Ivan, when drunk, which was regularly, would go down to the bars in the red-light district and loudly perform decidely second-rate renditions of everyone's favorite arias. One day after I arrived he borrowed a neighbor's broken-down car and took it to his usual haunts. As Ivan stepped out of the car, which had somehow become steeped in gasoline fumes, a small kid tossed an enormous firecracker inside. The result was the biggest explosion in Palmira that New Year's. Fat Ivan, with the legendary luck of drunks, was unhurt, merely having been blasted through the door of his favorite bar to the largest round of applause he had ever received.

Another suffering man at New Year's was Don Alberto, Camille's bodyguard-driver. A man who resembled Friar Tuck, Don Alberto had two wives and two families, each unknown to the other and living at different ends of town. In addition, he was strongly rumored to be involved in numerous unspecified illegal activities. Camille and I spent part of the night

147

with one wife while Don Alberto appeared intermittently to down a drink, twitch, and run off again to his other wife. Being a bigamist at New Year's was certainly no fun.

The day after New Year's, Camille, astounded and incensed that no one had yet exploited the commercial potential of the walk on my behalf, announced that he was going to do something about it himself. As a first step he arranged an interview with Big Dan, a "big-shot American promoter" from Cali. On the big day he even made me shine my shoes and gave me his Arnold Palmer shirt to wear. Florencia, the one of Don Alberto's wives with whom I was now staying, ironed my trousers, and Alberto drove us all over to Big Dan's hotel suite.

Big Dan was all one might expect. Middle-aged and silver-haired, he was wearing jogging shoes, shorts, and a sun visor. If he hadn't been on a health kick, doubtless he would have been chomping on a Havana as well.

We withdrew to the suite's balcony, and Dan whipped out a yellow legal pad. Camille opened with "Er, Dan, this is George, the man I was telling—"

"OK. Got it." Big Dan forged on: "Glad to see you brought the product along—hey, George, you don't mind me calling you the 'product,' do you? Of course, it's just PR shorthand."

I ventured a reply: "No. Not at all. Back home everbody calls me the prod—"

"Got it. Let's begin. Now the way I see it, Camille, you've stumbled into a potentially very valuable product, and all we have to do is *market* the product. This is achieved by putting him on all the TV talk shows, radio, et cetera, et cetera— and buying off the newspapers. I have friends who can handle that."

Camille: "You're going to *buy* . . ."

"Yes, yes, *buy* journalists. Do it all the time. Now shut up, Camille, and let me finish. *Now*—all the money. Lots of big beautiful bucks for testimonials, advertising various products, using our product to sell their product. Understand?"

"No," Camille said.

"Camille, shut up. Now, where was I? Hiking equipment

firms are obvious, but anything from unicycles to Dixie Cups
will do."

I stopped the whirlwind with a word: "Cosmetics."

"Pardon?" said Big Dan.

"You could use me for selling cosmetics."

"Well, I don't really know about that . . . but we *did*
give the K2 mountaineer plastic surgery . . ." Big Dan bolted
on like a rabbit after rest. "My business is producing/direct-
ing/backing films, and in this connection I know the men at
Twentieth Century-Fox who do the ten-minute fillers while
the crowd is out peeing and buying popcorn before the main
feature . . ."

Big Dan suddenly stopped talking. I thought he had just
had a heart attack. What had happened was that while Camille was taking pictures of Dan and me with his motorized
camera, Don Alberto had slipped in close to Big Dan.

"Good *God*, Camille, are you trying to get me *shot*, putting me in the same picture with *Alberto!*" Big Dan then beat
the amiable Alberto back to a seat with his sun visor.

"Now, Camille, don't waste my time with that camera.
I'm a two thousand-a-week man. I won't waste my time. Now,
where was I?"

"Pissing and buying Cokes before . . ."

"Got it. Now—money. I require five thousand *now* to fly
to Chicago and make a preliminary investigation to see if this
scheme is serviceable. I'll get a hold of Donahue and Carson.
I also have friends in the biggest advertising house on Mad-
ison Avenue. If the investigation proves positive, then we let
the product walk or do whatever the hell he wants. Our business will be in the U.S., and we need nine months' lead time.
This is expensive."

Camille: "How much will . . ."

"Right. We need three-quarters of a million . . ."

Camille nearly swallowed his whole can of beer in one
gulp. Big Dan impatiently clarified the situation. "Syndicate.
Very simple, gentlemen. Fifteen rich bastards all put up fifty
grand. No problem. Done it before."

He continued. "If the kid dies, nobody loses, except per-

149

haps the kid, of course, ha, ha! Actually, the English are very good at heroic failure, ha, ha!"

Big Dan then slapped me on the back, and on that jolly note we went to dinner, where Camille got so drunk he wanted to accompany me through the Darien, while Big Dan began ranting about hiring a helicopter to follow me. Over dessert they shook hands, and slowly but noisily Camille slipped to the floor drunk.

On the bus back to Medellín, I slept fitfully, with my mind full of movie stars, helicopters, and millions of dollars. At a night stop, feeling financially secure for once, I splurged on a ham sandwich. But, of course, I never did see Big Dan again.

Back in Medellín, I became the guest of the Montoyas, the family of two youngsters I had met on the road. What luxury! A real house, complete with two showers, two maids, and two singing birds, plus a young tree, which the grandfather, Don Pedro the poet, watered every morning. During my weeks with this splendid family I slept in Don Pedro's library, I had free use of the telephone, and I was even allowed to cook up my monstrous stews. I settled in well—and so, for part of an evening, did another fellow, Don Alfonso, known locally as "Don Alfonso the Drunk." One night, chancing to notice the Montoyas' front door open, he entered the house, meticulously took off his shoes, and went to sleep in Uncle Ivan's bed. Doña Rosa, Don Pedro's wife, discovered the intruder snoring away and let out a scream that mobilized the entire household. Without much discussion, young Augusto and I gently removed Don Alfonso and lay him down, like a sick man, on the grass outside.

My mind was now preoccupied with two pieces of unfinished business: completing the South American leg of the journey, which meant walking to El Tigre at the edge of the Darien Gap, and making preparations for the crossing of the Gap itself, which above all else required finding a reliable guide. As gathering information about the Darien proved slow and I was having no luck finding a guide, I decided to put the preparations on hold and finish the walk.

I left Medellín on January 22 and climbed out of the beautiful valley in which it sits, pausing only long enough to look back down on the city set among the darkening mountains and marvel at the crimson sunset reflecting off the soaring white buildings. After two days of climbing over the central cordillera in the cool of the mountains, so reminiscent of England in the springtime, I reached Santa Fe de Antioquia, which sits in a narrow, hot strip of land between the central and western ranges and seemed hardly to have changed since colonial times. The entire department of Antioquia contained a startling number of blond-haired children with dark skin. Why this should be I don't know. Scandinavian shipwreck? Pirates? One can only guess.

Crossing the western cordillera was an 80-km hike almost straight uphill and down. As I moved slowly north the people became more wretched and filthy. At a two-hut town named Tascón I tried to erect my tent, but so terrible were the swarming insects—at one point there were three in my eye— that I abandoned the idea in hand-over-face misery. Just the noise of insects constantly buzzing in one's ear is tormenting. I eventually was permitted to place my sleeping gear on a pile of rusty bedsprings in a corner of one of the huts. Once I entered, the couple barred the door with a hunk of timber, leaving the three of us inside an airless, windowless, stinking hot room.

In the morning, as the family and I were standing outside, an Indian family came out of the Chocó region to the north, dressed in rough red cloth with double bands of zigzags drawn on their limbs in soot. The hut dwellers, themselves living in squalor scarcely credible, openly mocked the Indians, shouting, "Primitivos!"

Farther north, Indians along the road became commonplace. I spent an hour with an old lady who might have been Sitting Bull's mother. She told me, "We were warned that a lone inglés walking had entered these lands and was coming our way. Our men told us you are a loco inglés walking from the moon, but are not dangerous. We were not to run away but to help you." She gave me a half a banana, said, "God be with you," and returned her large Castro cigar to her mouth—lit end first!

On the tenth day out of Medellín, I banged out a symbolic 40 km, my favorite distance, and camped out that night in the tent. Actually, I camped *on* the tent, as the insects were unaccountably absent, perhaps because of the heat. The tent, which had served me well, was now torn beyond repair and blackened by a thousand candle flames. I looked across the flat swamps to the horizon, a pale moon, and twinkling stars. I felt ecstatic: I was on the far edge of South America.

The next day I walked 7 km to the El Tigre turnoff. My South American road, 11,454 km long, had ended. As if in knowledge of this, my faithful water bottle expired, leaking a puddle into the soft sand of the road.

I took the bus back to Medellín, sleeping most of the way on the floor amid orange peels and cigarette butts. No sooner had we settled in than a squad of soldiers scampered aboard, searching for terrorists. With all the hubbub, retrieving our belongings after they had left was nearly impossible: My coat was somewhere in the back, and the chickens were now with the driver. Fifteen minutes later, yet another army contingent boarded, and by the time this crew had finished their ransacking, all was pandemonium. My new water bottle had been kicked over, someone sat on a chicken, and a lady was screaming that someone had stolen her bottle of beer. Before we reached the city, there were yet two more military roadblocks, and one of the bus's tires blew out. It was a completely normal South American bus ride.

Back in Medellín I again took up residence with the gracious Montoyas. Waiting for me was a letter from Yoshiko, which, I knew, must contain her response to my declaration not to return home. I apprehensively tore open the envelope to read, "Yes, I wrote you, 'Come back home'—because I thought you were waiting for me to say so, so you could come back because that is your wife's hope. But no, you will not. To say the truth, I had not thought that you would, you've got such a strong will."

Dear Yosh—she knew me so well.

In her letter, she went on to discuss our plan for her and Ayumi to fly to Panama:

> . . . Many times I changed my decision "Shall I go or not?" but at this stage I'm going to meet you with Ayumi in Panama. However, in case you could find some place where we can live comfortably, know that Ayumi needs her own quiet place.
>
> In the house, can I use kitchen to cook baby foods? Probably I'll have to make milk hot in midnight. In every midnight she cries loudly.
>
> Please let me know the weather and other every thing that you know about Panama. I do not know even what clothes I shall take for Ayumi and myself.
>
> George, can you understand how much I love you? Of course no . . . But no matter, you will see soon.
>
> I nearly forgot to say—Merry Xmas and a Happy New Year! and Happy Birthday!
>
> You are now 26 years old aren't you? If you want to kiss your baby, keep your lips clean till you meet her. Don't kiss any pretty girls, even if they're sexy and have big busto!
>
> Yoshiko, XXXX

The next three weeks were occupied with frantic preparations for the attempt on Darien, for I had to get through before April's rainy season, when the floods would shut the place up like a dropped portcullis. Even in Colombia very few people seemed to know anything about the Darien. I had spent days combing the city for Michael Hill, who was one of the few authorities on the frontier region. And I finally did discover him after a long search. He was living only a few yards up the road from the Montoyas!

Hill expressed his regrets that his work schedule didn't allow him to accompany me, nor could he recommend a companion: All his guide contacts had moved on, including Don Lubin, Snow's guide. I enlisted Don Alberto, Camille's bodyguard, to help me find someone. He contacted his hairy *contrabandista* friends, but it seemed they were all "occupied."

153

In desperation I phoned Camille in Palmira, who hastily dispatched his brother-in-law, Jairo.

Hill was nevertheless a source of much valuable advice, and he obligingly spent several days with me helping me map out details. We decided I should carry fifty-five pounds of food, mostly canned meat, fish, sausages, etc.—plus two kilograms of milk powder, two kilograms of sugar, and a pound of salt. My addition was twenty-five pounds of peanuts in one-pound tins; in a pinch, my guide and I could live off these exclusively (nuts contain more protein per ounce than any other food, including beefsteak). This lot was to be bound up in two rucksacks.

The question of the best route through the Darien boiled down to whether I should follow the Atlantic coastline or plow straight through the center. Hill vetoed the coastal-route idea, saying that although he didn't know central Darien, he did know the Atlantic and Pacific coasts and that they were impassable. A map of Colombian Darien was presented to me by the Instituto Geográfico Augustín Codazzi. When I couldn't get a map of the Panamanian side, even from the Panamanian consul general, Hill loaned me his.

There was more: I had to secure permission to cross a stretch of Colombian national perserve. I was also given references from the Colombian Ecological Society and the Development of Uraba Corporation, and the Panamanian consul general added a note to my visa stating "*Apia Todo Sur América*" ("Walking All South America").

The local agricultural institute gave me an anti-snake-venom kit, complete with hypodermic needle and serum. "But don't get bitten by the red coral snake," Hill cautioned, "because the kit doesn't cover that one. Also, if you're allergic to horse serum, this stuff will kill you quicker than any snake."

"Charming! How can I know if I'm allergic?"

"You can't . . . at least, not till it's in you." As a going-away present, Hill gave me a copy of *The Idiot*.

The Yoshikart had to be temporarily ditched—not much use for wheels over mangrove roots and whatever other tangled swamp vegetation lay ahead. My sleeping bag and tent were also indispensable, but I decided to take a stab at shipping them ahead to some point in Panama past Darien where they could be held for me. I decided to try the mails. This was a Big Mistake, for I ended up visiting more offices than when tracking down my marriage certificate. Five days after I first attempted to mail it, the parcel finally went off.

Jairo Molina, Camille's brother-in-law, was a powerfully built, somber lad of twenty-eight. I had high hopes for him as a companion for Darien: He had jungle experience, he had been in the police, and he seemed to have a practical mind to boot. At our first meeting, in a touching sort of ceremony, he presented me with a machete. Then, as time wore on, I became increasingly uncomfortable with his sullen demeanor.

Michael Hill told me, "Don't move without five hundred dollars U.S. cash and another several thousand in pesos," and so I had wired England for money. Pennington at the Banco de Londres was incensed with his home office for already taking forty days to respond to his repeated Telexes on my behalf. "Worse than the Middle Ages," he fumed. I decided the bank money would not come in time and so I phoned Camille, who agreed to fly down the next morning with the needed cash.

Camille arrived at the Montoyas' looking like a mafioso: dark glasses, gold medallion around his neck, and his bodyguard Don Alberto in tow. I was relieved to see my old friends, as Jairo had been acting strangely, brooding and mumbling. I had even mentioned my moody companion to the banker Pennington, who remarked, "I don't envy you, old chap, he's a manic-depressive, you know—could do anything."

That evening I spoke to Camille about his brother-in-law. "Oh, he'll be OK once you get moving, I promise you. Don't worry, he's under my control. He won't let you down." Over dinner Jairo visibly brightened enough to crack a half-smile, while I pondered for the first time why he was no longer with the police.

The one remaining bureaucratic hurdle was obtaining exit visas. Jairo and I went to the Documento Policía in Medellín.

They were adamant in their instructions: "You must go to Turbo." Turbo is a nasty, notorious dope port on the Golfo de Uraba where four U.S. federal agents had once mysteriously disappeared. I was in no mood to go there.

"But in Turbo they will tell me to go to Medellín."

"That would be stupid."

Who could disagree? The next day, February 21, I bade farewell to the Montoyas and together with Jairo caught the bus to Turbo, where the customs chief, a part-time bullfighter, said, "This is *stupid*. You must go back to Medellín. There *is* no Documento Policía here."

After a lot of begging and three trips between the police in Turbo and the customs post just up the coast, we got our exit stamps. Among the new marks on each document was a scrawl by a sixteen-year-old policeman stating we weren't criminals, plus an irrelevant squiggle contributed by a taxi driver, deemed necessary by a junior customs officer "because the policeman forgot to sign his writing." When all was decided ready, the customs chief—only after dinner, of course—signed his own impressive *firma*, and we finally left the aspiring torero in peace.

Just before reaching El Tigre, Jairo and I were hauled off the bus by soldiers in steel helmets, members of the Condor Battalion, who first demanded our machetes but eventually settled for our rain gear—a letter from their commander that Jairo had chanced to obtain impressed them not a whit. Only after the bus had long gone did they let us go. We ended up hitching a lift the last few kilometers to El Tigre. The assault on the Darien was on.

Darien Gap

At El Tigre, I found my two-month-old mark, and as it was now growing dark, I began jogging westward, toward a red-soaked sky, into the Darien. Jairo, having remained with the gear on the truck, would meet me in Barranquillita, 9 km farther on.

Two years of walking and even more of planning had brought me to this crucial leg of the journey; my mood was one of nervous expectation. I had no illusions about the possible dangers that lay ahead, but something else, an element never in the original plan, now counterbalanced my former fears—the knowledge that after this one last hurdle I would be reunited with Yoshiko and at last experience the joy of holding our child in my arms.

Sweating, puffing, bombarded by insects, I eventually groped my way into Barranquillita well after dark and stumbled upon Jairo, who greeted me with his usual vague, cheerless acknowledgment. The village was a few unlit hovels, rough one-story affairs, including two cowboy bars complete with horses tethered to rails out front. I stopped a drunk who was just emerging from one of the bars and found out from him where we might spend the night. Then, with the drunk's "assistance," we manhandled our mountain of gear along a grass trail to the stables of Don Dario Zapata.

Don Dario—who owned a string of mules, had a very large stomach hiding beneath his torn vest, and carried on his shoulder a red and white macaw that roundly abused us throughout our conversation—not only allowed us to sleep in his stable but proposed to supply us with a mule for the day to carry our gear, plus a rider familiar with the region.

The next morning, the mule was loaded with our two thirty-pound sacks of stores plus half of Jairo's personal kit. Jairo had packed his belongings in two small bags, which I thought was an unnecessarily cumbersome arrangement. (In one of them, he was carrying his bedroom slippers!) I settled for a standard backpack.

The dirt road that ran into Barranquillita from the south ran out at the bridge over the Río León at the northern edge of town. Once we passed this point, I had the eerie sense of leaving civilization behind—at least what little of it I had seen in Barranquillita. Now our ad hoc trail was a track of matted grass, but not through thick jungle, as I had imagined. All about, the land was undergoing slash-and-burn operations, being cleared for grazing and farmland; the forest was literally being smashed to death. Felled trees lay everywhere, and in areas where the vegetation had very recently been burned off, tree trunks still lay smoldering. In the distance one could hear the roar of earth-moving machinery and the whir of chain saws.

With the mule and rider leading the way, we had started out very quickly. But as there was no forest canopy overhead to protect us, the combined heat of the sun and the glowing timber soon made it a hot, silent march. After an hour of this, Jairo and I were reduced to stumbling after the mule through the heat haze.

Water, always a special consideration for me while walking, was obviously going to be a problem here, and so it came as a shock when Jairo unrepentantly announced that he had no water in his half-liter canteen. Had he forgotten to fill it? No, he *had* filled it—with rum! By the time we reached a finca hours later, my half-pint for the three of us was long gone. To go thirsty because of another's stupidity is one matter, but then to have to share your water with that person is particularly galling. I didn't push the point. I needed Jairo's—someone's—company if I was to get through the Darien in one piece, and obviously the only way to get along with Jairo was to compromise. I decided to give him a free hand so far as was reasonable.

The finca provided us with all the sugar water we needed and another mule for our personal gear. This spared my already sore shoulders and gave Jairo a rest from his small load, which appeared to give his strong frame more trouble than it should have. One thing was clear: Jairo would never make a porter.

Many of the posts through the Darien had no names as such, but were identified in terms of the nearest kilometer marker. On the 3-km march to KM 27, we walked most of the way through tall elephant grass. Only a few enormous trees here were still untouched, the last survivors of yet another massacred section of jungle. At KM 27, we found Finca el Darién, where we rented a horse and arranged to stay the night. When I said I was going to sleep outdoors atop my sleeping gear rather than in the hot, sticky rooms, for some reason Jairo became upset. But perhaps he was right, for the night grew so cold that I had to put on my old torn coat, my constant companion since Ushuaia.

The first question I asked myself upon waking was: Is Jairo feeling "up" and playing the noisy critic, or "down" and sulking in some dark corner? This second morning it was the former. After rising I came upon him sitting with a group of woodcutters, stabbing his finger at the map and loudly exclaiming, "The center route's wrong. My Peruvian friend says the coast is the only way. The way the inglés proposes is stupid."

I had gone through all of this with him before. Now I repeated the story of my exhaustive inquiries and why Michael Hill had severely discouraged taking the coastal route. Jairo glared at me with a familiar fix of self-righteous anger and contempt. "Look, Hill is a fool," he said. "You always think that you, an inglés, know everything and that I as a

Colombian in Colombia know nothing." I began wondering when the other shoe would drop.

Another visitor at the finca was a man in his fifties. Despite his appearance—his skinny frame made him look ludicrous in knee-length shorts—he impressed me with a certain air of authority. To my surprise and delight I discovered he was none other than Don Lubin—I had found Snow's guide! (Jairo had learned who he was the previous night but had neglected to tell me.) Without hesitation I offered Don Lubin an open-ended commission, which he accepted after a fashion—he could only spare me two days. Nonetheless, I was overjoyed to have run into this remarkable man, who was a legend in Colombian Darien; he once spent six years straight in perfect solitude deep in the jungle. There is even a settlement here named after him.

Perhaps now Jairo would be defused, at least momentarily. Before we set off, I filled up my canteen—almost apologetically, as Jairo, the "professional," had patiently explained to me that I was wasting my time, there being plenty of water nearby. There was, in fact, water, but it lay in a filthy canal, and so Jairo ended up drinking most of my canteen.

The land became increasingly wooded and boggy, and at one point we had to unload the horse to make progress when the frightened animal began flaying about in mud up to its hocks. Our route passed by the enormous earth-moving machines that could only be heard the day before. It was a brutal sight, watching men in hardhats and leather gauntlets driving these roaring monsters straight into the virgin rain forest, mowing down everything in their path (although it would be hypocritical for me, an Englishman, to deliver any final judgment, considering that my forebears had already deforested most of my land centuries ago).

After three hours we had passed the last of the forest-clearing operations and finally entered unadulterated rain forest. At KM 29, we came upon a hut beside the brown, turgid river; inside was a boatman, a Colombian with fair hair and blue eyes whom Lubin introduced as "El Mono" (translated for me as "fair one," although it also means "monkey").

For a fee El Mono agreed to ferry Jairo and the provisions upriver to KM 40 in his motorized dugout canoe while Don Lubin led me overland through the jungle.

What a relief to lose my human burden! And what a joy to be traveling with Don Lubin. As we walked, he would point out exotic birds, a particularly colorful explosion of jungle flora, an animal camouflaged in the underbrush that I had failed to see, and entertain me with elaborate discussions of the same. The forest soon conspired to produce an air of delicious mystery: tangled shadows playing over the rain-forest floor, strange birds caw-cawing high up in the canopy, the intermittent jabbering of howler monkeys hidden from our view. In contrast to the sun-blasted open country we had crossed, the jungle, shaded by a near-impenetrable roof of greenery, seemed almost cool.

As we neared the Atrato Swamp, encroaching water became more of a problem, and at one point we had no choice but to take a canoe in order to cross a river—I swallowed hard, for it was the first time since the Strait of Magellan that I had made progress in any way other than on foot.

The 11 river kilometers that El Mono and Jairo were traveling to KM 40 translated to 26 km along the jungle trails for Don Lubin and me. We nevertheless succeeded in hitting our objective, Don Doria's finca, before nightfall. Don Lubin immediately set out to locate my cargo while I waited in the main house, a one-room mud-and-stick hut. At first I found this place oppressive, but as night fell, the room, under the weak flicker of the homemade oil lamps, took on a more homey aspect.

When it came time to eat, swampfish were dealt out like so many sticky playing cards. The creatures were so shot through with bones that I gave up, and the rice, like cold gravel, might have better been used to resurface Watling Street. Don Doria stuffed this rubbish in with a will, bones and all, observing, "Best food in the world!" I nodded weakly in reply. When Don Lubin returned, having satisfied himself that Jairo and the stores were secure with El Mono, hammocks were rigged, and by eight o'clock the hut fell silent.

On day three I got up at the crack of dawn—i.e., my crack of dawn, 9:00 A.M.—in order to create a good impression. (Of course, the whole family had been up for three hours.) While two of the daughters pulverized maize into flour in the hollow of a tree stump, Señora Doria, an elephantine woman, sat delousing one of the kids. A chicken had the misfortune to peck under her chair, and quick as a bullet she collared the unfortunate bird and wrung its neck. That was noon dinner solved. A fire was laid and the fowl consigned to it. For anyone wondering how one skinny chicken serves five adults and eleven children, I will tell you—one mouthful apiece. (My hungry stomach resents a large family as much as my brain resents overpopulation: Ultimately it will mean one mouthful for all of us, and not for only two-thirds of the world's people, as now.)

In the afternoon, Jairo reappeared with El Mono and some of his family carting all our gear. I was particularly pleased to be reunited with my Lee and Perrin's Worcestershire sauce; I could now splash this on almost everything and make it palatable. Jairo then left with El Mono to get petrol for the trip to the Atrato the following day, which meant another relaxed night without him.

I showed my family photos to the Doria family that evening and even gave a couple away. All of this caused such excitement that the grandmother was specially ferried from across the river—she wanted a picture, too. Don Lubin took a shine to a snap of Yoshiko's mum giving a bath to Ayumi, so I presented it to him; in return, a delighted Don Lubin gave me a yellowed photo taken of him while on some long-forgotten expedition.

From KM 40 the shortest distance to grandly named Puerto América on the Río Atrato, our next objective, was a straight-line distance of 23 km due west. In between, however, lay nothing but dense swampland. No one could ever "walk" across this soup. I proposed to do what Snow had done and what everyone else still did—bypass the whole appalling mess in a dugout. If we proceeded north through the series of four lakes that are connected by rivers and swampland, we would eventually reach the Atrato by a roundabout route.

El Mono arrived along with my grim companion before dawn, and just before moving to the river with our gear I paid my respects to Don Doria's family and regretfully bade farewell to Don Lubin, who now had to leave to fulfill a prior commitment—guiding a party of engineers in search of a route (still!) for the Inter-American Highway.

The thirty-foot canoe was driven by a powerful outboard motor that sped us along at a handsome eight knots, and by sunrise the interlacing channels opened into the first of the connected lakes. There was no recognizable shoreline, as the perimeter was blurred by swamp vegetation. Sitting, almost floating, at the lake edge were desperately poor huts occupied by black fishermen; at one of these El Mono exchanged plantain for fish.

After four hours we reached the Río Atrato, over three hundred yards wide at this point, and the canoe took a pounding as it punched through the powerful current while waterbirds swooped down overhead. We finally reached our objective, a spit of land sitting at the confluence of two rivers. Getting here had taken two hours of traveling due south down the Atrato—a direction I had been assiduously avoiding for the past two and a half years! The convoluted nature of this leg of the journey left us 5 km north and 23 km west of the now clearly visible hill at La Islandes, our starting point.

El Mono wished us luck and, his outboard purring, set off back home, leaving Jairo and me at Puerto América—at least that was what the bleached and broken wood plank nailed to the signpost said. Puerto América is—well, there's no way around it—simply the most miserable place I have ever clapped eyes on: a dozen wretched huts in a line, each raised two feet above the ground, the steps leading up mostly broken or missing—an insurance man's nightmare. As it turned out, I was probably lucky to have escaped there with my life.

The villagers, all black, gathered about us excitedly. One of them, an outgoing fellow named Byzantine, welcomed us to share his one-room shack, where we deposited our valuable sacks—an operation that immediately gained everyone's rapt attention. As luck would have it, the part-tin, part-thatch roof was in such disrepair that when a torrential rainstorm struck a half hour later, our bedrolls and gear were heavily soaked. (To live in a rain-lashed area and tolerate a leaky roof, I thought, is to raise indolence to new heights.)

Food was now prepared: a watery mix of rice, bones, a small fish, and more bones, all washed down with gallons of water freshly scooped from the Río Atrato. If the water doesn't kill me, I thought, the filth from the cooking pot probably will. In the meanwhile, Jairo dispatched his portion with gusto. Seeing that I was only picking at my serving, my host offered me, at a price, one of the supposedly edible black turtles kept in a box out back. No, thank you; for some reason I wasn't hungry anymore.

By nightfall, the rain was still pouring down mercilessly. Jairo and I were left alone in the pitch-black hut when Byzantine and his family went to visit all their neighbors to tell them all about the crazy gringo in their midst. Heat, humidity, rain, insects, squalor—these were the ingredients of the hellish stew in which we now almost floated. Jairo was getting more jittery by the minute, pacing back and forth and mumbling about not being appreciated. All I could think of was that I was hungry and tired, but most of all desperate for privacy, for some clean, clear space where I could rest my boiled brains. I told Jairo I was going to sleep alone in a nearby abondoned shack; at least I might find an uncontaminated corner there.

Jairo, losing the last of his patience, launched into an animated lecture, harping on the fact that his job was to protect me and that my proposed move was the height of irresponsibility. I started to speak, but my words were cut short by a terrific impact in the center of my chest that sent me crashing into the wall behind me. It took some moments before I realized that Jairo, whom I couldn't see at all in the darkness, had punched me with all his might. (At first I thought I had had a heart attack.)

Bouncing off the resilient wall, I had been sent hurtling to my knees. I stayed in a crouch, frozen to the spot where I had landed. Despite the roar of the heavy rain bouncing off the roof, I could hear swooshing and rustling noises: Jairo frantically seeking me out in the near-total darkness, circling the floor and flailing about. Looking up, all I could see was a dim, gray, rectangular patch—the door. Escape! I sprang out the door, stumbling down the steps and landing on all fours in a putrid mash of mud, twigs, leaves, and garbage.

As I scrambled to my feet, Jairo came bounding after me, and I splashed down the line of huts and eventually lost him in the dark. Jairo had obviously lost all reason, and I was convinced if he found me now, he was crazy enough to kill. Circling the settlement at a short distance through the jungle, I suddenly recognized the hut of a local functionary. The rain had stopped, and this "policeman"—he was the only villager who owned a rifle—was sitting outside, an oil lamp resting on a stump nearby.

I burst upon the scene like a bit-part player in a disaster movie. "Sorry to bother you. You have a rifle, don't you?" I asked by way of introduction and confirmation. The man slowly looked up from his scrapwood seat and vaguely nodded. "Good!" I blurted out. "My friend has gone loco. He is man- ico-depressivo—he's just attacked me." The "policeman" re- acted hardly at all, as though this sort of thing—nuts on the loose and all that—happened all the time around here. And when I asked permission to sleep in his hut, he agreed in the same matter-of-fact manner.

To his eternal credit, however, he did offer to recover my belongings from Byzantine's shack. Unsheathing his an- cient carbine, he silently inspected it all over, set out down- river, and returned later with my gear. He had actually seen Jairo, he said, and he had been sitting in brooding silence. By now I had calmed down and felt I was safe, at least for the night. But once inside the hut I was again overwhelmed by the filth, which was as appalling here as in the rest of Puerto América. To compensate I hauled a bar of Lux soap out of my bag and sniffed at it like a drug, hoping the smell would somehow keep me in contact with a real world I knew must exist somewhere outside.

There was a lot to think about that sleepless night, including an aching, bruised chest. My journey was foundering. In one insane instant everything had gone up in smoke. What if Jairo had attacked me with his knife! (He normally carried one.) I should have seen this coming, but despite Jairo's moods and antics, I still couldn't believe that my "bodyguard" would turn on me. But this was all academic now. I had to figure how I was going to fend for myself, far from friends and assistance and any form of long-distance communication. It was already late in the "dry" season. Should I go on alone, or should I return to Colombia and lose several months waiting out the monsoons? I saw myself in grave danger not just from Jairo but from the villagers as well. I was carrying sixty pounds of valuable stores and, it had to be obvious to everyone, large amounts of cash—a king's ransom out here. Had a better target ever wandered this way?

Morning brought a bright, hot sun, welcome for once. When I finally saw Jairo, he was "down"—i.e., in a subdued mood. Incredibly, he spoke to me of going on, as if absolutely nothing had happened. I couldn't even be sure he remembered the events of the previous night. I told him bluntly that I would travel to Panama alone and that he was welcome to take whatever he needed. (He eventually took three cans of food and the large water canteen and reclaimed the machete he had presented to me in Medellín.)

Jairo said he also intended to travel on to Panama. (Of course, disgrace alone awaited him if he returned to Colombia.) He had been carrying some of my money, and as he would now need money of his own, I chalked this sum off—for services rendered. This finished our business together. At midday he left, accompanied by two villagers, Don William and his son. As I joined the assembled villagers to watch them leave, I wished them luck. In reply, Jairo, without looking back, shouted to the assembly, "He hates all of you! He thinks all blacks are fuckin' animals."

Later that day, sitting atop my pile of gear on the steamy

166

banks of the Atrato, I wrote across the top of my map, which was temporarily serving as my logbook: "I have no option. I cannot turn back—the bureaucracy would finish me. There is barely sufficient money. Things will be harder, more dangerous now. Alone. Much glare from a hot river sun. At last the final challenge."

Jairo had spent most of the morning spreading lies about me, and now the hostility toward me was palpable. My first challenge was winning back the villagers' trust; to this end I went into each of the twelve huts, explaining my walk and answering the people's questions. Next I found Byzantine and proposed that he and his friend, a man named Sheep, accompany me to the Panamanian border at five dollars a day; to show my good faith, I gave Byzantine's wife two tins of meat. The pair immediately smashed open the tins and proceeded to fight over the contents. Good moral fiber here, I thought—must have served at sea.

Byzantine was hesitant to move immediately, fearing Jairo might take out his revenge on him for helping me, so we waited throughout the long limbo of scorching afternoon. Came five o'clock, no one wanted to move: "Mañana, boss!" Maybe they were content to rot here, but I certainly wasn't. If I didn't make progress, however small, I felt I would go mad. Summoning up my best pep talk, I managed to load my reluctant guide, his friend, and all my gear into Old Jim's leaky canoe, and the three of us paddled across the river.

It was a grim little voyage. With an uneasy mind, I sat in the water that was slopping around the bottom of the leaky dugout. Byzantine and Sheep, if not actively hostile, were certainly indifferent toward me; what alarmed me most was that they wouldn't meet my eyes, but would always look away. Perhaps, after all, Jairo's tongue would do me more damage than his fist. It seemed to me ludicrously easy, even logical, for these two men to move a small distance into the jungle and cut me down with their machetes for the relative fortune I was carrying. My body would never be found. The grisly image of the Medellín corpse kept floating into my mind.

These thoughts were put to one side when with utter

amazement we stumbled across a research station run by the Colombian government. So this is where it was! And so near! The level of information on the Darien obtainable in Colombia was pitiful, and while I knew of the existence of this outpost, I hadn't the slightest idea where it was—nor, apparently, did anyone I had spoken to at the various Colombian government agencies. After Old Jim set out for home in his sinking canoe, Horatio, a young naturalist from Medellín, showed me around the station, which was equipped with motor launches, a helipad, fully stocked kitchen, radio, and even a TV!

Byzantine and Sheep were meanwhile stripping the bark from trees for straps so that they could convert the two food sacks into backpacks. Horatio kindly offered us all dinner, and my new guides visibly brightened under the glow of a full stomach. Then Byzantine and Sheep asked for permission to cross the government's wildlife preserve when it came time for them to return home (thus saving the cost of a boat fare). No, they couldn't, came the unequivocal answer. I pressed their case vigorously and even applied a strong dose of namedropping by mentioning my dealings with the agency's top man in Medellín. ("Very agreeable chap he was—yes, indeed!") This did the trick. By winning this concession I also seemed to win the loyalty and respect of my guides. I slept much better that night.

The next day, March 1, as we moved off on foot I was astonished by the speed of my companions, which left me gasping at their heels. This proved to be a five-minute wonder, however, and when the march had settled down, I was leading the way. The track we now followed through the close, shadowy jungle was an inexplicably superb "highway," a swath recently cut by some vehicle or vehicles. Sheep explained that a squadron of jeeps had been partly driven and partly hauled through here only weeks before. This was confirmed by midday by the appearance of a red Land Rover inching along the trail toward us; on its side was written "Swiss Toyota Tokyo-L.A.-Brasília-Zurich Expedition"—in very small lettering, of course, just to get it all on. Out hopped a jovial Swiss with a broken leg in a plaster cast and a very large camera, and we chatted awhile before going our separate ways. (I asked him if he had dropped the camera on his foot, but he didn't see the joke.) Now I had real cause for elation—this could mean a tunnel had been chopped out of the undergrowth all the way to Panama. It hadn't. After half an hour, the "highway" petered out near a watercourse.

I had noticed for some time that Sheep, a large, powerful man, carried his load easily and without complaint, whereas Byzantine, who was slightly built and had never walked long distances or carried a load before, was visibly wilting under his forty-pound sack. Byzantine caused me further worry when he became sicker by late afternoon, although I wasn't surprised—he had already taken more medicine in two hours than I had in two years. Rest stops increased from every hour to every five minutes, and then Byzantine collapsed entirely. Fortunately, although we didn't know it at the time, we were within a few hundred yards of the Río Crystal. It was a lucky stroke, for we were all dehydrated, and a waterless night would have greatly added to our sufferings.

With some effort Sheep and I lugged Byzantine to the river and laid him out on some giant leaves under his mosquito netting before setting up hammocks for ourselves. Byzantine, who still couldn't move, was stoic, even apologetic. I sympathized, for I, too, had problems: My wretched shoulders were now a mass of ulcerous sores (it was to avoid just this that I had devised the Yoshikart).

Promptly at sundown the mosquitoes zeroed in, fighting their way under the netting and even biting through the hammock bottom. This continued all night—the repellent (claiming "preventive action guaranteed") seemed if anything to encourage them. At one point I was being so badly bitten that in frustration I threw myself out of the hammock altogether.

Dawn finally brought relief from the mosquitoes, but Byzantine still lay stock-still, complaining of stomach pains. He was obviously out of the game, at least for now. We discussed the situation. He would be fine in a few hours, he assured me, although not in any shape for portering. When

Sheep pointed out that there was a Chocó settlement a short distance ahead on the banks of yet another river, Byzantine suggested that Sheep and I take half the gear to the village and leave him here with sufficient food and water; then I could return with a Chocó porter to retrieve him and move the rest of the gear. "Bring an Indian!" Byzantine shouted after Sheep and me as we moved on.

After an hour of very steep going, Sheep and I were within earshot of the settlement. In the near distance, we could hear children splashing about in a river, the music of pure innocence—and relief. At last I could dump my backpack and ease the ghastly rubbing and pain on my shoulders. Terrified of a crippling infection, I gobbled down a fistful of penicillin. Then, eager to get back as quickly as possible to my man in the jungle, I immediately enlisted a Chocó teenager to accompany me back to the Río Crystal. The boy refused to move before upgrading his apparel, however, and so I was forced to wait the five minutes while he dispensed with his loincloth, pulled on a pair of torn trousers, and meticulously buttoned up the front of his shirt—which already had a rent completely down the back! By the time we returned Byzantine was up and around, and so the three of us without delay made our way back to the village. During this shuttling operation, I was tremendously impressed by the young Chocó's strength and speed. Even when he was carrying a forty-pound load and I nothing, I had trouble keeping up with him.

I was still apprenhensive about encountering Jairo. Although he had said he was going straight through to Panama, I couldn't be sure he wouldn't circle back and try to ambush me if the mood struck him. I was therefore somewhat relieved when late in the day Don William and his son limped into the Chocó village and reported that they had left Jairo far ahead in Panama. Later I learned that Jairo had reached Costa Rica, where he signed on with a Greek ship, and most recently I have been told that he has settled down in Brazil, where today he is an elephant trainer in a circus! Jairo's brother-in-law, Camille, who was shocked and humiliated to hear of the "incident," eventually passed along to me the let-

ter of justification Jairo had written him. The letter—in translation by the Reverend McLean from Quito—reads in part:
"That insect George doesn't appear to be a walker. By the
little I walked with him, I know I have more experience than
he. . . . I put up with him for long, and then I lost my
patience and finally gave him a punch by which he will remember Colombians for all his future."

The Chocó settlement consisted merely of two huts—but
what huts! Each stands on stilts eight feet high, leaving room
underneath for the occupants' pigs, dogs, and other animals.
The thatched roof of each hut, which slopes down from a central beam raised eighteen feet above a square floor thirty feet
on a side, leaves a three-foot gap where there otherwise would
be walls, making the whole an open-air arrangement that is
still protected from the rains. Around the floor a raised perimeter about a foot high serves as table, seating, and so forth,
for there is no furniture. Off to the side of each hut is another
structure holding an enormous box of packed earth upon which
sit the cooking fire along with the various pots and utensils.
And that's the whole plan. (You can now build one in your
garden—given zoning permission, of course.)

When I first climbed the tree-trunk ladder and entered
the faintly dark but spotlessly clean Chocó great-hut, the real
attraction and excitement was not so much the architecture
as the Indians—well, to be precise, the ladies, who were naked to the waist (although ever so particular on covering up
their thighs). With the arrival of evening the homemade tin-
can oil lamps were lit and things took on a rather festive air
as food appeared. I even tucked into a well-cooked iguana,
which I found very good, my only complaint being that the
skin was like oily sandpaper. In fact, it was the best food I
had in Colombia. At nine o'clock the Indians all disappeared
behind huge white mosquito nets, and soon afterward, with
the fire dying slowly and the moon rising, the great-hut fell
silent.

Up with the sun. Roosters crowing, pigs grunting, babies
crying, half-eaten banana breakfasts, chaos, preparation, and
confusion. Byzantine, much improved, could now carry my

light twenty-pound rucksack, while Mr. Sheep and two Chocós, the boy of the previous day and his elder brother, split the rest of the provisions among themselves. I gave one Chocó grandmother nearly a kilo of milk powder for the happy kids already playing in the river before making a thorough nuisance of myself trying to get a water container. "There's water on the trail," I kept hearing. I'd heard that before.

We moved quickly, overtaking a poor family of Colombian blacks who were seeking to enter Panama illegally; they were carrying a large suitcase, two sleeping babies, and a bucket of fish. I wished them much-needed luck. I had already found the route here exhausting, even though I was only carrying a machete. The trail led over what seemed an endless series of short, steep embankments. I had been racing for two years to reach the Darien in the dry season; if anything, I had been too successful. The streams here were all dried up; there was no water anywhere.

After four hours one of my knees started to seize up, and I was becoming desperately weary—I just couldn't seem to raise the energy to catch my men strung out far in front—when a shout ahead told me that we had reached Palo de Letres, the frontier. Glowing inwardly with pride, I stumbled over to the broken stone plinth that marked the border. I had reached the Isthmus of Panama—Central America.

The triumph of the moment passed quickly, for our mutual misery over water dominated us. My pathetic half-pint was now passed around the five of us, like something at a wine tasting—one sip each for a morning's hard jungle struggle. The only answer was to continue on to the Río Paye, an estimated three hours away. Byzantine found this particularly hard to take. "I'm never, ever gonna walk ever again for no money never," he moaned. Me neither. On we marched.

Throughout Darien my traveling companions regarded my valuable peanuts with something less than enthusiasm. Byzantine, especially, often addressed the matter: "Hey, boss, the nut things—is that all you eat?" or "Oh, boss, not nut things again! Haven't we got any bananas?" My reply was invariably the same, somewhat in the style of Field Marshal Montgomery: "Good Lord, man. Just think how *lucky* you are—it's not every gringo who carries nut things!" To which Byzantine would reply, as though acknowledging the ultimate tragedy of life, "Yes, boss—I know, I know."

Back in their village the Indian boys had quickly developed a passion for my drink of milk powder, sugar, raspberry concentrate, and river. I promised them a whole bucket of the stuff once we reached the Paye. In the meanwhile the elder Chocó found a particular vine and slashed it open. To my wonder, water gushed free, nearly a quart, but so quickly that the boy was the only one to get any.

Unburdened, I moved far ahead of the rest of the party. The questionable wisdom of this was driven home when I heard a strange rustle just behind me. I shot a backward glance and saw a flat black snake about four feet long. I had blindly stepped over it. There is no way (for me, at least) to see a snake lying motionless across a trail; most are perfectly camouflaged under the broken branches, huge leaves, and other rotting vegetation. I moved on very, very carefully, but almost immediately caught sight of the Paye far below in the valley floor. Throwing caution to the wind, I ran all the way to the bubbling water and jumped in. After filling the canteen, I dashed back up the steep side of the valley, passing the tired porters who were sliding down one by one. Each asked me for the canteen, but I was keeping it for the last of my party. After half an hour I reached him, the elder Chocó, who was moving slowly because he had gashed open his leg when his machete bounced off a hollow vine. He drank the half-pint in one draft.

The joy and relief of reaching the Paye was somewhat marred when a border guard poling a dugout through the rapids beached his canoe next to us and brusquely ordered us to walk to the *comisario* some 2 km away. As this was in the opposite direction from our night objective, a Kuna Indian village, we deposited the injured Chocó and his brother under a tree before plodding on. At the frontier post they promptly took my belt and boots and soaked them in disinfectant as a precaution against the invasion into Panama of hoof-and-mouth disease. One guard, spotting my kilogram tin of milk powder, triumphantly shouted, *"Prohibido!"* He then seized the tin and went out back to build a fire for the purpose of burning the dangerous contraband. I tried to explain that a new, unopened tin couldn't carry disease, and when this failed to persuade them I pleaded with them to let me give the milk to Byzantine and Sheep so that they could bring it back to Colombia—or at least to let us drink some on the spot. The morons only laughed at all these suggestions and then unceremoniously committed the Nestlé's to the pyre, throwing in my anti-snake-bite kit for good measure.

When we returned to the waiting Chocós and described what had happened, they found it difficult to believe. Coming from a paperless, bureaucrat-less, identity-card-free society, they simply could not fathom why anyone would burn a valuable tin of milk, nor could I give them an explanation. The only redeeming feature of this episode was that Byzantine, unseen, had taken one of the officer's boots, which had been standing polished in the sun, and tossed it—just that one, mind you—into the river.

As we straggled into the village of Paye the Kunas' dogs began barking and nipping at the heels of the Chocó boys, as though confirming the sometimes hostile relations between these two rival tribes. Although they live near the Chocós, the Kunas are strikingly different in several respects. Families live in rows of neat, low huts made of short poles rather than the raised constructions of the Chocós. Also, they are lighter-skinned than the Chocós, with finer features that make them look more Asiatic. Finally worth mention are the workaday clothes of the Kuna women, which make a Harlem pimp look dull by comparison: midlength patchwork skirts and vests constructed of the most intricate patterns in various shades of red and yellow, a similar cloth covering the head, and broad bands of multicolored beads wrapped around the calves and forearms. The fabrics' unique patterns, called *"molas,"* date back centuries and are so vivid and stunning that they have become the de facto symbol of Panama—no tourist can leave without at least one. The women wear their hair with short back and sides, which sets off beautifully the gold ring worn through the nose. The men, while they have similar haircuts, wear mostly Western-style shirts and pants.

The village chief gave us all bananas and told us we could sleep the night under a giant coconut palm. That night, by torchlight, I bandaged up the injured Choco's leg one last time, and a large crowd of Kunas gathered round to witness the curious spectacle. Afterward I paid off my four porters, and finally, to the sounds of cards being dealt and bets made, I fell asleep. When I awoke late the next morning, Byzantine, Sheep, and the Chocós were gone, and I was once more left with the strange, sad sensation of always ending up alone.

A black man in his forties sat leaning against a nearby tree trunk listening to his portable radio. "Fancy a walk?" I asked. "Yeah, man!" In a short time we were plodding into the jungle, with my new porter carrying the single pack of stores, which were now down to forty-five pounds. The going was tough, almost continuously uphill and down. Much of the time on these breathtaking gradients was spent on hands and knees. My new companion, Tizzard, had brought along his radio—not quite a "ghetto blaster," but incongruous enough in the steamy rain forest—and now the machine seemed to mock us by bashing out inner-city rhythms in time to our jungle struggle.

By midafternoon we were within sight of the Kuna village of Pucara, across yet another river. As the current was swift and deep, we hailed a canoe. In midstream the boatman suddenly let out a desperate shout, and just then two shots rang out from the direction of the village. Tizzard hunched down in the bottom of the canoe and simultaneously slung one leg over the side—he was getting out, radio and all. I bent down and interrupted his agitated departure by casually inquiring, "Is somebody shooting birds here?" "No birds, boss. Us. Two shots—that's a warning. Third shot—Guardia shoot to kill." The instant the dugout hit the opposite shore we were prodded up the embankment at riflepoint by a guardsman dressed in full uniform—except for the fire-engine-red swim trunks he wore in place of trousers. The "guardsman" in fact was a

Kuna villager who had been given a shirt, a rifle, and some vague instructions, and was now scattering my gear to the winds in his zealous search for drugs before we should be let go.

The next morning Tizzard contracted to do another day with me, and so on we marched to the next village, three hours distant. It was a relentless, exhausting business, livened by a single moment of sheer terror. I was grappling up an embankment on my hands and knees, unable to concentrate on anything except my wretched knee and the damned humidity, when I came face to face with a green tree snake perhaps eight feet long that had risen up directly in front of me like a cobra. For a split second, I stood frozen, as we confronted each other eye to eye. Then with a gasp I threw myself backward and went sprawling down the steep embankment that I had been struggling to ascend. Landing in a heap on top of my gear, I looked up to see the snake slithering away.

Tizzard looked down the slope to check after me. "Did you see that?" I yelled up to him.

"Yeah, boss."

"Poisonous?"

"Yeah, boss." We continued.

When we reached Barzal, a small, pleasant Chocó village, Tizzard and I parted company, as he had other work the following day. Toward evening the village men returned in a flotilla of canoes from their day's hunting. It was a strange sight, one not found in a textbook: barefoot hunters with Beatle haircuts clad only in red loincloths and toting antique rifles. The village chief gave me a riverside hut to myself for the night, and in the morning he volunteered his youngest son, Hilberto, to be my porter-guide to Boca de Cupe, a settlement a day's march away. The boy, although just fifteen, was stocky and tough-looking in his torn vest emblazoned with a picture of the Panama Canal. After we had walked two hours, my barefoot companion asked where I was ultimately headed, and when I told him "Panama City," he excitedly asked whether he might accompany me all the way. It seems Berto had never been to the city—indeed, anywhere very far from his river. Glad to be relieved of the chore of finding a new guide every day, I signed Berto up at a wage of four hundred eighty plantains (about five dollars) a day—the plantain was not only his tribe's principal crop but their unit of currency as well.

We reached an enormous clearing in the forest where the devastation was total, as if a giant meteorite had fallen, flattening the area as far as the eye could see. We had to chop our way through the tangle of uprooted vegetation and toppled trees, and we were constantly forced to stop so that Berto could dig splinters out of his foot with a knife. Eventually we lost the trail altogether and wandered about aimlessly until finding a desolate hut. The Indian family ushered me inside, where an old woman lay naked in the dark, pitifully emaciated, her legs cruelly swollen. Beriberi or elephantiasis?—I wondered. I gave the poor thing a two-week supply of multivitamins and left, deeply saddened by a sense of helplessness.

From here we passed into a treeless landscape more familiar to Berto, and by midafternoon we reached Boca de Cupe, which actually featured two stores and even a girlie bar, complete with a hostess. As we passed the bar, who should creep out but a priest—"Padre Denis," a charming missionary from Spain. "I'm the priest from down below," he volunteered once we had introduced ourselves.

"What—from hell?"

"No, but very close—El Real, down the river." (El Real was ransacked by Captain Morgan and a few friends in 1673, and they say it's been going downhill ever since.)

As Berto's traveling wardrobe was limited to the rags on his back (his joining me had been a spur-of-the-moment decision), I bought him a few items, including his first pair of shoes. It was an exciting occasion for him, our trip to the shoe store, where he instantly zeroed in on some bright red plimsolls, rubber-soled half-boots with beige canvas tops. Another new experience for Berto was sleeping in a bed. The one we found was a rusty wreck belonging to Maria, the black cook at the café; it was in fact the first bed Berto had ever seen. I preferred the floor.

On we marched, crossing a series of rivers, most of them shallow enough to ford, all of them offering a different adventure. After a while I didn't even bother taking off my boots—they were going to get soaked anyway. Either I would fall in a hole or slip on a wet rock. Crossing one stream, I cut my bare foot on a hidden boulder and fell in. At the next, yet another snake just missed us. At the third, Berto spied his aunt whizzing by in a long dugout full to the gunwales with bananas. And at yet another crossing, too deep and swift to attempt by foot, Berto whistled up a lovely topless Chocó maiden, wearing a necklace constructed of dozens of silver coins, who ferried us over in her canoe. Also in the canoe was her mother, who like the Indians in northern Colombia sported patterns drawn in soot on her skin, not only on her legs but over her entire body.

At Yape, Berto proudly introduced me to his mother, two sisters, and elder brother. Berto's father, being a man of substance, owned two hectares of rice paddies, three hectares on which he grew bananas, and another five for plantains—and had two wives as well, living in villages twenty miles apart. When the nagging in one household became too much for him he would simply shift his hammock to the other.

The rest of the hot afternoon's journey was a steeplechase in and out of shallow valleys cut by rivers and streams. At each river Berto would strip, jump in for a quick bath, and just as quickly jump out again. He never used a towel; he would just shake himself to near-dry before putting his clothes back on. All along the route, we kept dodging columns of soldier ants, so huge you could see their black eyes, feverishly busy clearing perfect highways through the debris on the jungle floor. Another insect had four transparent wings about four inches tip to tip. At the end of each wing were black blobs, so the whole contraption in motion looked like airplanes flying in ever-changing formation.

Pinogana was just another grim backwater, and so we charged headlong into the forest to Yaviza, the capital of Panama's Darien Province, a short way off, running to beat the darkness before we lost the trail. The walk should have taken ten minutes, but it was only after two hours of near-hysterical progress that we emerged from the jungle and reached the town. While we sat on a porch swilling colas and catching our breath, a policeman stepped up and ordered us to the police post—"Now!" Here, without delay or courtesy, my gear was kicked all over the floor, the police pecking at it like scavenger dogs nosing about in the rubbish. My money belt was seized and its contents, about three hundred dollars, counted no less than five times, during which process twenty dollars disappeared. I suppose I was lucky. Snow had been carrying thousands of dollars and said he had been lucky to escape with his life—the police had set him up with two local hit men as guides.

Yaviza was not much better than the rest of the hellholes along this route, its population of about three thousand mostly black with some Chocós and two fat Chinese provisioners doing a brisk trade. Grim as this dump was to me, to Berto it was Paris in the spring. Such miracles as electric lights, TV, and movies were all first sights here to his quickly expanding mind. We watched interference on TV for fifteen minutes, which he pronounced "good." That night we went to a broken-down, beat-up "movie house," not much more than a reclaimed Chocó hut—yes, it was on stilts—and sat among a predominantly Indian audience to watch *Dr. Diabolico*, which fully lived up to its title. The movie, probably made in the 1930's, was apparently a new release in this neck of the woods, and Berto loved every second of it, especially the part where the doctor, with obviously malign intentions, strapped down the diaphanously clad blonde to the operating table in his rec room.

In Yaviza I met some gringos, one a Californian named Upton who had tried to cross Darien before but was defeated by early rains and the unfortunate loss of his companion, who was murdered. Another American, a professional Christian who had passed this way, was Arthur Blessit, the self-proclaimed "Priest of the Sunset Strip." Throughout Darien I kept finding his "Smile—God Loves You" stickers; they popped up even more frequently than all the rubbish—discarded chocolate wrappers and food cartons, etc.—that I had been shocked to see littering the trail. Blessit was reputed to have hauled a ten-foot cross weighing over fifty pounds across Darien. (It was, in fact, a smaller version, especially constructed for the occasion, of the twelve-foot model, weighing twice as much, that he had carried across Europe and Asia—or, rather, rolled, for the foot of this original cross had been fitted with a small wheel.) I met a man in Yaviza, however, who claimed to have served as Blessit's porter—that is, to have carried the cross while Blessit (no fool, he) had "supervised" the operation.

We left Yaviza on a bulldozed dirt road that was as good as many I had walked in South America, which was a surprise, for I had expected to be negotiating jungle terrain for at least another week until the next settlement. For all practical purposes the Darien Gap was now behind. As if to confirm this, after we had been a half hour on the road a beat-up Panama City taxi bounced by, honking as it went. Berto had never seen a car before, and the fact that it was a taxi made it doubly exciting, for he had heard the word all his life without ever knowing what it meant. In celebration, he spent the next fifteen minutes imitating the horn: "Bip bip! Bip bip! Bip bip!" Later that afternoon, when a pickup from a construction site stopped to offer Berto a lift, there was yet more excitement. Watching him clamber aboard, I could see that this was a real adventure for him, like flying a Spitfire or going to the moon.

After spending a night in a woodcutter's hut—I had failed to connect with Berto, but something told me not to worry—I set out the next day along a newly graveled road. This should have been cause for celebration, but my physical condition, which had been tottering for days, now nearly collapsed completely. Groggy and barely moving at all, I stumbled into a scraggly hut, and without explanation—all the owner had to do was take one look at me—I joined the company of two skinny dogs lying under the table. After sleeping and sweating in this kennel for the duration of the long, hot afternoon, I inched another kilometer to Mutate, where a kindly family gave me soup and rigged up a cot for me in their well-founded hut.

I left my benefactors with a souvenir postcard of Rainham, High Street, and moved off late the next day, slightly improved. In my usual hunchback, head-down walking style, I didn't see Berto until he gave me a strange birdcall signal from down the road. Then with a great yell he ran toward me while I hobbled toward him as quickly as I could, and when we met we shyly bashed each other on the shoulders, almost afraid to admit how glad we were to be together again. Berto relieved me of my pack, and we walked on into Santa Fe, a construction camp 4 km farther on. Berto had been so overwhelmed by the experience of riding in a car that he had forgotten to get off until Santa Fe and had spent the next two days sitting beside the river, loyally waiting for me.

Little by little, Berto and I had established an easygoing friendship. We had been traveling together a week before he even thought it worthwhile to ask me my name, but now he chose to walk with me from one construction camp to the next instead of making his own way. As we walked we would take turns singing our favorite songs, he in Chocó and I in English; he particularly liked "Tea for Two," for which he learned the words and joined in. Our common language was Spanish, but because neither of us spoke it very well, most of our conversations took place on the level of an introductory high school course. "All Chocós have big feet and need a haircut," I might say (good-naturedly, of course), which Berto would counter by saying, "All gringos are bald and have soft, baby-pink feet." Then, with a flourish, he would illustrate his point by mimicking my limping gait and shouting a long, pained "Arrrghhhh!" (my standard reaction when a stone popped through the gaping hole in the sole of my boot).

Berto was looking a good deal smarter than I these days. He was now wearing my fire-brigade shirt, a new pair of white trousers I had bought for him in Yaviza, and a Sony baseball cap that he had paid for himself. His pride and joy, however, was a pair of my long blue nylon socks, which he wore over his trouser legs, making him look like a 1920's golfer. When his unlaced plimsolls became too much trouble for his broad feet, he would take them off and walk along in his stocking feet. While sartorial considerations seemed hardly to move Berto at all, carrying a full pack of cigarettes was always important—in fact, the ultimate status symbol. Whenever he posed for a photo he would not only light up but would make absolutely sure his pack of Viceroys was visibly poking out of his shirt pocket—he might even hold up the pack in front of him, like a policeman showing the necessary identification.

North of Santa Fe we ran into a flurry of construction on the Inter-American Highway; everywhere there were huge machines, resembling insects in their mindless industry, ripping through and flattening the forest in a frenzy of activity as everyone rushed to beat the soon-expected rains. We continued on to Chepo, the largest town south of the Canal, with about twenty thousand inhabitants and, it seemed, twenty thousand jukeboxes, all playing at once. (You could hear the place from miles out—the noise guided us in.) Here we stayed the night with more missionaries and more mosquitoes. One of the missionaries, Jim Enermark, told me of once sleeping three nights on the banks of the nearby Río Bayano, where he was so tormented by the insects that he was forced to seek refuge, despite the incredible heat and humidity, by crawling into an oversize plastic garbage bag!

Oddly enough, certain nights, or at least part of them, could get very cold. One night I awoke shivering, put on my old coat, and, still not happy, finally settled for unhitching my hammock and wrapping that around me, too. My sleep was a hard but warm one perched atop sacks of maize as hard as rock. (And I had thought that jungles were consistently steamy!)

Berto, carrying a thirty-pound pack fitted out with improvised straps made of tree bark, walked with me the 38 km to the new airport at Tocumen, each step impressing me with his endurance. I wouldn't have been able to carry this load more than a hundred yards. At the airport a dolt of a soldier gave us the most infernal set of misdirections to reach the terminal—he sent us across the main runway, a fact we discovered only when a 747's route on descent very nearly intersected our own. Whether the pilot noticed two weird figures straggling across his landing site I couldn't tell. Berto, nearly hysterical, hit the deck as the big machine crunched to a landing thirty yards past us. "Just an airplane, Berto," I confided with all the authority of Inspector Clouseau.

Talk about culture shock! While I bedded down in an inconspicuous corner of the terminal, Berto spent all night contentedly sitting in the lounge of this great air-conditioned palace, sipping Cokes, watching the jets take off and land, and every so often strolling through the duty-free shops to stare at the fancy watches and examine the liquor bottles that lined the walls. When I woke in the morning he showed me the postcard he had bought of the near-naked members of his tribe, now ten thousand years away.

"19 March, 25 days out of Barranquillita and 780 days out of Ushuaia, I entered Panama City!" Thus reads the last notation I made on my map of Darien, the same one I once thought might be my last testament. Having completed what many would consider a colossal walk, I felt not wild excitement, but merely relief, glad that my luck had held out this far.

Berto and I made our way through the crowds on Central Avenue in our rotting, stinking clothes, drawing stares everywhere from the immaculately dressed shoppers. Berto, in his shoeless stocking feet, seemed to puzzle them especially. When we reached the Plaza Cinco de Mayo, I touched the monument there—it was now my mark. Good God! After two years of appalling work I had actually completed South America and the Darien Gap. Now I eagerly awaited reunion with my new family. After that I would have plenty of time to contemplate Central America.

Panama

It is late evening. While I update my journal, Yoshiko is in the next room singing Ayumi a lullaby with sweet words and a haunting Oriental melody:

> Why do you cry, Baby Crow?
> He cries for wanting
> Uncle Cockle-Doodle-Do's
> Red cap and red boots.
> Why do you cry, oh, Baby Crow?

Soon mother and daughter will be asleep. I keep scratching out words hour after hour into the chilly night as thoughts of a warm bed and even warmer arms beckon.

We have been reunited; the long separation was forgotten in one long moment's embrace. What a delightful existence we now share—the self-indulgent pleasure of waking at one in the afternoon and listening to the eternal music of the stream rushing outside our bungalow and the hooting, singing, and whistling birds of these northern tropics. Great chunks of our day break off and float away under roaring waves of laughter. To Yosh and me, at last together with our exuberant child, the world indeed looks a wonderful place. A reporter in the local newspaper has characterized us as "the happiest couple in all Panama." We disagree: We are the happiest in all the world.

Ayumi-chan, a year and a month old, wants all our attention and tries her best to dominate our days. Her only store-bought toy is Mr. Fang-Fang, her teddy bear; otherwise, when we are not playing with her ourselves, we encourage her to amuse herself with an assortment of paper cups, plastic containers, and like household objects, which at the end of the day are gathered into a box marked "Bum Chewing Gum" that sits in the corner. Yesterday we heard her first sentence: "Boo, daddy" (*boo* is Japanese baby-talk for "drink"). We are all incredibly happy.

The day I reached Panama City, the satisfaction had been almost immediately lost in a series of hassles as Berto and I, still caked in jungle mud and sweat, set about searching for accommodations. When I finally got an address from the Salvation Army, it was early evening, and by the time we set out, it was almost dark. Only later did I learn that *everyone* knows that the neighborhood we had been sent to, the Marañon, is a notorious district chock-full of thieves, muggers, and murderers; I got to find this out firsthand.

Toting our gear on our backs, we had no sooner crossed over into the Marañon than without warning I was overwhelmed by an explosion of flying fists and kicking feet. As I struggled to recover, I saw that Berto had been smashed to the side and that four wiry, pop-eyed teenagers were zeroing in on their target: me. Suddenly I found that I was immobilized—two of the thugs, who had circled around behind me, were holding me by the frame of my backpack. I was entirely at their mercy. First my watch was ripped off my wrist, together with a bloodied patch of skin, and then my camera bag was cleanly snatched away. I fought hard to keep on my feet; to stumble to the ground now would surely mean the end. Then, under the weak yellow light of the lamppost, I saw the glint of steel.

One of the teenagers facing me had a knife and was tossing it menacingly, tauntingly, from hand to hand. My thoughts moved in slow motion; events seemed to be unfolding in a thick fog. I thought: This can't be happening—am I really to be stabbed here, just after having survived the Darien Gap? I watched, frozen with horror, as the steely glint came straight for my chest. At the last second I made an attempt to turn away and then stiffened, preparing for the inevitable, as the knife pierced straight through my pack and hit the edge of the aluminum frame and stopped short with a metallic *clink*.

"Muthafucka!" my assailant spat out, apparently as surprised as I was at what had happened. Struggling to withdraw the blade from the fabric, he backed off, preparing for another assault. The pair behind me set me up again, locking my twisting body four-square in front of their accomplice, who let out a terrifying grunt as he made a sweeping lunge across my guts. I winced. What, no searing pain? No spurting blood? Not even nicked? Miraculously, the blade had somehow become entangled in my mud-encrusted shirttail. My slovenly road attire had actually saved my life!

Just then, from around the corner came the wail of a police siren, and the four fled, spitting and cursing, to the oversize shack across the street. Someone had alerted the police, who arrived at the scene of the crime in a remarkable thirty seconds. What happened next was yet another surprise. When the vehicle, an armored pickup truck, trundled up, one of the officers casually got out and, following my frantic directions, approached the door where the criminals were hiding—and knocked ever so gently on the door. I wasn't very much surprised when no one answered—but I was when the police, without even taking our names, told us to wait where we were, drove off, and never returned! They had a watertight case, including at least a dozen eyewitnesses, and our assailants holed up directly under their noses—and yet did nothing. When I considered the fact that the police are part of the Guardia Nacional, who actually run the republic, I shuddered for poor Panama! That same night the Salvation Army hall was broken into, as was a church nearby, while the top prize went to two drunken seamen found in a locked room with their throats cut. Jolly place, Panama City.

Berto, totally shaken by this experience, wanted to leave Panama City immediately. I was no less shaken—and felt bad for Berto as well. Here I had taken an unsuspecting lad from his quiet riverside home in another world and watched with fascination as he became acquainted by degrees with the attractions of twentieth-century living. Now he had been subjected to the dark side of industrialized society—the fear of every city-dweller, unprovoked street violence. I wanted somehow to make this up to him, to prove to him that "modern civilization" had something positive to offer that he could take back with him to his village.

I persuaded Berto to stay on a few days longer, with the understanding that I would pay him for this "overtime." We secured reasonable lodgings for the night, and the next day visited the National Museum. Things got off to an interesting start the moment we rather casually entered a tiny room. As soon as the door slid closed, Berto fell to the floor, grabbed his head, and began moaning in a mild panic. The idea of an elevator had never entered his imagination, let alone his experience—nor had I thought to warn him. Berto did eventually calm down and become more or less acclimated to the "flying room."

When we reached the exhibits, Berto was especially intrigued by the section on primitive tribes. He studied the Chocó exhibit intensely, while I read the placards to him as best I could. It was an odd experience to be in a museum looking over artifacts fashionable thousands of years ago while next to me stood a boy who considered these objects as contemporary as freeze-dried coffee. Berto even unabashedly wanted to buy a grinding stone and take it home. "How much?" he asked a startled attendant, explaining to me with an aside, "It's better than my mother's."

Very few Chocós have ever visited the capital (Kunos, on the other hand, are a fairly common sight here). Most Panamanians are not even familiar with Chocó territory; to the average citizen, Panama ends at the Río Bayano. Consequently, Berto attracted considerable attention on the streets. People would stop him and ask, "Where are you from?" At first he would say Barzal, but no one would recognize the name, so he would progress from Chocó Union to Boca de Cupe and even Yaviza while his questioner would keep shaking his head. Astonished that no one knew of these places, Berto eventually settled for simply answering, "Darien."

After four days Berto had had his fill and prepared to leave. It was thus payday. He was almost rich; he had earned a whopping 11,520 plantains, which, thank goodness, he took in balboas (the nominal currency in Panama, which are in fact dollars). There were certain difficulties in paying him, however. For one thing Berto could not decipher the numerals above five, and while he could count confidently up to twenty, he hesitated in the thirties, skipped the forties entirely, and petered out in the fifties. Berto was no fool, and was certainly of at least average intelligence; it's just that he had no formal education. "How can I know for sure," he said, "that when you tell me this is a twenty-dollar note that it is not a ten-dollar note?" How, indeed! From earliest childhood he had been told, probably with justification, not to trust anyone outside his tribe. He needed some guarantee that he wasn't being hoodwinked.

We agreed that he would be paid $120 in singles, which he would have no trouble recognizing. But there was more: "How do I know when you give me a hundred and twenty bills that they are not thirty bills or some other number?" He came up with the solution for this himself: I first tore a piece of cardboard into 120 bits. He could trust me to do this honestly, he reasoned, because the operation didn't involve money and its corrupting influence! Then he matched the bills to the bits of cardboard. But even this wasn't a simple matter. First, he counted out 20 bits of cardboard and placed a dollar bill on each, then made five similar piles, placing one pile on the bed, two on the floor, and so on. To his delight the cardboard bits ran out exactly on a count of 20. He then counted the piles, six, and thus proved to himself that $20 \times 6 = 120$, as I had maintained two-and-a-half hours earlier. With a roomful of torn-up cardboard, Berto at last felt assured that he had not been cheated.

Berto's last day in the city was an orgy of unbridled spending. He particularly wanted, he said, to bring back some dress material to his mother. (Chocós regard cloth as the most desirable of commodities.) Before getting around to this purchase, however, he bought a pair of sunglasses, a watch (after some instruction he could read hours, but still not the minutes), six pairs of long socks, six tropical shirts, three pairs of trousers, several yards of trouser cloth, a set of suspenders, and a plastic water pistol. I called a halt to this frenzy of consumption just as he was about to dip into the funds for his fare home, and when he realized that he had overlooked the cloth for his mother he was overcome with remorse.

While we waited for his flight at the airport I asked Berto, "Any disappointments?" His answer amazed me: What he really wanted was to have his front teeth (which were so white and perfect as to be a Hollywood star's envy) extracted and replaced with gold ones. Apparently gold teeth were all the rage in Darien.

I was saddened to see Hilberto Kondi board the small aircraft, nervously clutching his nineteen-dollar ticket to Yaviza. I would have liked to take him traveling with me in the United States (I had happy visions of Berto in Disneyland or meeting the astronauts). He was an extraordinary companion, and I was honored to have been his twentieth-century guardian. Good fishing, Berto!

My full attention next swung to a house search, for Yoshiko and Ayumi would be arriving soon. After days of futile inquiries and follow-ups that never materialized, a new acquaintance offered to let us stay in his bungalow in the mountains. This was an absolute godsend, but the house wouldn't be available for a week and Yoshiko was due to arrive in two days—not much time for me to convert my present lodgings—a small, unused storeroom in a high school—into the grand suite I had dreamed of for her. I pushed together a couple of old beds that were collecting dust in the corner and with the help of families I had met in the nearby Canal Zone found sheets for the mattresses and pillows for the bed. I arranged flowers in a beer bottle, set a bowl of fruit on a card table, and bought new, bright bulbs for the lights. Done! The effect was rather good.

At the airport, I waited anxiously. Pacing about the terminal, I certainly must have seemed a bizarre specimen in my campo outfit: ruined boots, baggy Darien trousers, straw hat, and blue workshirt, my very last Navy Number 3s, the one I had worn at our wedding. This last item had made the entire journey from Ushuaia and was now a mere rag, the entire back gone, but I knew Yoshiko would be amused to see me in it. There was some confusion about where her plane was to disembark. When I went to the announced gate and didn't see Yoshiko, I figured she was on a later flight. Walking down a stairway I passed a long line of Japanese passengers climbing up—but there was no one here who looked like Yoshiko. Or was there? Was that her? I stopped on the landing, walked back, and approached a woman who was smiling, even laughing at me. Hesitantly I spoke:

"Is it . . . really you?"

"Of course, George!"

I took a long breath. Such a change! Where was old, rugged Yoshiko, the Yoshiko of my dreams, Yoshiko with long black hair, blue jeans that she had pestered me to buy her, and a fat bottom? The new, elegant Yoshiko standing before me was a slim beauty wearing a dress, makeup, and designer eyeglasses. She, in turn, scanned me from head to toe, laughing at my appearance, nodding her head in acknowledgment of everything my outlandish getup implied. Without further hesitation we made an attempt at an embrace—quite an awkward attempt, in fact, because my darling wife was all this time carrying a little bundle in her arms.

"Look, George, I've brought you your daughter—look how pretty she is!" said Yoshiko, swinging a severe little girl onto the floor in front of me, where she stood resolutely and glared at me, unsmiling, while clutching the white teddy bear slung over her shoulder.

"That's Mr. Fang-Fang," said Yoshiko.

"Oh!"

I hardly knew what to say or do. I had dozens of photos of Ayumi, but this was a completely different experience. Here, at last, was my real-life daughter, my own flesh and blood— and without a doubt Yoshiko's, too, as her beautiful almond eyes attested. Still, I remember wondering, what, or who, *did* she look like? My confused mind was brought back to reality when a passing porter good-naturedly called out to Ayumi, "Hello, Chinita!" (Chinita means "Little Chinese"). Gosh! I thought, I guess she *does* look "Chinese"!

The friends who brought me out to the airport now took us in their van back to the storeroom. After we piled into the back seat, I said, "You look different in those glasses, Yosh— like Rocky's girl."

"Spectacles," she corrected me. "Glasses are for drinking from—I've been studying English, you see! They're not really necessary, but they're a current fashion in Nippoń. They're Christian Dior, you know."

"Oh."

I had so much to say, so much to ask, that I couldn't think of anything to say at all. Most of the way we sat silently, holding hands, with Ayumi sitting on her mother's lap gazing at me with a mixture of curiosity and wariness. Once at the school, we had to climb over a badly parked van to enter the storeroom—how embarrassing! To add more misery to the moment, the day was especially hot and humid, and the water in the adjoining sink and shower had been shut off. Yoshiko, always the trouper, laughingly shrugged everything off as part of the madness of being married to a madman and told me how much she appreciated the fruit and especially the flowers-in-the-beer-bottle arrangement.

After a short time Ayumi, fed up with all the attention her mother was giving me, an interloper, began bawling.

"What's up, Yosh?" I asked, unnerved to hear our child cry for the first time.

"Nothing, silly. She's just too tired—she hasn't slept in twenty hours."

Yoshiko laid our daughter down on the bed, and it was then that I first heard her sing the lullaby about Baby Crow

191

and Uncle Cockle-Doodle-Do. When Ayumi was finally asleep, Yoshiko turned to me and said, "We've done it, George! Can it really be a dream that we are at last together?" And then, in that terrible hot little storeroom, we euphorically embraced.

In the following days, Yoshiko took in hand what she considered the top priority—fixing me up to look more nearly human. After forcing me to shave, she cut my hair and trimmed my mustache. Next she threw out all my ragged and torn clothes and gave me my presents: dashing new white trousers, white socks and briefs, and a flashy green Hawaiian shirt. Then, at her insistence, to top this all off I bought a pair of blue-and-white supersneakers. The new George was so different from the old model that my new friends and acquaintances at first did not recognize me.

While supervising my transformation, Yoshiko asked, "George, why is your left sock so much higher than your right?"

"No reason."

"Let's see," she said, suddenly grabbing hold of my leg and pulling the sock down in a single motion. "What is *this?!*" she demanded, pointing to the map of South America covering the lower half of my calf. (I was, of course, leaving the upper half free for North America, later.)

"Just a tattoo, love."

"You up-to-no-good urchin boy," she said sharply. "Who told you to mark yourself, eh?"

"It's a . . . reminder of my sea days," I said, and then added, as if in apology, "It's not finished yet—needs a few more touches." With that, Yoshiko slapped my leg, more in resignation than in anger, and went off to change Ayumi's diaper.

That evening we went into the center of Panama City to visit Vilma, an acquaintance who boasted over a score of tattoos scattered about her person, and she accompanied us to Jim's Tattoo Parlour in the red-light district. Jim's had been founded by an American who settled in Panama during World War II. As Jim's is reportedly the only true tattoo shop in all Latin America, the establishment can probably take credit for the designs on a hefty percentage of the world's seamen. While "Doctor" Andres Suchy (the current "Jim" and son of the founder) set about finishing his job on my calf, Yosh and Vilma perused the designs lining the walls. Vilma, like a child let loose in a toy store, took an immediate fancy to the thirty-dollar "Jesus Christ Loves Me" (complete with head-and-shoulders portrait of the Son of God), left Jim's in a rush to raise the cash, and returned with it within minutes.

Meanwhile "Jim," who had previously inscribed the map of South America (with a hiking boot in the center), now added the important place names and traced my route in red. This business really hurt, and my face was so contorted in agony that Yoshiko came over to hold my hand. "Really, George," she said, "you're such a coward. You could never have a baby! Look at that boy—he doesn't make such a fuss." Sure enough, the seaman seated opposite had been sitting stolidly through the hour and a half required for the huge black panther to take form on his broad upper arm.

We moved into the bungalow high in the mountains of the Panamanian interior, where we stayed for several happy months while the dreaded rains I had succeeded in avoiding came down full force every day. The first few weeks were a crash course in the joys and drawbacks of fatherhood. When Ayumi woke up early in the morning, we had no option but to get up, too. Then, once she was fed and her blue booties laced up, she would invariably lead me on a hundred-yard gallop across the lawn. She had been walking for three months when I first saw her, and was now moving strongly, if clumsily. On one occasion she fell five times in a row, the last time badly scraping her knees. Despite this she rejected all offers of assistance and never cried. It surprised me to see just how resilient a baby could be.

I observed certain changes in Yoshiko. Whereas in Argentina I constantly had to monitor our provisions to make sure she wasn't sneaking out large amounts of food to eat in secret, now it seemed that all the energy she once expended to fill her own tummy was being directed toward feeding our baby. And while I could never rouse Yoshiko at a "decent" hour during our tenting days, now she would instantly scramble out of bed whenever Ayumi woke up crying, even if it meant dragging herself out of a deep, exhausted sleep.

"Where's your busto gone, Yosh?" I asked her one day, saddened by the loss.

"Oh, yes, such poor tits," she acknowledged. "That's from feeding your greedy daughter. Still, next time they will get huge again."

Next time! All of a sudden, I remembered having seen the famous thermometer among her personal effects.

Yoshiko responded to the wonder and curiosity in my eyes. "Of course, I will not bring next baby to see you for at least a year, when you reach United States, because of all the work of watching new baby."

This was interesting on at least two counts. Since Yoshiko's arrival I had not said a word about the future of the walk, but apparently she considered the matter settled. (Not long after, she told me, "George, this is no proper place to end your dream.")

Then, of course, there was the matter of another baby. I hardly had to give that a second thought. We got straight to work.

We have been preparing for Yoshiko's return. We agree that this place is one of the prettiest we have ever seen or could even imagine. Nature herself seemed to confirm this when she allowed Yoshiko to conceive here: A second bundle is on the way!

A few days before her flight, as I put the finishing touches to my South American journal, I listen to the rain drumming off the tin roof over my head, droning a hypnotic lullaby. In the next room Yoshiko is asleep; asleep also is my baby, Ayumi-chan, my joyful dictator. Too tired to continue, I finally put the pen down. This morning I'll sleep well, the luscious sleep of a weary man who has long been lonely but has now found his family.

September 24, 1979. The British Airways jetliner with

Yoshiko and Ayumi aboard lifted off the runway, and when the thunder of the giant engines was reduced to a whisper and the aircraft had faded into a dot and disappeared, I was left shaking sick . . . alone. After five glorious months they were gone, and perhaps the best of my existence gone with them. When would I see them again? It wouldn't be for at least a year, when I hoped to reach the United States. Only one thing was certain: I must go on, chasing my improbable dream, until I planted the Union Jack on the shore of the Arctic Ocean.

The afternoon humidity again turned to rain and held me in its gasping, warm grip. That night, my first alone in months, seemed to take place in an empty wasteland, and so I resolved to press on immediately. I just simply had to break with this place full of memories.

By next day's sunset I reached the Thatcher Ferry Bridge, which spans the Panama Canal. (Paradoxically, crossing the Canal to reach the northern part of the Americas requires that you travel south!) From the bridge I crossed 11 km of open land, part of the Canal Zone—although in a few days the Americans were scheduled to return the Zone (and, in the year 2000, the Canal itself) to Panamanian authority. There was no gate or fence at either border of the Zone, but there was no doubt about when I had again entered Panama proper. The loud, pulsating jukebox salsa and the reflection of glaring lights off tin roofs introduced me into yet another seamy evening in a Latin American republic. Among the noise and sweat I found a lone gringo, an American ex-army sergeant selling hamburgers, and spent the evening chatting with him before turning in on the floor of a firehouse. The night brought little sleep, however, for the heat was stupefying and I was continually troubled by mosquitoes. Worst of all, I had been off the road for five months—I had grown soft.

October 1, 1979. One of the greatest days in Panama's history, the return to Panama of sovereignty over the Canal Zone. At midnight, the air above the Canal town of Ancon was torn apart by a brilliant, thunderous, window-shaking barrage of exploding fireworks. Panama had now officially reclaimed the

195

Zone; a new era had begun. Among other changes, the Zone post office, formerly well run by the U.S. Postal Service, was now the property of the inept Correo Nacional de Panama, who, like commandos, had taken over the building at the stroke of midnight October 1, installing their own rubber stamps, flags, and signs—and doubtless seeking out new corners to lose mail in.

I spent the last few hours of the official American occupation of the Zone at the home of a Zonian, Dr. Ken Lake, dean of faculty at Panama Canal College. Lake, like his fellow Zonians, remained at home. The Americans were to a man silent, some fearful of harm at the hands of the celebrants. In fact, nothing untoward happened that night. And the next day, as I took a stroll to the post office, the neat suburban streets were as quiet as ever—no sign of the hordes that were reportedly going to uproot all the trees.

Antagonism runs high between Zonians and Panamanians. Both groups were among the unfriendliest and most discontented I encountered anywhere during my journey. The Zonians acted as though they had been backed into a corner and needed to defend themselves at every turn against the Panamanians' ill will, which in turn was clearly nurtured by envy and resentment. The Panamanians' attitude was understandable. Most of the gringos they encountered cruised by in expensive cars, earned salaries several times theirs, and could even buy cheaper food shipped in from the States. Ironically, and perhaps because of the example of the relatively wealthy Americans in their midst, the Panamanians are the most avid chasers of the Big Buck in Latin America.

My road now ran virtually straight for several hundred kilometers, clear to the Costa Rican border. The absurdly narrow two lanes hummed with traffic dashing with speed and true Latin bravado. The favored few drove the preferred Cadillac, while the majority took buses—American-style school buses, just as elsewhere throughout Latin America, with gaudy portraits of Roberto Duran, Farrah Fawcett, and other superstars of the time painted on the sides. One such bus just a few days earlier had skipped plum off the Canal bridge, killing all aboard save one fortunate baby.

The combination of speed, narrowness, and some drunkenness spelled danger. For two and a half years I had walked on the edge of the road (on the side facing traffic, naturally), but now there was a problem: This road had no shoulder. The tarmac edge ceased with an abrupt drop of several inches into boulders, debris, and stunted greenery. After an hour of leaping out of the way of the oncoming vehicles, I gave up and sought shade and respite at a dance hall, a peculiarly bleak sight in the daytime. I sat down at a table, but soon fatigue forced me to the floor, where I lay weakly for an hour or so, completely ignored by the indifferent patrons. Toward midafternoon I staggered on, feeling even more broken than earlier, and finally lay my sleeping bag in the corner of an abandoned shack. I had scratched out a bare 12 km that day.

For the next few days I limped onward; a crushing lethargy dominated my body and soul. I had expected that, once back on the road, with time I would gain strength; instead I grew weaker. The hot tarmac blistered my feet badly, and food didn't interest me at all. Most afternoons it would rain, as if in response to the colossal buildup of heat during the day. Outside Chorrera a savage rainstorm blotted out everything about me. My waterproofs had been stolen the previous year by the Colombian army, but in this humidity they would be nearly useless anyway.

Chorrera looks a tin-shack mess at any time, but now, as I almost floated in, saturated, my boots squelching, she indeed looked "down." My neck was enlarged and my throat so swollen that it took forty-five minutes to get a half-slice of damp toast into my reluctant system. I pushed myself into a hospital, where the efficient American-trained woman doctor checked over my symptoms—chronic throat infection, vitamin deficiency, rotting mouth—and diagnosed it as incipient scurvy. At first I thought she was joking. After all, Yoshiko had fed me so well!

197

"Really?" I asked.

"Really!" she said.

Perhaps this had been coming on for a long, long time. It's amazing how the body can go to pieces under emotional stress. When she gave me an injection of penicillin, I almost passed out, strict coward that I am when it comes to needles or any other kind of pain. I was glad to escape back onto the blistering *camino*.

I continued moving forward in the same grim way, through the same pulverizing heat. That night, hours before dark, I acknowledged my near-total exhaustion and flaked myself out on the filthy, glass-strewn floor of an abandoned warehouse. I lay on my sleeping bag hour after hour, too tired even to turn over, great lakes of sweat soaking through my shirt and into my bag. Daylight faded, and with the darkness came the dreaded whine of mosquitoes flying through the broken windows. My perspiration mixed together with the spray-on repellent, forming a lather that was only partially effective in warding off the bugs. Throughout the long night I slept only intermittently. Somewhere just this side of consciousness, in the near distance, I could barely make out the rising and ebbing sound of men playing cards. My mind drifted back to Rainham and home and happy childhood days—knockout whist with Mum in the sitting room, and, of course, tons of tea and biscuits always at hand. Now it was all so far away. I felt weak and alone and was longing for companionship.

Life in the bungalow in the mountains with Yoshiko had been so good that I keenly felt the loss when it came to an end. And in fact, as I slowly began to recover, women were catching my eye more than usual. Yoshiko had dealt forthrightly with this general subject long ago, before leaving South America. She had said, "George, I know you will be tempted by other women, and I know you may do it. Do not be afraid, for our love is greater than all this means."

There were encounters, some. One such occasion was somewhere before Penonomé, where I encountered a brown-eyed mestizo girl in shorts and T-shirt standing astride a rusty bicycle. We nodded at each other as I passed. In spite of (or perhaps because of) my weakened condition, as I plodded on, my thoughts lingered on her. And then I heard her cry, "Hey! Hey!" and, turning around, I saw to my happy surprise that she had pedaled after me. When she got close enough she shouted, "Come home! Come to my home!"

Leaving the road was one thing, but walking back in the direction I had just come was something I loathed—in fact, something I almost never did. But a girl! I instantly turned and followed, expecting I knew not what.

Her home was a grass-roofed stick hut set in a small grove of palm trees some thirty yards off the road. A vegetable patch nearby looked pitifully vulnerable in the poor, baked earth. The skinny mother, barefoot and wearing a colorless rag for a dress, cheerily bustled about, with a listless dog constantly in tow, and intermittently poked at the fire that had been built on a small tin-sheathed platform. She waved as we made our way across the yard, which was strewn with chipped enameled bowls and pecking chickens. The girl led me down a tree-lined trail to a point in the brook where a pool had formed behind a rank of boulders. Without hesitation she jumped in, clothes and all. A portrait of Panamanian strongman General Torrijos was printed on the front of her T-shirt, and when she surfaced, the general's face had all but dissolved, revealing even more clearly the form of a girl emerging into womanhood.

We splashed and played beneath the sun's punishing glare for a half-hour, perhaps more—who knows? I could have spent a lifetime there. For a precious moment the road seemed far away. After skipping out of the pool, from somewhere in the foliage my girl produced a damp comic book. She pointed to one of the panels. "Look. Do this—it has never happened to me." After a pause, she added sternly, "But no more!" The picture showed the Man of Steel locked in a powerful kissing embrace with Lois Lane. With water in our hair and the babble of the brook in our ears, "Lois" and I shared an innocent kiss—and no more. Finally it was time to go, and so I bade good-bye to Lois Lane and silently hoped that one day she would find her Superman.

The landscape through which I now hobbled was tamed and parched—too near civilization to be rampant. Trees were few, and only occasionally did I reach a hill, from whose crests I could spy the deep blue of the Golfo de Panama. The only change in the unflaggingly blue sky came in the afternoon, when the colossal buildup of clouds would precede yet another violent storm.

Toward Santiago, the countryside grew greener, and there were more Indians, for this was the land of the hopelessly impoverished Guayamis. Tin-roof settlements appeared at frequent intervals, and in every last one of them there was a roadside truck stop, complete with lazy ceiling fan, serving chop suey and chow mein—whether or not there was a Chinese in sight. At one stop I asked a customer about this common fare and learned that these dishes are not indigenous to China, but had been more or less invented at the turn of the century to feed the large gangs of coolie labor imported to work here on the Canal.

Once I had passed Cruz de Mesa, the high point of the morning was when a tiny cloud drifted between the sun and my back. I rejoiced in the shade, but five seconds later the wisp had blown on, leaving me more desperate for shade than ever. At last a fantastic crack of thunder heralded a break in the heat, and soon the warm rain was falling. (As usual, I felt cheated that it was not cooler.) The rain grew heavier, and eventually cascaded down with such force that the fat drops ricocheted off the blacktop a full foot and flattened the broad, downturned brim of my sombrero. For over a half hour the sky was crisscrossed with sizzling lightning bolts, the heavens roared, and all about me the land steamed. When the frenzy subsided, the sun once again bore down on the saturated landscape as though nothing had happened.

The road now passed through an increasingly hilly region, and as walking became harder, I grew thirstier and more frantic to find the ever-dreamed-of Coca-Cola. One promising hut showed the familiar red sign. Half-paralyzed by the climate, I burst in on the dozing owner and asked if they sold cola: *"Vende cola?"*

"Why, of course, señor. We have the red sign, don't we?"

"Good," I rasped gratefully. "Give me one, please, cold."

"Why, of course, señor, but we don't have one," he said, adding that they would come tomorrow: *"Mañana."*

"Well, give me a Sprite, then . . . something . . . anything."

"Why, of course, señor, but we don't have any now."

"I suppose they come *mañana?*"

Why, of course, señor."

"This is bloody murder. I don't give a damn about *mañana.* It's *today* I'm here."

I stormed out and sat sulking on a log under a banana tree. Slowly all the numerous family came out of the hut and from among the surrounding trees and stared at me in expressionless silence. One of the naked kids came forward with a grimy plastic bowl, placed it near me and bolted. Full of red-faced, gritted-teeth outrage, I drank the liquid. It wasn't bad, actually. In fact, it was very good: thick lemonade, infinitely better than any soda pop. I slowly began to smile, and the kids smiled in return. Then I nodded, and they nodded, and we all laughed together

A fat, motherly woman came over to me, offered me a banana, and said, "If the gringo is happy, then we are happy."

As I was leaving, the owner embraced me and said, "Why, of course, señor, you will never forget my family and me."

"Why, of course, señor," I said. "I can never forget you."

Incidents like this took place almost daily. I was always thirsty—I would even leave the road to find my beloved Coke—and always the soft-drink truck had blown up or was due *mañana.* I would become angry and abusive, but these great-hearted people would merely nod and smile until the rage subsided. By the time I left there was nothing but goodwill, and a flock of fat elders, shy daughters, proud sons, and naked toddlers would wave and laugh and shout, *"Adios! Adios!"*

Finding the elusive Coke became even harder in the Chiriquí Gap, the strip of rain forest between the Golfo de Chiriquí on the Pacific and the inland mountains. Vehicles were few here, and most stopped to offer a lift—I counted eleven in one morning. With a cheery *"No, gracias,"* I would wave the bemused motorists on. Taking a rest at a roadside shack, I was trying to break into a reluctant orange when a small boy wearing nothing but a pair of ragged shorts courteously offered to lend me his penknife for the job. The irony didn't escape me: Here was the Professional Traveler, encumbered with nearly fifty pounds of gear, relying on the tools of a penniless lad to accomplish the simplest of chores. He sold me the knife for one balboa.

The rain forest was overrun with insects. Farther on, I walked straight into a blizzard of thousands of brilliantly colored butterflies, while on a tree trunk I saw a spider eight inches across. At one point I spied something more hospitable—a glint of red metal, a Coca-Cola sign—through the thick greenery, well off the road, and set off straight for it. Just as I reached a clearing, two Indian boys astride dappled ponies emerged from the foliage on the other side. Their mounts were frisky, but the youngsters, who could not have been older than twelve, rode them bareback with great style and pride. Halting directly in front of me, for a frozen instant they seemed almost to be painted there, precisely centered in a framework of tropical forest—brown, white-teethed Indians against a background of giant green and yellow fronds: "Youth at One with Nature" might have been an appropriate title, I thought. They stopped hardly a second and said not a word before galloping off. Immediately my imagined painting shifted into a surrealistic mode as I was left standing there, motionless, alone, holding a precious Coke in a clearing in the forest, so apparently out of harmony with my—their—surroundings.

Over this stretch it rained most of the day, every day. Would these rains ever end? By the time I reached the neat, quiet town of David I was wracked by fever. Despite my lack of money—seventy dollars had to last me until I reached my next dropoff in Costa Rica—I was desperate enough to consider renting a hotel room, if I could find one. Instead, I found myself tightly hanging on to an iron door knocker, for my head was spinning and I would otherwise have toppled to the ground. Luckily for me, the concerned, white-habited nuns took me in at the Hogar Santa Catalina, a rest home for the elderly destitute, where I lay in a tiny cell, stretched out on a bed, for several days.

While my stay at Hogar Santa Catalina was in the main recuperative, my rest was disturbed every night when the man in the next room would begin screaming, "Water! Water! Please, for God's sake, someone give me some water!" Every night I would bring the tormented man a full cup. "*Muchas gracias,*" he would say, his voice suddenly taking on a matter-of-fact tone, and he would uninterestedly put the water to the side. Then, as soon as I closed the door, he would return to his desperate wailing: "Water! Water! . . ." Poor fellow, he was perfectly able to walk to the tap and get water himself, but was apparently at the mercy of some cruel inner demon.

By and by I regained my strength and eventually felt well enough to go shopping at a food store in the center of town. Behind me at the checkout counter stood a distinguished-looking middle-aged man wearing a pleated bush shirt, worn outside the trousers in conventional Panamanian semiformal fashion. The man struck up a conversation, introduced himself as a doctor, and invited me to his surgery nearby. In his dimly lit air-conditioned office he opened a can of beer, slumped back into his black leather highback swivel chair, and began to ramble in good but slurred English. "So you live with the sisters, eh? That's very good." He slumped farther down in his chair. "I've been a doctor now for twenty years, and I'll tell you what: It bores the hell out of me. In fact, I don't even take patients anymore." He straightened up and

203

leaned forward with a newfound intensity. "My interest now lies in the spiritual side of man."

He took a long swig of beer and belched. "When I was traveling a few years ago, wandering around Argentina, I was led—it must have been God Himself Who led me—to a small junk shop in Buenos Aires." With this he pulled himself up in his chair, and his voice rose with emotion. "And He Himself led me to *this very book!*" He picked up a book from the desktop and lifted it aloft. "This book tells the truth—just watch." He shut his eyes tight, flipped through the pages at random, and then opened his eyes to read a passage: "'You, therefore, My son, give not into your lusts, but discipline your will.'

"You see! You see! The book never lies. It's all here," he exclaimed. He closed the book, moved it to the side, and reverently squared its worn edges with the corner of his desk, his hands moving so gingerly that one might have thought he was handling a letter bomb. "This book," he said solemnly, "means more to me than anything else in the world."

But oh, dear!—his right elbow somehow nudged over his new, nearly full beer can, and the bubbly liquid gushed out all over the sacred tome. At the sight of this the doctor sucked in a chestful of air and rolled his huge, agonized eyes heavenward, his face transformed into a mask of unaldulterated horror. I had to bite my lip and tighten my stomach muscles to keep from exploding with laughter. From somewhere the man found a long bandage and began desperately swabbing the sodden, injured masterpiece. As he was trying to stanch the flow of beer down the leg of the desk, gravity took over and seemed to haul him out of his chair and onto the carpet. Now on his knees, he took the opportunity to entreat his mentor for forgiveness and then peeled open a damp page. "Look! Look what it says!" he gasped, and proceeded feverishly to recite: "'Wherefore I am worthy only to be punished because I have grievously and often offended You, and in many things greatly sinned. . . .'"

A frantic few minutes later, with order restored, the doctor leaned back in his chair, new beer in hand, and became lost in deep thought. I took this opportunity to take my leave, and was only momentarily delayed when he scribbled out a prescription for my ills and handed it to me. It read: "Book: Imitation of Christ. Author: T. à Kempis."

Central America

Costa Rica

"Can anybody here change dollars?" Work came to a halt in the Immigration Office, sleepy eyes opened a notch, and from every corner a swarm of deadbeats were soon descending on me, waving fistfuls of local currency. A corpulent captain of the Customs Service waded his way through the throng. "No, no, no, no!" he shouted at me above the din, "you must do this officially." Hustling me into his office, he slipped surreptitiously into a space between the filing cabinet and the wall and, hunching over, produced a wad of colons from his pocket. "Eight and a half to the dollar," he said, eyebrows arched, as he peeled them off. "OK, eh?" And so with a minimum of formality I entered Costa Rica.

The heat on the road was as stifling as an elderly couple's living room in winter. After just a few kilometers I was sweating so profusely that I had to stop at a bar for a long cola refill. I had hardly taken a seat before I was assailed on all sides by several Ticos (as Costa Ricans are affectionately called) plying me with food and raving about the benefits of democracy—Costa Rica is one of the few successfully functioning democracies in the region, perhaps in part because it abolished its army in the late 1940's. One gabby fellow put his case eloquently: "Democracy is great! I can get drunk here, and later go to San Isidro and get 'legless' there, too!" Thomas

Jefferson could hardly have said it better. My "legless" companion ended his speech with a flourish by crashing back to the bar, punching the air with his fist, and bellowing, "Fuck communismo!"

Outside the uproarious bar, the heat on the road was intensified by the lush foliage growing straight up to the edge, at places even encroaching on the narrow road itself. Throughout Panama gangs of workers could be seen hacking away with machetes at the roadside vines and branches. Costa Rica apparently couldn't be bothered with such niceties. The end result for me was claustrophobia; it was like walking through an open green pipe—very difficult to see oncoming traffic. While the traffic was light, the occasional tractor-trailer racing by would invariably blow the hat off my head—and me nearly off the road. A more promising development was that physically I was feeling better than I had in months. After Villa Neily I began to bash out my first 40-km days since South America.

Deeper into Costa Rica, huge stands of bananas became more evident, their heavy green fingers curving up to the light in apparent contradiction to the law of gravity, held aloft by a broad, rotten-looking trunk that looked like it could be toppled with a slight shove.

Then there was the rain—always the rain, sometimes three cloudbursts in a single day. As I crossed one large hill after another, the swollen streams would gush forth torrents, creating small waterfalls all about. Every day I would get soaking wet at least once. My only consolation was that the showers seldom lasted very long and I could depend on the sun, once it reappeared, to bake my clothes bone-dry within a half hour. Approaching Palmar Norte at night, however, I started across a small bridge in the "dry" condition and was caught by a flash shower which was over before I cleared the bridge a bare few seconds later. Damn! This meant sleeping in wet gear, as there was no way to get completely dry until mañana's heat wave.

It took exactly a week to reach the provincial capital of San Isidro del General. San Isidro sits at the base of the immense Cerro del Muerte, the Mountain of the Dead, most of which is perpetually shrouded in mist. It derives its name, not, as I first thought, from some horror story of colonial genocide, but from the fact that so many traffic accidents take place there—cars plunging off the fog-bound cliffs and the like. I didn't especially look forward to tackling this monster, but there was no other practical route to the Meseta Central (Central Plateau) and the national capital, San José. (I was especially eager to reach San José because I had been reliably informed that I could find a Kentucky Fried Chicken there— my passion at the time.)

The damp, circuitous road upward was soon engulfed by low clouds and swirling mists. All along the route, great twisted trees loomed out of the fog, their tangled green-gray foliage dripping with cold dew—an altogether eerie place that seemed more like a Tolkien fantasy than anything one might imagine in the blazing tropics. After 40 km of continuous upgoing, I finally stopped at an inn to warm myself for a few minutes by the fireplace and drink hot milk before completing the 6 km to the summit (almost eleven thousand feet above sea level, the highest road point in Central America). The view, as could be expected, was nil, just sheets of rain and drifting fog, and so without pause I began the long slide down to the Meseta Central and the heart of Costa Rica.

After walking four hours in freezing rain, I chanced upon a Tico family's hut; nailed to the outer walls were flattened five-gallon oil cans that gave the dwelling the appearance of a medieval siege engine. The family didn't seem at all surprised at my request for shelter—nothing was too much trouble for them.

The father, Don Carlos, was a man of dignified appearance in his fifties. His plump wife was twenty years his junior; when they were married she was barely fourteen. Don Carlos owned the land surrounding his home, a good-size parcel where he raised cows; with their milk he made cheese, which he sold profitably in the capital, clearing several thousand dollars annually, far above the average per capita income. With productive land, healthy sons, a comfortable home, and even a small TV, Don Carlos was apparently that rarest of beings, a truly contented man.

The mother's passion was for royalty. Pasted on an entire wall were magazine photos of kings, queens, princesses, royal couples, royal families, even royal retainers. Before leaving the next day I examined her display and I noticed that the picture of Elizabeth and Philip was quite faded—it was one taken at the time of their wedding, in 1947. Throughout South America I had carried in my kit not one but two postcard portraits of Her Majesty (in the now-tempered conviction that my endeavor was in some sense "for Britain") and this gave me a sense of connection with home. I was reluctant to part with even one of the cards, but now this seemed an appropriate way to repay the hospitality of these fine people. When I presented the portrait to the mother, her misty eyes and slight coo convinced me that the picture really did belong here, in this armor-plated hut halfway up the Mountain of Death in Central America.

Most of the rest of the way down the mountain the air was clear and cool, but the last few miles before the capital found me reeling through a choking fog of car fumes. The pollution was so great that a team of technicians were roaming the roadway testing for exhaust emissions. I reached San José November 9, 1978. The city and the date were special to me, for reaching this capital meant that I had finally exceeded Sebastian Snow's limit of 1974—almost 13,000 km. No one had ever made a longer uninterrupted journey on foot in the Western Hemisphere.

For once I had a solid contact, an introduction from a couple in the Canal Zone, and on its strength I took a mini-bus to the pleasant village of Escazu, more or less a suburb of the burgeoning capital. My hostess in Escazu, Margaret Boudoin, an expatriate American, was a teacher at the Universidad Nacional and one of those remarkable people who open their homes to an outlandish variety of guests—for a day, a week, or a month—and still manage to keep everything on an even keel. Her household was a bustling crossroads of exchange students, Ticos, and for a while a group of grizzly prospectors who were camped out in the living room. Among the permanent occupants were her two teenage daughters, two birds, three fish, nine cats, one dog—plus Eugene, a Japanese-American who had popped in the previous year and decided to stay forever—all under one roof, in a modest bungalow. Margaret was such a generous heart that she carried leftover bones with her on the way to work— just in case she ran across a needy stray.

From my base at Margaret's I took the minibus to San José and went to a bank to cash some newly arrived drafts. At the British Embassy I requested they draft an official letter that would help me in my dealings with the new power governing Nicaragua, the Sandinista Revolutionary Front. The vice-consul's initial reaction was the same as the British ambassador's had been in Panama: He told me to forget the whole thing. "Perhaps you could fly to Mexico?" When I answered (with all due respect) that I of course simply must go on, and that was that, the vice-consul resignedly agreed to draw up a letter for me, thus making a visa unnecessary. I had anticipated problems in Nicaragua for some time, and back in Panama had even sought help from the Nicaraguan consul—this was shortly before the ultimate victory of the revolution. The nervous, morose Nicaraguan consul, doubtless a Somoza appointee, seated in a darkened office and flanked by large wall maps, took one look at my outfit of faded Salvation Army cast-offs and the spent remains of my fourth pair of boots and advised me, "You must dress correctly in Nicaragua, not as you are now. Otherwise," he said, "the Guardia—the national army—might mistake you for a mercenary, a guerrilla. They may kill you—but by accident, of course."

"But, of course," I replied. "But, Consul, if I look correct to the Guardia, I may look sort of incorrect to the rebels, and then . . ."

"Yes," interrupted the consul. "Yes—and they may kill you, too."

I rather liked this man, with his ambling, tragic manner. Later, when I saw the black and red Sandinista flag fluttering over his office, I wondered how he had fared.

At my mail dropoff I found two letters from Yoshiko. I read them on the spot and was immediately puzzled by their uncharacteristically brief and businesslike tone. In one she said she planned to leave Rainham and return to Japan with Ayumi as soon as possible, no explanation why. Something was obviously wrong, but what? Was Yoshiko's love weakening? I had no way of knowing—and no way of finding out. I couldn't call Rainham, as Mum didn't even have a telephone (with her poor hearing the instrument only frustrates her) and brother Anthony had a new, unlisted number. I felt not only dispirited but helpless, and when I got back to Margaret's I dashed off a letter asking Yoshiko why the sudden change in plans.

Soon after, I received a letter, a bolt from the blue—not from Yoshiko, but from my brother Anthony whom I hadn't seen in six years. He wrote to say that he was flying over from England to visit me in Costa Rica—on a whim; he even (rather imperiously) instructed me to have a "*good* hotel ready" for him. I found him a room for the astronomical price, to me, of four dollars a night, hoping he wouldn't mind that it was in one of the poorer parts of town. (It turned out he had made reservations at an expensive hotel anyway.)

Rather than just kick around for six days waiting for Anthony to arrive, I decided to gain distance by walking to the road fork leading to Puntarenas and returning to the capital in time to meet him. I was intrigued by a Tico saying that I had heard, "Only a Costa Rican can love Puntarenas," and so set aside a whole day to find out why. Certainly this depopulated, ghostly quiet port town had seen better days. Still, to the visitor it had a few redeeming, if humble, charms.

I ate a fish dinner in a seaside café listening to the waves break against the litter-strewn beach, while across the blue waters of the Golfo de Nicoya I could just make out the Nicoya Peninsula cloaked in a watery haze. A pleasant and pure peacefulness reigned here—that is, for me, who was just passing through. To the townspeople the place probably stank of decay and despair, and their lives were only aggravated by widespread food shortages. A freighter from Chile was shortly due to arrive here carrying a full cargo of beans. Costa Rica was now dangerously low on this important staple, and everyone was nervously following the daily reports of the ship's progress in the national media. At this same time, to the north, Nicaragua was not only out of beans but critically low on rice as well.

Although strikingly different in manner and life-style, Anthony and I share a common philosophy of living life to the limit, which inevitably involves a greater-than-normal amount of risk-taking. During our brief times together—he is nine years my elder, and for most of my childhood he was away from home serving in the RAF, where he established the basis for a later career as a munitions expert—we have always enjoyed a splendid relationship based on whoopee-cushion humor and gently provocative one-upmanship.

After sixteen years in the service, Anthony worked at the Chatham dockyards, specializing in naval ordnance—and occasionally, when the shipwork slacked off, sawing up wood shelving. This was his situation when I had last seen him. Since then we had exchanged exactly two letters, and he had amassed a small fortune working for British Aerospace in Saudi Arabia.

No matter how much or little Anthony was earning, he always maintained a certain stylishness; whether he was well off or flat broke hardly affected his polished appearance. Even while sawing wood, he drove an elaborate late-model Citroën (which he got cheap in France), ate at fashionable restaurants where he ordered the finest wines, and was impeccably suited out. Anthony is not only a crack bomb disposal specialist and at home with any kind of munition, including handguns, but also a self-styled expert in just about everything else as well.

From among the milling crowd of travelers at the San José airport stepped an immaculate gray-suited figure, sort of a cross between Roger Moore and Terry-Thomas. "Ah, there you are, Brother!" (He has always addressed me as "Brother," never "George." I have always called him "Anthony," because Mum does, instead of "Tony," which everyone else does and which he prefers.) All about us shrieked weeping Costa Ri-

215

cans hugging their kin in hysterical reunions. Many had un-doubtedly returned from shopping junkets to the capital of Latin America, Miami. None of this emotional rubbish for the Brothers Meegan, however, six years' separation or no. With Margaret looking on, we were content to shake hands—after all, we *are* English.

"Look!" he said, and pointed at the black leather tag on his pigskin valise. "It's the Concorde name tag. First Class only, you know, Brother—all the champagne you want." An-thony wanted to take a taxi, but Margaret would have none of it, and on the two-hour bus ride Anthony rambled on about how Ayumi was a "problem child," how Yoshiko insisted on picking her up whenever she cried, how Yoshiko was again smoking cigarettes. Now I was beginning to get a picture of what was going on in Rainham: Yoshiko was suffering from that dreaded malady, only too familiar to me, of "guest com-plex"—the total loss of freedom one experiences after staying too long in someone else's home.

Anthony brought me up to date about his life since the dockyard days. While in Saudi Arabia he had somehow wran-gled an extra job teaching European-style show jumping to the Royal Horse Guard and had made close friends with one of the numerous princes of the extensive royal family. All told, his tax-free salary and sensible investments had allowed him to retire at the grand old age of thirty-five. Thanks to his generosity, I was a thousand dollars richer on his arrival; without it, I would have had to walk Guatemala and Mexico on zero funds.

Anthony was under orders from Mum to feed me and smarten me up. First I was taken to a barber, then to the tailor, where I metamorphosed from a roadside caterpillar into a jet-set butterfly. Now at last I looked smart and dignified. It was awful. As if the populace smelled betrayal, the friendly waves I was used to getting from Ticos in the streets of San José abruptly ceased. Next followed a series of lavish meals. It was days before I could get into the decadent swing of three-hour lunches, and I never became comfortable with the idea that nearly a hundred dollars a day was being spent on food. My delicate system and whole approach to food, developed over several hundred days, simply collapsed and was washed away with the white wine.

After twelve days of such extravagance, I saw Anthony off at the airport. As I handed him his pigskin valise, he pointed to a black leather tag and said, "Have you seen this?"

"No, Anthony. What is it?"

Anthony rolled his eyes toward heaven. "It's the Concorde name tag, silly. First Class only, you know, Brother— all the champagne you want." We shook hands, and he was gone.

After weeks of basking in the balmy climate of the Meseta Central, it was a rude shock to descend four thousand feet into the torrid coastal lowlands, but it felt wonderful to be back on the road again. I was jubilant; I was free. And at last I was once more making progress.

At the Puntarenas cutoff I headed northwest along the Inter-American Highway and was still walking by nightfall— but nervously and oh, so cautiously. Twice drivers stopped to warn me that at several points they had seen hundreds of yard-long snakes slithering across the road. In the hour before sundown I counted eight snakes on the road, both dead and alive. Fearing they might still be out after nightfall, I stamped and shouted as I walked along, hoping this would somehow save my legs from being a target. A light appeared ahead and led me to the sanctuary of a hacienda owned by a Cuban exile, where I spent the night in a hammock. The morning was reminiscent of a biblical plague as I stepped on and over dozens of crushed, dull-colored snakes.

I was now making my way through the foothills of the country's northern mountain range, the Cordillera de Guancaste, cattle country. As it borders Nicaragua, during the recently concluded civil war it had been the site of training bases for the Sandinista rebels. On several occasions the Nicaraguan dictator Samoza had even threatened to "liberate" the province.

Slowly I was returning to my old regime. Again I could

take real pleasure in satisfying my hunger with a raw onion on bread. Now that food was less easily available it took on dearer meaning, and I might desire a tomato at day's end far more than lobster thermidor. My clothes were again the familiar faded and tattered ones; the new clothes Anthony had purchased for me I redistributed en route. It wasn't that I didn't like or appreciate them, it was simply that to wander about dressed like Beau Brummell was the most blatant invitation to robbery.

Ensuring my safety on the road consistently required a combination of planning, observation, and an indefinable sixth sense. This last factor had come into play several times, most recently three days out of San José. Reaching a roadside tienda at sundown, I had no sooner bought a Coke than the storekeeper offered me some floor space for the night. I was about to accept—indeed, this was my target for the day—but something inside stopped me. Perhaps I wanted a few extra kilometers. Who knows? In any event, the next morning a driver stopped to tell me that the storekeeper was dead. During the night a burglar had broken in and buried a dagger in the man's back. Had I narrowly escaped a similar fate by chance alone? Or did some force prevent me from staying there? Whatever was responsible, dozens of similar incidents on that seven-year trek eventually persuaded me that I had been surrounded by an "envelope of protection." After completing the walk I no longer sensed the presence of this envelope, and I never again felt quite so secure as when I was walking, perpetually walking north.

By the second week of November, I reached the town of Liberia. The week's progress had been terribly slow. But progress was progress, I rationalized—at least each step that never had to be repeated was a step nearer home. Outside the last town, I spied a surprisingly familar orange glow: a tent like mine. Of all improbable combinations, inside were three Health Department inspectors from Southampton. They invited me to share their dinner, and I was amazed to see how willingly they tucked into the local rice and slop, as though they had been brought up on the stuff and not good old fish-

and-chips. After two months they had perfectly adapted, while after nearly three years I had perfectly not adapted. Much of the time on the road I would yearn for Yorkshire pudding or Irish stew. On parting, we all shook hands, and I watched them cycle away into the east. In a few hours they would cover the distance that had taken me three days to hack out, and with that thought in mind I turned and marched north-west, toward Nicaragua and popular revolution.

Nicaragua

I crossed the muddy *frontera* into Nicaragua in the company of a small group of international flotsam—two German hikers, perhaps a missionary or a nurse, no one you could really call a tourist—while battle-equipped soldiers of the Sandinista Front spaced at short intervals glared at us with mock sinister purpose. As everyone was aware of the recent triumph of the revolution, we all walked in respectful silence. Talk was replaced by staring—at a child, no more than ten years old, in full uniform; at a portrait, nailed to a telephone pole, of César Augusto Sandino, the martyred hero of the half-century-old revolution; at the posters, tacked up all about, shouting out their revolutionary slogans—"Death to Somoza," "No More Yankee Puppets."

At the chaotic Immigration control, an ad hoc affair consisting of two mismatched tables set up in the roadside dust, a bearded soldier in olive drabs spoke to me in English: "Welcome to the new Socialist Republic of Nicaragua." He then took me aside and whispered, with an anticipatory nod, "Have you any pot for your friends?" In another world he might have been a laid-back, doped-up product of American higher education (which, for all I knew, he was). But here in his homeland he was the very model of a modern revolutionary. He went through my gear in a perfunctory manner.

No bombs here, nor, more importantly, dope or dirty books. He was clearly bored with this routine—it was just another job. No more the heady days of guerrilla raids or of bloody battles about León.

A girl so plump she was nearly bursting through her green fatigues took our passports and disappeared. After a fretful half hour the soldier who had searched my gear reappeared carrying an armful of passports and unceremoniously dumped the load on one of the roadside tables. Almost immediately pandemonium broke loose.

"I had a bus ticket in the back of mine," screamed one girl. "Now it's gone!"

"What about the two passports he dropped in the road?" shouted someone else.

"Anybody seen any vaccination certificates?"

The terms of the visas granted us were as mixed up as the documents. The German couple were told they had forty-eight hours and then had to leave the country; I was given no time limit at all. Whatever you got or needed, it was arbitrary, no reasons given. I asked my laid-back soldier friend how long I actually had. "Who knows, man? Perhaps you'll stay forever." I hoped not.

Suddenly a shout arose; the soldier unholstered his pistol and began firing it into the air as he ran toward his compatriots. It was four o'clock—time to close the border. All hell broke loose as rifles, machine guns, absolutely everything ripped into the air and raked the surrounding bush, hundreds of rounds spent in a display of revolutionary bravado. Clearly this was not a place for an afternoon walk with the family dog.

Past the frontier, once the huge tractor-trailers with their hooting, waving drivers had stopped passing my way, the road became desolate. The countryside appeared to be littered with burned-out and abandoned huts. I was told that the ebullient National Guard leader "Commander Bravo" had run wild and roughshod over this region (in return he was tortured to death in Tegucigalpa, Honduras). Only slowly were families returning to their homes to restore something of their ruptured lives.

Halfway into this ruined land I suddenly beheld, like a

vision from another world, a vast blue body of water, its surface laced with shimmering streaks of silver beneath the afternoon sun—Lago Nicaragua. Poking up from the center of the lake were two great, green cones—the volcanoes Concepción and Madera, standing free and clear like two gorgeous breasts. As I gawked at this sight, while billowy white clouds drifted behind the twin peaks, to my utter delight a puff of smoke escaped from the cone of Madera.

Back to political reality, all along the road to Rivas I passed bullet-riddled wrecks of vehicles that had been brusquely pushed over to the shoulder. On the outskirts of town, next to a well-tended garden, an armored car lay overturned, its rusted, wounded side open to the sky. An elderly woman who reminded me of Mum momentarily left her garden-tending and spoke to me over the wood fence. "Two boys from the 'Front' came into the house and waited behind my bedroom dresser for two hours. When this armored car drew near . . ." and she paused, recalling the scene in surrealistic wonder, ". . . when it drew near they blew it up with their bazooka. Then they machine-gunned the ones running away."

In Rivas the roadside was strewn with broken stonework, scraps of metal, smashed glass, and the odd plastic bucket. It was nighttime, and because the town was poorly lit—there was only an occasional weak lampbulb swinging in the breeze from the broken lampposts—I moved cautiously through a veritable minefield of potholes. Roads in Latin America typically abound with unexpected protrusions and hidden holes, war or not, but throughout Nicaragua many of the streets had clearly not been maintained in years. (The Inter-American Highway here was especially bad, with long stretches of broken *pavimento*.) None of the cafés was open. I could find no eggs, no chocolate, pretty much nothing. I spent the night on the floor of the Cruz Roja (Red Cross) building, one side of which was entirely blown out. On the remaining walls I could still see traces of splattered blood that soap had diluted but could not completely remove.

In daylight, Rivas was an even sorrier sight. The church by the main plaza was scorched black by the fires that the

Guardia Nacional (National Guard) had set in their failed attempt to torch the town. The rebels had seized the initiative and gutted the Guardia post, which now stood in silence while grass grew atop the collapsed rubble. All of Rivas—indeed, much of Nicaragua—was riddled with bulletholes. An otherwise unremarkable wall might have a hundred or more. Passing the Memorial para las Madres (Mothers' Memorial) in Rivas, I saw that even this hallowed monument had been indiscriminately raked with machine-gun fire.

Just beyond Rivas stood a fort—now a jail filled with Somocistas—guarded on all sides by sentries with fixed bayonets. Formerly used to hold captured Sandinista rebels, it was now filled to bursting with Somocistas awaiting trial, including one hapless old general who had just been called up out of retirement only to suffer this ignominious fate. Had this been an Iranian-style revolution, everyone would have been taken out and summarily shot. The Sandinista Front, to its credit, had no truck with this sort of thing. They had even abolished the death penalty.

On this stretch of the Inter-American Highway, I was the constant object of insults and threats shouted at me by the drivers and passengers of passing vehicles. To them my blond hair marked me as just another "Yankee bastard." This virulent anti-Americanism didn't arise solely from recent events— the United States had been arming Somoza's government until Jimmy Carter, in response to reports of human rights violations, cut off aid altogether—but had roots in events going back a century. In the mid-1800's an American mercenary, William Walker, was hired by local politicians to settle a squabble and ended up running the country; the United States even recognized Walker's short-lived regime. In 1909, when the Nicaraguan government defaulted on several large loans, a consortium of New York banks literally appropriated the nation's economy. And when a rebellion threatened the status quo in 1912, the United States sent the marines into Nicaragua, where they remained, except for a short break, for twenty-one years.

After the departure of the marines, American interests

were effectively protected by Anastasio Somoza, head of the Guardia Nacional, who eventually emerged as the government's strongman and ruled as president from 1937 until his assassination in 1956. (Sandino, one of the most effective dissidents in the 1930's, was captured and shot by Somoza's Guardia, and his name has been memorialized ever since in the name of the opposition, the Sandinistas.) Two of Somoza's sons succeeded him as president, and the last Somoza was holding office right up until the Sandinistas' ultimate victory.

During the afternoon heat, with Rivas at my back, I stopped for rest at a stick hut. The hut's barefoot owner was desolate. "Today they took my last, my only cow. What can I do? How can I approach the authorities when it is they who took her?" Despite his painful dilemma, he bade me climb the tree outside his hut for a papaya so that I could enjoy its sweet orange pulp. The magnanimity of his gesture touched me; I couldn't even be certain that he had much else to eat. He refused to take money, so I left some in a tin mug where he could find it.

My night stop was the village of Belén, a wretched place whose mud streets were populated by starving, sad-eyed dogs. I wandered about until, as often happened, a family's questions turned into an invitation to stay the night. But first, by way of *turismo*, they took me to the local church, whose walls had been chipped by a thousand bullets and cratered by cannon shells. A few months before, I was told, a small band of guerrillas, women among them, had been surrounded here by a unit of the Guardia, who blasted their way into the church, cutting throats and slashing off women's breasts as they went. While standing at the site of this atrocity, I asked one of the daughters what she had missed most during the civil war. Her answer might have been that of women everywhere: "Well, for me personally, it was the shortage of, how you say . . . Max Factor."

During the long walk back to their house, night drew on, and with it wild drinking in a makeshift cantina on the tall, uncut grass in the center of the town. Curses flew through the air in my general direction; everyone who spotted me seemed to be in a belligerent mood. I kept my silence—one garbled Spanish phrase from me could have been turned knife-quick into a minor incident. It was with great relief that the nervous family and I managed, backs to the wall, to edge away from the throng and into their house.

The father told me that his youngest son, a thirteen-year-old boy, had been given a five-year government scholarship to attend school in Cuba. (I had already seen Cuban school-teachers in Rivas, and read reports that there were two thousand Cuban professionals in the country—engineers and doctors as well as teachers, all sorely needed. Commandante Humberto Ortega, I'm told, had said that American doctors were most welcome, but he personally doubted they could leave their fat salaries behind.) This man's son was, in fact, now in Cuba, in the thick of his studies—mainly Marxism-Leninism. The boy's latest letter included a postcard showing a portrait of Lenin, which the boy had colored a poisonous green. The situation appalled and saddened me—why wasn't he being prepared for a career in, say, civil engineering? The parents refrained from making judgments. They were content knowing that their son was special, that he had been chosen. These were simple folk and trusted their new leaders—who, after all, were from the people.

"Strap on your pistols—we march on Masaya," are the words Somoza, resplendent in the uniform of a five-star general, was reported to have told his demoralized officers. They did, the assault failed, and the civil war ended shortly thereafter. I, too, marched on Masaya, but with a more benign purpose. I entered the provincial capital through the hills to the south and was given a U.S. Army camp bed for the night by the Cuerpo de Bomberos—the firefighters. During the heaviest fighting, part of the firehouse roof had been blown off by an artillery round. Even the fire truck had received a tank shell. "Had the Guardia no respect for the fire corps?" I asked an officer. "Oh, no," he said, "not at all. They shoot at us, la Cruz Roja, anything."

Near the firehouse, a Made-in-U.S.A. "purely defensive"

bomb, a five hundred-pounder, had been dropped, killing and mutilating a lot of ordinary people. This sort of thing, when combined with the unfortunate history of Americans in Nicaragua, only served to pour gasoline on the smoldering fire of anti-Americanism.

A fork in the road lay just ahead, and I faced a major decision. For months I had been asking myself: Should I walk through El Salvador, or walk around it, through Honduras? For three years I had looked forward to walking El Salvador—certainly not because of its appalling political situation, but because of its distinction as the smallest nation in the Americas. I could be through the whole country in a week! (It had taken me over a year just to traverse Argentina.) But three hundred civilians a week were reportedly being killed there; I might just be number three hundred and one.

But what about Honduras? Taking the route to Honduras would mean making a huge detour over to the Caribbean. Moreover, Honduras, after Haiti, is the poorest country in the Western Hemisphere. Taking that route would probably mean going hungry much of the time. In Nicaragua I had already lost weight in places where I had had absolutely none to lose. I kept wavering in my decision. No, I did not want to walk Honduras.

The fork was upon me. Without hesitation I glided to the northerly course that by and by would bring me to Honduras.

With little traffic to watch out for, I dashed on at a good lick. A tiny Swiss flag that I had attached to my gear fluttered behind me. I had picked up the flag at L'Escargot, one of Anthony's swank restaurants in San José, and was displaying it on the theory that it would defuse hostility; after all, Switzerland (unlike Britain) had no imperial background to raise a revolutionary's ire. (In fact, I could claim some right to carrying it, for Mum was born in Switzerland.) The flag now drew the attention of a Sandinista toting a submachine gun, who signaled for me to pull over and addressed me forcefully. "You are not a Swiss. You are a Yankee bastard—pretending to be a Swiss."

"I'm not, I'm not," I protested strongly. "I'm an *inglés* bastard pretending to be Swiss." My clumsy admission apparently disarmed the chap, who motioned me with his gun to pass.

The region I was now moving through vibrated with a denser population, and their dwellings were everywhere to be seen along the road. Above each humble mud *casa*, on a tall bamboo pole, flew the colors of the Sandinista Front. There were hundreds of them, as far as I could see, clear to the horizon. I was alive and aware beyond words. The scene was absolutely medieval. I imagined them to be the huts of the serfs of old, dominated by the sinister-looking red-black banners, which streamed and danced in the wind, their cracking the only sound in that silent countryside beneath the cobalt-blue sky. I felt I should have been astride a white horse, part of a conquering army, perhaps the Moors on their glorious ascent of the Iberian Peninsula.

At last I reached Managua. The sight of the capital city came as a shock. All indications told me I was in Managua, but where was Managua? The streets were silent. Where were the hundreds of thousands of inhabitants? I wandered about and found a fire station. From the roof I could see the lake, a crisscross of empty streets, and what looked like a grassy plain, and in the midst of this surreal landscape, where a city once stood, a large cathedral that stood out almost rudely in its naked exposure. Back down on the street, upon closer inspection I saw that the grassy plain was overgrown vegetation, which was gradually enveloping the debris of block after block of flattened buildings. Here and there stood jagged pillars of rubble, like solitary teeth in an old man's mouth. Particularly eerie was the almost total absence of normal city noise. Nature was reclaiming the city: Plants grew stoutly through the wreckage, and the song of woodland birds drifted through the air.

This state of affairs was only partly the result of civil war; even more devastating had been the 1972 earthquake. In a span of less than three hours a series of catastrophic tremors had virtually obliterated the city, leaving tens of thousands dead and injured, most of them in the poorer barrios where the adobe-brick dwellings had crumbled like cheesecake. Not much later, before any real effort at rebuilding could be made, war trundled through, with its grim toll of yet more destruction. Poor Managua! In short order, the Four Horsemen of the Apocalypse had ridden straight through.

The situation was fraught with ironies. Nicaragua today sees its greatest threat coming from the United States, with some reason. Yet in 1972, the first tangible aid for the earthquake victims began arriving within twenty-four hours of the initial tremors from those same United States. The arrival of food, clothing, and medical supplies at the surrounding airfields for once galvanized the Guardia into action. They organized the transportation of these materials and in their zeal even commandeered private vehicles. Many in the Guardia, however, were thinking not about the desperately needy, but about the desperately greedy—themselves. With suffering all about them—seven thousand eventually died and two hundred thousand were left homeless—the Guardia, it was reported, were busy looting the destitute and actually hindering their relief.

A final irony: As in any earthquake, in 1972 the residents of Managua panicked, many running into the safety of the streets to escape collapsing buildings. In the midst of this, perhaps the most improbable and bizarre sight was the pathetic form of a man more emaciated than a Managuan beggar: It was billionaire Howard Hughes, who had been shaken out of the penthouse suite of the capital's Inter-Continental Hotel.

From the main cathedral, where a twenty-five-foot-high painting of Sandino stood propped up against the shattered stonework, I strolled over to the General Assembly building. This had been the scene of a famous episode at the start of the civil war when a handful of Sandinistas had taken over the entire institution, holding as hostage about twelve hundred parliamentarians and office workers—a world record. The whole incident was negotiated smoothly by the rebels' "Comman-dante Zero" and a lady lawyer, and miraculously no one was hurt.

Across town the offices of the newspaper *La Prensa* were not hard to spot. Outside stood an enormous rusted printing press, almost half a block long; wrecked by the government, it had become a de facto memorial to all the victims of cen-sorship. The day I visited was the first anniversary of the murder of Joaquín Chamorro, the paper's owner and editor-in-chief, the incident that had finally sparked all-out civil war. Chamorro's widow, Violeta, had become a member of the rul-ing junta—its most liberal member, in fact. (After eight months she resigned in protest.)

To get a breather from the squalor, I spent most of an evening hanging around the Inter-Continental Hotel (the same of Howard Hughes fame). Because it was the only first-class hotel in the city, the Inter-Continental was a revolving door of domestic and foreign dignitaries. As I lounged about the lobby I recognized the black-bereted Nicaraguan minister of culture, Ernesto Cardenal Martínez, who was also, I was sur-prised to learn, a Jesuit priest. (Later the pope ordered him to resign his civil office, and when he refused he was sus-pended from the priesthood.)

In the lobby I picked up a copy of the *Miami Herald*—the most popular American newspaper in Latin America—and was shocked to read for the first time of the Soviet invasion of Afghanistan. My first reaction was one of indignation and outrage, and my feelings for the Soviets hardly improved when a moment later three men in business suits speaking Russian stepped off the American-made elevator. I could understand Nicaraguans' feelings about Americans, even if I violently dis-agreed with the popular characterization of them as "enemies of humanity," but what-in-hell's-name good could the Rus-sians possibly do in this smashed nation? Greatly saddened and fearful for decent, ordinary Nicaraguans, I left the hotel and kicked a stone all the way back to the darkened fire sta-tion where I had been allowed to spend the night.

Before leaving Managua I picked up my mail at the prearranged dropoff and found a letter from Yoshiko in Japan. In it she chastised me for thinking the worst—"You surprised me that you did not know or doubted me if I don't love my husband!"—and went on to explain why she had left Rainham:

> Mum and I did not have any troubles, but only pressure each other because of the different way to live and think. Also Mum is a person who worry about others very much—you know this. She was always trying to do her best for me and thinking of me and Ayumi. To me this was too much and she is too perfect person to me to feel comfortable. Because as you know I am a such "mas-o-menos" woman for housekeeping.

Yoshiko went on to discuss the matters Anthony had mentioned, such as her cigarette smoking—"Yes, I started to smoke again in Rainham and still do just occasionally when I really want. I believe this does not hurt our new baby." She ended by reassuring me about the walk. "Yes, I want to live together with you as soon as possible, but I want you to finish your walk only when you feel content."

Never mind a strained leg and back pain. After a period of inactivity, it was a joy to be trudging the endless road again. The sun was strong, and a fresh breeze picked up the dust in the increasingly lonely landscape. Yet as the houses and huts became fewer, food became a problem. Rice and beans, the two staples that represent the bulk of the grim fare of the average Latin American, were both in short supply. These were hard days to be a Nicaraguan. In Costa Rica I had bought a twelve-ounce tin of Planter's peanuts for a crushing five U.S. dollars. Now I was glad to have it, for it proved to be my principal food for five days.

Once back in the countryside, I resolved to march through the rest of Nicaragua quickly. My appearance, indistinguishable from that of the hated gringos, made me a target here, and there was no reason to prolong the situation. The problem wasn't the Sandinista troops. They were for the most part friendly. In fact, one of them literally gave me the shirt off his back. "Hey, gringo, where ya going?" he first said. This was on an empty stretch of road high above a valley before the town of Darío. Two young military police of the Liberation Front driving by in a jeep had stopped to question me. They got out while their girl companion waited in the vehicle.

"I'm walking through Nicaragua, your republic." At this the three of them let out a spontaneous cheer. The girl now got out of the jeep and offered me a plastic bag full of sweet ice, bound at the neck, with a straw dangling into the slush. As I gratefully sucked the synthetic udder dry they asked me more questions: "Where are you from? What are you doing here?" Prodded by their enthusiasm, I revealed more than I normally do. When they learned I was English, this pleased them enormously—at least I was not an American. (I met only two other Englishmen in my entire walk of Nicaragua.) I finished my story: ". . . and I'm the only man to have walked from Argentina to Nicaragua—and I'm going to try to reach Alaska." They were speechless, simply overcome with joy. My original interrogator, a well-built fellow, now introduced himself as Bismarck, removed his shirt, and with great ceremony placed it on top of the ragged one I was wearing—"for friendship's sake," he said.

"You must be careful, Jorge," were Bismarck's last words to me as he did up the buttons. "Our sun will burn you." To this day I clearly remember, in the magic moment that followed, the chill wind singing past the telephone wire high above us. As we stood on the bleak hillside, a shirtless Sandinista and a double-shirted Englishman, we were one. He had never asked, "Why?" He knew. We were brothers; he had seen the dream.

Past Darío my dash to beat dusk one evening found me in San Isidro. The entire town was a vast junkyard, the streets littered with debris and boulders. There was no electricity, and so the only light came from a few dim oil lamps. A revolutionary unit that had seized a dank stonework one-story building for their headquarters gave me permission to lay down my sleeping bag and gleefully showed me their huge collection of guns, knives, and cudgels. Most of them were boys, some of them barely in their teens, all seemingly out of place in their green fatigues, black boots, and cartridge belts. One soldier, a girl, wore a six-shooter strapped to her side that had notches carved in the handle. Despite the arms spilling about everywhere, I felt absolutely safe here. (At least they exhibited none of the arrogant swagger of the military elsewhere.)

The soldiers, like so many kids left to their own devices, lived in shocking filth. Here (and, unfortunately, everywhere else in Nicaragua) I couldn't even find a place to put my toothbrush. Every surface within range of a sink, bucket, or faucet was perpetually covered with either dirt or debris, or both. The headquarters' backyard was a no-man's-land of latrines choked with refuse. Despite the staggering stench I managed to sleep the night through, awakened only when the troops assembled to sing a patriotic anthem as they hoisted up the Sandinista flag in the morning (I never once saw the blue and white national flag flown).

Over the hills and through intermittent showers, I pushed on. Food was becoming even more of a problem. Sifting through the trash thrown from the few southbound cars, I deduced from the evidence of a discarded hamburger wrapping that there must be a McDonald's in the next town, Estelí. I was sadly mistaken. Estelí, badly smashed about and in parts even blown to bits, had nothing to offer at all. I searched about for milk. *"No hay, señor,"* I was told. *"Solo para los niños"*—only for the babies. Eminently reasonable, but bad news for an exhausted tramp. I approached a noisy dining hall and kept on going when the patrons began screaming abuse at me through the smashed windows. I began to nurse my few remaining peanuts with still miles to go before the next town.

Lack of food had an unintended benefit: My senses were

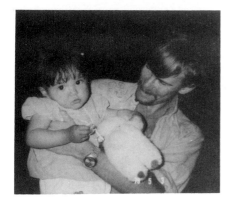

At long last I hold my daughter Ayumi-Chan. Panama. April 1979.

Together with Choique in Patagonia.

Bedtime with my daughter Ayumi. Central Panama mountains.

Family in Panama. August 1979.

Right: With brother Anthony in Costa Rica. November 1979.

Below: "Any dope for your friends?" asked the Sandinista border guard. Nicaragua. December 1979.

Below: A moment of rest. Honduras. January 1980.

Hot as hell. Mexico. March 1980.

Right: The endless road north. Guatemala. March 1980.

Below: I clear the tropics. Mexico, June 1980.

On the road in Texas, family together. November 1981.

Reunion. Texas. August 1981.

In President Carter's garden, Plains, Georgia.

Happiness on the road. Virginia. May 1981.

Senator Dale Bumpers (D. Arkansas) wants to know "Why?" The Capitol. Washington, D.C. May 1981.

Crossing the George Washington Bridge. New York. September 1981.

Toseko and family in British
Columbia.

Yoshiko camping on the Alaska
Highway. May 1983.

Sloshing through British
Columbia. July 1982.

Left: Looking toward the last frontier. Alaska. June 1983.

Below: Last full day on the tundra. Alaska. August 1983.

Yoshi's Mazda. Yukon Territory. Canada.

Above: Celebrating the last steps of the 19,091 mile walk.

Right: The bitter end. Beaufort Sea. September 18, 1983.

Below: All my family together aboard the *QE II*, October 1983.

exceedingly clear and sharp these days. The entire country-side vibrated in extraordinary Van Gogh colors as I marched under a powder-blue sky dotted with powderpuff clouds. The brisk breeze seemed to blow straight through my body and mind. Truly, I was alive and living my dream.

That was during the daytime, but Condago at night was as black as hell. In a dark alley I couldn't see my hand as I urinated against a chipped wall—but a young soldier saw me. He criticized me for my antisocial conduct and said it was unbecoming in the New Nicaragua. I apologized to the child with the rifle, and made sure to address him as "sir."

The road to Ocotal was peppered with billboards advertising a swank hotel with a swimming pool. What luxury! Alas, my funds would never cover this. Still, judging by the ghastly state of the rooms I had seen so far in Nicaragua, they would probably have to pay me to stay there. Fate lent a hand, however, and I did in fact end up staying at the fancy hotel of the billboards. The premises, after all that, were in a state of near-total collapse and had been most recently commandeered as a Red Cross center. The glamorous furnishings were all smashed or had long since been taken away. The water supply consisted of two halves of a forty-five-gallon oil drum that had been sawn in two and filled with a nasty brown liquid, and the once-regal swimming pool was clogged with turgid muck and rusting bedframes.

The most common sight in Ocotal was of the townsfolk transporting five-gallon bottles of water on their heads—there was no permanent supply of tapwater. This supplemented the water that was brought up from the muddy river by mule trains, each animal burdened with two large, rectangular, decapitated paint cans. Each trip saw perhaps a third of the water lost as it slopped over the edges—an endless, heartbreaking business.

At the border were gathered large units of troops; some even recognized me from various points on the march, and we exchanged joking greetings and waves as I passed. It was always a minor celebration when I had crossed another country, and whenever I reached a border I would try to sum up my feelings. I had heard so much about Nicaragua, both pro and con, and yet if I had been pressed to make some snap political judgment or philosophical reflection after this strange passage, I would have come up empty. Rather, what stood out in my mind were the people themselves, like the old peasant who bade me climb his tree for a papaya, and young Bismarck doing up my shirt buttons. Good-bye, Nicaragua—and good luck.

Honduras

Past the border, I kept pace for a while with some Hondreño troops on the march and swapped banter with the friendly young men. When the squad finally peeled off into the bush, their bayonets glinting red in the setting sun, I once again settled into my plodding rhythm. Once again, this time with some relief, I was alone.

My horizon was filled with Honduras; the clean, sweet smell of pine and fir trees filled my world. My spirit soared as I skipped and jumped and made animal calls all the way down into the dark valley and town below. Even in the dark, El Paraíso seemed brighter and somehow more hopeful than any place I had seen in ravaged Nicaragua. No wreckage or rubble littered the streets, some of the *casas* had even seen a lick of paint, and to my amazement I soon stumbled upon a *supermercado*—a supermarket—complete with strip lighting and shiny turnstiles. Food! I'd been longing for it, dreaming of it, for endless weeks.

Temporarily passing up the supermarket, I went straight to a hotel, where I ordered dinner and sat waiting for it, almost quaking in anticipation. When dinner arrived I tore into it. After a ravenous initial burst I suddenly felt breathless and bloated. My enthusiasm wilted on the spot; I pecked a little but soon gave up altogether. Defeated and mystified, I scraped the plateful into my kit and departed. It was days before I could even approach a proper meal, for my stomach must have changed during the silent, hungry days just past, and all I could manage for nearly a week was a little soup and milk.

The police post let me stay the night; the corporal in charge even made a token effort to sweep the dust off the cement floor where I was to bed down. The gesture was well taken, coming as it did from the unexpected quarter of government authority. I slept well enough, if somewhat stiffly. As I lay there before drifting off into sleep, my mind echoed the sentiment of the name of a Honduran *departamento: Gracias a Dios*—Thanks Be to God.

Leaving town, I headed inland through rich timberlands along a road that led in the direction of the capital, Tegucigalpa, which I estimated to be at least a three-day walk away. On the outskirts a group of Latino hitchhikers subjected me to a familiar good-natured jeering as I trudged by. One of the crowd stuck out, his slicked-back haircut making him look like a swarthy James Dean. James Dean hollered after me, "In two hours, *amigo,* we will reach La Capital!" Not long after this, the hitchhikers shot by me in the back of a flatbed truck, hooting with gusto and leaving me coughing in the wake of their exhaust fumes.

That night, finding myself short of my day's objective, I was given a berth in the corner of a rude stick hut—a small bed made of sticks tied together with leather thongs and topped off by a straw mattress. Several children pottered about, while one clung to a woman in a dusty, dull blue smock. The woman retrieved a couple of half-burned twigs from the deadened cooking fire (to conserve fuel in the Third World, fires are dampened the instant food is cooked). She proceeded to fry an egg for me, taking her cooking oil from a gallon jug that shone like a golden treasure under the dim lamplight. Examining the container, I saw the same phrase printed on its side in several languages, headed by the bold notice, "SOYBEAN OIL. A GIFT OF THE PEOPLE OF THE U.S.A." When she saw what I was doing, the woman ran her hand over the polished metal and, smiling, said, *"Regalo de la gente de los Estados Unidos."* I thought it unlikely that she could read (nearly half of all Honduras cannot), but she still clearly knew where the oil had come from. At least this particular item of foreign aid had found its way exactly to where it was needed. American taxpayers can share in this poor campesina's happy pride and my own gratitude for an egg cooked in soybean oil.

Indeed, throughout Honduras I never heard the usual scapegoat claptrap about evil Americans. Almost continuous goodwill was expressed toward Yankees, something most of Latin America (and much of the rest of the world) considers almost unpatriotic. As one storekeeper said to me, rather in the manner of showing off a favorite operation scar, "In this *república* we Hondreños actually *like* the Americanos."

After traversing and climbing out of the Zamorano Valley, I finally spied Tegucigalpa below; it was now plain-sailing, downhill all the way. Ever since the outskirts of Danlí I had regularly caught up with, passed, and in turn been overtaken by the young hitchhikers, who each time were more footsore and dejected and fewer in number. Just before the suburbs of the capital, I spied a familiar figure, the last of these hapless travelers, now only a few yards ahead—"James Dean," of course. As I, the tortoise, drew abreast of the hare, I winked and could not for the life of me resist saying, "In two hours, *amigo, I* will reach La Capital!"

Tegucigalpa is a small, unpretentious city of less than a half-million that sits smack in a basin surrounded by mountains. The skyline is unbroken by the towering shafts of glass and steel that everywhere else are taken as tokens of "modernization." Instead, small whitewashed houses with red tile roofs still hide behind barred courtyard gates, just as in colonial times.

My walk about this quiet city should have been pleasant, but my condition was still weak—due to a series of severe bouts of diarrhea—and so everything seemed just a distraction; even the grand presidential palace reminded me of an elaborate wedding cake. The day before I was stricken yet again, and the night had brought me another worry, a nightmare, all in muted, hellish hues, in which I saw the corpse of my beloved Yoshiko in a black plastic bodybag. I was scared, and the next morning, still troubled by my dream, I shot off a desperate note to Yoshiko. My morbid state of mind was such that when I strolled over to the British Embassy—for the usual reasons: to get a taste of home, perhaps read the London papers—I ended up asking the ambassador, in the event of my death in Honduras, to ship my body back home to Rainham.

On a side street I ran into an American doctor and his blond Russian wife who seemed to be wandering about with no special purpose in mind. We chatted, and he took a serious interest in my health, telling me to watch my diet very carefully. "Your bowels can kill you," he said. "They're a perfect breeding ground for lethal infections." I thanked him for his advice but could not bring myself to tell him that it would do me no good. Most travelers—by which I mean tourists and such—can monitor what they eat. I could not. I ate what I could, when I could, where I could. A good proportion of what I ate was food that poor people shared with me, and to start sterilizing proffered food would be an appalling lapse of manners. The loss in goodwill would far outweigh the gain in hygiene. My defense against all manner of imbibed bugs and filth was my constitution—my immune system—which so far seemed to rejoice in its own evolutionary brilliance, although lately it hadn't been acting so wisely.

At nightfall on the cracked road leading out of Tegucigalpa, the terrain all about me became menacing, and progress, especially downhill, became increasingly uncomfortable as the nagging infection inside me worsened. I began seeing things. Great bulbous hills became deep black shadows under the light of the full moon. The crash and roar of water warned me only a few yards before I drifted across a bridge. Far ahead, stark and horrible, stood a solitary white cross; the moon picked it out like a spotlight. Whichever way the trail happened to twist, the ghoulish symbol remained in view, as though waiting for me. As is often the case in Latin America, this isolated cross marked the spot where some fellow soul had perished, most likely in shock and pain. Someone, just here, had stared death in the face and then seen no more. As I drew close an owl hooted, and the chill fingers of a shiver passed over me.

As I looked up to the luminescent clouds drifting across the blue-black sky the thought drifted across my mind: Perhaps *my* name is written on the cross. Terrified yet fascinated, I reached the foot of the hill and drew abreast of the cross; now it and I were alone in the universe. It shone like the dried bones of dead men, calling like a siren song, but I absolutely refused to pause—dared not pause. To look is to confirm. With an energy that astonished me, I fled to the other side of the hill, nervously singing Christmas carols as I went. Between the face of the cliff and the long drop below, the circuitous trail kept bringing me back into taunting view of the cross, a bleak reminder of my mortality. It seemed to mock me, perhaps laughing its stone pants off to have so rattled a lone Englishman beneath the huge, twinkling stars.

I camped beside a stream, the full moon now high above me. The tent, my friend and home for so long, was now a pathetic sight, so fragile that simply by crawling inside I tore yet another rent in the rotted fabric. As soon as I put my head down to sleep, the ants appeared. There seemed to be hundreds inside the tent; I had probably camped close to a nest. I began sweeping them out, and I inadvertently killed some. As if on command—I saw this clearly by the candle-light—they simultaneously hunkered down and began biting me. Anguished, I addressed the tiny, courageous creatures: "Sorry, ants. I didn't mean to kill any of you. Please, leave me alone, and I'll leave you alone." It was a night for mystical occurrences: I don't know whether ants hear or not, but if they do, these ones clearly understood English. The remaining foragers left me in peace, and I wasn't bothered anymore that night.

I reached Comayagua in the afternoon; the walk had taken much less time than I had expected. Apparently the map I obtained in Tegucigalpa was in error—but for once the error was "in my favor." Wandering the ancient cobbled streets for a place to eat, I found it hard to accept that this nearly empty and desperately quiet town, over four centuries old, had once been the nation's capital. (It lost this status a century before because, as the *South American Handbook* cryptically puts it, the puritanical townspeople "would not tolerate the governor's mistress.")

My next introduction brought my sleeping bag to a spectacular and unusual home, no less than a palace, this one occupied by a bishop. The squat building, complete with two massive wooden doors, sat forlornly behind a maze of ironwork and was now little more than a sad reminder of the city's former glory. No gilded casements here now—just the usual dust and peeling paint. The bishop wasn't at home, but I rested happy: I had a big onion and bread in my bag.

The next day, while I was quenching my thirst at a wayside *pulperia*—the local version of a *tienda* that would have fruit for sale and perhaps kerosene, a few canned items, that sort of thing—a burly man in a cowboy hat struck up a conversation, and before long he invited me to his home a few miles down the road, where I ended up staying two nights. Dr. Jerome V. Mankins, who was half American Indian, had left the States to study tropical insect life. Jerry spent his days, as he put it, "among my bugs," and had established a reputation as the finest entomologist in Central America. His ungainly appearance, however, especially his sausagelike fingers, made him an unlikely candidate for handling tiny insects. He looked more like a boxer, which in fact he had been—among the memorabilia lying around his house was a trophy for winning the middleweight championship of the Pacific Theater in World War II. Other interesting items in his collection included an arrow symbolizing the office of Chief of the Maidu Plains Indians (an office he once held) and another item which he mischievously produced as proof of his favorite hobby, lion taming: a photograph that showed his bald head smack inside a big cat's mouth!

The sky looked threatening when I left Jerry Mankins,

and soon I was sloshing through chilly mountain rain. On the heavily wooded slopes, every now and then I could just make out, through the pervasive deluge, a smoldering charcoal fire being tended patiently by a solitary *campesino*. The crimson glow of one of these fires under a cooking pot filled me with a nostalgia for the baked potatoes and lackluster bangers (sausages) of home, now so dearly missed.

Walking in the interminable cold rain all the way through Taulabe and past Lago de Yojoa hardly helped my still-suffering bladder, and the medication I had been given by a doctor in Comayagua was boldly ineffective. My insides felt like a warm dishcloth in the process of being wrung out. At the same time, my foot, the same leading left that always seemed to be the source of trouble, was causing me to limp badly, which in turn threw my entire body off balance and left my joints aching. On top of this, my right hand was infected and I was covered all over with irritating insect bites. The whole Caribbean coastline was rotten with mosquitoes. Just reading the names off the map could curdle the blood. The Costa de Mosquitoes, with its much-harassed Moskitos Indians, ran straight north from Nicaragua; Honduras even had its own Departamento Mosquitia. And off the coast lay the Cayos Mosquito—Mosquito Islands—and beyond the Darien Gap the entire coastline of Panama sat on the Golfo de los (what else?) Mosquitos.

Beyond Potrerillos, the road dropped down into the hot and muggy lowlands; at least now I wasn't shivering. But after Pimienta, as I headed toward Guatemala, each single step shook up the inside of my bladder. For twelve million paces, it seemed, I had never noticed the continuous shakeup the body gets from walking. The last mile before the road fork took so much out of me that I had to stop and drop to my knees every few minutes just to regain my senses. After I did this a few times, I began to imagine, as I squatted motionless and delirious on the blacktop, that the passing mestizos must regard me as some religious nut who had suddenly found enlightenment. Mind you, such bizarre behavior of the "gringo hippies" was generally tolerated, even expected. To the good-natured masses of this continent, it was a humorous diversion, a welcome break in their humdrum and often hard lives.

In the closest town, San Pedro Sula, the bomberos favored me with a dusty, ancient cot in the corner of an unlit storage closet full of fire equipment. Although it was not yet evening, I slumped down on the top of my bag and stayed in the jammed closet until morning, neither eating nor sleeping, just feeding on a headful of nagging fears. Overwhelming anxiety had become my steadfast companion. Were my kidneys on the verge of falling apart? Would I be able to reverse the course of this decline? Could I walk even a few more miles under the present distress? The idea of crossing another country, let alone the immensity of another continent, was staggering. Tomorrow for sure, I kept telling myself, I must find a doctor.

For hours I tossed sleeplessly, helplessly slapping the incessant mosquitoes. From the depths of my mind arose the most frightening question of all: Are you losing your grip, old son? Maybe a few marbles loose? Perhaps going bonkers? It's amazing how an abstract idea like that can take hold, attracting your attention and just floating about in a soup of brain waves and electrons, saying, "Hey, look at me!" It seemed to color my every thought. Not even the *Time* magazine I read intermittently by candlelight could distract me from this devastating idea. My inner dialogue appended every thought with the comment "You are going mad." My mind raced. I could concentrate on nothing save my plummeting mental state. Like parting a curtain, I glanced back at my family background, which now appeared to be strewn with disturbed people: a dear aunt, institutionalized; a poor grandmother forever remembered in a dressing gown, babbling and senile. When I was eleven a telegram arrived at our house, always a harbinger of doom. Mum stated blandly, "Oh, Grandfather is dead," which to me was news indeed. As I had never heard him spoken of, I naturally assumed him long gone. The very confirmation of his life was his death notice! The only explanation I ever got was that this unfortunate man died in Broadmoor, the national hospital-prison for the criminally insane.

I reflected on the throw of the genetic dice. There was part of a certified madman in me, perhaps even set to go off after a prescribed interval, like a time bomb. In my troubled state of mind and body, this didn't seem unreasonable, not at all. God, how utterly sick I was of all this—the insects, the heat, the ordeal of living seemingly forever among poverty and squalor, longing for order and finding only chaos. Along with Lord-knows-how-many other loonies in the world, I whispered through agonized tears, "I can't take any more!" After three years on the road, I was cracking up, and I knew it.

So terribly I missed my home and family—things so many seem driven to escape were, for me, my solid foundation. In the ever-changing tides of the sea of life, I swam constantly toward this rock of hope. Even a good booze-up with my pals at the corner pub would have seen me right, but this was no option here: I lay in the tropics, naked and alone, fighting to regain my balance, fighting for a future. Better than most I knew the power of that mighty organ, the brain. To date *it* had carried me nearly nine thousand miles, while the great towering column of atoms labeled George just followed. Was it now going into reverse, working against me? "Why *shouldn't* I be mentally ill?" I asked myself. Had not the colossus Snow suffered from "illusions" or "delusions" or something of that sort? What allowed me to think that *I* was so perfect? I had seen people go mad at sea. Why *not* me? A ridiculous-looking fireman's helmet sat in one corner of the closet, and I couldn't take my eyes off it. It became an act of will not to put the damned thing on and prance about. No one would be surprised. "Oh, yes," they would say, "George went bats in Central America, the poor fool."

Toward morning, my prayers were answered by a few moments of fitful sleep. In the new day's sunlight I felt a little better, although still as fragile as an old lightbulb. The fireman's helmet seemed to have stayed in its corner. Now was the time to get out of this place. I made my way through close, quiet streets lined with brightly painted *casas* streaked with the dark shadows of tall, slender trees. San Pedro Sula is a small, pleasant city (just as Honduras is a small, pleasant country), and so it is a pity that it will always remind me of my personal crisis. That peaceful day I was seeking out Anglo-Saxon types, the sort who might recognize Jackie Charlton—the Babe Ruth of British football, if you will. I needed my people, more than ever before.

First I tried an English mission. The staff there were "busy"—but at least they let me use their washing machine. I left the machine running and on the way out made friends with a fat mongrel with a slobbery tongue. Returning later from my other errands, I found the mission gate locked. They wouldn't allow me back in, but instead pushed my sopping wet clothes through the bars of the gate. Where to hang the stuff? No one cared. Even my friend, the mongrel dog, was gone.

Neither the cool English manager at the tiny Banco de Londres not the British honorary consul could oblige my desperate need for some quiet conversation. The latter, sporting a long gray beard and shod in rope sandals, looking every inch the ancient mariner, would not even deign to acknowledge the considerable coincidence that we both served as officers in the same shipping company. When I asked him if he knew of a doctor, he said, "I don't go to doctors—I never get sick."

"Well, if you ever did get sick, who might you go to?" He wrote a name on a scrap of paper and dismissed me with a curt "I'm very busy. Good day." No Jackie Charltons here.

Rather than continue chasing a will-o'-the-wisp, I went straight to the Escuela Internacional (International School), seeking a new berth. I found the principal in his office and learned coincidentally that the man, an American, was a psychiatrist. What a stroke of luck! I felt suddenly relieved; of all people, a "trick cyclist" was just what I needed—and right now. On the spot, I spilled out my troubles, confessing that I had somehow lost my former inner tranquility, the calm acceptance of circumstances that had so far permitted me to forego career and income and submit to growing old quickly while chasing a dream.

The man listened to me with the same look of grave yet detached concern that I had seen on the ambassador's face. I knew it meant he had bad news for me, and he delivered it more as an apology than a comment: "I wish I could help, but I have to fly to the States tonight—and, oh, yes, you can stay here." On top of my despair I felt a tinge of hysteria. Here I had stumbled across almost certainly the only English-speaking shrink in Honduras, and he had to rush off to catch a plane!

I waited out the afternoon siesta and visited a doctor whom I picked at random, a handsome black Colombian from Cali who wrote out his prescriptions with a flashy fountain pen. My mental state interested him not at all. "You have a persistent infection, are greatly malnourished, and are suffering from exhaustion," he told me. All of this I already knew. "You must rest for three weeks."

After dark, I gravitated to the open door of a church and peered into the bright interior, where people were jumping about, wailing, and waving their hands above their heads. I slunk back into the darkness. It was not for me. I drifted on and about before finally coming to rest at the bolted door of the cathedral. Here I crumpled down behind a convenient boulder and wept, praying that a selfish man's selfish journey might continue. It had become my life, my reason to exist.

That night in my room at the International School, the temperature broke a hundred. I tried to eat, but the food just stuck in my gullet, choked off by resurgent panic. Again I couldn't sleep, just sweat and worry while an occasional twitch flickered across my face. I was reminded of an unfortunate lad at sea whose face twitched on and off like a signal lantern. Was this to be my fate, too?

I felt as though I was struggling to hold on to the rim of a giant funnel with greased sides that was suspended over an abyss; if I slid down much farther, I would never be able to haul my way out again. Recovering my sanity was battle enough—what beyond that? Now I began to calculate the astronomical odds against my completing the journey. I had always half expected destruction from without, but the idea of

245

destruction from within had never merited a ha'pennyworth of consideration. I took a sleeping pill for the first time in my life. It was a total failure, and for the first time in my life I didn't so much as nod all night.

Daylight has the power to bring its natural peace to the world's unbalanced. I knew very strongly that the doctor's advice was wrong. To stay here for a "rest" would finish me for sure. The only cure for my condition was its indirect cause— walking. I must walk again. I wrote a letter to Yoshiko, pouring out my problems and telling her—as well as myself—that I had to return to the road if I ever was to find peace:

> Dear Yosh,
> . . . We must meet—it's a race to get me to the U.S. before I totally collapse. PRAY for me. This is the turning point of the whole three-year effort. These are the most important and indeed unhappiest words I've written you. God help me. I'm looking at my own shattered dreams. Give me strength!! Yoshiko, I love you.
>
> A nearly beaten
> George XXXXXX

For once I was on the move at the very crack of dawn. I returned to the road south of Sula and recommenced my march, now as much for therapy as for distance. At first I moved tentatively. Ultracautiously I inched along; it was as though I were feeling the road through someone else's legs. But it felt good once again to knock off another kilometer, even one. My insides felt terrible, but at least there was scenery to help distract me. Feeling at last the satisfaction of progress, I made my way past Santa Bárbara and a few hours later reached the sleepy village of Quimistan, where a district nurse in the tiny *clinica* overflowing with peasants whopped a syringeful of glucose and vitamin B into my rear.

According to my new road map, tiny Sula lay 24 km distant from Quimistan; it turned out to be only 20. This may not seem much of an error, but it nearly brought on another crisis, as I arrived in bright daylight and all but panicked at the thought of being alone with myself and my symptoms.

There were no kilometers to hide behind, nor darkness—nothing to do but sit in the town's only cantina for four solid hours while a deep-breathing *borracho* (drunk), standing the regulation two inches from my face, "talked" to me.

Sitting there in the half-light, I realized how much I needed people, any people, even the voluble piss-artist now beside me prattling on and on. When I attempted to write a few lines to Yoshiko, my friend El Borracho followed this (to him) mysterious procedure with deep and animated enthusiasm. He couldn't have been more excited had I turned one of our fellow patrons into a block of stone. Eventually he passed out, and not long after that the rest of the cantina fell silent as well. What grinding monotony life must be here. A cockroach scurried across the littered floor. Was its life any drearier than those of these muted people?

Beyond the village the countryside was flat, the foliage dry and yellowing under the overpowering sun. The forest that once dominated here had long since given way to peasant holdings and fincas whose buildings, set amid stately shade trees, could be seen as far as the washed-out horizon. Populating the approach to each stick-and-mud dwelling were always the few uncaring pigs, the watchful, scratching dogs, and a tolerant cat or two. These small plots of land were typically given over to bananas or any of a dozen other crops that the hot weather draws forth. I took so many rests at these poor but peaceful places—ubiquitous not just in Honduras or Central America but throughout the vast supercontinent of Latin America—that in my memory they have merged into one.

From La Entrada I trooped 44 steep kilometers over to the mountain town of Santa Rosa. As I was moving well again, I kept walking the following day well past sunset. It was a dark, cloudy night and I found myself shuffling cautiously along the *pavimento*, literally feeling my way. Just outside Lucerne I marched straight into someone's back. The figure violently swung around and hit me in the stomach with something hard—a submachine gun. It was a soldier. As we tumbled to the ground, his helmet clattered along the road, and I began shouting explanations in Spanish, acutely aware that this was a deadly situation. As I staggered to my feet, hands held toward the sky, I heard safety catches clicking off all around—I still couldn't see anything or anyone. Lights began playing upon me and voices screamed out orders in the night. Things finally calmed down when I was allowed to explain who I was and why I was wandering in this sensitive border region under such improbable circumstances.

My abominable Spanish may actually have saved me, for no spy would so mangle their language. I was also fortunate in that it was the commander I had stumbled into—a conscript might well have shot me down in panic. Eventually the lieutenant and I fell into friendly conversation, and together strolled over to a hut that had a few items for sale. He courteously knocked on the door, and when a ponchoed Indian slowly and warily poked his head out, he asked, *"Tiene aspirina?"* ("Do you have aspirin?")

"No hay," came back the inevitable reply (and here I had been thinking it was only I that got the negative for every piffling request).

"Oh, no!" moaned the lieutenant. "I've had this steel helmet on all day," he confided to me, "and it's given me a headache." For once I could be useful. From my medicine bag, well stocked these days, I dug out an envelope of aspirin tablets. The lieutenant was overjoyed. In return he bought me three warm *refrescos,* and then wrote his name and address in my diary: Primero Teniente Manuel Antonio Amaya Hernández—Ejército, Honduras, Centro America.

The road map indicated that the distance to Nueva Ocotepeque was a manageable 40 km, but I had no way of knowing that this included a mountain range—this meant that half the route was grueling uphill going. Tired or not, I forced on to the top of the range and then rolled down the other side like a rubber ball. "You vicious bastard!" I screamed at my map when I hit the 40-km mark. There was a town on the map here, but none on the landscape, just a passerby who informed me that my objective was "at least two hours away." When Nueva Ocotepeque finally blinked into view, it was late, and I was exhausted but triumphant. It had been a stunning 52-km day, and I had succeeded in circumventing the murderous situation in El Salvador. I slept at a pension, under a sink, having neither the money to spare for a room nor the nerve to ask for one gratis. By midmorning I returned to life and marched on, into Guatemala.

Guatemala

I was trying to keep a low profile at the Guatemalan Immigration Office at Agua Caliente, as the authorities here were notoriously capricious. Back in Tierra del Fuego, a couple from Switzerland had told us that the Guatemalans arbitrarily refused them entry—no reason given. And these people were nationals of a neutral country. Who knows how much more horrible to Guatemalan eyes I, a Briton, might appear? Guatemala has long coveted neighboring Belize, formerly the crown colony of British Honduras, and in 1964 even broke off diplomatic relations with Britain when Britain granted Belize self-governing status.

The sight of the Immigration officer wasn't encouraging. He wore unpolished shoes and an ill-fitting uniform, and his shirttail was hanging out; he looked almost as bad as I did! When the officer signaled that I was next, I placed my embarrassingly conspicuous passport on his desk and he proceeded to examine it with special care. This requires some explanation. The passports of most nations are handy shirt-pocket-size documents. But Britain's is larger—just large enough so that it won't quite fit into a shirt pocket (and it's printed on a stiff water-vulnerable cardboard that quickly disintegrates when exposed to moisture). The covers of most passports bear just the country's name, perhaps with a simple insignia; Britain's sports an elaborate gold-foil seal depicting a chained unicorn and crowned lion rampant, with Latin script.

So much for my low profile. The glare of the glittering heraldic animals certainly caught the eye of the official, who now bore down on me. "Belize is part of our republic of Guatemala!" he bellowed, apropos of absolutely nothing. With a wave of his hand, he indicated a large wall map on which Belize was indeed depicted as one of Guatemala's departments. "It's the same as with Gibraltar," explained the officer.

The absurdity of this pricked the devil in me. I couldn't help asking, "You mean Gibraltar is part of Guatemala?"

"No, inglés fool. It's part of *Spain*."

"What? Guatemala is part of Spain?"

"No, no, idiota imperialist!"

The man then turned around and tapped the plastic sign hanging from the pillar behind him. Written in English was the admonition, almost certainly intended to discourage irate gringos from seeking just redress, "THIS OFFICE WILL NOT HEAR SLANDER." Apparently satisfied that he had made his point, the official smartly stamped my passport and sent me on my way. I considered myself lucky.

As a kind gesture, the monks in the shrine town of Esquipulas offered to set me up at a nearby pension for the night, but the place turned out to be an evil pit. Eventually I found safe haven at another pension for several nights, gratis. With a fixed base, I was now free to wander the down-at-the-heel streets in my down-at-the-heel boots.

One of the institutions of the town was Padre Geraldo, an American who had resigned monkhood (on medical grounds, he assured me), married a local woman, and now operated a café. Between serving the customers, Geraldo struggled in the back of the café with his nine-year-old son over a school lesson he insisted the boy finish. The youngster's task became even harder when music came drifting in from the street: the thump of a big bass drum and the tinny whine of a cornet. A procession was approaching, and from the back room it could be heard but not seen.

The boy now squirmed all the harder, and only reluctantly settled back to his lesson when the drum had faded away and the cornet was nothing but a memory. I witnessed all this with more than a little sadness, thinking: How lucky I was to be free. How difficult it is to break with set routines, even when we want to, and join life's parade passing just outside the door. The job, the mortgage, and a dozen other considerations mute the big drum, and only rarely does the trumpet call prove irresistible.

The towns and villages past Esquipulas were nicely spaced on my map, which afforded me a series of convenient, reasonable objectives. One of them, Chiquimula ("chee-kee-MOOL-ah"), was my favorite place name in the Americas, but my initial impression made it less than my favorite town. In fact, it was a fantastically stinking-hot, bug-ridden mess. First thing, I ducked into an alley and, like a snake molting, peeled off my nasty sweat-drenched shirt and replaced it with a marginally less nasty one—a routine I had lately adopted upon entering towns, and something I never felt compelled to do in South America. Times had changed; I felt I had to look better these days.

It was early evening and still oppressively hot as I wandered the cobblestone streets. I happened upon a market in a poorly lit corner of the plaza. Most of the stalls were shuttered for the night, but at one short row of tables the vendors, still selling their fruit, juices, and ices, invited me to draw up a box to chat. They were dirt-poor, these jovial men in their pants of coarse, stained cloth, ragged, buttonless shirts, and torn vests, and the women among them were prematurely aged, but they all exuded great warmth and dignity. They plied me with questions and even more fruit—rich, sweet, and sticky. I was an attraction, a foreigner, and a foreigner from wherever was always considered great entertainment.

When it was heard that I was making my walk alone, a girl shouted out from the darkness through the babble, "Take me with you!" Her plea went straight to my heart. In the two years I had been walking alone, several youngsters had half-jokingly asked to join me, but something in the tone of this girl's voice made her appeal different. The girl shyly approached and told me her name was Lola. Perhaps fifteen, she stood awkwardly in her plastic flip-flops. She had spindly ostrich legs and no figure to speak of, her knees were rough and callused from working on her knees, and only a few teeth remained in her mouth. To me she was beautiful, however. "Lola, do you *really* want to come with me?" I said. By this time, dozens of people had gathered around, and everyone was waiting for her answer. Lola gestured at her cart with its two muddy turnips, single green papaya, and bunch of bananas, and said, "I can't leave, for this is my life—but I will travel with you in mind and spirit." I understood her completely, and later, when I moved onward, I was not alone, but accompanied by a small bundle of bananas, a green papaya, and the memory of yet another kindred soul on this planet.

One nightfall, I found myself far off my route and in the company of a mysterious priest at his church in the mountains. All about, votive candles were fixed into spent artillery shells. "I have been transferred," he told me by the flickering candlelight. "When the revolutionaries took me away, they gave me three choices: I could be buried alive, chopped to bits with machetes, or hanged. Fortunately, I have friends in the army, and they staged an ambush and rescued me. Then my bishop sent me here—to be forgotten."

I felt now more desperately then ever in need of what I call civilization—something like a morning newspaper and milk brought to the door. I even chanted the word while I marched ("Civilization . . . civilization . . .") as a sort of mantra of hope. Toward this end, I raced a powerful 48 km to Sanarate, well on the way to Guatemala City, the capital, my brain pushing my legs all the way. It was after dark when I beat on the wooden side of the only café open in town.

"Got any food?"

"Sí."

"What have you got?"

"Tortillas." (I knew it—no "real" food.)

"Got anything else?"

The man heard the undertone of despair in my voice and shot back, "Why? What do you want, elephant?" The wit then sent me packing. Another hungry night—and certainly no newspaper or milk deliveries that morning.

Next day I moved on to the capital, a large, modern city with a population of one million (the largest in Central America), where I had numerous pieces of business to transact. First to the British consulate to pick up my mail and the new pair of boots that Berghaus had sent there. I urgently needed the boots, and so of course they had not arrived—although the letter sent to accompany them had.

Yoshiko's letter concerned me, for she seemed set against the idea of bringing both our children to Texas (God willing, there would be a second baby). I wanted to persuade her otherwise, but decided not to bring up the subject with her until nearer the date. Meanwhile, I was happy that she was well and her usual wonderful self.

Financially I was near the end. My original eleven thousand dollars plus Anthony's one thousand had been reduced to what I had in my moneybelt—about fifty dollars in cash and a four-hundred-dollar money order. And this had to last me until the States, still some 2,500 km and four months distant. (In that Promised Land, I was naïvely hoping, corporations would sponsor me in return for endorsements, etc.) All told, my original stake had lasted very well—and most of that had gone for the family's airfares! Yoshiko would even have to rely on her father's help to get to Texas.

Most recently, I was desperately cutting corners, and now in Guatemala City I was faced with my standard big-city problem: no place to stay. The police wouldn't have me, the *bomberos* wouldn't have me, and the newspapermen I contacted said they didn't care. Actually, I could sympathize with the local press, who sat in their fortresslike offices half-scared to death. Highly visible journalists in this country stood a good chance of being on at least one faction's death list. Some had in fact been assassinated—victims of the ultimate act of censorship.

Guatemala seemed to be a land of contradictions. Economically it was the most dynamic country in Central America—on paper. According to statistics, the economy was growing annually at a healthy rate of 5 percent. The fact that most of the cans of food that came my way in Central America were stamped *"Hecho en Guatemala"* (Made in Guatemala) seemed to confirm this. Yet in the Guatemalan countryside I couldn't get cheese, or ham, or peanuts (and I could never get used to the grim, ubiquitous tortillas). In the meanwhile, the cost of the supposed economic dynamism was a repressive military dictatorship that ruled by terror and threats of terror, which perhaps explains why I found people cautious in their dealings with me and other foreigners.

The situation was nowhere so strained as in the capital, where rumor had it that death squads were operating directly out of the president's palace. The streets, while neat and clean, were filled with menace. Armed troops constantly cruised the city in jeeps with machine guns fitted to the rear platforms. Soldiers in steel helmets and flak jackets idled away their time on streetcorners, a sight I hadn't seen since a voyage to Ulster years before. Sometimes, always unexpectedly, I would run into one of these contingents, perhaps in the shade of an overhanging tree in a well-to-do neighborhood. Like the Guatemaltecos, I always avoided looking at them directly and settled for furtive glances.

I had finally found a place to stay when a stranger, in a gesture of support for my enterprise, gave me 2 quetzals ($2 U.S.), "for a room." After almost two weeks, I paid one last visit to the consulate, hoping that my boots had arrived and perhaps more mail. With great excitement I found a letter full of congratulations and encouragement from none other than Sebastian Snow, who more than anyone else knew what I was going through. But—what was *this?* . . . a note from Anthony scrawled on the back of an envelope containing a letter from Mum: "George: Yoshiko had a baby BOY. Congratulations!" I wanted to tell the whole world. I started with the people at the consulate. I should have known better; none of these cool fish was moved in the slightest. I left, and roamed the streets walking on air. I thanked the fates. Surely, I was

255

the luckiest man on earth, with the privilege of having a son to go with my daughter, my remarkable wife, and this our journey, our dream.

After a stopover, it always felt good once again to be making progress. All in all, things were looking up: The sore throat brought on by the city traffic was clearing and the sun shone warmly. Memories welled up within me of the long break from school, of relaxed, warm days when I would ride my bicycle over the gently rolling hills of the North Downs. How impossibly huge Kent had seemed to me then; how impossibly small it seemed now.

At Patzicía, past Chimaltenango, I left the Inter-American Highway and branched off onto a very narrow *pavimento* that leads to the tourist mecca of Lake Atitlán. The Indians here were stunning in appearance, especially the womenfolk, clad in a riot of colors that varied from village to village, along with the language. Most wore red or gray-green cloaks, some a dozen silver necklaces, yet others red-and-white strips braided into their long black hair. Each turn in the hilly road would reveal yet another living spectacle. Along the route to the lake, many Indian women I passed were burdened under loads of water or sticks, and occasionally one would gesture at the Yoshikart—as if to acknowledge how practical an arrangement she thought it was. Whereas a typical motorist would hardly even notice, these people spend all their lives on foot; this was our common bond.

The vision of Lago Atitlán emerged through the trees as a belt of cobalt blue with three volcanoes standing sentinel in the background. The hills I had been following were the steepest I had encountered yet in Central America. Tipsy with fatigue but exhilarated by the view, I took a shortcut through some thick woods, guided by two small boys and their nannygoat. (When they conversed in their language, it sounded to me like a tape recording being played backward.) At one point we came to a clearing, where a girl was sitting on the grass, weaving, holding the warp lines taut with her bare foot. Charmed by the scene, I asked if she minded if I took her photograph. She refused unless I paid her. Alas, such is the corrupting force of tourism.

There were horrifying stories circulating in Panajachel: The military were taking suspected revolutionaries up in helicopters and pushing them out while hovering over active volcanoes. Word was also out that the government had massacred a village of Indians somewhere to the north and were warning people to stay clear of the area. A friend from Guatemala City, Joanna Codrington, counseled me to end my walk at the Mexican border—"for your health's sake, George," she said, cautious not to offend me. Her concern for my health was well founded, but I knew I wasn't ready to go home. From day one and before I had been totally committed. I felt that to go home now with two legs still functioning would be to court mental trouble forever after. I would never find peace. I would be a doomed man.

In Nahuala, I stayed with missionaries recommended to my by a clergyman in Panajachel: Alan Edwards and his wife Pat were both medical doctors and operated a dispensary as well as a small church for the Indians. Apart from an administrator, these two Americans and their teenage children were the only non-Indians in the community.

At last, after years of journeying, I had found "civilization"—and where, of all places but in a mud-hut village in Central America. Nonetheless, here it was: a home with electric lights and food, real food—even Yorkshire pudding (God bless them, they looked up a recipe specially for me!)—and family entertainment. In the evening Dr. Alan leaned back in his easy chair, eyes shut, lost in Karajan's Beethoven pouring out of the stereo, while one teenager regaled me with magic tricks and the other demonstrated his latest hobby on a newfangled thing called a skateboard (I had been away so long that I had never seen one before). The whole family was so active they didn't even seem to notice their semi-isolation or miss having a television. The two boys and I quickly became firm friends, and like young boys that I met everywhere, they expressed great enthusiasm for my journey.

One day the Edwards boys took me about the pueblo. A particularly bleak sight was a cracked concrete courtyard sunk ten feet into the ground—a jail, into which the administrator periodically threw drunken Indians. As I peered into the hole, where the hung-over occupants seemed like so many sad birds of paradise at the zoo, a woman dressed in dazzling blue lay in the dust around the edge and lowered a bucket of food to her interned man.

I was next taken to the home of a neighboring Indian family. It was not much different from those I had seen before. The single low-ceilinged, windowless room was dark and thick with smoke and the walls blackened with soot, as the chimney was far from the open fire burning in the center of the packed-earth floor. One striking difference, however, was that the furnishings, such as they were, seemed almost like toys. The stools, for example, stood only a foot off the ground. The local Indians, by Western standards, were almost miniature people, the women standing under five feet, the men not much taller. This particular householder spoke little Spanish, his wife none at all; this was the norm. Literacy was nil, not just in Spanish but in the native languages as well, since there were few if any government teachers who spoke these tongues.

Upon my departure from the Edwards', I kept noticing Indians on the high mountainsides, so far off they were barely more than dots, and they waved to me throughout the day; it was a glorious show. As I moved toward San Cristóbal, my route took me to the top of a huge 12-km hill and a settlement called, of all things, Alaska. (So no matter what happens, I thought then, I could say I had walked to Alaska.)

Yet another village found me handing over an introduction at the door of yet another missionary, where I had an experience of an entirely different order. The man's wife ushered me into the living room to await her husband's return. After half an hour the front door swung open and in marched the missionary in the company of three other men, whom he introduced as visitors from the mission's home church in Milwaukee. The man's fierce, determined manner—he acted more

like a four-star general geared for battle than a man of faith—
immediately brought to mind General George S. Patton. This
Patton was so invigorated and refreshed, I learned, because
he had just finished giving some unfortunate soul a two-hour
Bible beating with the Book of Enoch. My heart went out to
the unknown victim of this barbarity, and I steeled myself for
a gritty evening in the trenches.

Grace at dinner, led by Patton, was interminable and included a special plea for me, his uninvited guest—"Dear God,
make this man a Christian . . . bend him to Thy will" (he
had never asked me anything on the subject—he just assumed, the way people do, that on sight he knew everything
about me he needed to know)—followed by a prolonged entreaty concerning a window being installed in his church.
Throughout the otherwise superb meal, Patton found it difficult to conceal his contempt toward my pagan presence. And
the moment that his rather pleasant wife asked me a question
concerning my journey, Patton instantly raised his voice and
drowned her out. The lady never broached the topic again.

After dinner the missionary read a passsage from the Bible and became so moved by the Spirit that he offered up
yet another prayer. It covered much the same ground as the
earlier supplication, including a throwaway for someone (guess
who?) who needed to be "broken to Christianity," followed
by further appeals to the deity concerning the wretched window. A prayer meeting was scheduled for that evening, and,
despite his obvious distaste, Patton extended me an invitation
to participate. Walking had made it a hard day, as it usually
did, and so I passed over the opportunity in favor of bed.
Patton seemed mildly pleased by this, as it no doubt under-
lined my doomed and sinful nature.

The following morning I approached the Milwaukee trio
and offered to buy one of their Guatemalan cowboy hats—I
had lost my sombrero and was sorely in need of head covering. They declined (not unexpectedly), and so I mentally
noted for future reference that the sun in Wisconsin must be
exceedingly strong. My kind hostess, however, without any
prompting from me, donated an old sombrero she found lying

259

about the house, and even made sandwiches for my departure.

I was fast approaching the frontier, and with the gain in latitude I became more exhilarated. In 1524, a conquistador had written to Cortés, probably from somehere in this region: "We are the wildest country we have ever seen." Today, tourists in vehicles that ply the blacktop would call it just scenic. I preferred to think—I *knew*—that these dried-up riverbeds, yawning gorges, and blistered valley deserts were wild country still.

Two days out of Huehuetenango, I was toiling through the rocky, windblown Selegua canyon at nightfall when my latest hat blew into the deep yonder. My spirits were liberated; indeed, they soared, for, God willing, *mañana* would find me in Mexico. For another half hour I followed a full moon while the puffy cumulus darted by, until I fetched up, windswept and bedraggled, at a pleasant *casa*. The hour was late, but the family bade me stay.

I was happy that my last night in Central America had struck this kindly note in this disturbed, rather frightened nation. As I lay about to doze off on the living-room floor, I recalled a fantastic sight in the settlement of San Sebastián, miles behind me, when I chanced to walk right into its teeming Sunday market. It was a sight that probably hadn't changed from before the conquistadors. You could hardly slip a banana leaf between hundreds of milling Indians. The scene was dominated by a riot of exploding colors, babies in back bundles, baskets of fruit, bolts of burning-bright cloth, Panama hats, armfuls of sullen inverted chickens, here and there a snorting, grimy pig, and above it all vegetables, in headloads, by the dozens. It offered a total saturation of the senses.

Despite my petty woes I knew that one day I would miss all this, that all life is to be cherished, and that surely this was life in one of its more glorious manifestations.

North America

Mexico

The border was casual to the point of a holiday. Three inspectors, after cursorily checking my gear for illegal fruit, plied me with tequila for a solid half hour. Then one of them dragged me along behind him, squealing, "Come—come see my mother." This was Romeo Guillén Guillén. (Latins take two surnames. The first, from the father, is the one mostly used as a last name, while the second is the mother's. Illegitimate children take the mother's name twice. This appears to be no disgrace, perhaps because so much of the population are illegitimate.) By the time we reached Romeo's room a short distance away, he was still exclaiming, "You must come see my mother!" In the room he made a great ceremony of throwing himself on his knees, still drunk but now contrite, before his mother: a framed photograph of the Virgin of Guadalupe that hung on the wall. I left him to settle his family business. Clearly Mexico, much touted by visitors and media alike, was going to be fun.

The villages I now passed through were populated mostly by Indians. Nothing looked "Mexican" to me; it was as if I hadn't left Guatemala. My intuition wasn't far off the mark. Picking up the *South American Handbook,* I read that until 1821 this region, the state of Chiapas, had been part of the colony of Guatemala, and then joined Mexico over something

having to do with the machinations of an irate headmistress—
a historical quirk that helps explain why relations between
these two countries have not always been the friendliest.

The president of Mexico was scheduled to visit nearby
Comitán, ostensibly to open a new military base, but almost
certainly as well to reassert, by his very presence, central
government authority in this tentative border region. I became caught up in the celebratory atmosphere and put off the
walk for a day so that, along with the populace, I could take
one of the free buses arranged by the local branch of the PRI,
Mexico's ruling party.

In Comitán we were let off near a luxurious, sparkling
white colonial-style hotel. Letting my rampant imagination take
its course, I pictured myself inside, wearing a white dinner
jacket, on my arm a sultry countess dripping with dia-
monds—I had just bailed her out of the massive debt she had
incurred at the baccarat table. Alas, that night found me in
less chic circumstances. There were no colonial-style arches
at the local billiard hall, nor much else to speak of, and my
suite was located under one of the billiard tables, just near
the urinal.

The presidential progress the next day was an impressive
and exhilarating show; low-flying helicopters circling noisily
overhead, bands striking up one lively march after another,
banners waving, and José López Portillo, El Presidente himself, in a white suit, streaking by in the back of a jeep as
thousands of cheering Indians lunged forward en masse in an
attempt to catch a glimpse of "El Jefe"—The Chief. I myself,
from thirty feet away, could just make out his waving hand
above the throng.

Back in Ciudad Cuauhtémoc near the border, the air was
hot and dry. From the edge of town I could see that the
landscape beyond was flat and featureless, the road empty,
with not even a *tienda* in sight. It was like a sweaty Patagonia. At daybreak the next day, before leaving the protective
shade of a parched tree, I downed four colas in a row to play
it safe, and lucky I did, for once on the broken road I was
immediately attacked by the punishing sun. There was nearly

total silence out there as I tottered along while iguanas and olive-drab lizards, some a foot-and-a-half long, scampered about my feet.

The third day out, I passed through Comitán for the second time, but now I first noticed that, compared with similar towns on my route, the trees here were few and skimpy; only occasionally was there a bush with bright flowers. Because I was now walking, I was able to view the town and countryside with a more discerning eye. Now I saw more than just narrow streets and pastel *casas* with red-tile roofs and enclosed courtyards, the standard features of most Latin American towns.

I felt cool for the first time all day. It was sundown, and the sky glowed a soft pink. The village of Amatenango del Valle, shining in that magical light, was alive with red cooking fires and draped Indians scurrying among their mud huts and stocks of earthenware pots. Once again I had the strange sensation of peering into another age while traveling a twentieth-century blacktop. Before I reached Teopisca, a pickup stopped beside me. Out of the darkness of the cab, a worried voice questioned: "Are you armed?" (Of course I wasn't—not even a plastic teaspoon.)

"No. Why?"

"Los Indios. They are very dangerous. You must be afraid."

I had never really considered the matter. The incident reminded me of the man I had met on a Peruvian mountain road who strongly advised me to carry a machete, like him, *"por los tigres"*—for the jaguars. (I heard the same thing again in Darién.) I had seen many Indians armed with machetes, but it never occurred to me to fear them. I just waved my hat and passed cheerfully on. If anyone had wanted to do me in, there was nothing I could do about it. Moreover, pulling a cart behind me raised no one's ire; I couldn't have seemed any more harmless had I been a mole.

To reach the family of David Jarvis (another introduction), I hitched a lift along a scarred and bumpy dirt road in a truck that stopped every half mile so that another load of barefoot and muddy Indians could clamber aboard. In the growing chill of twilight, I was left off at an empty void, allegedly near where the Jarvis clan hung out. After some searching, I found a trail leading down to the rush of a river. Leaving the cart behind for the moment, I felt my way in the darkness, slid across a pipe that spanned the river (surprising myself when I didn't fall in), and then scrambled up to the top of the riverbank, where a large, goofy hound kept nipping at my heels before I finally found the house and was escorted inside.

David Jarvis—called Don David by the local Indians—was sitting like a smuggler in a dimly lit room that might have been a cave, and was only just visible behind an assortment of articles on a large tabletop: seeds, plants, books, tins of food, nails, the odd wrench, and even a few dinner things. Don David and his wife were English missionaries to the Tzeltals, and so during the days I spent with the Jarvises, I learned much about this tribe, as well as the neighboring Chamulas. I even became familiar with the various tribe "characters" and learned where they lived—the tribe's assassin, the tribe's thief, the tribe's knife sharpener, etc.

The Chamulas not only refused to be photographed, but could be expected to exact a high price from anyone who neglected to respect their rule. I had frequently observed an aversion to the camera among Indians, many of whom believe that to have one's image so captured is to lose a part of one's soul. The Chamulas, according to David, were especially adamant; one transgressing tourist had in fact been hacked to bits. I thought David might have been exaggerating until I read in the *South American Handbook*, hardly a sensationalist rag, that two gringos had been killed in a Chamula church under similar circumstances—specifically, for ignoring the "No Photos" sign. Perhaps, I thought, this was a touch excessive for disregarding a sign, which we all do from time to time; it's like walking on the grass and finding yourself beheaded on the spot. But then, the Chamulas have a long history of hypersensitivity. In 1868, it is recorded, there was a massive Chamula uprising, provoked by a dispute over the ownership of a speaking wooden idol; finally, the Mexican army was called in to crush the insurrection.

The Tzeltals were a gentler lot, although in some ways not much less superstitious than the Chamulas. David held the local Catholic church partly responsible; their practices, in his view, flirted with idolatry. During dry spells, for instance, the Indians were allowed to take the statue of their rain goddess from the sanctuary and parade it around to make rain. Even so, most of the community remained pagan, and Tzeltals were still being knocked off by their own people for the crime of embracing Christianity.

When he first arrived here, David said, the Tzeltals would not look at him directly, for fear of the evil eye. Eventually David—in fact, everyone in his extraordinary family—learned to speak the Tzeltals' language. However, his conversations with the Tzeltals could be incredibly vague, often running something like this:

Tzeltal: It looks good today.
David: Yes, it does.
Tzeltal: It looks good.
David: Yes, it looks good.
Tzeltal: The sun will shine.
David: Yes, it will shine.
Tzeltal: It looks good . . .

and so on for perhaps an hour.

Women's lib here was, in Don David's words, "cut up on the wrong side of a black snakeskin whip." For marriage, the suitor has to present a long list of gifts (silver coins, perhaps a year's worth of free labor, and, among other specified items, one hundred hard-boiled eggs and forty pounds of dough) to the girl's father—while the girl hides in the bushes awaiting the result of the negotiation.

The Sunday before my departure was Easter, an occasion for the Christianized Indians to conduct their own five-hour-long service. David and I joined them—near the end, thank God. The tiny white chapel, packed to overflowing with hundreds of brilliantly clad Tzeltals, sat atop a steep hillock, strategically isolated from the bulk of the huts, which stood on pathless pastureland. The scene inside the chapel was a kaleidoscope of dazzling humanity; the overriding impression was of a storm-tossed sea of yellow ribbons. When Don David was invited to say a few words to the congregation, to my great embarrassment he introduced me from the pulpit; although I don't understand a word of Tzeltal, I knew what he was up to when I heard him say "George Meegan" and saw him point in my direction. He then asked me to speak to the assembly while he translated. My legs were shaking badly as he asked the congregation to repeat my name by way of extending me a welcome, which they did in unison, pronouncing it something like "Joje Mogga." Utterly charming.

When it came time for me to set out to the north, David made my departure somewhat of a ceremony, which served to remind me once more how messy and difficult good-byes can be. As we took our parting, seven or eight Tzeltals watched from a short distance. I was particularly touched when David said a prayer of protection for me on my "walk through Creation." As we shook hands a final time and I was just about to walk off, David leaned over, nodded in the direction of the Indians nearby, and said softly, "George, don't forget these people. Nobody thinks they're worth dirt—shake their hands." I was instantly shocked by my oversight. And so, of course, I shook their hands—it was my honor. I considered this a timely lesson, and I have never forgotten it. I simply never thought before that there were people who might regard my handshake as significant.

Progress continued through the Indian country of Chiapas State, and so my days were never dull; one comical sight was a barefoot Chamula mother carrying her baby on her back and her shoes on her head. Nights, however, had an endless low-order variety about them. My night in San Cristóbal de las Casas was spent in a Red Cross center trying to sleep amid roaring dance music and rowdy teenage volunteers. Ixtapa found me in a distrustful café-owner's yard, while Bochal saw me bedded down at a gas station in the oil-soaked pit under the grease rack.

By the time I rolled down onto the valley floor and into the town of Pichucalco, the distance logged was 15,000 km, over 9,000 miles. So many people, so many pueblos, barrios, and shanties; a full dozen republics. On completing tiny Tierra del Fuego, I had been ecstatic; it was my first milestone, and it was a great achievement for Yoshiko. I was also proud to have crossed Argentina—sad that I no longer had Yoshiko's companionship but still feeling a sense of accomplishment. Now with every milestone, instead of looking back with pride, I looked forward to seeing the family with eagerness, but also with anxiety. How much longer could I go on? Did I have the stamina to last another three or four years? Could I survive the realization of my own inflated dreams?

I descended to the state of Tabasco, and now I was violently sick. Over the years I had built up a strong resistance to this sort of thing, but now I had been pole-axed by the poisoned fish I had eaten the previous evening. I lay on a bottom bunk at the bomberos on Avenida de la Constitucíon in Villahermosa, a hot and steamy coastal city. Sleep came and went like a drifting ghost. Darkness overtook twilight; the sun expelled the night only to be transformed in its turn back to darkness. Meanwhile, the firemen were playing cards nearby. To block them out, I hung a cotton poncho from the top of my double-decker bunk to establish some "privacy" in my illness. Throughout the night they played, and the sounds of their shouting and the lulls in between would come and go as though from across the water somewhere in the distance.

The second morning brought just enough energy to propel me, vomiting all the way, into a farmacia, two blocks away. Quaking, I eventually succeeded in getting the dope inside my flaming guts. Now I began to recover, but my newfound good health of Chiapas was knocked for six.

Once I was free of the hothouse city, my every step was tracked by the sun. Sweat trickled off my nose, breathing became a conscious act, my stomach trembled, and the blisters on my swollen feet made the miles dreadful. All about me were oilfields and swampland; the region was a barely controlled jungle. Along the roadside sat dank pools of still water, like so many harbingers of incipient plague. At twilight the mosquitoes began their attack, and without net or repellent I suffered badly.

As darkness fell and the flares of the oil burn-offs lit the northern sky, I forced my way into an abandoned warehouse while trying to nurse a hundred bites. In an attempt to escape the insects, I built a cardboard cocoon from the cartons that were lying about and lay down inside. When the mosquitoes still got through, I was forced, despite the insufferable heat, to put on my coat and boots.

All next day the road weaved between clusters of ghostly-still pools harboring I-knew-not-how-many-millions of breeding mosquitoes. I found myself walking on tiptoe, dreading the possibility of being found out. As long as I was walking, everything was fine, but to stop and rest beside the road invited harassment. I could hardly breathe, the heat was so stupefying. (Several people told me that it was Mexico's worst heat spell in a century.) At one point I became aware that a group of women doing their washing at an ancient handpump down the road were intently watching my slow, staggering approach. As I passed, I begged them to toss a bucket of *agua* over me, which they did with relish. "Now, that feels better," I immediately said to myself. And I staggered on, like a drenched (and marginally happier) beetle. Finally, in Cárdenas, I found a place where I could buy repellent, mosquito netting, and quinine.

At the crossroad leading to La Venta I put down for the night at a café, draping my new mosquito net over two benches. One grim hombre lazing at a table seemed quite content to let three mosquitoes sit on his face and drink his blood. Was I alone troubled by these bastards that others could ignore?

This was my last night in Tabasco. I shuddered at the thought of having to put up with these conditions until the

United States, still about a thousand miles away up the Gulf Coast. It was almost May, the worst month, when the humidity would rise even higher before exploding into the next wet season. As I plodded along, I assessed my situation. My health was taking a worse beating than I had ever expected; my prospects were looking grimmer.

Then, like magic, the moment I stepped out of steamy Tabasco and entered the state of Vera Cruz, the clouds overhead formed a broad protective shield and the resulting drop in temperature produced a bearable, almost pleasant day. On I pressed, and for the first time I spied the Gulf of Mexico, which meant that I was looking on the Atlantic again.

Invigorated, I pushed on over the scraggly hills and over the toll bridge into the port of Coatzacoalcos. Here, the editor of the local newspaper took such an interest in my journey that he gave me two hundred pesos and allowed me to sleep out back in the tiny yard, where I made myself comfortable between the noisy printshop and the brick toilet. These accommodations may not sound like much, but it was always wonderful when I could get a "private" space, no matter how humble. I also appreciated the editor's story on me in the paper. It began: "There is a man walking the length of the planet—an Englishman, of course. . . ." The story then went on at length about the great English travelers of the past and suggested that I was continuing this tradition. It's a rare spirit, I thought, that can read such things into a bag of bones sleeping alongside his toilet.

In the distance puffed the giant oil refinery of La Cangrejera on the Bay of Campeche. Making my way to the open shoreline, I walked along the spray-blown rocks and drank in the open horizon. As I listened to the gulls shrieking overhead, my thoughts wandered back to the last time I had smelled the Atlantic, years before, beside Tierra del Fuego.

Southern Vera Cruz is dotted with towns packed close together. Once or even twice a day I would enter another pueblo, each more tumbledown and grimier than the last. The overall impression was of dusty decrepitude. In each town was a *parque:* a central, tree-lined plaza with a church at one

end and shops on the other three sides. They are cool and
tranquil focal points, with ornamental lampposts, flower plots,
and sometimes a band playing in the early evening. Every
Saturday night the parque would be the scene of a prome-
nade, as the young men would circle clockwise while the girls
walked counterclockwise, warily eyeing one another—the only
"legitimate" way for young people to become acquainted
without their parents fluttering around. In the meanwhile, on
the sidelines, the drunks also cruised about, like so many
wobbly sharks, asking anyone at all whether he would like to
have a tequila in their company.

The next blot on the map was San Andrés Tuxtla. The
center of this town contained a few moldy three-story buildings, while the hillside was stacked with shanties put together
from scrapwood and tar paper. In homes of this sort, millions
of Mexicans live without running water or even windows.
Surprisingly, in view of such squalor, the country has an ad-
mirable literacy rate (by Latin American standards) of almost
70 percent. One result is that the nation is comic-book-crazy.
Serious adults on buses, in cafés, or on streetcorners can be
seen engrossed in "*Super Hombre*" or "*El Incredíble Hulko.*"
In the larger towns there are even swap shops, which thrive
on buying and selling new and old comics, including expensive collectors' items, and where put-upon parents can be seen
flipping through endless stacks and comparing the issues with
lists of numbers their children have given them.

I was desperate to cool down, and the only place in San
Andréas Tuxtla that would let me inside was the jail. What
an evil place: men lying about half-naked on rusted bunks
with dirty flattened cardboard boxes for mattresses while clouds
of mosquitoes drifted randomly over them. These were the
guards! Behind them, dozens of sweat-glistening prisoners
peered out at me through the bars. The only water was an
exhausted trickle dripping from a nub of pipe poking out of
a rotting wall. As I took my "shower," in full view, the inmates' constant requests for cigarettes gave way to jeers and
shouts from prisoner and guard alike. Just as long as the liq-

uid touched my blazing brainbox, I couldn't give a damn about any of it. That night I slept adequately on the cathedral steps.

Santiago Tuxtla is remarkable in at least two respects. In this small pueblo of colorful villas with chipped paint, there stands a stone Olmec head, reputedly two thousand years old, that stands ten feet high—the largest ever found. Also, I never tasted better medicine than the elixir compounded by Padre Manuel Alvarez Zarola, the village priest. Perhaps it was because each test tube of the good father's potion was topped with gin. In any event, it seemed to keep my bladder in normal functioning order as I walked by the sugar plantations of Lerdo, across the Río Papaloapan, and into Alvarado.

The land had become increasingly swampy; at one point I passed the aptly named Motel Swamp. I briefly examined the city of Alvarado, a run-down fishing port, from the vantage point of the Disco Apollo IX, a second-story dance hall I had been led to by a character named Jimmy. One stranger or another—often, it seems, wearing an oversize gold medallion on a chain—always seemed to be towing me off to strange places.

I finally reached Vera Cruz, Mexico's principal port and the site of Cortés's original landing (not to mention the 'anding, in this century, of the U.S. Marines). I headed for the British consulate, a crumbling centuries-old stonework building that is dominated by a colorful coat of arms displayed beneath a wrought iron veranda. Inside, I discovered that my new boots had arrived; they had actually been delivered to the address on the package, and to my further amazement there was no duty to pay.

I was also happy to find the following letter from Yoshiko waiting for me:

Dear George and Father,
This is first letter after we had a new baby, Geoffrey Susumi. Congratulations! You've got a son now!
Last night you came to me in my dream, but with black

hair like Geoffrey. When born he was 4.110 kgs, even bigger than Ayumi. (Both were biggest in hospital.) He drinks so much milk.

I got your tee-shirt, it still smells of road. I will wear it as a part of you in this summer. Ayumi loves to see your snaps. I want you to see her watching at you in photo so seriously.

I love you so much.

Yoshiko, Ayumi
and GEOFFREY now!

Heartened by such joyful news from home, I moved on. But this coast, too, was hot and fly-ridden; the Gulf, now constantly visible, gave a sharp blue hint of tantalizing coolness through the shimmering haze. The days moved like a slow dream; nights were spent wherever I could, sometimes on an isolated beach, where I would feel marooned and think on the days spent with Yoshiko on the Fuegian shore, where she used to build driftwood fires.

From Papantla and its vanilla fields I moved on to Poza Rica. Here I took a trip out to the pyramids at Tajín, the ancient capital of the Totonacs, once the proud possessors of a thriving civilization at a time when my forefathers were living in rude forest settlements under Saxon rule. The present-day Totonacs are a slightly different story, a dirt-poor lot in white cotton garb and straw hats—the people who are usually victimized by both the gringos *and* the bandidos in the movie westerns. Nevertheless, I was lucky enough to see the Totonac rain-making ceremony. Five men in colorful costumes climbed a thirty-foot pole. While one of them, standing on a tiny platform at the top, stamped his foot in time to an eerie tune that he played simultaneously on a pipe and drum, the other four gracefully wound down to the ground, head-first, at the ends of ropes that were attached to the top.

I reached the port of Tampico, the last large city before Texas. At the British consulate I found more mail. The news was that Yoshiko was busying herself in preparation to meet me in Texas, and that she was bringing not only Ayumi, but also our newest, Geoffrey—*and* Dr. Matsumoto, my father-in-law!

Ayumi, it appeared, was also busy:

> This morning your silly daughter took a soap and sponge and a big bucket and went to tulips in garden. And can you imagine what she did? Yes, she started to wash them, and then she gave them a lot of water, so kindly. This is your genius daughter.
>
> So you lose my watch again. You'd better wear a big, big clock which nobody can carry away. Oh, George, I really need you, your hands, your existence.

> Love,
> Yoshiko XXX
> Ayumi, Geoffrey

Also, Mum wrote to say that both she and Anthony were flying over, too. What a reunion! In his letter, brother Anthony, the financial savior of this journey, enclosed three hundred dollars, a whopping sum for me; with this loot I could now easily reach Texas without concern for finances.

North of Tampico there was nothing but flat, empty desert; apart from the low scrub there was no other variation in the landscape. This bleakness was somehow a relief—few new people or places to absorb or negotiate a way past. I took some medicine, some liquid calcium a dentist had given me, and my mouth was so parched that I drank half a large bottle before I noticed the warning label—I had taken enough for two months.

In Estación Miguel, I spent two nights in a Mennonite mission. The administrator, Linwood Koehn, wore a black beard and dark, simple clothes, and his home was similarly stark and orderly. During my stay I was struck by the fact that his wife, as well as other women of the Mennonite community, almost never spoke to me directly (although they did betray some emotion by singing religious songs while doing the washing). I sensed there wasn't much equality of the sexes here; there was, in fact, none. Linwood educated me in this regard by showing the passages in the Bible where God has given man dominion over woman.

While Linwood Koehn's views and life-style differed greatly from mine, I remember him above all as a gracious and sympathetic host. Just as I was leaving the mission, he slipped ten dollars into my hand—one of the most heartfelt votes of confidence I ever received. Scores of missionaries along the way had dismissed me—and particularly my vocation—the second I failed to embrace their faith. Many wouldn't content themselves on being merely humorless; they had to try to scare me to death in the bargain. One in Central America told me point-blank, "If you don't accept Jesus Christ as your personal savior and become a born-again Christian, then it's the big fiery pit. And when you get there, don't say I didn't warn you!" For many of these Bible-beaters, the only route to salvation was *their* way. Bless you, family Koehn.

Past Estación Miguel, I put in at a poor finca belonging to one of the families Linwood had converted. A rickety wooden bed was set up on the dusty grounds—it was much too hot to sleep inside—and there I spent the night. In the early dawn, the mother threw a blanket across my bare legs—she didn't want the children frightened. With a mixture of pride and sadness, she showed me a picture of her eldest son, who had left home two years before to join the flood of "wetbacks" who venture north and enter the States illegally by fording the Río Grande. In the photo he was grinning as he stood next to the symbol of newfound success, a bright red secondhand Ford.

For those living in poverty, the lure of the nearby Land of Plenty is understandably irresistible, but here I saw the other side of the coin: the despair of those who had been left behind, a despair rooted in the knowledge that they would never see their family together again. The pueblos that I now walked through were largely empty; they are dying, I thought. It was as though the region were being sucked into a whirlpool.

July 12, 1980, I crossed the Tropic of Cancer—4:36 P.M.,

to be exact. Marking the spot was an ugly yellow cement ball, supposedly representing the earth, with a black line, representing the Tropic of Cancer, scored into its surface. In 1977, in northern Argentina, I had entered the tropics wondering if I would ever get out of them in one piece. Now, as I left the torrid and entered the temperate zone, the climate seemed, if anything, more torrid. A hot wind arose, and by sundown the air was full of whistling sand. Suddenly, just in front of me, a stray dog stepped in front of a speeding car and was killed instantly, as if by execution. The sight of that dog lying there, still and silent, milled in my mind with the vision of the dozens of mashed armadillos I had seen along the same road, a poignant reminder of my own mortality.

In a restaurant that evening, I felt compelled, before I should die, to tell someone about my accomplishment. I decided that the dim waitress would do. "Do you know," I boasted, "I'm the only man in history ever to walk from . . ."

She cut me off with a "*Sí, señor.*"

I persevered. "Nobody else has ever . . ."

"*Sí, señor,*" she cut me off again. "We know you have been out in our beautiful countryside enjoying perhaps too much sun, *señor.*"

I thought: Beautiful countryside? But it's just desert!

She then admonished: "You must wear your sombrero always, *señor.*"

In contrast with my recent itinerary, Soto la Marina was such a pleasant pueblo that I spent several days there. The highlight of each day would be late afternoon, after siesta, when I would sit in the parque drinking lime juice, idly listening to a medley of sounds—the chitchat of the juice-cart vendor and his customers, the tinkle of ice, and the slap of the ladle as the man stirred up the lime juice in the oversize glass pitcher.

This town was just the right size for the amenities—food, shelter, one good store, a working refrigerator somewhere— and for getting to know everyone. An important feature of such settlements that made this possible was that they were all town, no suburb. The city limit would be nothing like the usual featureless merger of more highly populated areas. Rather, the road would come to an abrupt halt. The concrete would just stop, and then there would be nothing but desert sand and cactus.

On the road to San Fernando, I stepped out of the noontime glare and into a café that seemed nearly blacked out. In the corner, *camionistas*—truckdrivers—sat at a table, gossiping. From out of the chatter I managed to hear the familiar words *"caminar"* (walking) and "Alaska." They were talking about me. As the men rose to leave, I stopped one and asked, "Why are you talking about Alaska?"

"There is an inglés walking there from South America."

As he obviously didn't associate the skinny gringo before him with the gentleman in question, I saw this as a golden opportunity to find out what people really thought about this journey. Playing devil's advocate, I asked him, "Is he crazy?"

The burly *camionisto* glared at me. There was a pause as he seemed about to say something in anger and then changed his mind. Still agitated, he finally said, "No, no—he does what he must," and then added with some force, "It's very hard and very hot out there, you know." As he left, he slammed the door behind him. Clearly this soft gringo had insulted him, the man on the road—how could he ever know his tribulations?

Later that day, the evening was in the process of forming red and gold while the scrub-brush desert remained unchanged; I could see for miles. After the liberation of tearing off my sombrero and sunglasses, I felt larger and fresher than life itself. There was no traffic; I was alone.

For some time now, perhaps years, I had been trying to pin down the real significance of this journey, this prodigious output of energy. Now, as I paused to rest, I began to read a magazine account of a Russian pilot who had defected by flying his MIG-25 to the West. As I pondered what this Soviet air force lieutenant had to say about his country's system, I suddenly came to the realization that under a Communist or any other totalitarian form of government, my journey and

dream would have been vetoed by some middle-level bureaucrat. From that moment on, the walk became what I perhaps always sensed it was: a Celebration of Freedom.

I reached San Fernando, a near-empty junkyard sitting
in a glaring sandscape. Just as I entered the town the power
failed. (This was becoming so common that I had once again
taken to carrying candles in my gear.) The farther I walked
from the tropics into the North American summer, the more
blazing the climate became. (Some leagues to the north, people were literally dropping dead in what was eventually dubbed
the Great Texas Heat Wave.)

My berth in San Fernando was in a garage attached to
the church. I literally had to shovel a coffin-size space out of
the accumulated debris to get in. Even this token shelter didn't
last long, however, as the church was being used by loud,
all-night worshipers. I couldn't sleep, and so retreated, like
Scaramouche, up to the cramped belltower, but this, too,
proved a disruptive bedroom. Every fifteen minutes the bell
would ring: first once, then twice, and then three times, all
the way up to the hour—or almost up to the hour. About
five minutes before the hour the bell would chime the hour—
plus one! The same number of chimes would be repeated,
God knows why, five minutes *after* the hour. Get it? Midnight was the jackpot. At 11:45 P.M., we got three *dings;* at
11:55 P.M., thirteen *dongs;* and at 12:05 A.M., yet another
thirteen *dongs.* In the morning, the villagers occasionally
stopped on the street below to gawk at my stooped form—I
had become the Hunchback of San Fernando.

North of San Fernando, in the midst of more barrenness,
cars from the States twice stopped to ask me where "the town"
was—"any town." For hours they had seen nothing. With one
I had to share my water.

My last night on the Mexican open road was spent sleeping on the ground alongside a kiosk that seemed to be mostly
held together by the cola signs nailed to its walls. At dawn,
I was surprised to hear movements of people stirring inside—
an entire family was living in there. The sleazy householder

stepped outside, and spying me, thundered, "I will call the police!" I laughed in his face at the very idea of it. Today I didn't give a damn; today I was exultant; today, barring a catastrophe, I would complete the first-ever foot-slog of all Latin America.

It was three and a half years to the day since I had left Ushuaia at the tip of South America. That I had earlier been tossed out of a Red Cross clinic on suspicion of being a drug addict might suggest my appearance and condition. At 5 feet 8-1/2 inches I was a tailor-made trashery, and decidedly underweight at 8 stone, 1 pound (113 pounds). My mouth was a bloody mess. I was losing my hair, now bleached blond (to everyone I was "the Swede"). The bones in my hip joint ground together. My face was riddled with various holes, spots, and scars, my eyes deeply lined from years of squinting into the setting sun. My bladder malfunctioned. Everyone I met took me to be forty. (I was twenty-seven.) All in all, I was damned lucky to be here at all. Could it really be luck? By now I had dismissed this idea and come to the conclusion that I was being looked out for and that the prayers and good thoughts of so many were somehow protecting me.

I was coming to an end—an end to chaos, filth, and squalor, of course, but also, sadly, an end to the warmth of these little-known Spanish-speaking peoples of the Americas, an end to the sight of mud huts on a hundred hillsides, bravely poking out of the mist at the beginning of yet another harsh day—an end, too, to that cool young Englishman who began this march.

So many ends, so many feelings, but ahead, very close now, awaited my family and a hundred new beginnings. The smudge on the horizon before me was Matamoros, beside the Río Grande. At the sight of this long-sought goal, my heart glowed cherry red with the relief of having seen my dream half-accomplished and the pride of personal achievement fulfilled.

Texas

It was my last day in Latin America. Just across the Río Grande was Brownsville, Texas, the long-dreamed-of U.S.A.; and there also my waiting family, including little Geoffrey, the son whom I had yet to hold.

I had just finished packing my gear in the dormitory of the Matamoros Red Cross center when I heard a commotion in the corridor, and then a familiar voice: "Are you there, Brother?" Into the room burst Anthony, puffing, soaked with sweat. Something terribly urgent had clearly propelled him here, across the border.

"Here," he said, and then caught his breath. "Thank God I've caught you in time!" He then unceremoniously pressed a small package into my hand—a dozen condoms. It had not escaped my protective elder brother's attention—God bless him—that Yoshiko had already returned home pregnant twice in a row.

The shallow, muddy Río Grande ran slowly beneath the bridge. Compared to the crumbling façades I had left behind, the clean, sharp lines of the U.S.A. seemed almost painfully inhuman. As Yoshiko and I marched side by side across the International Bridge into the United States, we were bursting with happiness; we were together again; again the journey was ours, not just mine. Atop my shoulders bounced little

Ayumi. The stumbling baby had grown into a loose-limbed, free-running tot.

And what a relief it will be, I thought, once again to be able to converse in my native language. Left behind in Matamoros was my tattered copy of *Spanish in Three Months*, folded open to page 8, as it had been for the past year. No need for that again.

We reached the far end of the bridge. A burly American border official in uniform strode forward to meet us.

"Good morning," I said.

"*Buenos dias, Señor el caminante de Ingleterra, vengo aquí!*"

"*Sí, señor, sí . . . ,*" I replied in resignation.

With a minimum of bother I was granted a full year's visa; the friendly officials even waived their authority to search my gear. (Or were they just avoiding my socks?)

Outside the Immigration Office, we were at last all together. I hugged Mum, the brave, tiny lady who later admitted that she had waited constantly in fear of the black-bordered telegram announcing the worst about me. Hanging back only slightly was Dr. Matsumoto, my father-in-law and staunchest supporter; when others had counseled me to end the journey and rest content with one record or another, it was always he who, reflecting the tradition of his culture, insisted that I must keep my word, uphold my honor, at all costs. "George, you must keep going to the end," he had said.

And of course there was—dare I believe my eyes?—five-month-old Geoffrey Susumi (his middle name means "keep going"), here in his stroller in the Texas dust looking like a punchball bladder about to burst, the most cuddlesome bundle I have ever beheld.

America only really began for me, however, in Room 112 of the Brownsville Ramada Inn. To a tramp who has never seen its likes before, an American motel room is surely one of the wonders of the world: wall-to-wall carpeting; a banana tree outside the French windows, and beyond, sparkling through the foliage, a swimming pool; running hot water, with ice close to hand; enormous beds with cushiony mattresses, box springs, crisp, spotless sheets, and heart-stopping soft, deep pillows. Just to submerge into all this starched hygiene was heaven.

There was no lightning bolt of realization that, yes, I was north of the border; rather, there were a series of unique American moments. Perhaps that strip of paper across the toilet seat swearing an oath to the god of sanitation—quite a novelty after years of bushes and buckets. As time allowed, I stole a few moments away from my family in order to wander the streets of Brownsville alone. What struck me was its stonelike silence—no street music, no central plaza like that pulsating world across the river; just a few stores catering to day trippers from Mexico.

Otherwise, everything in Texas was just as portrayed in legend—nothing but the biggest: the endless rows of huge cars that sat in runway-size parking lots, monstrous malls that housed acres upon acres of merchandise, and the vast horizon that seemed to stretch to infinity.

In different ways we all experienced culture shock, perhaps none so much as Dr. Matsumoto, who acclimated by falling in love with everything American (and especially everything Texan), from Big Macs to J.R. Ewing on TV's *Dallas*. He even got to wearing a stringy Texas-style necktie and ten-gallon hat, the sight of which sent Texans in their turn into culture shock.

During our two-month stay in Brownsville, I became reacquainted with my family in a variety of ways. One afternoon after returning from a short tour of Brownsville, to avoid a quarter-mile detour I had crossed directly over a six-lane expressway and, unaware that the heavy-gauge wire was sheared off at the top, punctured my hand in climbing over it. I was hurt and angry—and scared. My first thought was that I would die of lockjaw if I didn't get a tetanus shot immediately.

Back at Room 112 of the Ramada Inn, everyone reacted in character. Anthony, taking on the role of Meegan, M.D., insisted that there was "absolutely nothing to worry about."

283

Mum, a former nurse, glanced at my minor wound and simply exclaimed, "You silly fool!" Only my father-in-law seemed both concerned and sympathetic; he asked after my condition for days afterward. Yoshiko, busy feeding the children, looked at me with that half-smile that told me her thoughts—"Yes, I really do have *three* babies."

Anthony finally agreed to drive me to a clinic for a shot. No sooner were we out of the door than we were almost blown to the ground with a violent slap of windy rain. It was the harbinger of Hurricane Allen, which would turn out to be one of the most destructive of the century and was at this moment ploughing a lethal path through the Caribbean, savaging Santa Lucia and Haiti with 185-mile-per-hour winds. Brownsville was being evacuated. By the next day two hundred thousand people had fled inland from the vulnerable southern Texas shore. We made a calculated decision to stay on at the inn, which even now the owner was busy boarding up.

Things were getting exciting. The night clerk burst violently into our room and gasped desperately, "We're abandoning the top levels—everyone to the ground floor immediately!" With Ayumi in a blanket and my journals under my shirt, I ventured out into the raging weather en route below. Outside, I looked down the road and saw no cars, no people, nothing; only the driving rain blowing horizontally down the expressway.

The power was out. The water was out. From somewhere Anthony found a flashlight and was now in his element marshaling and ordering about the few guests who remained. I said to Anthony, "I'll bet you fifty cents it doesn't get any worse." "You're on," he replied with a smile. Just then a palm tree crashed through the nearby window.

For three days and nights, the seven of us remained hunkered down in our candlelit room, listening to the latest weather reports on a portable radio; without air-conditioning we were sweltering in the insufferable heat, and it was all we could do to keep the children happy. Our life-style was much like mine of the previous road days. For years I had longed to escape the life of bottled water, canned food, and flickering candlelight. Texas had been the doorway to that escape, and now this great wind had carried my past ahead of itself.

We were spared the full force of Hurricane Allen (much to Anthony's and my disappointment) when it stalled just off-shore, and all we got was a savage storm with eighty-mile-per-hour winds.

Soon after all the excitement died down, the grandparents and Anthony prepared to leave. For our last evening together, we dined at the local restaurant specially chosen by Dr. Matsumoto as his favorite—Pizza Hut. Always ready to make the most of any occasion, and inspired by the new sense of family that we had all experienced over the past two weeks, I had composed little rhyming tributes to everyone, which I now recited between bites:

Dr. Matsumoto, I presume, what a grand surprise
To see you sitting down here before
    my very eyes . . .

and

With all my heart, Mum, I'm happy you're here,
You've traveled so very far, to be so near . . .

and

Now, to my brother, who is never bored,
For he flits about on BAC Concorde . . .

and

So you think I'd forgotten, Yoshiko?
But really it's only my little trick, you know.
For you, Yoshiko, are my wife
    and number-one Queen,
You're the finest woman who is or has ever been . . .

It was often gratifying to receive publicity, but the little I got didn't always produce the desired results. About the third week in Brownsville I began getting indecent phone calls

285

of a gay nature. They persisted. It seemed that whenever I went out and returned the phone would ring immediately. I deduced I was being watched.

The idea that some man was in pursuit of her shaken husband considerably amused Yoshiko, who giggled when I would return to the room and nervously triple-lock the door. (She even made up a nickname for my secret admirer: "Blow-job.")

What made it all the more chilling was that the voice was vaguely familiar. The phone would ring, I would lift the receiver, and this treacly-toned voice would somehow make a direct connection with my inner brain. The voice began to haunt me. Christ, the voice was like the one on the TV commercial—it *was* the voice in the commercial! *That was the fellow!*

Knowing the culprit's identity neutralized my fear. At the next call I lunged at the receiver.

"I know who you are!"

"No you don't," hissed Blowjob, "I'm from out of state."

"No you're not—you're on the local TV commercial for . . ." He hung up, just as I was about to identify the sponsor, an insurance company. (No, it wasn't the "Good Hands" people.) He never called again.

I had to get moving again. Yoshiko knew this and volunteered that it was time she take the children home so that I could continue with the journey. Yet I didn't feel the time was quite right. I still hoped to pick up some form of sponsorship in the States, perhaps even get the use of a car to ferry my family along for the rest of the walk, or at least part of it. When nothing came of this, we decided to experiment with Greyhound buses and leapfrogging from motel to motel in a kind of upgraded version of our Argentine campsite-to-campsite routine.

To resume the walk, I first had to return to the border yet again and walk the uncompleted distance to the Ramada. I decided to get as many of the family involved in this as possible, and so on this stretch I pushed Ayumi along in the stroller, duly noting in my ledger that she had covered miles 10,409, 10,410, and 10,411.

Yes—"miles." How awful! I hadn't seen them in years, but now I was finally forced to use them. One mile took me sixteen minutes to walk, four miles per hour and four minutes. How messy when compared with a kilometer every ten minutes. My day's work might now be a miserable twenty-five units, whereas it could be a healthy-looking forty other units. A paltry 10,408 miles paled in comparison to a brilliant 16,653 kilometers covered so far. My efforts had been arbitrarily demoted. In my upcoming year in the United States, I never felt I was making sufficient progress walking distances reckoned in the American (and British) style.

Before me, stretching to the horizon, lay the vast Texas flatlands. The great road embraced me once again. My feet swelled up, my face hurt from the burning sun, and warm sweat dripped off my brow. Ah, yes, the road! After sixteen grueling miles, I bused back to the family.

The leapfrogging began. I moved the family to a motel in Raymondville. As we could only afford a single tiny room, the children had to sleep on the floor. At least there they had no place to fall; already Geoff had a gash on his face after falling out of bed. It was clear this strategy had its limitations, but we continued with it, not wanting to separate again so soon.

As my daily progress increased, I began to regain strength. The road ran true north, straight as an arrow across the scrub-brush-dotted chaparral. Occasionally I would pass stagnant pools filled with water lilies, their surfaces peppered with red, green, and white butterflies. Sometimes the land reminded me of Patagonia, especially when I passed through the low-lying towns and villages, except here there were groves of palm trees. Wood is at a premium in both places, and so substitutes have to be used in construction. In Patagonia, the people had resorted to adobe and tinplate, whereas Texans favored concrete blocks, which paradoxically made their buildings uglier, junkier, more temporary-looking. The facing boards on the sides of otherwise respectable motels in southern Texas were of such poor quality that they would be used for firewood anywhere else.

Money is not at a premium, however. I was amazed and annoyed to see that public funds had been used on one long, totally empty stretch of nowhere to erect a low concrete structure identified as a "Dog Comfort Station." This "nowhere" was in fact so total that most days the only thing breaking up a day's march would be roadsigns counting down the miles to a "Trash Disposal Station"—a little curve of extra road with a plastic-lined bin set at an angle to facilitate dumping without having to get out of one's Oldsmobile.

I was nearing the King Ranch, nearly one million acres of fenced-off land—large even by Texas' bloated standards. I had learned something about this stretch of land earlier, when stopped briefly by the Border Patrol, federal agents who have been given the thankless task of stopping the unstoppable— the flood of Mexicans who constantly cross into the States seeking work. One of the officers had told me that the ones who are caught and sent back to Mexico just try again the following week. Some of those who are not caught end up trudging the King Ranch backcountry and never come out again, the unfortunate victims of starvation, exposure, or rattlesnake bite.

It took several days on the road for me to negotiate the King Ranch and reach Kingsville (owned, of course, by the King Ranch). I moved the family up here to the Sage Motel (owned, of course, by the King Ranch), and we had a look around; aside from Texas A&I University, it seemed a bleak place. There was one taxi in town, its driver a woman.

"Aren't you frightened to drive alone?" Yoshiko asked the señora.

"No. I carry this," she said, pointing to the Colt .45 resting in her lap.

By the time we reached Corpus Christi the expense of keeping my family on the motel circuit was draining our funds—actually, my stalwart brother's funds (he had generously lent me money again). Now there was obviously no alternative but to make plans for Yoshiko and the children to return to Japan.

In the meanwhile, I was still looking about for a sponsor. During the past two months, I had been following up dozens of leads nationwide, in the process spending a small fortune making long-distance calls and sending letters, trying to capitalize on my endeavor for some backing—any kind of backing. I never got past the executive secretaries; the entire corporate world was "taking a meeting."

The effort to "sell myself" was repugnant; it was having a worse effect on me than the traumas of the road. I became a chronic worrier; I developed a facial tic. The last night Yoshiko and I spent together, I angrily accused her of paying more attention to the baby than to me, which, of course, was true—and totally irrelevant to anything. Yoshiko's response was to slam the door in my face. Within moments, the firestorm had passed and we locked hands. Last days often seemed to be like this; we were both on edge. I finally decided sponsorship could go to hell. Negative reactions, no reactions—all these were signs, I decided, that not only would I never be sponsored, but I shouldn't be. I must complete the journey with the same backing that had brought me this far: the people.

About this time I received a letter from Maud Copeland, an elderly widow living in a hot and poor part of Panama City, which moved me very deeply. She had enclosed a single dollar bill—"to buy some milk." This kind lady's pittance meant more to me than any commercial sponsorship. If a corporation couldn't underwrite my trip, the goodwill and prayers and gestures of a thousand ordinary folk became that much more meaningful.

"How long to the end, George?"

"I don't know . . . about four years, I suppose."

"Could you possibly make it in three?" Her mood was quiet. I quickly dug out a map and using my hand as a "year-stick," considered the situation. It looked almost possible.

"OK, love . . . I'll go for three years."

She smiled, and just then the family's flight was called. As the queue rapidly reduced, I bit my lip. Yosh looked sad, too, as she headed with the children for the loading corridor. Ayumi trooped resolutely into the jumbo jet, her huge new toy, without looking back, and then Yoshiko and Geoffrey were suddenly gone also.

Now my thoughts dwelt on how I was going to reach Alaska in three years' time on the $330 stashed in my money belt.

"Wow, can we give you a hand, Mr. Meegan?" an editor at the *Corpus Christi Caller* kindly asked. Forced to practice a new economy, I took the bait. "Perhaps something to buy a meal?" It was the first time in my life I had asked, however obliquely, for such assistance. I didn't get it.

That night, to cross the bridge over the Nueces River I had to negotiate a tiny eighteen-inch strip of concrete for a solid half-mile, fending off the mesmerizing glare of hundreds of oncoming headlights. The whole time I tottered barely six inches away from the roadway—and so close to the crash rail that the friction scorched a hole in the nylon rucksack—while a steel ribbon of two-hundred-horsepower machinery screeched by at the regulation fifty-five miles per hour.

Reaching Sinton, I immediately set out to find shelter. During the journey I had certainly slept in a variety of odd places: hidden by a blanket draped over a table that was supporting a crèche in a busy street in Colombia; inside a giant pot in Peru; in a burnt-out movie house in Nicaragua. I would have preferred a luxury bed every night, but who can argue with Providence? In Sinton I slept on a judge's lofty bench, directly beneath a photo of LBJ.

In a shower of mosquitoes I hit Refugio, a town with a Spanish name just southwest of Calhoun County—an Irish name. An American pilot with the Dutch name of Hans Vandervlugt took me home. I thought: This is America; America contains all the world.

Farther on, my idealism took a battering. As I sat inside a general store in Colet Creek, seeking momentary escape

290

from the sun and insects, the owner brought out a rifle and ordered me off the premises. (I naturally complied, and without hesitation.) A few miles down the road I turned off at a gas station and told the boss what had happened. He knew who the man was, he said—a newcomer to these parts, from somewhere up in Illinois. Then he bit his cigar, spat, and snapped, "Goddam Yankee!"

In Victoria the church elders sniffed at my press clippings before declining to let me sleep on the Sunday School floor. The fire station just gave me a crude "No." (This was going to be harder than in Latin America, I thought.) And so it went with the police as well, but not before one of the officers, after hearing my story, snapped, "Yessir, I sure as damn hell know where Tara Dee El Fargo is!"

It was growing dark. Reluctantly I crashed my fist on the heavy door of the Salvation Army emergency center. The grim custodian, looking suspiciously like an ex-bum himself, signed me in and mentioned that there would be no food until breakfast at five-thirty the next morning. This was bad news, as I was famished and it wasn't yet nine. Even at that hour my fellow paupers were already making their way to the dark, dank bunkroom.

While stripping for bed, one deadbeat making idle chatter said he had been an extra in the film *The Alamo*. A few of his cohorts gasped. "Were you one of Travis' men, Willie?"

"Nah, I was a Mexican," he admitted dejectedly. "They put me in the back," he added. "I didn't even get a uniform." Everyone nodded in an understanding way. There would never be any uniforms, not even Mexican ones, for these unfortunates.

A middle-aged man in the next bunk, whose face was the same gray as the dormitory wall, removed his broken boots from his sockless feet. Glancing down, I noticed that his big toe was missing. "Walking must be difficult," I said, more as a question than an observation.

"Sure is," he said in the sweet, nasal accent of the region (where "sure" sounds like "shore"). "Lost it on a farm machine as a kid." His name was Jim, and as we talked I saw that he was not only a sad but a decent man.

"Want a watch, Jim?" I chirped. For some reason I had three on me.

"Gee, sure do." My reward was seeing the flicker of a smile illuminate his face.

At nine o'clock the lights were turned off, and soon most of the men were asleep. I lay awake for hours, keenly missing the opportunity to watch TV, especially Johnny Carson—a newly acquired habit from the Brownsville days.

At 5:30 the lights came on; by 5:31 Jim was frantically shaking me. "Guy! Guy!—you gotta get up and hand in your sheet and pillowcase!" Grunting some sort of acknowledgment, I fumbled through this exercise and then made my way to the mess hall. Everyone else was already up and eating, in total silence; as I entered I felt several eyes staring at me. It was a dreadful 5:40. At the counter stood a glowering, thickset cook wearing a stained apron and chef's cap and rapping a wooden spoon into the palm of his beefy hand like a billyclub. "Wadja think this is—a hotel?" he said.

I passed up the opportunity to make a sarcastic reply and instead stared downward in humble silence. A bowl of cornflakes, presoaked for at least half an hour, was vigorously pushed my way. I joined the others and ate in silence.

By six o'clock the residents were leaving. Jim was pulling a well-worn knapsack over his shoulders. "Where to, Jim?" I asked. He said he had heard a rumor that there were fruit-picking jobs maybe a hundred miles to the east, in Brazoria County, and then limped off into the chill darkness of the early morning, a gallant and tragic sight.

I resolved never again to resort to one of these places: It was just too dispiriting to see so many sorrowful, defeated men.

The countryside was now more populous. I was in the heartland of the Texas agribusiness as well as the richest urban-industrial region in the state. Whenever I looked at my map, the great yellow splotch of Houston lay up ahead like

a burst fried egg. Houston is urban sprawl taken to its furthest illogical conclusion, and although it was still over a
hundred miles away, Interstate 59 was already sucking me
into the city's yokey orbit. I decided to reduce the effects of
its gravitational attraction by taking loose aim at the fringes
of Galveston Bay and thus skirt Houston's epicenter.

With relief I moved onto a tranquil byway in Jackson
County, and for the next 30 miles I passed only two stores.
At intervals the flat landscape was broken up by farms and
paddocks and stands of trees that seemed to float in the distance. Past Midfield, I sailed along a little-used farm road for
hours, past a sea of rice paddies. The first Europeans to come
here, shipwrecked conquistadors in the sixteenth century, had
found only cacti; now a passing farmer told me, "This is maybe
the most productive rice land in the world. I get three tons
an acre on my one-man operation—and the average everywhere else is only half a ton. Ya know why? Chemicals and
specialized machinery."

It was becoming a thirsty march. I approached a matron
sitting in a deck chair in her garden and asked if I might have
water.

"No."

I was flabbergasted. No one had ever denied me this ba-
sic request. How could anyone be so far removed from reality? I concluded that only a supermarket mentality of the worst
order would refuse water to an obviously weary traveler. Shame
on you, lady of Texas!

I had always thought that the southern United States was
relatively warm year-round, but now, in late November, I could
feel winter fast approaching. A cold front settled over the region, and sharp winds rattled through the gray skies. On the
news, they were reporting that the Texas panhandle, barely
600 miles to the north, was already under snow. Entering
West Colombia, I could hardly function for the cold and was
eager to find a motel.

By this time, I had more or less developed a standard
approach to asking for a room. At the check-in desk I would

293

ask to see the manager, explain my walk with the visual aid of one or two press clippings—a front-page item from a nearby town's newspaper was always best—and then ask if I could stay the night, making it clear that I didn't need a regular room. I didn't mind if it wasn't made up. It could even be an out-of-the-way storeroom—anyplace I could put my sleeping bag down in relative privacy.

Ironically, the lower the staff position of the person I was talking to, the greater my chances for being refused, which is why I always asked to speak to the manager. In the same vein, the fancier the accommodations, the better my chances were for a room. The people who ran fleatraps would often be hard cases, having been approached so many times before, while the managers of the posh hotels, perhaps anticipating some publicity, seemed honored to have me.

The manager of the Twilight Motel, D. L. Wilcoxson, not only gave me a room gratis but treated me to breakfast. D. L. was a no-nonsense, let's-roll-up-our-sleeves fundamentalist. It was his practice every evening to stand outside the motel, resolutely face the horizon, and deliver the following exhortation: "Devil and thy work, begone!" This was more than an exercise in faith. Before he accepted Jesus, D. L. told me, there had been occasional trouble at his motel, and after one incident, when an irate whore threw acid in his face, he decided to keep a gun hidden behind the front desk for protection. "But I dumped it," he said. "I would get a bad attitude. A customer would come into the office—nobody special, maybe just somebody who I didn't like the way they walked—and all of a sudden I'd be thinking, 'I can blow your damn head off,' and it might be just a normal guest."

I was getting closer to Houston in spite of myself. When the farm road I was walking suddenly veered off and ran smack into the madness of the Galveston Freeway, I gave up trying to avoid the inevitable. I set my mark, phoned a friend's son, and was soon driven to the center of town. Through the suburbs we passed mile after action-packed mile of spanking new development and half-flung-up construction. No public transportation to speak of here, however. In the building frenzy that was going on, city planning became obsolete even before the requisite surveying could get under way. Services like municipal bus lines simply couldn't keep up.

Houston is quintessential Oil Boomtown, U.S.A. And even though it lies 10 to 20 miles inland (depending on how you define metropolitan Houston), the ship canal linking it to the Gulf of Mexico makes it a major seaport. Houston remains a depressing memory for me, but not because of the hyper-development and the boastful attitude of the citizenry (epit-omized by the overblown Astrodome with its four-story-high scoreboard). It was here that my worst fears were confirmed about the prospect of walking through the United States, where a stranger on the city streets after dark might be someone out to buy a pack of cigarettes or—who knows?—a potential assassin. In the few days I spent in Houston, someone I just met was shot in the stomach—in a dispute over a parking space. Shortly after, I heard on the radio that John Lennon had been gunned down by some maniac in New York City.

It was then I decided that once I reached the north-eastern United States I would cross the continent by way of Canada, which at least had had the sense to outlaw handguns. Some time ago I had made the decision to aim for Washing-ton, D.C., and then make tracks for Alaska. This would em-ulate, somewhat, Tschiffely's ride from Buenos Aires to the U.S. capital a half-century before. If successful, this massive dogleg would make the journey the longest single march ever. The gamble, entailing an extra year or two of exposure, was enormous. I knew that if I kept on that road enough days, enough years, something or someone might eventually kill me. Now I was beginning to feel totally vulnerable; aware that America has more than its fair share of evil cranks, I planned to continue north after reaching Washington and get out of the country as soon as the journey allowed.

Returning to Galveston, I found my mark stuck amid the junked-up construction site by the freeway and resumed the march toward Louisiana. I crossed the San Jacinto River by going underneath it, through the tunnel, but not before hav-ing to make a half-dozen phone calls to various officials, who finally waived the no-walking regulations for me. In the Land of the Car, I was learning, bridges and tunnels can be severe obstacles to the pedestrian.

In Beaumont, which was choked with industry, I had trouble finding food—that is, the food I wanted. Throughout Latin America I could have killed for a McDonald's. Now there were at least a dozen fast-food chains in every town, but nowhere was it possible to get proper food, like a decent boiled cabbage, the way Mum made it.

The Deep South

No arid plains here; this was Louisiana bayou country—Calcasie Parish, to be exact. (In Louisiana the counties are called parishes, a vestige of the days when this territory was part of France's New World empire.) The landscape was half-drowned. Beneath the concrete piers of the elevated highway lay rotting wood, tangled vegetation, and a half-submerged confusion of trees struggling toward daylight. It was my first day in Louisiana, my first state of the Old South. Hoping to sample some of that legendary southern hospitality but not counting on anything, I got off the highway near Vinton and knocked on the door of a rectory. After a minute it cracked open a few inches, barely enough for me to see the bespectacled priest peering out at me. "Ahem . . . excuse me, Father. I'm walking the length of the Western Hemisph—"

"Good—keep walking!" the priest snapped. Then, without waiting to hear the rest of my standard introduction, he pulled three singles out of his pocket and shoved them into my hand before slamming the door shut. Down the road I tried another church and was again rejected. The old biddy in charge there was also of a mind that I shouldn't leave unfulfilled, and so she gave me a stern lecture on Christian values.

I finally struck paydirt at the Vinton police station. A

couple of the fellows on the late shift were nice enough to let me camp out in a back room. In the morning, however, I was rudely awakened by an officer who had just come on duty and whose way of introducing himself was to kick his shiny black boot into the mattress beneath my head. "What the sonuvabitch are *you* doing here?" he growled.

"But, sir," I protested groggily, "I was invited . . ."

"Shut up, hippie! Get over here," the man barked, motioning me into the office. I finally got to blurt out the events of the previous night, and at my insistence the officer made a series of radio calls to confirm my story. I began making notes in my diary, and when he noticed this, the man said, "What the hell you doing *that* for?" Word started coming in that I was "all right," and the bombast grew more sheepish. Then a couple of the officers from the night before drifted in.

"Hey, Bob, he's writing a book," one of them shouted from across the room. "You're going to be a star!"

"Oh, hell! I didn't know that."

"Too late, Bob," the man gloated, "you're in there now." Then, addressing me, he said, "Hey, Limey, see you spell his name right. It's Sergeant R. Miller: R for Robert, M-I-L-L-E-R."

"Oh, hell!" whined Miller. "God, I just fly off the handle. I'm sorry." We got to talking. Under his prickly exterior Bob Miller was a pure softie with a heart of gold. Afterward he even had me look up his mother-in-law in a small town along my route; she and I ended up joking about Bob's famous temper.

Interstate 10 through Calcasie Parish had a paved shoulder, which in effect provided me with a lane of my own. Aesthetically, however, this was Standard Superhighway. The "landscape" basically consisted of a galvanized, waist-high crash barrier between the westbound and eastbound lanes and, flanking these, ranks of threadbare trees whose leaves were grimy from constant exposure to exhaust fumes. The only variety in all this (aside from the traffic) was the litter. It's amazing what one finds dumped on the roadside: kitchen appliances, carpentry tools, books, magazines, and even pornography— lots of pornography. At one point along this road I found a Polaroid snapshot of breasts—just a huge pair of breasts. The fantasies provoked by roadside trash can be hard on a long-distance walker. Just as the hamburger wrappers I had found along the road in Nicaragua turned out not to lead to a McDonald's, neither did I find those breasts up ahead.

At the beginning of the new year, 1981, I reached the outskirts of Baton Rouge. The state capital sat just across the Mississippi River, whose slow-moving gray-brown waters had barely come into sight when I began contending with three jam-packed lanes of speeding traffic. Worse, the New Mississippi River Bridge had no walkway. I summoned up all my concentration, as clearly one side glance could easily spell disaster. The officer in the passing Highway Patrol car looked at me aghast, and seemed to want to arrest me, or at least warn me, but even he could not control the traffic, and so he disappeared, swept along in the flood of speeding metal, leaving me only with the mental image of his despairing glance. After fifteen solid minutes fearful of even blinking, I finally reached the east bank and slipped off onto one of Baton Rouge's quiet side roads, rather like a calm lagoon behind the thundering surf on a reef.

Route 190 out of Baton Rouge was a more humane road to travel. The problem was that the motels, whose comforts I now sorely craved, were all on the interstate two miles to the south. So that I could enjoy the best of both worlds, the Highway Patrol often courteously ferried me the two miles to and from my mark. I resented the very idea of walking any distance off my route. The miles either counted on the grand total or they did not, and when they did not it was an utter waste of energy and knee cartilage.

Just beyond the aptly named town of Walker, I racked up 11,111 miles. The numbers appealed to me. At no other time on the journey would five digits on the mile scale be the same. I vaguely recalled 1,111 km in Patagonia long, long before, and this thought brought home to me the magnitude of what had been achieved so far. I thanked the great power for my survival and hoped for future benevolence.

In Covington, however, the motels wouldn't touch me. The sheriff, his paunch bursting through his shirt, threatened, "I'll drag you across the state line, boy." He emphasized his point by slapping his hand with a long flashlight, which apparently doubled as a cudgel. The local priest gave me a fifteen-minute lecture from his porch entitled "Looking After Yourself," the substance of which was that I should write ahead to every point on my itinerary stating my intentions, etc., etc. I might as well work in an office, I thought.

To many Americans and most Europeans, Mississippi represents what is most shameful about the "southern mentality"—poverty, illiteracy, racist rednecks, all mixed up in a subtropical stew. For me, clipping along I-10, however, there was no obvious difference between this state and Louisiana; it was the same endless steel stream of mobile America.

With relief, I slipped off the federal artery and onto a pleasant side road that led down to the sea and my old friend, el Golfo de Mexico. (I never could get that language straight when I was there, and now that I wasn't I couldn't get it out of my mind.) Flanked by yellow pines and green meadows, I reveled in the silence of my new road and the salt smell of the ocean wafting my way.

Resting on a hummock beneath a tree I finally took a look at the newspaper I had picked up earlier that day in Slidell, back in Louisiana. A few days before, the *Slidell Sentry-News* had sent over a reporter to interview me. Fed up with hearing the same old question, "Why are you doing this?" I had answered, "Because I'm a professional nut." I was interested to see the story, but the front-page headline came as a real shocker:

"Professional Nut" Living the
Dream That's In His Heart

As if that weren't enough, above the contents listing was my picture with the caption

Professional Nut Visits Slidell

This time they didn't even grace my "nuthood" with quotation marks: It was no longer alleged—it was fact. The story ran over to page 4, under the heading

Professional Nut (cont.)

Such press would make motel rooms hard to come by, I thought, although there was doubtless a psychiatric bed waiting for me back in Louisiana.

Blue moods usually left me after a few hurried miles, but today the cool gray sky and the soggy white sands along the Gulf permeated my being. For days I had been out of kilter, suffering from sort of ground-level vertigo. The cart trailing me was as much support as burden.

For two days I moved weakly along the rock-strewn shoulder of Route 10, listening to the muffled dash of el Golfo against the shore. As I approached Biloxi, out of the mists, like a sinister apparition, rose Beauvoir, now a museum but formerly the residence of the president of the Confederacy, Jefferson Davis. Inside, I was enthusiastically shown about by several Daughters of the Confederacy. "Yes, sir," one of them told me, "our Jeff Davis was restored to U.S. citizenship by our Jimmy Carter in 1978." In my weakened condition I could hardly pay attention to what she was saying. I had to hold on to the wall from time to time to keep from falling down.

I sought out a pharmacist and related my symptoms: dizziness, weak appetite, and, particularly unnerving to me, a tremor in my left hand. The man urged—nay, ordered—me to see a doctor. Having neither the money to pay for a doctor nor the patience to follow the inevitable prescription ("You need rest . . ."), I fell back on my standard remedy—the road. I was simply addicted to miles.

301

Two days later I reached Pascagoula and crossed the state line into Alabama. Mississippi had taken just five days to cross. Now I was planning to take even less time crossing Alabama—not its entire breadth, but just the little foot that juts out around Mobile, giving the state its sixty mile coastline.

I marched across the gentle, green lowlands of southern Alabama for two days before encountering an obstacle, which finally materialized in the form of a tunnel leading to the port of Mobile. There was no way around it, and prominently displayed signs made it clear that it was closed to "foot traffic," as the humble walker is known hereabouts. In Alabama I had already been kicked off I-10. The officer had said, "No walking on the Interstate," which I found odd because the police in three previous states hadn't said a thing. By now reluctant to seek special permission and risk the attendant hassles and delays, I circled around the tollbooths and dashed through the tunnel illegally.

The next two days found me scrambling around the city from TV set to TV set. Ronald Reagan's inauguration and the release of the American hostages from Iran was a double bill I wasn't going to miss. I heard "America the Beautiful" played so many times that for days afterward I was unconsciously humming, ". . . and crown thy good with brotherhood, from sea to shining sea."

In the distance I could see a town, and then I heard the wondrous noise I always associate with Europe: Churchbells were ringing throughout the town. The American hostages had just been released by Iran. I wondered when again I would hear the bell of my own beloved St. Margaret's in Rainham.

On my way to Spanish Fort, I climbed the first hill since Chiapas Province in Mexico, some two thousand miles back down the trail. Small-town, rural Alabama was glorious. Great puffy clouds, driven by a brisk winter breeze, charged across the great blue dome of sky; the overpowering scent of southern pines filled the air. The pity was that I couldn't really enjoy it: My bladder was again in poor order, and just outside the village of Loxley, with no cover in sight, I was forced to relieve myself on a nondescript post by the roadside—it was the tenth time in three hours.

Farther down the road I stopped at a dreary little café for a bite to eat. I went inside and ordered a corn muffin. The other customers sat in silence and stared glumly at me. I hadn't taken two bites when a pudgy woman came over to me, introduced herself as the owner, and proceeded to unburden herself. "This town's got problems—brother against brother, friends that don't talk—all 'cause of the election, the mayor and all his friends. I'm tellin' you now for your own good, the police, they're gonna arrest you soon as you're outta here . . ." And here she leaned close to me and said in a conspiratorial whisper, ". . . 'cause you're a *stranger*."

I chalked it up as more of the nonsense that a traveler has to endure, paid my bill, and left. "Hey, boy," hailed the policeman as he pulled his cruiser up alongside me, "*you* are going to *jail*." I was dumbfounded; the Cassandra in the café was right after all. I glanced back over my shoulder and could see her even now peeping through her plate-glass window.

"What for?"

"What *for*, boy? I'll tell you what for—public lewdness, that's what for." An arrest warrant was waved in front of my nose; it bore not only the town magistrate's signature but my name as well (I never did learn how they found this out). Checkmate. I was locked into the back of the cruiser along with my gear and sped off to the police station. In the back seat I took a second look at the warrant, and this time saw the crime I was accused of:

A person commits the CRIME of Public Lewdness if HE exposes HIS ANUS or GENITALS in a public place and is reckless about whether another may be present who will be DISGUSTED by HIS act.

"You see, boy, you done gone and pissed on our City Limit sign."

My farcical interrogation took place at the stationhouse a half-hour from Loxley. As there was no judge sitting locally, one on the coast was phoned up. I put my weak-bladder case strongly, and the judge (no doubt a specialist in lewdness) ordered that I scrub out the jailhouse. By this time my captor had taken an interest in my adventures, and so mercifully ignored the order and whisked me back to my mark in Loxley. The officer was extremely courteous, and on our return trip he shyly questioned me about a town in Yorkshire—Batley—because that happened to be his name.

My entry into Florida could have been orchestrated by the Florida State Tourist Board. At the state line the country road stopped abruptly and the route became a wide slash of concrete highway stretching straight to the horizon. Alabama's overcast day had been so cool that the brisk wind forced me to zip up my jacket, yet hardly had I crossed into Florida than the sun burst forth. Down came the zipper and off came the jacket. Sweat began forming on my brow. It was like jet-hopping from northern Europe to North Africa. Although it was midwinter and much of the United States to the north was under several feet of snow, here in laid-back western Florida—Burt Reynolds country—it was all suntans, short shorts, and cotton candy.

Encountering little traffic, I skirted the city of Pensacola and was put up at the Rodeway Inn far outside town in exchange for some publicity from the local TV station. The next morning the TV reporter arrived with his "Eyewitness News" crew and set up for a taping on the road leading to the motel. The timing of the interview was appropriate, for this day marked exactly four years since leaving Ushuaia. The occasion was marked by suitable theatrics.

Halfway through the taping, an uninvited participant began yelling off-camera, "Love Jesus, you shit-heads!" The reporter blinked several times, trying to maintain his composure. Then I noticed a barefoot man in clerical robes standing on a grassy slope nearby, and recognized him from a recent newspaper picture—a cult member who went by the name of Jesus Christ.

The two-minute segment was hurriedly concluded, but

not quickly enough. The high-pitched, ear-piercing scream of a woman now rent the air: "Wake-up—for Christ's sake!" The force of the shriek apparently sent the audio meter dials off the far end, for the sound man winced and tore off his head-phones. This new voice belonged to Mrs. Jesus Christ, who had been hiding in the bushes and now, together with the Savior, came straight up to the reporter and stared at him with an expression of pure, concentrated hate. The reporter, in turn, with his two-minute brain, simply blinked. The interview was aired on "Eyewitness News" later that day, alas, with Mr. and Mrs. Christ scissored out.

Little by little, I was beginning to get the hang of what the local TV news crews wanted. Often they were a couple of hacks, with six more segments to tape that day, who asked that I "do something physical" for them in order to impart an idea of my years of travel.

In Crestview, I picked up my first mail in three months. Back at my motel room I found true contentment, with letters scattered all about my feet and the local specialty, souse (pickled pork trimmings), sticking to my ribs. What a joy to hear from Yoshiko: "Hello, dear George . . . hello, my love," she wrote. "I'm in Tokyo staying in a hotel alone and thinking of you so much. I'm watching TV in this room alone and realize your feeling staying empty, alone, terrible! I want you!"

Here and there on these flatlands, I would see some great tree streaming with heavy gray-green beards of Spanish moss and pass one of the coconut palms that dot the roadside. Occasionally I would imagine that I was back in Spanish America (as Florida once was!). The landscape and the humidity had something to do with it, but so did the sight of signs pointing the way to Valparaiso and Panama City.

In Funiak Springs, I exhausted all my possibilities for accommodations before ending up at the local jail. Although all the cells were full, the sheriff offered to let me share one. First, however, he warned me, nodding in the direction of one cell, "Don't get too friendly with this guy. The sonuva-bitch in there stomped his pal to death." Moving to the next cell, he said, "If you think that's bad, this guy's ninety-three-years old and he killed his goddam brother." I idly pondered: Could this man's mother, giving birth to two sons before the turn of the century, have possibly imagined that both of them would live past ninety—and then that one would murder the other? How mysterious our destiny!

Crossing a corner of Alabama to Columbia, just west of the Georgia state line, I took the narrow blacktop leading to the Chattahoochee River and crossed the bridge into the Peach State. I moved on to Blakely, whose distinction was a Confederate flag flying from the last rebel flagpole erected during the Civil War. I saw the Stars and Bars—the Confederate insignia—everywhere throughout the Deep South, not just printed on T-shirts and bumper stickers but flying in town squares. As with other "foreign" flags, federal law requires that the Stars and Bars be flown lower than the Stars and Stripes; in some cases here, this might be an eighth of an inch.

As I moved north, the rain came down in massive sheets, one day nearly five inches of it. My morale was so high these days, however, that no flu bug stood a chance with me. Come Cuthbert, I desperately charged out of the rain and into a general store, and without making the slightest explanation grabbed a can off the shelf, tore off the cap, and sprayed my legs up and down. "Ants," I told the clerk, as I paid for the medication. Crawling throughout my wet long johns was an entire regiment of them, lost and biting—they must have leapt onto me from the tall grass to escape the flood rising over Antland.

After a local motel owner called me a bum, I ended up at Cuthbert's Andrew College, where a passing student let me dry out and berth in his room for the night. This was the only time I ever managed to lock into the extensive American college system—and this was a fluke. Generally, I avoided colleges, as most seemed to be away from the center of town, my usual day's objective. Also, dealing with enthusiastic students after a tough day is very draining.

The next day I was sneaking away, congratulating myself on having avoided creating a stir, when I walked slap into Dr. Greer, president of the college. Before I knew it, I was addressing the student body, who applauded and cheered this "bum" of the night before. I was amazed. Some even asked for autographs.

Long before reaching Plains I was intrigued with the possibility of meeting Jimmy Carter, who had only just returned to settle down in his Georgia hometown in retirement. I realized I wouldn't be able just to march up his front walk and knock on the door, but then neither did I regard my idea as a foolish dream. After all, I had a remarkable precedent—the fact that Calvin Coolidge had granted Tschiffely an audience at the conclusion of his ride. What a thrill it would be to meet a leader of Jimmy Carter's stature! I decided that when I reached Plains, I would make a major effort to see him.

My heart skipped a beat when I saw "Visit Billy Carter's Gas Station" on the billboard on the approach to Plains. (That this billboard was the only one I ever saw for miles around may have been an indication of the Carter family influence—although, ironically, I later was told Billy had fallen on bad times and the station was no longer his.) Plains, set among the Georgia flatlands, is a very charming and very small town, with barely more than six hundred inhabitants; in one sense, it is not much more than the place where Route 280 temporarily becomes Main Street. While the town had only a few hundred residents, however, it had four churches, which for so small a community gave me an unusually wide choice in my eternal search for shelter.

I stopped at the first convenient parsonage and rang the doorbell, and when the young minister appeared I launched into the latest of my hundreds of introductions, this one beginning, "Hello, I'm English—and . . ."

The man nodded tolerantly as I rambled on. "Well," he finally said, "you might as well come in anyway!"

With minimum formality he ushered me into his bedroom. "You can sleep here," he said. "But what about you?"

said I in protest. "I'll put a sleeping bag on the living room floor—the experience will be good for me." While neither of us knew it then, the Reverend Thomas Quickel was to spend the next two weeks on that floor, during which time he became my guide to Plains and its people, late-night confidant, and ultimately my top adviser in the effort to meet Jimmy Carter.

"This town's going to be pretty hard to impress," he told me when I first mentioned my ambitious project to him. "For the past few years they've seen every kind of celebrity run backwards down Main Street with the same thing in mind."

Undaunted, I set out the next morning to the mayor's office. Boze Godwin III (he was also the town pharmacist, as had been Boze I and Boze II) was receptive enough to my presence—he was already aware of me from an earlier press release—but when I told him of my mission he came straight to the point: "I have absolutely no influence on anyone about getting you and the President together," he said. Then, as though giving me a consolation prize, he produced a blank, presigned certificate and intoned, "I hereby officially make you an honorary citizen of Plains, Georgia," adding with a gentle apology, "You'll have to fill in your name yourself— my printing's awful." At least we didn't waste each other's time: The whole transaction must have taken a mere two minutes in and out. Back at Tom Quickel's, I showed him my honorary-citizen certificate. "This is quite an honor, George," he said as he filled in my name with his fountain pen. To me it had seemed like the clap of doom.

Renewing my resolve, I next stopped in at the offices of the local newspaper, the *Plains Monitor*, where I no sooner walked in the door than I overheard two women in conversation, one of whom was saying, "Do you know, people come in here all the time wanting us to get them near Jimmy? I mean, the very *idea!*" Finally noticing me, she turned and smiled broadly: "And what would *you* like?"

I was shown into the office of the owner, "Brother" Sheffield, who had gotten wind of my passing and was glad to spare a few minutes telling me about the paper's checkered history. The *Monitor* was formerly owned by Larry Flynt, the same of porno magazine publishing fame. "The way I got to own it," said "Brother" to me, "was I said to my daddy one day, 'Daddy, I want a newspaper'—and so Daddy bought me *this* one." I was slightly encouraged when "Brother" assigned one of his reporters to write a story on my walk.

The Reverend Tom lived the proverbial bachelor's life amid a seeming blizzard of paperwork—every flat surface in the house (excepting the bathroom) was continually covered with papers. Tom's casual habits were a great relief to me, for they drew attention away from my own. Nevertheless, one evening he casually mentioned, "George, you know that green garbage bucket?" Indeed I did—it was rather a large one, and I had been throwing my chicken bones and other refuse into it for the past three days. "Well, it's not really for garbage. I use it for my incoming mail." Red-faced, I made straight for the bucket and frantically began sifting through its contents to retrieve my chicken bones. Tom stopped me with an outstretched hand and added quickly, "but it doesn't matter."

Over the days I began to settle down into the quiet life in Plains. I took walks through the town's few streets, past modest white clapboard houses, and occasionally strolled over to Reese's, a small supermarket near the black community at the edge of town, to buy cabbage and souse. By the end of the week, the townspeople got to know me. The Main Street Café was even providing free meals, and just about everyone I met seemed to be rooting me on. "Have you seen Jimmy yet?" they would ask. Alas, I would have to tell them, "Not yet." Perhaps not ever.

Mayor Godwin, among others taking up my cause, even went to the trouble to write a letter to the Carter staff, but no one there was responding. This was understandable. *Time* magazine reported that the former President was now in "semiseclusion." It was certainly well earned; if anyone ever deserved a rest from people like me, it was Jimmy Carter, now only a few weeks out of office. As the days rolled past and nothing happened, my chances seemed to be disappearing. I began taking evening walks past the Carters' low brick house, which after dark was perpetually drowned in flood-lights and patrolled by Secret Servicemen, heavily armed and constantly alert. Perhaps the only way I was going to see the President was to disguise myself as Willie Nelson and para-chute into his backyard.

My last hope seemed to lie in the nervous hands of Kath-ryn Addy Wall, the reporter who had been assigned to write up my story. I wasn't encouraged at our first meeting at the Main Street Café when she immediately got up on the table and shinnied up a pole—to prove she was sober. After sev-eral informal interviews, however, she became one of my strongest supporters. Over beers one night, with her deadline fast approaching and my time in Plains running out, she asked me to answer a two-pronged question that we both hoped would do the trick:

"Tell me, first, exactly why you want to see the former President, and, second, why he should bother to see you. Here," she said, pushing her notebook toward me, "write your answers out."

I jotted down a few sentences, noting that by coincidence I had started my walk the same week as Jimmy Carter's in-auguration in 1977, and that by meeting me he would be honoring the diverse peoples of the Americas, so many of whom have shared and continue to share my dream—my Celebra-tion of Freedom. "Some have prayed," I wrote. "A few have wept, but all have cared. I think Mr. Carter cares."

The very next day, I read my exact words in print in the *Plains Monitor*—a new kind of experience which I found nothing short of amazing. Even more astonishing, however, was the message scribbled on a notepad by Tom Quickel which I found (by some miracle) in his living room that Sunday morning: "George—Miss Alton [Jimmy's aunt] called. Also Miss Allie [Jimmy's mother-in-law]. Jimmy says meet him at the church. Victory in sight! Tom." In a panic I bolted out of Tom's living room and rushed over to get a haircut from No-rinne, a hairstylist who worked out of her mobile home and was known to "do" not only the local farmers but the Pres-ident as well. While I was there, I mentioned that I was looking for a camera. Perhaps I could even take a photograph of the President. For eight dollars, Norinne's son sold me his grimy Instamatic, complete with frayed holding strap.

I hurried over to the Maranatha Baptist Church, where the Carters worship, without the slightest idea of what kind of arrangements had been made, and arrived just as the congregation was filing in. All the while, in contrast to the devotional atmosphere, Secret Servicemen were busily scouting the area and working their walkie-talkies, which would periodically come to life with bursts of garbled static. A black limousine pulled up and a slightly stooped, gray-haired man holding a little girl by the hand walked down the path to the church entrance. Despite the tight security surrounding him, he looked curiously alone and vulnerable, certainly different from the Jimmy Carter familiar to me and to millions of others from years of media exposure.

Finally I sighted some friends who had come to worship and who knew my situation. We entered the jam-packed church together and took seats not far from where the President and Amy were sitting, near the front. From time to time during the sermon, I glanced at the man in his severe blue suit and ancient spectacles, and noticed that every so often he would put his arm around his daughter. When the service ended, Jimmy and Amy began walking back down the center aisle, and then a kind of muffled hysteria broke out from a group at the back, apparently tourists and well-wishers, who began cheering—one even shouted, "Hey, Jimmy, we all love you . . . we're from Illinois!"—while the congregants looked on with stoic tolerance. Jimmy continued down the aisle, supremely relaxed, smiling confidently, gently acknowledging the hubbub and shaking hands on all sides—including, for one electrifying moment, my own—and then he left.

This was *it?* But this was a disaster! Sensing my disappointment, one of my supporters approached the President's cousin, Hugh Carter, and I overheard Hugh say, ". . . Yes, a nice lad, but he's not seeing anybody—just transition government people." I glanced over at Dr. Collins, the pastor, who gave a despairing shrug. Jimmy Carter's aunt came over.

"I saw that you shook Jimmy's hand—did you get what you wanted?"

Who in hell was I to say the President's hand wasn't good enough for me—that what I really wanted was an audience. "Yes, thank you, Miss Alton," I responded bleakly. I left the church, crestfallen—at least, I tried to leave the church, but a young Baptist, so moved by the spirit that he was weeping openly, chose this very moment to latch onto my arm and try to convert me.

Back at the parsonage Tom Quickel asked me, "Well, George, did you get what you wanted?"

"Well, yes and no . . ."

When I explained what had happened, Tom took me to the Kentucky Fried Chicken in nearby Americus, but not even Colonel Sanders could lift the gloom.

"You know, George," said Tom, "the problem is that when you go after what you want, you're too reserved. You've got to be more outgoing, more forceful—like those folks from Illinois who shouted out in church. You've got to speak up for what you want. Be more assertive!" Perhaps Tom was right. I thanked him for his advice and said I would try to follow it.

Later that day I was at the home of yet another minister (and supporter), the Reverend Barrett. "Any luck—did you meet Jimmy?" he chirped.

"Well, yes and no," I said, and then explained what had happened.

"Why not say a word to Murray," he said, referring to Rosalynn's brother Murray Smith. "He's in the garden, over there."

Downcast, I wandered over to where Murray was energetically cutting the grass. "Did you see Jimmy?" he cheerfully asked.

"Well, yes and no," I said, and then explained what had happened.

"Well . . . he's seeing nobody. We've even had folks here who put him up for the night on the campaign trail—no luck for them, either. It's my guess that when you shook hands

Jimmy didn't have a clue to who you were. I believe *he* would be the one honored by meeting *you*." (I was thunderstruck by the compliment, especially from one of the family.) He went on: "I'll tell you what. I'll tell Momma. She might be able to help."

"Momma" was Miss Allie—Allie Smith, Rosalynn's mother.

The next day in the company of my stalwart friend Tom Quickel I went to see Miss Allie. On the walk over, he advised, "Miss Allie is the kindliest lady in the world, but she won't waste a single word. She doesn't engage in small talk— you'll end up answering your own questions."

We climbed the two steps to the porch of a white clapboard cottage, and Tom knocked on the door. It was a long wait, and I was getting edgy, but finally a curtain moved and then the door squeaked opened. A small, neat, white-haired woman stood there, staring at me full in the face. Tom made in introduction of sorts to which Miss Allie gave a slight nod. All the while her clear blue eyes never left me. Ignoring Tom, without preamble she went straight to the point.

"Did you see him?" And then, to make sure I knew which "him" she was talking about, she said, "The President?"

"Well, yes and no," I said, and explained everything. Miss Allie never said a word, just slowly nodded.

"Do you want to come in?" she finally said.

"Well, yes and no. You see, right now I have to go the the dentist, over in Americus. But I'd like to come back later, maybe, if it's OK."

She shrugged. "OK—but not for long. I'm going to Murray's for dinner."

Tom drove me to the dentist in Americus, and later that afternoon I returned alone to the white clapboard cottage. Again I found myself on the porch nervously waiting for Miss Allie to answer the door.

This time there was no hesitation. Excited, she motioned for me to get into the car sitting in the driveway. "Quick, quick—let's go. I've just heard that Jimmy is out in his backyard, and we might be able to catch him."

313

My heart stopped momentarily. The next thing I knew I was sitting beside Miss Allie in her subcompact and we were driving (at surprisingly high speed) along the streets of Plains toward the Carters' house. "I called Rosalynn," she explained, "and she said Jimmy's been doing some woodworking and right now he's in the garden."

In practically no time we were at the Carters' single-story brick house just off Main Street and were waved through the barricades by the Secret Servicemen. After parking the car, Miss Allie quickly disappeared into the house, leaving me in the tree-shaded backyard, alone . . . But no—there he was, Jimmy Carter in jeans and red lumberjack's shirt, barely a few yards away on a small rise.

My heart began thumping. He approached with immense strides, a solid, sleek Jimmy Carter, moving as relentlessly as a naval destroyer, bearing down on me, appearing even more self-assured in work clothes than when I had seen him suited up for church.

The strangest feeling came over me. I felt numb. Perceptions of everything about me were unpredictably altered— movements alternately slowed down or seemed to be instantaneous, as in a herky-jerky home movie. My systems were running on raw nerve, my mind on automatic pilot. Whatever thoughts or impulses had brought me this far—curiosity, compulsion, admiration—now faded, and I was seized by the overwhelming realization that I was absolutely unprepared for whatever was about to happen. Attempting to slow down the man's inexorable approach—for a panicky moment I thought he was going to trample me—I was amazed to discover that I still had a voice as I shouted up the slight incline, "Hello, Mr. President!"

"Hi! Nice to meet you," said the President, beaming and moving ever closer. This is uncanny, I thought: the smile, the voice, the small wave, the tilt of the head—all precise copies of Rich Little, the impressionist!

He ground to a halt just inches from me. We shook hands. Something in me—perhaps my upbringing, or the English tradition of deference—amazingly prevented me from looking him in the eyes. To regain my composure, I ventured a declarative sentence: "I have made such efforts to see you, sir, because by meeting me you recognize the thousands of ordinary people of my journey in South America, Central America, Texas . . ."

For a fleeting moment I dared to look straight into his face, at the great smile more than anything, to gauge his reaction, and then my eyes retreated to the safety of staring blankly at his shirt pocket. His eyes suggested he hadn't the foggiest notion of what I was talking about.

I also sensed that he was impatient to go. But wait . . . out of the corner of my eye I saw something that gave me the chance to hold him a little longer. In the driveway, one of the President's sons and a handyman were struggling to lift something large onto the back of a pickup—from where I stood it appeared to be an enormous doghouse. Then I noticed the President furtively glancing in the same direction, as though eager to help, and so I blurted out, "Shall we lend a hand?" He muttered a noncommittal "Ummm . . ." and taking long strides charged off to the action, while I trotted along behind like a faithful gun dog.

We reached the pickup, and as he stood there assessing the situation I felt compelled to say something—anything. Unfortunately, I should have heeded the advice of one of Carter's predecessors, Abraham Lincoln, who remarked that when someone thinks you a fool, remain silent so as not to confirm it. For in all innocense, I breezily offered, "This must be the biggest doghouse in the world!" The President's only response was a stupendous silence and a slight movement of the head in my direction. Then I saw what the object was: Amy's dollhouse. What a stupid remark!

Things grew worse. No longer paying any attention to me, the President joined the two men in an effort to lift the awkward load and began heaving. Horror of horrors . . . there was no room for me to push! This was undoubtedly the low point of a lifetime full of looking on helplessly from the sidelines. I had no choice but to stand aside and bleakly watch a President of the United States lift and shove barely two feet away.

The job done, the Great Man turned and retreated to the garage and the woodwork he had been doing before all these interruptions. Remembering Tom's admonishment to be forceful and shout for what I wanted, I made a desperate appeal: "Mr. President!" He stopped dead in his tracks and spun around. Screwing up all my courage, I said, "Mr. President, can I have a photo?" He grimaced.

"I don't have a camera," he said, a little apologetically.

"But I do!" His face dropped as I reached into a plastic bag and pulled the Instamatic out by the filthy string attached to it. "I bought this from Norinne the hairdresser's boy for eight dollars," I said, hinting at the fact that the same person had cut his hair as mine (and perhaps hoping he would regard it as happy coincidence).

"Eh!" And then, with an imperial wave of his hand, the President put an end to this trivia. Heaving a sigh, he pointed to the beat-up carpenter's apron about his middle. "But I'm wearing *this*," he protested with a soft moan.

"It's fine!" this tramp offered in consolation to the statesman.

"Chip!" he bellowed. "Come take this picture!"

Chip Carter appeared momentarily and took the camera by the filthy string as he would a dead mouse by the tail. Now the President was standing by my side—whether it was with or without the carpenter's apron I was too shocked to notice at the time. (In fact, he had taken it off.)

Click! The picture taken, his duty done, Jimmy Carter was gone in a flash, and a moment later, after handing me my camera, Chip, too. I was left standing in the backyard alone. I glanced about. A security-system TV camera bolted to a tree peered down at me.

As Miss Allie was nowhere in sight, I concluded it was time for me to get out. I walked among the leafless trees around the side of the house and reached the path leading to the road, my composure returning little by little with each step toward freedom.

Behind me I heard a shout. I halted. It was Miss Allie; she was beckoning me to come back. I reached her just as someone rushed out of the house and dashed toward us, an attractive girl wearing a red kerchief and sunglasses. She wasn't any Carter that I could recognize, and as she approached I tried to figure out who it could be, perhaps an aide, or a student, or—Good Lord! It was Rosalynn Carter, Miss Allie's daughter! Suddenly, I was back on automatic pilot.

"*Very* nice to meet you," she said, cocking her head slightly and taking my hand. There was warmth and sincerity in her manner, and as I stumbled over a few words (much the same ones I had recited to her husband) I sensed that she actually knew what I was about. (Only much later did it occur to me that it was, in fact, Rosalynn who had agreed to let me come over—basically as a favor to her mother.) After a few sentences my voice began to crack, and Miss Allie kindly came to my rescue, addressing me firmly: "We must go— they are preparing for a trip to Atlanta tomorrow."

Miss Allie drove me back to her house, where at her invitation I spent the remainder of the afternoon chatting about our respective families. At one point she browsed through the scrapbook I had brought along with me and came to a stop at one of the recent headlines. "Professional nut, eh?" she asked.

"Well, ah . . . yes—a misquote."

Miss Allie nodded in apparent understanding of the occasional cruelty of the press. "You know," she said, referring to reporters, "they sometimes say such terrible things." As we continued talking, however, it became clear that world affairs held less interest for her now than the annual Peanut Jamboree parade down Main Street, and Jimmy's decision where to locate his new Presidential Library concerned her less than the new dentist she had found for him in Macon.

Throughout that long afternoon chat I sensed that Miss Allie enjoyed sharing this time together almost as much as I appreciated the honor. Outsiders who came to Plains to see the Carters, I had been told, were invariably "Jimmy's people," or "Rosalynn's people." Perhaps now I could be considered one of "Miss Allie's people."

As I began to leave, Miss Allie asked me to wait a moment while she went into another room, and when she returned she shyly pushed several tightly rolled cylinders of paper into my hand—several ones, and a five. Quickly taking my hand, she said, "To help you on your way," a phrase I had heard so often in Spanish and numerous Indian tongues.

I stood again on the doorstep, but now the small white porch was flooded with gold as the sun set across the red clay fields of Plains. As I took my leave of this gracious and unassuming lady, I asked if she would mind if I kissed her on the cheek. "Of course," she said, and so I did.

Among my partings in Plains, there were many heartfelt ones, from so many wonderful people: Tom Quickel (who was as choked up as I was), Boze Godwin, Kathryn Addy Wall, and, of course, Brother Sheffield, who wrote in the *Plains Monitor:* "We salute you, George Meegan. You are a jewel in the crown of your Queen and country." And when I left town the next day, I still had, in my imaginary kitbag, the memory of a kiss for Miss Allie.

Eastern Seaboard

Past Savannah and the Georgia state line, I passed through South Carolina and kept heading up the Atlantic coastline, invigorated by the clear sea air. Just as I entered North Carolina on a glowing spring day, with new leaves casting shadows on the narrow road, the words came over as clear as a canary's song: "Get out of the road, you fuckin' asshole!" Normally, if a passing motorist shouted something at me—and most likely it would be an insult—the words were mercifully lost in the roar of the traffic, and in any event I had long since become inured to this kind of thing and tended to dismiss it. But hardly a day went by in North Carolina when I wasn't the target of some sort of hostile gesture or insult from passing cars. In my book, this state leads the league in this sort of nastiness.

As I approached Folkstone a car sped right up to me, stopping barely a foot from my knees. Though it had happened before, it was still unnerving—usually overzealous people wanting to chat or get an autograph. One of the two men in the car got out, and I extended my arm for a handshake, but he charged straight through the gesture, spread-eagled me facedown across the hood of the car, flashed a badge before my eyes (on which I just managed to read, "Food and Drug . . ."), and bellowed, "You cocksucking sonuvabitch acid-

319

head!" Still pinned against the car, I glanced around. The men wore no uniforms; the car bore no special markings. In the shock of the moment I considered that the ID badge could be phony. But there was nothing phony about the wicked-looking revolver stuffed in the madman's waistband.

"OK, you motherfucker, where's the dope?" demanded the official—or was he a nut? He glanced at his silent companion. "Search this shithead's gear." Bringing his face to within three inches of mine, he shrieked at the top of his lungs, "You! One peep from you and I'll stuff you in the fuckin' trunk and haul your ass over to the Onslow County jail."

"Hey," shouted the number-two man. "I found something."

"Whatcha got? Dope?"

"No—this dude's got a picture of him and that Jimmy Carter."

"Well, Jimmy Carter can come and get his goddam ass out of jail."

The two conferred on the roadside and finally retreated to the car, all the while shouting at me, "OK, cool it. Just cool it now"—and they drove off.

It hadn't taken me very long to get sick of North Carolina. I couldn't even find a single sixteen-ounce Coca-Cola bottle with its screw-on cap, so convenient for the road. As far as I was concerned, the South (as in "southern hospitality") had ended. And the North was still hundreds of miles away.

To avoid problems with North American traffic, I customarily sought to walk either the back roads or, oddly enough, the superhighways, where the paved shoulder gave me a lane of my own. The ones in between were the backbreakers. I was no sooner in Virginia than I found myself on one such hellish road after a nervous highway patrol officer ordered me off the interstate, forcing me onto the narrower and more dangerous Route 301, where I was far more vulnerable. With the chaos of bumper-to-bumper traffic swirling about me, I pushed on.

I arrived in Petersburg at night. In the United States,

entering a fair-size city after dark was always a nerve-wracking experience for me. Here, in a run-down neighborhood, I stopped in an illuminated sidewalk phone booth. While I kept fumbling around for a pen to take down a number, all about lurked fearsome night creatures, staring at me. How easy to imagine that every last one of them was a homicidal drug addict contemplating whether or not to strike.

By day Petersburg was not much better. A predominantly industrial city, it had that sooty look I associate with the mill towns of northern England—except that here there seemed to be a teenager bouncing a basketball on every street corner.

After I got the Yoshikart fixed up—a wheel had yet again collapsed—I took the walkway on the bridge crossing the Appomattox and continued past Colonial Heights and through mile after mile of grime-covered smoke-stacked industry. Toward evening Richmond appeared on the horizon, a smudge of dark shapes against the skyline. Little by little with the falling light, the buildings in the distance lit up. As I passed the fringes of Richmond and entered the metropolitan area, my ears were greeted with the inner-city "music" of howling police sirens.

In Richmond, while sipping a cider at the Penny Lane Pub, I fell into congenial conversation with a bulbous character named Andy Zavoy and his friend, a gray-haired gent named Les Ball. Les was a Scouser—a native of "La Pool" (Liverpool; scouse is a Lancashire hot pot stew)—who had served in Burma in World War II, of which he had many an interesting tale. The two eventually introduced me to the pub's owner, Terry O'Neal, another Scouser who once played Division I soccer with the greats. During Liverpool's pop-music glory days of the early 1960's, Terry retired from soccer and became manager of The Cavern, the club where the teenage Beatles got their start. At the time, they were earning, according to Terry, ten pounds (about twenty-five dollars) a man per night. All of this fascinated me greatly.

I ended up staying with Les and spent several nights camped out on his couch. When I left Richmond, my gear was loaded down with presents, including a clean white shirt from Commander Zavoy "in the event of meeting any brass in D.C.," fifty dollars, a Penny Lane Pub T-shirt from Terry O'Neal, and a photo from Les Ball of himself as a professional footballer. One of Les' neighbors wrote me a touching farewell letter, which included the following old Irish blessing:

> May the road rise up to meet you.
> May the wind be always at your back.
> May the sun shine warm upon your face,
> And the rains fall soft upon your fields.
> And until we meet again,
> May God hold you in the palm of his hand!

Route 1 out of Richmond was relatively tranquil compared to the traffic that I could see hurtling along the interstate just to the east, and north of Ashland the countryside became even more pleasant as the pastures became fewer and the road wound through hills carpeted with thick woodland. Approaching the District of Columbia, however, the road (at least my part of it) inexplicably got worse, and I had to contend with a soft, sandy shoulder with road ballast strewn all over it—tougher going than anything I had yet encountered in the United States.

As I climbed and stumbled up the road toward the crest of the last ridge on the approach to the District of Columbia, everything looked so temporary on this hill, like so much else on the outskirts of America's cities. The slope was awash with junk-food stops, gas stations, and windowless, corrugated steel sheds; it all could have been put up in a single afternoon.

At last the crest opened up to reveal the city sprawling out below, with the slender Washington Monument and the white dome of the Capitol standing bold and clear above the plain of the city. I rolled down to the Potomac River; far to my left was Arlington National Cemetery and straight ahead the Pentagon. When I reached the latter, I actually got lost for a frustrating quarter of an hour in its immense parking lot before being set straight by a stray lieutenant colonel.

An introduction found me at the doorstep of the house

shared by Billy Hall and Gerald Smith, two gracious madcaps who gave me space to sleep for several weeks behind the couch in their living room. My stay there, as it turned out, was fortuitous, for my long-unavailing PR efforts took an unexpected upturn when Billy put me in touch with an editor at the *Washington Post*. As they say, success breeds success. In chain-reaction fashion, the *Post* ran a feature on me which caught the eye of the editors at *People* magazine, who in turn decided to publish a story on the journey.

As the *People* article was not to appear for two and a half months, in the meanwhile I decided to explore similar avenues. For years, someone or other would inform me (daily, it seemed), "George, the *National Geographic* ought to do a story on you." In fact I had written them in 1975, even before I started the walk; they wrote back saying they weren't interested. After completing South America in 1979, I wrote again. This time I didn't even get an answer. Throughout the United States, I was asked one question so often that it almost became a drumroll: "Why doesn't the *National Geographic* follow you?" Well, the National Geographic Society was headquartered in Washington. Now, I would go along and ask *them*.

Ideally I would get to see the *National Geographic*'s publisher, Gil Grosvenor, but I had to settle for William Graves, the Expeditions Editor. Graves all but threw me out of his office.

"I've had three heart attacks in five years!" he shouted—or maybe it was "five heart attacks in three years." "You've got thirty seconds," he went on. "We don't normally let people up here, you know." I quickly scattered about his desktop copies of the pages from a 1929 *Geographic*—Tschiffely's account of his journey. Several comments and observations that Tschiffely made half a century ago still held true when I passed through the same territories, I told him. My journey was a natural for the *Geographic*.

"You're too late," said Graves, ignoring the material spread out in front of him.

"But you did an article on Jenkins," I said, referring to the author of *A Walk Across America*, "after he'd been only

323

ten days on the road. I've been out there a hundred times longer than that—much longer."

"Well, Peter was lucky—he had a dog that happened to drink out of Gil Grosvenor's toilet!"

"Well, I *had* a dog," I snapped. "Too bad *he* never lived to drink out of Gil Grosvenor's toilet!"

This was obviously not going to lead anywhere, so I changed the subject. The *Geographic* had supplied Jenkins with a camera and film; perhaps they would do as much for me. "Can I have a camera?"

"No."

"Film?"

"Likewise. You're not a photographer, George. We would have to teach you. I'm sorry, George," he said, winding up our interview. "Your journey is a great one, but we missed it this time. Perhaps next time."

Next time! As a final irony, the receptionist slipped me a dollar on the way out.

I had hopes of meeting another President, the one in Washington—just as Tschiffely had done (he was received by Coolidge). A Texas friend contacted his congressman, Dan Archer, on my behalf, but when I went to Archer's Washington offices he told me, "I'm sorry, Mr. Meegan. The President of our great republic has not responded to my entreaty." He then turned his head to stare at the wall clock and didn't move a muscle. I excused myself, and left.

There was still a chance. A friend in Charleston had arranged a meeting for me with a fellow South Carolinian: James Edwards, the Secretary of Energy.

At the appointed hour I gathered up my portfolio of references and news clippings and was driven down Consitution Avenue by Bob Sherbow, the photographer assigned by *People* to cover me. The July morning air was as hot and sticky as ever (the humidity in Washington during my entire stay reminded me of the Atrato Swamp), and I was sweating straight through the white dress shirt Andy Zavoy had given me for just such an occasion. Sherbow noticed that I had no jacket. "You better wear a jacket, George," said Bob. "Remember— these guys are Republicans." He lent me his.

I reached Secretary Edwards' suite, where the reception- ist settled me into the luxuriously appointed waiting area. I didn't know how long I would be kept waiting and so decided to use the time to make a copy of a reference I had just picked up from the Voice of America, a new document that might help.

I took a knife and opened the envelope. But what had I done! I had sliced through the letter along with the envelope! The valuable reference lay on the chair slit into two sections, the top third rift from the rest. How could I be such a fool? In a few minutes I would be presented to James Edwards himself.

Casting Sherbow's jacket aside, I frantically got down on my knees and with some tape gingerly repaired the broken introduction, a ticklish job under the pressure-filled circum- stances. Every so often a Texas-oilman type would apologeti- cally step over my kneeling form. Eventually I managed to tape the letter back together, make a copy, insert it into my presentation, and get Sherbow's jacket back on—just in the nick of time, for just then the door to an inner office opened and I was ushered in.

Here I was confronted by the Secretary, a powerfully built gray-haired man who greeted me in a warm though wry man- ner. He began on an encouragingly light note. "So you're Harry Gregorie's friend, and I'm told you know Jacksonboro," he said, referring to a tiny hamlet that I had visited in South Carolina.

"Yes, sir, I saw a giant sturgeon there who looked a mil- lion years old."

His eyes lit up. "Uh-*huh!* South Carolina has the world's best caviar—that's sturgeon roe, you know." We seemed to be off to a good start.

"I believe you were at sea," he said. "Did you get your license?"

"Yes, sir, a second mate's—in fact, it's still valid."

"Oh, I was a third mate myself, but my license has unfortunately expired."

This was even better! But turning to the business at hand, he said, "I'm very sorry, young man. If I were the President, I would see you. But I've spoken to that fellow Deaver"— referring to Michael Deaver, deputy chief of the White House staff and unofficial keeper of the President's time—"and he said no."

"Well," I mumbled, "if I might show you my stuff anyway." Seeing him nod slightly, I opened a large envelope and took out the *Washington Post* story and a reference from the head of the Voice of America, which I knew to be one of Reagan's hobbyhorses. "And here's a letter of support from the British embassy," I said. Here he raised an eyebrow. (The embassy had cautioned me that Edwards, formerly governor of South Carolina, was a pol to his fingertips.)

Next out of the envelope was my formal letter of request, headed by some lines by Robert Service:

> There's a race of men that don't fit in,
> A race that can't stay still,
> So they break the hearts of kith and kin,
> And then roam the world at will.

"So you like Robert Service, do you?"

"Yes, sir." More importantly, I knew that Reagan liked Robert Service. I took my last shot. "Mr. Secretary . . ." I spoke up boldly, and motioning toward the enormous picture window, I made a melodramatic sweeping gesture with my arm that covered half the Washington skyline. (To my utter amazement, his eyes actually followed my hand.) "Mr. Secretary," I continued, "there are a great many people out there who want this thing to happen."

"Well," he said, stroking his chin, "I suppose we'll have to do this again, won't we?"

Just then the photo that Chip had taken of Jimmy Carter and me came tumbling out of my envelope. The look that came over Edwards' face was like that of someone who has just learned his next-door neighbor is Martin Borman. Leaning over to me, he asked rather archly, "And how is *he* doing down there?"

With that the gracious man ushered me out. The next day, according to the *Post,* he flew off to confer with King Khaled of Saudia Arabia—and I walked on to Maryland.

I had learned to live with loneliness, especially the loneliness of separation from my loved ones. I coped, but sometimes I went clean through the ice, as I did one night in my room at a motel near Baltimore. I was reading the latest letter from Yoshiko: "Dear Spanish Teacher—Geoff has 6 teeth now. The front ones are so big. My mother calls him Beaver-chan."

The TV happened to be tuned to a media awards ceremony, and glancing up at the screen I saw Shimada Yoko, co-star of the *Shogun* miniseries, trotting up to the dais to accept her award. I instantly thought of Yoshiko. Her very absence hit me like a jolt of electricity. I fell to the floor as though pole-axed. "Yoshiko, Yoshiko . . ." I screamed over and over again.

By morning, with my emotions back in the bag, I struggled on, fractionally deader, sustained only by a hope to finish. I crossed the otherwise insignificant northern latitude of 39°43′—the Mason-Dixon line, the Maryland-Pennsylvania state line that is the traditional boundary between the American North and South. As a youngster I had the mental picture of the South as a small corner of this country (where white plantation owners lived it up in their mansions while blacks toiled out in the fields under a hot sun and sang spirituals). Hardly. In truth, the South is immense; trudging from the Mexican border to the sands of Florida and then north to here had taken me nearly three seasons.

Pennsylvania wouldn't take long. I was only cutting across the southeast corner of the state, on the way to New Jersey and headed for New York City.

The Pennsylvania countryside opened up ahead; its

greenery had a parched look in the withering ninety-seven-degree temperature, the most gasping heat I had experienced since Tabasco, Mexico. Squinting under my sombrero I spied an amazing sight ahead: a horse and buggy approaching me on the road. Eventually I could make out the driver and his passenger, both of whom completely ignored me in passing—a bearded man with a dour expression and wearing a white shirt and black waistcoat, breeches, and hat, and, by his side, an equally severe woman in a black bonnet and ankle-length dress.

This was Lancaster County, the famous Pennsylvania Dutch country, and the horse-and-buggy pair were Amish, who together with the Mennonites and similar sects are known here as "the Plain People." (Nonbelievers, whether white, black, Hispanic, Indian, or anything else, they call "English.") The Plain People resolutely maintain their eighteenth-century life-style while shunning the benefits of the world of microchips and Big Macs, although most do not avoid all contact with the "English." At a village named The Buck, I found a baseball game in progress, and among the fans in the stands sat several of the Plain People somberly looking on, in stark contrast, in their homespun jerkins and breeches, to the brightly uniformed players on the field.

As I passed an Amish farm at sunset, on a distant hilltop, in dark relief against the reddening western sky, I could see a team of four horses dragging a plow and sending up small plumes of drifting dust—a scene deeply evocative of the mystical communion of man, animal, earth, and sky. Despite their self-imposed ban on modern machinery, the Plain People are superior farmers who take full advantage of Pennsylvania's rich brown soil. The entire countryside, in fact, looked landscaped, every corner well utilized, every hedge neatly trimmed; everywhere I went looked like a picture postcard.

Of all the counties in America, I had held a vision of just this one for years. I had read James Michener's *Centennial* in Argentina and longed to see Lancaster County—not for the Amish, but for the Lancaster town market. And now here I was wheeling the Yoshikart straight through the very brickwork gate described in Michener's book and right up to the cubicles of polished white tiles and red brick and the tables groaning under sumptuous culinary displays. At last I could satisfy my senses that this was real. Richly dressed meats with pungent aromas, brightly colored vegetables, juicy, over-stuffed sausages (I bought a bratwurst)—they were all here, just as Michener described them. What unadulterated beauty in this setting, what a welcome relief from the sterile, flu-orescent aisles of the typical supermarket.

Past Reading and throughout the Lehigh Valley on the road to Allentown I sensed a new outpouring of goodwill. Every ten minutes I was stopped to sign an autograph and some-times even given a few dollars. I was feeling so rich that when a bag lady asked for some change to buy coffee I gave her five dollars.

At one point a car screeched to a halt, and a man leapt out and introduced himself as Hank Naisby. Hank had been fascinated by the account of my journey in the *Washington Post*, especially as he had traveled extensively in Central America himself, and he had actually been making great ef-forts to find me ever since. And now we had finally met, purely by chance—the farther I went, the more I experi-enced this kind of coincidence.

Pennsylvania south of Allentown was mostly farmland. North of that city I walked smack into the state's industrial belt. Dreadful Route 22 took me past Bethlehem's steel mills, their smokestacks belching gray plumes high into the sky. Di-rectly ahead lay New Jersey, New York's smaller and reput-edly uglier cousin, one of the most concentrated industrial regions on earth. When I crossed the Delaware River into New Jersey near Phillipsburg, however, I was greatly sur-prised at what I saw. Instead of a continuation of Pennsyl-vania's steel belt, here were green pastures and herds of graz-ing cows.

Rural New Jersey gave way to suburban New Jersey, and soon both gave way to the chaotic urban nuthouse. In the distance I could see the sprawling squalor of Newark, the state's largest city. I didn't want to see Newark (just the week before, teenage vandals had drained a reservoir, and now the city was rationing water). Nor did I want to face the ferocious Jersey Turnpike traffic beyond it, and so I swung sharply north onto the Garden State Parkway—at least the name sounded tamer. Here I was immediately halted by a state highway patrolman, who apologetically issued me a warning ticket but let me keep walking his road anyway.

Past Clifton I veered off the broad Garden State Parkway and onto the broader Interstate 80 (when completed, this road would link New York and San Francisco). Nearer New York City the highway dipped into a cut a few feet below ground level; it was one of the uglier marches of the journey. Walking along the slightly raised shoulder, which in effect was a sidewalk (although pedestrian traffic is strictly prohibited here), I felt rather like a rabbit in a run. Towering above me on the far side of the high wire fence were the endless one- and two-story houses that line the highway. I waved a greeting in passing to a black teenager sitting on a stoop—his feet were just at my eye level. Surprised to see me (conceivably he had never seen anyone walking just here), he shouted to his friends, "Hey, look, I found a honky in the cage!"

New York and New England

Just as the world's most famous skyline came into view across the Hudson, thousands of blind windows glinted orange-red in the reflected rays of the setting sun. As darkness settled I imagined they were lighting up a twinkling welcome. To the southeast I spotted the twin towers of the World Trade Center and, north of them, a great flashing red beacon atop the Empire State Building. Reaching the George Washington Bridge, I stopped, set my mark of furthest progress, and plunged into the heart of darkness.

On the Manhattan side of the bridge I descended with the Yoshikart into the most infamous railway in the world, the New York subway system. While trying to get my bearings just outside the turnstile entrance, and probably looking lost—as indeed I was—a woman approached me, handed me a subway token, and just as quickly passed through the turnstile and was gone. I was gravely disappointed. This stranger's spontaneous gesture had in an instant destroyed my long-held notion that New Yorkers don't give a damn about people, especially out-of-towners. Another convenient stereotype right down the drain.

Through the sister of Billy Hall in D.C. I had obtained an introduction to Marne and Nita Camp in the North Bronx, where I ended up spending most of my long stay in New York. After taking the subway from Manhattan, I wended my way for a few blocks to a small house, complete with porch and a small American flag. Here, out back, wearing his Boy-Scout-commissioner khaki shorts, Marne Camp was hacking away at an overgrown bush. Over the weeks, many an evening I would find great delight sitting in this backyard in the shade of the overhanging trees. Especially when events grew frantic in "the city"—as the residents of the outer boroughs call Manhattan—this was a much-appreciated haven.

New York is among other things the publishing capital of the world, and I had mapped out a minor media blitz with the objective of obtaining a book contract on the basis of my South American journals. Not one power that be had ever expressed the slightest interest in such a project, however, and the very idea of the task before me—i.e., selling myself—was thoroughly repellent.

First I called *The New York Times* and spoke to a reporter who had been recommended to me. "Hello," I said, "I've walked here from—"

"Yes, yes. People do that all the time."

"No, you don't quite understand—"

"Look, we're not interested." *Click.* (Actually, *crash.*)

A few days later, with the help of a more influential acquaintance, I reached another party at the *Times* who listened a little bit longer. The upshot was a five-paragraph item under "Notes on People." Even in that short space, the paper that boasts "All the News That's Fit to Print" managed to botch the relevant information: In a kind of editorial Freudian slip, they identified my ultimate goal, Prudhoe Bay, Alaska, as "Trudeau Bay."

Things were much better over at *People* magazine. Their piece was almost finished; to round it out they scheduled a day to cover my official crossing of the George Washington Bridge. I was met at the Camps' by Peter B. Kaplan, an ebullient photographer, who drove me to the bridge in his van.

I wasn't expecting all the hoopla at the bridge, but there

were reporters and photographers from all the local media—plus a police escort to guide all of us across. Even the *Times* sent a man, although he apparently got lost on the way. "Typical," remarked Peter B. "The *Times* couldn't find a police car flashing its lights and going three miles an hour."

Once I had crossed the bridge and left the media behind, I began my walk through the South Bronx en route to the Camps', passing by hundreds of dingy tenements, many of their black and Hispanic residents standing about the streets in knots of twos or threes, or sitting on milk crates and staring into space. Every block or so there would be an open hydrant, most capped with nozzles that produced an arching spray reaching halfway across the street, while shouting, laughing, barefoot children in nothing but shorts or underwear would unselfconsciously dive in and out of the water jet.

Their momentary happiness was in stark contrast to the scowls of the adults who bothered to stare my way. Neither my straw hat nor the Yoshikart (not to mention the color of my skin) seemed to make the slightest impression on these dour characters—I was probably just another freak in a city where freakdom was the norm.

National television was an experience for which I was totally unprepared. But here I was, sitting in the Green Room on the sixth floor of the RCA Building in Rockefeller Center, waiting to be interviewed on NBC's *Today* show, my insides churning uncontrollably. A technician wandered in and remarked, "Ya know, eight million people will be watching this live!" Thanks.

I was led to a seat at the main desk. Events moved swiftly. I felt like I was in the electric shair and witnessing my own execution, an impression that seemed confirmed by the brief appearance of *Today* show regular Gene Shallit, his frazzled Bride-of-Frankenstein hair standing out so crazily that he seemed to have survived a charge of several thousand volts.

A microphone cable was gently let through my clothes. Powder was applied to my face—perhaps, I thought, to reduce skin resistance when the shock wave hit me. Dazzling lights were thrown on. Behind the glare I could see the stage manager counting down with his fingers: "Five, four, three, two, . . ."

Suddenly eight million people-volts were plugged in. Electronic images of my face popped up on two dozen monitors all around the studio. I could see myself everywhere. Death must be like this, I thought.

My interviewer, a cold, underfed strip of California beauty, launched into a facile presentation, speaking of my "remarkable walk from the South Pole to the North Pole"—nonsense, of course, but who was I to argue mere details in front of eight million Americans munching their All-Bran?

Two or three questions and then off. My handlers from Time-Life—the publishers of *People* who had arranged the appearance—said, "Marvelous!" "Fantastic!" I thought I stunk.

Eureka! I was offered a book contract and given an advance that would help finance the rest of the trip—and one of the keys was the piece in the wretched *New York Times* after all! Their snippet had caught the attention of an environmentalist in Brooklyn, who tracked me down at the Camps' buy phoning a TV newsman at home, rousing him from his bath. Such persistence marked him as a man after my heart; such serendipity was the hallmark of my journey.

The Brooklynite, John Muir, told me he had a friend who many years ago had had a school chum who now worked as a literary agent—maybe. After some days John managed to procure the agent's number for me. Over the phone the agent instructed me to leave the manuscript with her doorman— she was too busy to see me in person. There the manuscript lay, unread for days. In fact, the agent never did read the manuscript at all but, encouraged by the publicity floating about, volunteered to take on the project and sent it to a senior editor at a major publishing house. The editor didn't read the manuscript, either, but became interested when she just happened to see my appearance on the *Today* show. The result: In one week's time a first-time author sold an unsolicited, first-draft manuscript to a major publisher, surely a rare event in the world capital of publishing.

"A tree grows in Brooklyn," they say, but John Muir was a much rarer bird—an environmentalist in Brooklyn. On the strength of sheer enthusiasm and grit he had created single-handedly the Prospect Park Environmental Center, a non-profit corporation committed to developing people's appreciation of urban environments, both natural and created. He was a "reformed college professor," he admitted, much as one might confess to being a reformed bank robber.

Resembling a latter-day Pickwick, John welcomed me warmly into his brownstone near Prospect Park, where he enjoys the company of his attractive wife, Barbara. Barbara, whose family hails from Barbados, is the holder of an intimidating doctorate in mathematics—certainly an advance on Sam Weller.

One day John asked me what I most wanted to experience in New York. I didn't have to think for long. Charles Lindbergh had called it "the single most exciting and frightening moment of my life"—riding the Cyclone, Coney Island's famous and terrifying roller coaster. After half a century, it was still operating.

John's teenage son Johnny sat by my side in the front seats as our car was ratcheted to the top of the machine's first and steepest hill. John had compared that precipitous drop from the top of the Cyclone to bringing up teenage children: "A game you must play, but can never win."

Another side of John came out when we ventured out to Shea Stadium to see the Mets do battle with the world champion Philadelphia Phillies. Professorial Mr. Muir sat quietly eating a hot dog as we watched from the upper deck. At a crucial point in the game, he stood straight up, cupped his hands around his mouth, and in a voice that surprised—nay, shocked—not only me but the dozens of fans surrounding us, shouted at the top of his considerable voice, "Come on, *Kingggg-mannnn*, knock the sucker *outta* here!!!"

As soon as the issue of *People* covering my trip hit the newsstands its readers began writing and calling me, some to praise, others to criticize. One observation that (predictably) riled many people was my comment that I found the American suburbs the "most joyless places" of my journey. A psychiatrist from Chicago called and asked me what I dreamed about. I told him that I had one dream in which raised scars across my chest formed a map of the Western Hemisphere, and my chest was slowly blowing up, making the map more and more hideous and distorting the journey. In another I was sharing a hotel room with Idi Amin, and the problem was: Who was going to pay the bill? I had to get out of New York.

The radio broadcast a spellbinding story: "Today in Brooklyn a police officer was shot, and as his partner chased the assailant, a gang of youths attacked and robbed the wounded patrolman . . ." I had to get out of New York. I had to return to the road I loved, my true home in America.

From the Camps' tree-shaded garden with its scampering squirrels, my route progressed northward underneath the "El"—the elevated subway line—where every so often a train would rumble and rattle slowly overhead. The sticky-warm weather closed everything in, and I felt even more constricted by the superstructure over my head and the stanchions and the buildings and the bustle all around. By Yonkers the cramped city thoroughfares thinned out, and I marched along Broadway and into placid Greenburgh. I was back in the countryside. Upstate New Yorkers will tell you they are from *up*state, almost in a threatening way, a warning not to mistake them for Noo Yawkers, the inmates of that loony bin of skyscrapers and criminals; *up*state New York is not like that at all, they insist.

Hastings-on-Hudson and then Dobbs Ferry passed under my boots—and then an hour and a half later once again Hastings-on-Hudson! I had taken not one but two wrong turns, resulting in my making the only full circle that ever slipped into my walk. If one wishes, 1.6 miles can be removed from my grand total, but I prefer to leave them as a souvenir. In fact, I'm convinced that what I called my "envelope of protection" had somehow taken me in this misdirection, that had I *not* strayed some cruel fate would have been mine.

"I was at Woodstock," boasted the long-haired young man in a combat jacket. Ron McClendon wore, like a war medal, his participation at the rock festival that had been held nearby. He could also see my journey in bright lights. There, on the spot, at some intersection I have long since forgotten, he sang the chorus of his latest song:

> Dreamer that I am, and I am the dreamer,
> Schemer making plans,
> Visionary man called foolish believer.
> But if your mind can see it,
> Then I can be it,
> If only I'll believe it.
> So dreamer, dream on,
> And don't stop till you reach it.

The afternoon sun shone down on the gentle hills, glistening green after the rain, rolling away into the distance like some colossal golf course. Stately oaks dotted the fields, singly or in copses; at other points poplars lined the silent road like rows of sentries. In front of a red cottage stood an unattended table piled high with honey pots. A hand-lettered sign beside an empty cigar box read "TAKE WHAT YOU NEED. Leave The Money." And I was still only an hour's drive away from New York City! Upstate New York may be America's best-kept secret.

Past the small city of Poughkeepsie and stately Hyde Park, home of FDR, I arrived in the stage-stop town of Rhinebeck and found the local Catholic church, where the solemn priest said I could sleep in the church hall on the hardwood floor. The priest had left an urban parish for the countryside, he told me, because the pressure of the big city was too great. "All swinging singles, all youngsters, very few families—they were too busy for God."

Quickly becoming bored with the man's *up*state rectitude, I sought and gained his permission to make a long-distance call from the nearby office. (I assured him that I would reverse the charges.) I rang up Peter B. Kaplan to pass the time. Peter B., in a chatting mood himself, suggested he call me back direct to save money, and so I gave him the number and hung up. A minute later, he was back on the line, but even before he could say a word, I heard his pet parrot in the background distinctly repeating a single phrase over and over. Then I remembered that Peter B. had trained his parrot to respond to the question "What are your thoughts on the Ayatollah Khomeini?" and this was indeed the phrase the beast was now screeching: "the fucker . . . the fucker . . . the fucker . . ."

Another voice came on the line: "What?! What?!" The priest, hearing the phone ring, had picked up the extension in the rectory and was now shouting over the line, "What's that? *What* do you say?!" In an attempt to salvage the situation, I interrupted and blurted out the truth: "Excuse me, Father . . . ['the fucker . . . the fucker . . .' was still reverberating in the background] . . . excuse me, but a parrot has telephoned me from New York with some thoughts concerning the Ayatollah." He immediately hung up (the priest, that is, not the parrot).

Farther into the Catskills, without the slightest reason I crossed the Hudson River, first this way, then that—once over the delightfully named Rip Van Winkle Bridge. My route was irregular save for being northerly. I had become what the Latins might call—and they are expert on the subject—a *vacilado*, someone going in a general direction but not much bothered how he gets there. Perhaps I was just intoxicated by the beauty of upstate. I dozed here and there—in a motel, on a gas station floor, once on a pile of newspapers. It mattered not one jot. The sun shone.

Blast! My Mickey Mouse watch, my companion since Mexico, had finally hurled itself into oblivion—lost. For three days I had to use the map and mileposts to reckon distances;

it was so much more convenient to check them against time. But I knew something would turn up sooner or later.

I was passing a country garage along Route 40 just as a report of my walk came on TV. A mechanic working inside the garage instantly recognized me and then dashed out to greet me. "Great going, buddy! Can you use this watch? I found it around and I've been waiting for three days for someone to give it to."

"Thank you, sir. I've been waiting three days for you!"

Past Melrose and Greenwich I veered away from the Adirondacks directly to the north and toward the Green Mountains of Vermont. I wanted to see the change of the seasons in New England, that dazzling autumnal display when the trees withdraw their sap in preparation for winter and the leaves' green and brown are replaced by a riot of red, gold, and orange. The leaves were turning in New York State as well, but for sentimental reasons I had to see this in New England. I had been through a dozen countries and experienced nearly as many different climates, and all that time, through the deserts and forests, the mountains and plains, in freezing summers and hothouse winters, I had kept before me a vision of climatic reasonableness, of the regular procession of the seasons I knew as a boy—the climate of civilization, if you like. New England in the fall was the essence of that vision.

Crossing the Vermont state line, I jubilantly leapt skyward and plucked out of the air one of a dozen maple leaves that had been rattled free from the boughs by a breeze drifting down the roadside.

The road north took me between the Green Mountain National Forest and Lake Champlain; on the western horizon I could often catch glimpses of the lake, which forms the Vermont-New York border for almost one hundred miles. I reached a small town nestled against the lakeshore, Burlington, which with less than forty thousand inhabitants is nevertheless Vermont's largest metropolis.

North of Burlington I saw a snowmobile for the first time,

a chilling portent of the thousands of northern miles ahead of me. In a roadside store an elderly man in a black-and-red wool cap told me, "Us Vermonters have a saying: Up here we get seven months of winter and five months of damn poor sledding."

I crossed the bridge joining "mainland" Vermont to the Alburg Peninsula, which juts down from Canada into Lake Champlain and is connected to Burlington via a series of bridges over the Grand Isles. From that idyllic peninsula I carried away with me the mental image of the thousands of frogs and grasshoppers that scuttled about my feet as I meandered toward the border.

Push to the Pacific

The thirteen countries I had traversed to get this far were all republics. Now, in the autumn of 1981, at the Alburg crossing between Vermont and Quebec, just over the hill, lay my first nation of the British Commonwealth. I noticed the Queen's profile on some loose change lying on the counter at the border post, and it encouraged me to believe that I was practically on home territory.

But after examining my documents the Canadian Immigration officer shook his head. "*Entrée interdite*," he said—Entry forbidden! Canada wouldn't have me! I was thunderstruck. I had had some close calls, but this was the first time I had ever been point-blank refused entry to a country.

I drifted back into Vermont to find Clarke Washburn, an officer of the U.S. Immigration Service, who had befriended me on the way out. Clarke couldn't believe it, either. "They can't reject you, George," he exploded. "My God, you're the second one this week! The other one was an Indian, Chief Walking Wolf."

Whereas the Alburg crossing was a small post on a lonely country road, the Blackpool crossing in New York State was a bureaucratic beehive; perhaps there, authority would not be so arbitrarily exercised. Clarke offered to drive me there.

Despite his uniform, Clarke was brusquely ordered out

of the Canadian's Blackpool office. Immediately the woman officer laid into me with the whip end of her regulations: "You're in the United States illegally."

"Wait a minute, wait a minute . . . this is *Canada*," I protested.

"You are thirty-five days past the expiration date on your one-year American visa."

"Well, yes," I acknowledged. "It's taken me a little over a year to cross the U.S.A. But anyway, the U.S. Immigration brought me here at some personal cost. They don't care. Why should you?"

My protagonist abruptly changed tack: "You have no money."

"I've not had money for years. But my publishers in New York will confirm that I'm due several thousand dollars."

By now Clarke had somehow managed to get back into the office and began waving about the photo of Jimmy Carter and me. When the officers saw this, their attitude took an abrupt U-turn. Soon I was shaking hands all around and fumbling through answers to the question I always dreaded: "Why?"

In spite of the initially dubious reception, I couldn't help thinking: At long last, Canada, where border officials routinely ask one question, "Are you carrying any firearms?" It sounded like a reprimand to the citizens of the superpower to the south. Instantly, I felt safer. And there was a bonus: I was back to walking my favored kilometers.

It was still August, but when I set out the next day, I was wearing wool slacks and two pullovers. It was biting cold, barely above freezing. Puffing smoke, I clicked along an empty country lane past tree-lined meadows and quaint farmhouses of brick and stone. The chill gray skies, the rain and fresh wind—what a wonderful place. As I entered St. Jean sur Richelieu, cooking smells—French cooking smells—wafted through the air, and at the edge of town I passed a tall stonework oven by the roadside tended by a half-dozen women baking bread.

As I neared Montreal, rural Quebec began to dissolve

around me. It was still drizzling by the time I crossed the St. Lawrence River and passed the site of Expo '67, Montreal's World's Fair. The sight of the unfinished tower of the British pavilion made me yearn for home, but it would be at least two years, I guessed, before I could once again walk the white-chalk hills of Kent. Just the day before, to the east of Richelieu, I had reached my closest point of approach to England, but from here on I was heading west, in the opposite direction.

Leaving Montreal took me hours of walking an ugly freeway to reach Ville de Laval just beyond the city, and then more hours before the land resumed its rustic look, with the occasional square Norman church tower in the distance and several St. Bernard dogs loping in the fields. The roads were lined with poplar trees, and everywhere the tiny towns seemed like those of Western Europe; everywhere I heard French. Not that the region was totally free of the all-pervasive American influence. Occasionally I would stop at a roadside kiosk run by someone resembling a medieval peasant selling "La Hambourgeois" and "La Coke." Everything else smacked of the Continent, including the ditchwater weather.

Crossing the Ottawa River into Ontario and the nation's capital was a deadly quiet affair, unlike the entrance to any other capital I had seen, save perhaps Canberra. Beneath the highway bridge was a great raft of logs, tied up for the night: precisely my boyhood image of Canada—infinite trees, logs, timber. I crossed the lawn at the Ministry of External Affairs and wandered the empty streets. It was Sunday, and Ottawa was closed, like any other small town.

Ottawa, in fact, seemed for the most part a dull place overrun with bureaucrats. What compensated for the dullness was the time I spent with Antonio Mazza, a Canadian poet I had met in Mexico. Poets are normally the most cautious of civil servants, but one did pop in on us briefly, an official at the Ministry of Agriculture (he was to fly to the Soviet Union the very next morning to help set up a grain deal).

Antonio's visitor had read of my walk in the paper. After

343

we talked a few minutes, he said to me, "I see that in essence you're in a prison cell and banging your head against the same walls every day." Most perceptive, I told him. It was a rare person who could see this bleaker side of my journey. Most thought that I was as free as a bird—had I not dubbed my walk a Celebration of Freedom?—and couldn't see that at the same time I was a prisoner of my own dream. Others saw my walk as a voluntary undertaking. In my mind there was absolutely no option: I had to make this journey as surely as if it were programmed into my DNA.

I left Ottawa under a weak October sun, following the curiously ornate Rideau Canal. Beyond the city I set a course vaguely southwestward, toward Toronto—it was so vaguely southwestward, in fact, that I took a wrong turn and got lost. No matter; I was in no rush. Toronto was a reasonable year's-end objective, as winter was moving in and progress would be slowed to a halt anyway. Already the nights were bitter cold; in northern Ontario it was snowing.

I was nearing Toronto, where I hoped to wait out the winter with Yoshiko and the children before making the great push on to the Pacific after the new year. Just outside the city, however, I reworked the figures on my continental map and discovered with a shock that to honor my pledge to Yoshiko to finish the journey within seven years, I would have to press on for at least another 700 km before year's end. I was so concerned about the extra effort now demanded of me that as soon as I entered Toronto, I spent two hours late at night making sure I would be able to find the road north out of town.

I was now in the first city of Ontario and of all English-speaking Canada. The province of Ontario, once known as Upper Canada, dominates the nation in trade, finance, and the arts; almost half the country's wealth is here. With all this power and prestige, Ontario and particularly Toronto are held in little affection by the Canadians of other provinces, who view Ontarians as the "Texans of the North."

My overwhelming priority was now finding a place to stay

for my family when they arrived—and a way to pay for it and their passage. My money situation was as desperate as ever, as I wouldn't see any of my book-contract advance for months yet—my New York publisher told me that the necessary paperwork was tied up in Memphis or some equally unlikely place.

It finally happened on the third day out of Toronto. As the pale yellow sun disappeared over the rim of a hill, I stood in the chill twilight, reeling from the shock of realization. I appealed to the sky, "Oh, God, where *is* it?" The Yoshikart was gone, and with it my gear, my documents, everything.

I had left it beside the road leading up to Orr Lake while I inquired about accommodations for the family at the Little Banff cottages, and when I returned it was no longer there. I frantically combed the area and inquired of everyone I met; no one knew anything.

Feeling as though I had been gassed, I jog-trotted the few kilometers to the Waverly crossroads, my day's objective, where I knew there was a phone. With each bouncing pace— so strange, so unlike my walking rhythm—I was assaulted by waves of loss and despair. "Why *here*?" I appealed to the dumb trees. Throughout Latin America and beyond I had left my gear dozens of times in the most unlikely places—tiendas in Mexico, whorehouses in Peru, police stations in Alabama— and no one so much as touched that ratbag of rubbish. Why here?

With successive waves of despair passing over me, I considered what I had lost. My family photos—perhaps some could be replaced. But my address book was gone as well, hundreds of friends liquidated in an instant. And then the picture postcard of Her Majesty the Queen—I had carried that with me since South America. And my journal! Nearly all of 1981 also adrift. How could I possibly reconstruct my experiences in the United States without it?

I jogged on, feeling more wretched by the minute. I wouldn't be able to phone Yoshiko. (How would I get a number from Japanese information?) I couldn't even call brother

Anthony; he had an unlisted number (of course). The fact that I had no clothes in fast-freezing weather barely registered at all. But my papers! They were useless to anyone else. How unjust! How bloody rotten!

In Waverly, Constable Stafford of the OPP (Ontario Provincial Police) agreed to help, and we backtracked over my route in his patrol car. As the car's searchlight played over the roadside growth, he said, "This could be the worst place in Canada for people picking up stuff like that. After the weekend they just pour back to Toronto, taking what they can. Somebody made off with my garden hose. They even steal dustbins." ("Dustbins"! How long had it been since I had heard garbage cans called that?)

After a fruitless hour's search we returned to the OPP post in Elmvale. I was speechless with fatigue. As the patrol car crunched to a halt on the driveway gravel, an OPP sergeant approached and motioned for me to roll down the car window.

"You Meegan?"

"Yes . . ."

"Well, your gear's been located in Mississauga [a Toronto suburb]." Astounding! Perhaps Stafford was right—weekend vacationers picking up a "souvenir."

The next morning I returned to the OPP station. There was my gear, all right; the OPP had even gone to the trouble to transport it up here. All was intact, even the ham sandwich I had slipped under the top strap.

The OPP drove me back to Waverly, and I set out again, the Yoshikart clunking behind me feeling wonderfully heavy. I plodded on, totally contented. I had never thought of the cart as having a personality the way some car owners regard their machines, but it was an old and good friend nonetheless. Aside from my money belt, the Yoshikart was the only item that had started out with me way back in Ushuaia.

Past Parry Sound, I mulled over the idea of making a side trip to see the Ojibwa reservation nearby. "You don't want to go there," the man at a wayside store told me. "It's a mess, just tar-paper shacks and dogs." The man's description actually encouraged me to go there. Yes, the place was a mess, really no different from the typical Indian settlement (or most any settlement) that I had seen throughout Latin America. But here there was an up-to-date office with a radio and a telephone, while just outside I could hear the slap of a beaver's tail!

At the first plywood door I came to, I knocked; I was let inside and instantly made a dinner and overnight guest—no suspicion, no insults, no hostility, no questions asked. I was deeply honored to be with these people and share their food.

It first began snowing just outside Estaire, and beyond the town the snow continued to cascade out of the leaden sky. The temperature was below freezing, and I was having trouble keeping warm in my cold-weather gear, which now consisted of a greatcoat (courtesy of the Salvation Army), wool socks for gloves, and, tucked under my favorite straw hat, my father-in-law's underpants to keep my head warm. Surely this merited some kind of award from *Gentleman's Quarterly*.

As I sprinted along the Sudbury Bypass the countryside suddenly took on an otherworldly appearance—the trees and shrubbery simply disappeared. I may as well have been on another planet. The immediate cause of this odd circumstance lay in Sudbury itself, in the form of a thousand-foot chimney that daily spewed out tons of sulfur dioxide, not only rendering the countryside lifeless but also making a huge contribution to the acid rain falling on this continent and beyond. (This source had been implicated in the deaths of thousands of fish in European lakes and was even suspected of turning one unfortunate Dane's hair green.) The landscape was so barren that NASA had employed the site for training Apollo astronauts because it so closely resembled the lunar surface.

By the time I reached Massey I had settled on a goal for the year, Sault Ste. Marie, at the point where Lake Huron meets Superior, 200 km to the west. This would leave me well enough placed, I hoped, to reach Alaska the year after next and still leave time to arrange for my family's imminent arrival. The weather report from ahead was not good, however—it had been snowing in "the Soo" for eighteen hours nonstop. Vehicles coming from the west were heaped high with snow.

The road was a carpet of large descending snowflakes, and my progress slowed dramatically. That I made any progress at all was because the Trans Canada was well ploughed by giant machines—the same that I had seen in Patagonia being used as road graders. For the next few days the cold kept me constantly hungry. I was particularly in need of sugar. In this respect I was lucky, for the truck stops and cafes all had special homemade pies chock full of apples, plums, cherries, or currants. Great! At least the Canadian truckers hadn't sold out and settled for the gooey, processed, plastic-wrapped concoctions that pop out of the coin machine in U.S. pit stops.

I reached down and touched the gray waters of Lake Huron all the while thinking of Mohicans before slushing to the Soo. Then I marked my spot and took a bus back to Toronto, where I rented a cottage by Orr Lake, near Elmvale, the very same place where I had lost my gear a month before.

Yoshiko and the children arrived on a Wednesday in late November. It had been over a year since Texas, and it was a bittersweet reunion. "How's it been kid?" I asked my wife once the hullabaloo of hugs and kisses had died down and we were at last alone, sitting on the rug at the foot of the bed where the children lay fast asleep.

"Quickly time goes, but sometimes so hard," she whispered back in the darkness.

"For me, too."

Geoffrey suddenly woke up and crawled over to us, bleating, "Mum-mee, Mum-mee."

"No," Yoshiko corrected. *"Daddy."*

"Da-dee," he promptly responded. We all embraced. Another year was coming to a close.

With a break in the spring snow, it was once again time to walk. I flew with the family down to New York City, where we bade our sad farewells. After sleeping the night at JFK airport behind a kiosk, I flew back to Sault Ste. Marie and my mark.

Crossing the International Bridge at Sault Ste. Marie, Ontario, brought me into Sault Ste. Marie, Michigan. In the United States, I was always aware of the possibility, fueled by the media, of being shot on the road by any stray maniac who had bothered to get himself a gun.

I would rather have crossed the continent on the calmer, saner, pastures of Canada, but the fact that the route on the southern shore of Lake Superior is more heavily populated than the Canadian side was a strong incentive to move south at the tag end of Canada's worst winter in a century, when temperature readings of $-60°$ F had not been uncommon. I could plan for wet and dry seasons, but there was no way to foretell this.

This new year of 1982 was to be a speed year for me, a ruthless press for distance, for I had to reach the Alaska Highway before the snows if I were to finish by 1983. I needed every advantage I could get.

Even though it was March, in Upper Michigan it was still the dead of winter. The lumber and mining industries, which together comprise the backbone of the area, had been hit hard by the recession, painful evidence of which was to be seen in the great numbers of "For Sale" signs on display in front of houses and farms.

Thanks to a local news item, I was recognized by the customers at a bar in Michigamme (pronounced to rhyme with "fish-a-balmy") and given a barstool next to Ole Olsen, an old-timer who sang me a song from his school days:

> M-I-C-H-I-,
> G-A-M-M-E,
> That's the town that I was born in,
> One cold Jan-u-ar-y mornin'.
> There's lots of rocks and lots of weeds,
> And lots of Frenchmen, Finns, and Swedes . . .

Except for service in World War II, Ole had spent all

his life in this village. Ole mentioned that he had a friend "waiting about"—dead but waiting to be buried. "He's been waiting about since early winter. The ground's so hard we can't get him in. He'll have to wait about till late spring."

I zipped through the rest of the U.S. In Wisconsin the whipping wind was ferocious, like nothing since Patagonia five years before, an unrelenting, ghastly chilling headwind that pounded my face and the dripping, soaked gear with a mixture of rain, sleet, and driven snow.

Somewhere near Grand Rapids, Minnesota, I crossed a small, nondescript bridge. Although it looked no different from dozens of others in the region, this one was special. The stream issuing from under a shield of ice and flowing through the gunked-up reeds was North America's mightiest river, the Mississippi. I thought back one year to the time I walked across the bridge into Baton Rouge, and how I could barely spare a moment to glance at the slow, wide river below. It was hard to equate this with the cold, dark stream I now saw.

Just over the North Dakota state line was the Strategic Air Command (SAC) Grand Forks base, where I could make out, silhouetted against the dying light, a half-dozen B-52 bombers armed for Doomsday and all ready to go. A SAC staff sergeant I met on the road invited me to the base, where I was given an informal tour. Afterward, in the cafeteria, an airman asked me what I wanted to drink. "A Coke," I told him. He returned from the machine with an unwanted Sprite. "Sorry," he said, "I pressed the wrong button."

Bucking the fierce winds past Rugby ("Geographical Center of North America"), I reached the town of Berwick, which like so much of the area was reeling from the recession. "We used to have five grain elevators and two banks," the waitress at the Berwick diner confided sadly. "Now there's none of either." In this part of the country, grain elevators, possibly even more than banks, are cherished symbols, gauges of municipal prosperity. A "five-elevator town" was taken to be somewhat better off than a "four-elevator town," whereas a "one-elevator town" might be on the verge of sinking.

Out of Berwick and past Minot (a multielevator town), I swung north and left Route 2 behind. It was May. I was inching toward the Canadian border. The frost was gone. The grass once again reclaimed the prairie, a great yellow-green plain broken only by the occasional pond.

When I crossed back into Canada and entered Saskatchewan, I expected to see nothing but wheatfields, but on the approach to Estavan the countryside bore the grim evidence of open-cut mining. The terrain looked like the Battle of the Somme—brutal and lifeless. Farther on, along the empty road to Regina, the provincial capital, I at last found the expected wheatfields. Here I could see for miles and miles and feel the loneliness as clearly as the gentle wind whipping at my collar. Everything contributed to an all-cleansing feeling of peace.

Past Regina, the countryside was full of curiosities. Every so often I would see wood-lined tunnels under the highway, constructed especially to allow grazing cattle to move freely between fields. The same tunnels gave me an escape from the incessant drenching and the whistling wind. And before Morse (which was just a dot on the map), I spied what looked like a white desert in the distance. A little nearer, a sign identified this mirage. It was a dried-up lakebed, now a salt mine, from which three quarters of a million tons were scraped each year.

I was beginning to fall in love with this prairie, this rolling tableland that seemed to go on forever, as though it might stretch to the very end of the earth. Motorists I spoke to in passing almost always complained of the boredom of driving through such terrain and guessed that it was even worse for me. In fact, I was never bored on this (or any other) road— unless, oddly enough, I wasn't hauling the Yoshikart. Then the hours would drag on, and I would grow agitated because I just couldn't move any faster. Something like this probably happens to the driver: He can go just so fast on a given stretch of the road—seventy, eighty, ninety miles an hour—before reaching a limbo where he can't tap the car's potential to go any faster.

One night I dreamt in Spanish. The walk had been going on so long that my Latin American experiences of two and three years before now took on an aura of nostalgia usually associated with much older memories. Indeed, these days my thoughts while walking dwelt more on the past than on the present or future.

At Swift Current, I tried all day without success to reach Yoshiko on the phone. Becoming anxious, I finally phoned her mother and learned that Yoshiko had moved back in with her parents after a spell in her own apartment—she had been teaching English, but had too few students to pay the rent.

None of this surprised me, but it got me to thinking: If the journey could help me earn money, I would feel like a much better husband and father. Except for my book contract, however, I had virtually no support. How lucky I was to have a wife who never pressed me for things I could not give her.

I could live on dreams, but how could I expect my family to have to do the same? I began to be nagged by a question: Was the walk nothing but an ego trip, a lust for recognition and fame? Obviously I must have an overactive ego to have attempted this at all. But there were other factors. I have always been affected by wanderlust, from the time I was a child scurrying across the fields around Rainham all the way to the man wandering this great prairie. When I took a year off to study for my second mate's ticket in London, my body literally ached with desire to return to sea and visit far-off lands. The feeling was like being in love.

From the beginning, I knew that if I succeeded, I might gain some small celebrity—that itself would be nice, I thought. In New York, however, where I briefly stepped on the wild merry-go-round of national media exposure, I learned that the price of this status is a loss of one's privacy and freedom, which I value much too highly to trade away. Did I really want to spend the rest of my life talking about my journey?

Over the years the essence of the journey had changed from being the fulfillment of a simple, perhaps childish wish to being something that I chose to define as the largest work of abstract art ever seen, inscribed by the footsteps of a man in his self-created prison yard, the Western Hemisphere. I arrived at this after being hectored and badgered thousands of times by people asking the question "Why?" After all, who looks at an abstract painting—inherently no more useful or practical than my walk—and asks, "Why?" Or who would look at the twitching blobs of protoplasm under a microscope and question their "meaning"? My walk of umpteen thousand miles was of no greater or lesser value than those colorful blobs on the wall or those twitching blobs on a microscope slide. I was just another version of the same thing. It's the nature of the microscopic blob to twitch; it is my nature to journey.

Was I doing this just to write a book? I was often tempted to tell people this just to stop their pestering me. I even told people that I was making this walk to win a one-pound bet. (The bet was real! I had made it with a friend's father in a Rainham pub, before setting out.) Or was I looking for my long-lost father? (And would I even recognize him if I saw him?)

Then there is this whole business of "the longest march," of going for the limit, *Guinness Book of Records* stuff. Did I really want to be immortalized along with Reggie Graham (ate 37 doughnuts in 7 minutes, 5 seconds) and Ash Farmer (walked 38.6 km with a milk bottle perched atop his head)?

The real answer to why I walked was otherwise and had been reaffirmed to me a thousand times. One such time, I was alone on the dirt road somewhere far south of where I now stood. The moon was shining brightly, casting shadows with sharp edges; the stars were twinkling brilliantly. I looked into the vast sky, where perhaps lie all answers to all questions, and whispered to myself, "There's a hundred billion galaxies out there and a hundred billion stars in each one.

And down here there's nearly five thousand million people. I know that I'm less than a microbe in this great scheme of things. But I'm George, on my journey. I'm here. I'm alive!"

I reached Alberta. The days were hot, broken by heavy rainshowers. I didn't mind. I wore my straw hat and pressed on for distance. There are moments on the great North American plain when the quality of the sky, with its leaden glow, creates a strange, magic atmosphere. Through this dreamscape I would drift like a ghost, my endless horizon constantly changing—now green, now purple, now gold.

In Cluny, I stepped out of a huge storm and into a vast bar full of Blackfoot Indians. This tribe once waged war all over the territory, I was informed by the paleface who ran the bar; these days they were merely belligerent individually. At the table next to mine, an Indian woman smiled at me pleasantly, and we fell into conversation. The problem was trying to ignore the constant interruptions of her man, who kept pressing me for four dollars. Having no place to stay, I took the option, hesitantly put forward by Mrs. Jane Medicine Shield, to stay at the couple's home.

After a twenty-five-minute drive over a broken road in a dilapidated station wagon chock full of family, we reached the house. Once inside, I couldn't avoid noticing that everyone (except for Jane) was keeping a cautious eye on me—especially Jane's common-law husband, Mr. Harrison Bull Bear. It was as though I was the first white man to be invited into their home (which I later learned was the case). Feeling some responsibility for putting everyone at their ease, I brought out my family photos. This usually did the trick with Latin American Indians, so why not here?

Looking through my pack of smiling Ayumis, Geoffreys, and Yoshikos, everyone seemed delighted and satisfied—except for Mr. Bull Bear, who was staggering about and still hadn't given up asking me for four dollars. I finally relented and gave him the money—it was worth the privilege of being here—but Jane became incensed and immediately made him give it back.

I was comfortably set up in a bed for the night in the basement. Before leaving me, my hostess said, "I hope this is OK for you—I mean, I hope you don't mind staying with people like us Indians."

"Mind? There was nowhere I would rather be," I said. When I was growing up all my friends and I had nothing but admiration for Indians. We all played at being Indians—we wanted to *be* Indians (never cowboys). What a tragedy, I thought, for these fine people to buy their own bad press, even to the extent of apologizing for their own good heart and charity.

Upstairs, Harrison was playing Indian music on the stereo. I drifted off to sleep, the *THUMP-thump*, *THUMP-thump*, *THUMP-thump* of the recorded tom-toms accompanying me to oblivion.

The morning came cloudy, and the house was filled with a harsh light. Peering out the window and across the wind-swept prairie, I could see a few other dwellings, no direct paths connecting them, only a winding mud road snaking over the reservation. A scraggly, long-haired dog was asleep in the yard. He apparently always slept there; his jury-rigged kennel was filled to overflowing with beer bottles. Sheltered by a leeward wall was a front seat that had been ripped out of a wrecked car, a sort of improvised outdoor settee favored by many Indians.

Harrison Bull Bear was up and a perfect gentleman that morning. He spoke about his land, his family, and his deep concern that the youngsters were more fluent in the language of TV than in the language of their ancestors. Later, over dinner, Jane translated the names of her children for me. Elizabeth's Indian name, pronounced "ah-bew-ya-key," meant "Looks Like a White Woman," while Roena's Indian name meant "Yellow Old Woman." Then, just before I left, Jane bestowed upon my journey a great honor: "From now on you will carry a Blackfoot name, Ootascarapinny. It means 'Blue Eyes.' I will think of you as my son."

It was certainly summer now. Beyond Calgary, under the

scorching sun, the Rockies seemed to grow higher by the hour, gradually towering above my shortening horizon.

Now a huge storm was brewing, profoundly black and sinister. Great bolts of forked lightning blasted across the sky, and the thunder came rolling down the empty gray road like a barrage of artillery. This strange world seemed like something out of a medieval horror story; ahead might be lurking monsters, dragons, danger!

Raindrops began to fall, raindrops so fat they hurt my head. I struggled into my waterproofs, cursing all the while that they were too tight. I vaguely wondered whether I should take shelter—not that there was any. In the middle of this downpour, suddenly the grass was burning. The top of the telephone pole next to me spewed sparks and flame. A bolt of lightning had struck. It must have shot straight over my head. There was a strange smell in the air.

A split second later (and an eternity too late to make any difference), I flung myself into a roadside ditch. Feeling foolish, I eventually picked myself up and tottered on my way. Farther down the road, I found a lineman working at the top of a pole. "There's been a big one," he cheerily shouted. "It must have hit the line—this whole section's dead." At least I wasn't.

Now the road curved up to the left and then to the right, and soon I was surrounded on all sides by enormous peaks. It was as though a great mountain door had suddenly been shut without warning. The prairies might never have been. This world was so different. I spent the whole day with my head cricked to the sky, saying "Ooooh!" and "Aaaah!"

Near Banff, I camped out for the first time since Honduras. I had been lugging a new tent about, unused, since Ontario. Now I couldn't work out how to erect the thing—there were twelve poles, and I didn't know where a single one was supposed to go. I wished I had watched Yoshiko, who was always better at this sort of thing, when she put it up for the kids in our living room back in Elmvale. But because I had taken my usual noninterest in such things (I was reading the newspaper at the time), it now took me over an hour to get the damned thing together, and I still had one pole left over.

Near the extraordinary turquoise waters of Lake Louise, a motelier threatened to kill me. This was, unfortunately, something of a theme in Alberta—with notable exceptions. In Banff, for example, I was turned away from ten motel doors, in some cases hostilely, only to hear Mrs. Ullrich at number eleven say, "Why, Mr. Meegan, welcome! We have been waiting for you for more than a year now."

I stood astride the Continental Divide. From this point westward all water eventually flows into the mighty Pacific. Directly ahead lay British Columbia, where I was destined to spend the best part of a year.

Toward the Far North

Wherever my eye scanned, the great peaks of the Canadian Rockies dominated the skyline. In the early 1900's, the huge rock formations of Kicking Horse Pass represented a major obstacle to the completion of Canada's national dream, a transcontinental railway. Now, as I stood gazing from the head of the pass, one after the other the Canadian Pacific trains, enormous chains of moving steel, some of them two miles long with three engines sandwiched into the column, clattered along far below me, looking like so many toys. A million-and-a-half pounds of dynamite had done the job. Farther on, at the last great barrier to the railway on its route to the Pacific, Rodgers Pass, I spent four solid uphill hours before reaching the summit.

It was late July, and the Rockies were also full of tourists, campers, vacationers—and bears. In Albert Canyon a motorist shouted a warning as he passed: "Hey, there's a bear around the corner!" Further down the road he repeated this unnerving news to two cyclists. As soon as they had caught up to me, a young bear's black head popped up from behind a bush, sniffing the air. He had picked up our scent.

"Fuckin' hell," shouted one of the cyclists, and the pair furiously pedaled back in the opposite direction. There were still several cars on the road, and so I edged slowly past the bear along the other side of the road, using the passing cars as a moving barricade. I was exposed nevertheless—and none of the drivers seemed to notice my predicament. I just managed to pass the creature when it panicked, cannoned across the road toward me on all fours, bolted up an embankment barely fifty feet away, and disappeared. I stood there for a few more moments, dumbfounded. What had so shocked me, aside from the obvious danger, was the animal's amazing speed and graceful strength.

It had been three seasons since I had last made any northward progress; all that time had gone into the westward crossing of the continent. After briefly looking for winter accommodations for the family in Vancouver, on the Pacific, I backtracked to the town of Hope and again began gaining latitude.

At Lytton, which marks the confluence of the Fraser and Thompson rivers, everything that had been following the course of the Fraser downstream veered off upstream along the deep blue Thompson—the main road, the telephone poles, the railroad tracks, and myself as well. For miles the river and I, like jealous lovers, were rarely out of each other's sight. Then, at the town of Cache Creek, where both the Canadian Pacific tracks and the Trans-Canada Highway swing to the east toward Kamloops, I stayed north on Route 97, which follows the old Caribou Trail, the British Columbian gold-fever route of the mid-nineteenth century. Eventually the rugged landscape of South Caribou country gave way to green woodland.

The road now led in the direction of Prince George, a town that as recently as the 1920's was considered by folks in Vancouver about as far north as civilized people ought to go. The farther north I went, the fewer the signs of human habitation. With the decrease in the human population, I was warned, came a corresponding increase in the bear population. Several self-styled experts advised me to buy a gun right away for protection—a .30-.30 was the weapon of choice. But I abhor firearms and preferred to find some alternative; anyway, other "experts" were telling me that a gun wasn't needed at all. All the contradictory advice was very confusing. Only one point seemed certain: As the Parks Canada leaflet unequivocally stated, there is simply no guaranteed method of dealing with an aggressive bear.

I bought a whistle and hung it around my neck, where I could grab it at a moment's notice—the noise was supposed to frighten off the beast. My first opportunity to test this device was in Pine Pass late one afternoon.

There was a startling crash in the brush. It was hard to make out anything, because of the sunlight filtering through the trees by the roadside, which created a carpet of flickering shadows everywhere.

I looked around and glimpsed an arched, furry back. I saw it was a cub, but this was terrifying, for I realized that its mother must be at hand. In an instant I spotted her rising up on her hind legs in a patch of sunlight less than fifty feet away. I looked on aghast as this towering beast sniffed the air—she had caught my scent.

My knees were trembling. Some instinct told me that I was dangerously close to a terrible death. I struggled to gather my wits and sift through the barrage of information and misinformation I had been subjected to. I blew on my whistle, hard, to alert the bear to my presence, as I was once told to do. Nothing came out—not a peep. In my panic I had managed to get my little finger stuck in the whistle's hole! (I may have been lucky. A savvy woodsman later told me that a sharp noise in this situation might have driven the creature to fury.)

I fitfully glanced about to see if there was a tree whose branches might offer refuge. There was none. (Nor would it have done any good if there had been one—these were black bears, and they climb trees very well.) Only one warning from among the welter of conflicting advice seemed unanimous: Don't run. I held my breath and retreated an inch at a time, all the time maintaining eye contact with the mother bear. (Another piece of advice; somehow it made sense.)

Finally the pair, perhaps only mildly irritated at me for interrupting their sunning, slowly turned and disappeared into the forest. Relieved but still shaking, I thanked my lucky stars for my survival as I cleared Pine Pass, knowing that I would never again be so relaxed on the road as before.

I passed the 27,000-km mark; 90 percent of my journey was finished. I had entered a phase known in cricketing circles as the "nervous nineties," that point late in an at-bat when the batsman might take almost as long to knock up his last ten runs as he had the previous ninety. I was seeing banana peels at every turn.

And I was getting still more conflicting advice on how to deal with the bear threat. A Conservation Service officer told me there was "absolutely no need" to carry a gun; if I attached a small bell to my cart, he said, the constant tinkling as I moved along would be sufficient to warn off anything dangerous. A grizzled trapper, with a look of horror, told me a bell was "plain dangerous." What, then? "Mothballs—the smell will keep 'em away." And so I moved on, smelling like a chest of old clothes.

There were compensations. One cool night, the stars were out, and I lay on my back on the hard road surface. Two thirteen-year olds, Gavin and David, who had come down the road from a religious community to meet me, lay there, too. Together we marveled at the spinning cartwheel of glory above our heads, the aurora borealis—northern lights—an immense brightness you could read headlines by, with sectors of pale pinks and greens that cut into one another, continually changing shape, sometimes reverting simply to silver streaks in the sky. How splendid to share this spectacle with two growing minds. As we watched, illuminated by the ghostly light overhead, it was easy to imagine the awe of ancient man in the face of such magic.

In Sikanni Chief, a party of Beaver Indians in a car stopped to talk. There were eight of them squashed into a wrecked orange-red Pontiac—no plates, the exhaust pipe trailing on the ground—and they were as curious about me as I about them. The driver asked, "What tribe do you belong to?"

"English."

"Ah, they're a big tribe."

361

Indeed, yes, if compared to the Beavers, for there are only a few thousand of them left. On the other hand, there are native peoples of all manner in Canada, especially in the more remote regions. All told, there are 1.2 million (5 percent of the population). I met so many different tribespeople, from Stoney to Cree Indians, from the Thompson River to the Carrier Indians (so named because, until recently, widows carried the bones of the deceased husband in a pouch on their backs). For me, two of the biggest surprises about Canada were the large numbers of native people and the number of bears, both of whom I had imagined to be rare.

By reaching Fort Nelson in mid-September I far exceeded what I had hoped for this year. Feeling fit and optimistic, I decided to go on despite the fact that this was the last town before the Yukon Territory, over three hundred miles up the road.

Again I spoke with a Conservation Service officer about the bears. This one recommended, even urged, that I arm myself; he always had four shotguns on the rack in his pickup. I finally gave in and bought a cheap job, 12-gauge, single-barreled. I had never so much as held a gun before, and so in reality it constituted as much a threat to me as anything else. I promised myself—I rationalized—that I would use it only in the utmost emergency.

The road ahead was indeed fraught with hideous terror: loose gravel and biting insects. Deepening my misery was the journey's most error-filled road map, surpassing even those Latin American masterpieces of deception that typically landed me in some desolate *finca* when I should have been enjoying the comforts of town. According to my government road map, it was 64 km from Fort Nelson to Steamboat. Long past 64 km I still hadn't reached Steamboat. Well into the night I wandered on and on in vain pursuit of my lost target. I reached Steamboat exhausted. Note: It is 83 km from Fort Nelson to Steamboat.

The map's 84 km to Summit turned out to be only 67 km, the 76 to Toad River only 53, the 37 to Muncho Lake in fact 55. These had nothing to do with road alterations; these were the latest, "improved" distances!

Every day nevertheless yielded its treasure, at least one memorable moment that redeemed everything, even a horror like the vicious day I spent climbing up to Steamboat. Long after dark, almost despairing that such a place as Steamboat existed at all, I sat out a minute by the roadside to catch my breath and gather my thoughts. I was startled out of my reverie by an animal call somewhere above my head. Looking up, I saw a long-eared owl, silhouetted by the moon, sitting on a thin, leafless branch of the tree by my side, staring straight down at me with cool indifference. I couldn't suppress a smile. Nature can be like a lover who gently touches your shoulder and says, "It's all right."

At Liard River I paused and swallowed hard before crossing the tiny suspension bridge. The waters below flowed north, ultimately to the Arctic Ocean. The Yukon Territory lay just ahead. It was almost five hundred miles to Dawson Creek to the south; to the north was exactly one thousand miles of Alaska Highway left for the completion of this journey—if it even mattered anymore. I looked up the road and was overcome with emotion—choked with sadness at the thought that I was nearing the end and at the same time reluctant to leave the road knowing it would be another half-year before I could feel the pulse of a journey I had come to love. I crossed the bridge, and after a dip in the hot springs, I fled the area and began my return journey to Vancouver and winter.

Back in Vancouver, not only was I having trouble finding a place for my family—who would soon join me to wait out the winter—I couldn't even find a place for my own sleeping bag. I tried churches, the YMCA, social service agencies, the lot. For the first time in the New World I had to camp outside a city for want of refuge.

And it was raining. For the first winter in years, it didn't snow in Vancouver—but my goodness, the rain! Vancouver is famous for its rain, and for days and nights it seemed to pour without cease. A dry sidewalk was a matter for minor celebration. Yet if an outsider so much as mentioned this total deluge, Vancouverites would have none of it, but would say, "Well, you don't have to shovel it." One night there was so much water building up inside the tent that I punched a hole in the groundsheet to allow the water to drain out. Instead, it drained in!

My mail was a mixed bag. I had hoped to sell my story to a newspaper, as I had back in Toronto. In a jaunty letter, Lord Thompson of the *Times* of London wrote to say that he was sorry, but that no, his newspapers would not be interested in my journey. I got a similar response from the *National* ("Elvis Was a Martian") *Enquirer*. Nor would there be anything coming my way from the North American newspapers. I had exhausted every possibility.

In her letter, Yoshiko was her usual wonderful self. She told me, among other things, that Ayumi had asked her: "'Where do babies come from?' Shocked, I said, 'Of course, from Mother.' But she shouted, 'No, no, no! Where does the mother's mother's mother come from?' She is only four and thinking such a deep subject. Eventually, she answered it by herself. 'Didn't they come from the sky? Because the sky was there since long time ago when there was nothing. A stone in the sky exploded one day, and people were made by the stone dust.' I was shocked much more than before."

On the wings of chance, I took a very old bungalow in nearby Burnaby for five hundred dollars a month. In this little two-bedroom house I could see the makings of a cozy winter home. There would now be no money for us to return home. No matter. It was fixed. It was over.

This time, I went to the airport wearing a boutonniere and a rented suit, courtesy of a friend who insisted I look "presentable." When the plane landed, I was greeted by yet another surprise: As soon as the doors to customs swung open, I was immediately engulfed in the embrace of Toseko Matsumoto, my esteemed mother-in-law, whom I hadn't seen in seven years. Ayumi barreled toward me and skidded off at the last moment to hide behind Yoshiko, my smiling, laughing friend and lover. My debonair appearance was provoking not only laughs and comments, but consternation as well. Geoffrey didn't recognize me at all (although he was not too shy to pluck the leaves from my lapel rose one by one), and Ayumi, who at home regularly looked over the photos of me— always as the tramp—was puzzled by the sight of this spiffy impostor claiming to be her dad.

Back in Burnaby I had pinned a Welcome Home sign in Japanese on a decrepit garden shed near the house. So effective was this practical joke—the silence and suddenly long faces said everything—that the family truly believed this was the home I had promised them; indeed, wasn't this hovel in total keeping with my journey?

After a few moments of this fun, I relented and took them up the slope to the bungalow with its exciting pink bedcovers. I had balloons ready, food, toys, plus Yoshiko's favorite Robin Hood flour. The place was overflowing with floral displays, the kind gifts of friends and my landlords, the Rosenbaums.

That night, Ayumi confided to her grandmother, "Nana, this is a nice house, but I know he *borrowed* it."

Nor did my practical joke go unpaid. One morning close to my birthday I received a strange letter from my "wife in Japan" (Yoshiko had posted it before her departure from Nagoya):

> Dear my Only Husband,
> Hey! Who are living with you? I'm your wife in Japan. Don't you remember me? Someone told me you're living with an ugly Japanese family. I bet the most ugly fat woman is sleeping in the next room. OK, let her be alone. I'm not jealous at all. If you love her, kiss her. I'll find a better husband here. ANYWAY: Happy Birthday!! Have a good day with the family and a huge dinner—which of course you will cook for yourself.
>
> > Love,
> > Your wife in Japan. XXX

Over the next few weeks, I worked on my journals and we all did turismo—a bus trip to nearby Washington State and the ferry over to Vancouver Island and the provincial capital, Victoria, a small, most beautiful city, utterly English, with quaint shops full of such items as tatty imported tea biscuits, "sensible" shoes, and excellent fish and chips.

I was especially pleased that Toseko could see that Yoshiko and I really did run a proper home and were not just camping out in a house, and that the children were close to me. Geoffrey, now a mischievous two-year-old, finally now saw me as his father.

With the return of birds' song and longer days, it was time to think about moving on. I dearly wanted Yoshiko and the children to accompany me for the final stretch—what an experience it would be for us all! After bidding farewell to my mother-in-law, we shopped around for an inexpensive car and found one, a secondhand Mazda hatchback that was going for less than what the family's airfare to Alaska would have cost. We bought it on the spot. With Yoshiko driving, we would travel together after all.

Now it was the end of the first day of the resumed walk— the first day, I fervently hoped, of the last year. Heavily buttoned up against the cold, clear late-afternoon air, I rumbled down into the Smith River valley. In the near distance, beside the river, I could see a wisp of smoke rising from a campfire, and then three figures—my family—broke away from the campsite and rushed up the slope to meet me. I thought immediately of those golden moments of South America when Yoshiko would greet my arrival at the end of yet another long, arduous day. What a perfect way to end this journey, I thought, a wonderful coming-around to the beginnings.

Geoffrey and Ayumi, like two human cannonballs, lurched bucking into my arms, while Yoshiko, puffing, reached me a little later with a wide smile. "We are together again, George, on the road."

As evening drew on, the fir trees all around dissolved into the darkness; the only light remaining came from the

366

glowing embers of the campfire and the twinkling stars. Above our heads on that first shared night a little miracle occurred— the northern lights. What a wonderfully mysterious introduction for my family into this breathtakingly beautiful land.

Yukon Territory has very few roads of any description, but I fortunately got to walk on one that was at least partially paved. My spirits remained high as I clipped along toward my target. And even though my hands and face became numb in the driving slush, it was pure joy to be on the road again in this land of profound silence, and especially with the knowledge that there were family and hot food up ahead and a spacious tent in which to enjoy it all. All this and living a dream—what more could a mortal ask?

In Vancouver I had sold my first gun, never having had an occasion to use it, and I was scared of the thing anyway. On my way north this time, however, the incessant panic talk had stampeded me into buying a gross and unwieldy shotgun—a "Savage," so it said on the barrel.

To learn something more about the weapon, I took it to the local gun expert, which in this land populated with nothing but gun experts happened to be the assistant postmaster. He confirmed my worst fears: "It's factory-flawed. You've got one shot and then you might as well chuck it." We agreed that one shot would probably only enrage several hundred pounds of bear and all but guarantee for me a swift and messy exit from this life.

Fortunately, I chanced to meet a man named Leach, chairman of the Yukon Trappers Association. "I've been in the bush for getting on thirty years," he said, "and never have I seen anything I didn't want to see."

"Well, what did you carry?"

"A bell." He then added, almost defiantly, "You won't need a bloody gun!" That did it. I happily abandoned the Savage.

Beyond the small settlement of Upper Liard, I came upon a herd of horses grazing beside the road. They eyed me and my pinging bell, for they, too, wore bells, partly for the same reason. It was an odd musical confrontation as our different notes momentarily mingled on that cool spring day.

Adding to the pleasure of these days was having Yosh and the kids nearby. I might be walking along, and then, at no particular time, they would bowl joyfully up in the car to spend a moment with me. Out the children would charge, leaping and shouting. With wild, puffing runs, they would tag along for a kilometer or two before being swept up by Yoshiko and disappearing, waving, down the road, leaving me alone, in the silence, with my dreams and my world.

Each evening I would find the tent up and the campfire burning; hot food would follow shortly. Ironically, despite my love of fires, when I was alone I never built one. I was too tired to care. Now I wondered how, indeed, I had ever managed alone.

For the day, Yoshiko would make me fat, luscious sandwiches so substantial that, while I was doing marathon distances every day, I was actually putting on weight! My jaws were covering more distance than my legs.

The road was perfect. All traces of snow were gone here. In the meanwhile the news reported that in Steamboat the folks at the top of the pass were digging themselves out from under five-foot drifts.

Rancheria was the setting of the only road accident ever to befall the sturdy Yoshikart. We had stopped to pitch camp, and I slid the cart under the car and out of the rain—an open invitation for Yoshiko to drive over it, which she did, mangling my metal friend. By chance, this was one of the few places on the Alaska Highway with a welding machine, and the cart was fixed and ready to go by morning.

Why did I continue to haul the Yoshikart when I had use of a support vehicle? Three reasons, basically: In the event of a bear I could drop the thing, and this might at least distract the animal. Secondly, I had hauled it for so many years that it became a symbol of my identity—and of the journey. I had aged a great amount since the beginning, so much so that my face might not even be recognizable to someone who had only seen me then; nevertheless, a young lad would be remembered pulling a strange cart. And perhaps, I liked to think, the constantly turning wheels of the cart were like the spinning of a Tibetan Buddhist's prayer wheel.

Yukon is full of natural wonders—stately lakes, majestic cloud-shrouded peaks, swift, numbingly cold rivers. The great forests blanketed every horizon, with willow, spruce, and pine predominating. "Look at that!" I said to so many sourpussed sourdoughs, and they would invariably reply, "That's nothing—you should see north of here."

Forestry, mining, and catering to the hunting trade are the only real industries in the Yukon—and most of the mines were shutting down as a result of Canada's worst period since the Great Depression. Brave, hardy types who loved the territory were hanging on desperately; the poverty of some of their sod-roof cabins could almost be smelled.

We camped one night at Mile 747—postal addresses on the Alaska Highway are given in terms of the miles from Dawson Creek—and met a man whose business was conducting "safaris" into the north woods. The year's trade had been appalling, he told us, and the cabins he had built with his own hands had remained mostly empty. With true Yukoner spirit he was holding out as best he could; he wouldn't give up without a fight.

We finally reached Teslin, the first trading post in a solid week. The village sits on a picturesque headland that juts out into the long blue streak of Lake Teslin. Some few hundreds of Tlingit Indians live here in wooden shacks, some looking well constructed and comfortable, others less so.

On Sunday, I went to church. There was no music in St. Philip's service, and only a half-dozen stalwarts in attendance. As I knelt on the rough wood floor, I could see out a small window to my side. Down below sat the silent, brooding lake, and just across its deep waters, the steep sides of the Mountain of the Aces sweeping up dramatically to its snow-filled summit. In my side-glancing prayers I thanked God for the privilege of journeying through such grandeur.

Whitehorse, the territorial capital, sits beside the Yukon

River beneath a low cliff that hides it completely from view when one is approaching from the east on the Alaskan Highway. To fight, or at least contain, alcoholism, which is a major problem throughout the Far North, the city fathers have erected a bold notice: "No Drinking on the Road Within City Limits." The injunction covers a wider area than one might think, for the city limits (though the city has fewer than fifteen thousand inhabitants) reach out a full 18 km from the center of town.

Most of the town itself is a larger version of the settlements and roadworkers' camps that dot the highway leading up to it. Aside from a fair number of log cabins still in use and the odd clapboard store, the new construction is primarily of the prefabricated variety. The exception is the Yukon Government Administration Building, a superb example of ultramodern architecture.

The Yukon's Anglican Cathedral is a far cry from the lofty towers of Canterbury. In fact, it a pair of prefabs which resemble the emergency annexes thrown up by desperate school boards to accommodate classroom overflow in the big city.

Outside the "cathedral," I met Chappie Chapman, a tall, stooped figure in his eighties. When in his early twenties, Chappie had been a Mountie, when he would don a wolfskin coat and take four dogs and go out on patrol for months at a time, sleeping in a bag on a bed of spruce leaves in supersubzero temperatures. Later he took up the hardly less demanding occupation of miner.

But he only discovered his true vocation, as well as Mattie, his wife, after joining the Northern Commercial Company in the gold rush town of Dawson, which was once the territorial capital. In time, he became general manager, which meant that during the treacherous winters he would be responsible for supplying the needs of thousands in this last outpost of civilization. Once the Yukon River (the "Gateway to the North") froze over, the town was shut tight, and steamers wouldn't be able to reach Dawson until the big thaw in late spring. To keep alive the hundreds of miners during the winter, Chappie set up a chit system for feeding them until they could get south to sell their pelts and gold.

Gold is, of course, the reason there ever was a Whitehorse in the first place. In the 1890's, during the Great Stampede, Whitehorse, just downriver from the last rapids, was the initial target of the hordes of prospectors. They would have to climb over the Chilkoot Pass with a pack of mules, hauling a ton of supplies each (prudence dictated taking along a minimum of a year's food). To ensure their safety, the Mounties would check everyone out with scales before they were allowed to enter the wilderness.

Toting up my distances to Fairbanks, Alaska, I discovered that I would not complete 18,500 miles, qualifying me for the "longest march ever," until a point some few miles past that city. To make this come out right, I decided to add some arbitrary miles. I religiously trooped along the longitudinal streets of Whitehorse—without crossing my route, of course. The Mountie depot crossed the street, and so to maintain my integrity, I climbed over the fence and proceeded. Suddenly, from within charged a monstrous, yellow-fanged, howling huskie. I began backpedaling for all I was worth as I looked on in horror at the animal's great chain paying out like a ship's cable. (Huskies are as capable of eating human meat as any other.)

Thwack! The chain went bar-tight just as the dog was inches from my throat. I was spared. I continued my bizarre odyssey, without, of course, crossing my route.

I walked out of Whitehorse, returning a wave to all the cars that passed, and for the first two miles they constituted the Yukon's worst traffic—at least three or four every minute. Very soon I was totally alone with the frolicking rabbits in hot pursuit of each other and the rich smells of blossoming wildflowers. Spring had arrived.

My passing of a homestead generally led to a frantic commotion, as an entire team of agitated sled dogs, huskies and malamutes, would scramble the full length of their chains, hop onto their kennel roof, and howl mightily at me. How they would have envied my journey, this adventurous crew, for they lived for the trail.

With the coming of a warmer sun another annoyance was the onslaught of mosquitoes. One night, I arrived at the campsite to discover my family absolutely beseiged, prisoners in the tent, tormented by thousands of the flying dread. Even inside the tent the poor children had been blitzed—we counted over a hundred bites on Geoffrey and almost as many on Ayumi. It was terrible to see them scratching and tearing their skins so. While the mosquitoes in Canada were not the disease-carrying variety found in Latin America, they made up for that one failing by striking in full daylight and giving a bite that would itch up to three days. In the tropics, twenty minutes was the norm, and the mosquitoes struck only after dark.

The presence or absence of mosquitoes on this stretch could make or break a day's journey, which varied in difficulty depending on a number of factors, not just distance, that always came into play—weather, climate, terrain, the road, or just the way I felt, or any combination. After Whitehorse, the march into Haines Junction, for example, was an abomination. The assault of mosquitoes precluded rest stops of more than a few moments, and the temperature leapt to a muggy ninety-plus degrees. I was losing so much water that I knocked back most of three liters, more than any time since Mexico.

On the road to Kluane I passed through land of heart-stopping beauty. To my right stretched blue-green Kluane Lake, where ice still floated in the midregion. Climbing abruptly from the far shoreline was a string of small mountains with a salt sprinkling of snow, the peaks reflecting with crystal clarity from the mirror-still surface of the lake beneath a cloud-studded sky.

On my left stood the towering grandeur of the Front Range, beyond which lay the largest ice fields in the world outside the polar regions. The interior of Kluane National Park is so barren that no animal above the level of insect lives there save for the humble and remarkable iceworm. The joy of walking through this spectacular land kept my heart racing all day.

Later, under a dark sky, the whole family trundled along a mud track that led to the lake and an abandoned log-cabin settlement, Silver City. Where once there was life, now there was silence. Many of the sod roofs had collapsed, and grass and purple fireweed now grew through the ghostly remains. With a shiver, we quietly departed, as down on the lake black cumulus clouds sailed before the wind.

The next day, while crunching along the gravel of the highway near Sheep Mountain and admiring the day, I was startled to notice someone running toward me, waving. Helen Broomell was a total stranger who . . .

But I'll let her explain the encounter in her own words, as described in her book, *Alone on the Yukon Again*:

> I had seen a few news blurbs about a young man who was walking from Tierra del Fuego . . . to the Arctic Ocean, taking many years to accomplish it, but I had no idea where he was. Imagine my surprise when the Park Ranger looked down the road toward an orange-vested man pulling a small two-wheel cart with a pack on it, and said, "Here comes the hiker from South America!" . . .
>
> Obviously, after talking with him, one realizes that, undimmed by some threatening situations in South America, he is in love with the whole human race.

How did she happen to be exactly there at that time? "I was hitchhiking to Alaska," she told me, "and just felt compelled, by whim, to get off in this beautiful land." When you have an intense desire to meet someone, this is often the way it happens.

Helen hails from Wisconsin, but her blood doesn't nearly begin to run until she's north of the 60th parallel. She was returning to the Yukon River, all fifteen hundred miles of it, which she was canoeing in stages. The preceding year Helen, who was in her sixties, had spent several weeks alone on its empty reaches, and her many adventures had been published in the book quoted above. Pensioners whose idea of exertion is standing on the checkout line in the supermarket would do well to consider our resolute and wondrous Helen Broomell.

Burwash Landing is a Southern Toshone Indian village that clings neatly to the Kluane Lake foreshore. "We need little from the government," pronounced one of the elders. "So long as we catch the fish and hunt the moose, we make out." Dinner in the shape of an elk sometimes just wanders through the village.

We were all put up at the tourist lodge run by the To- shones. I spoke with one of the Indians working there, Wayne Reindeer, not a Toshone but an Athabascan from the North- west Territories. "They think I'm strange here," confided this strikingly handsome, tall young man. "You see, we eat seals, but down here they eat ground squirrel—gophers."

The next day we were all taken to the tribe's sacred burial grounds. Over the graves had been constructed miniature painted houses, complete down to the glass windowpanes; there were no doors, however, so that the spirit cannot wander off.

A few hours' march up the muddy road, the Burwash band kept a half-hidden camp, where we had been invited to attend a trout picnic. Several teenagers walked part of the way with me, and once we had all arrived at the camp one of them, Juniper, "married" Yoshiko and me in a teenage ver- sion of the Toshone wedding ceremony. It was all lots of fun with these good folk and their ever-circling dogs. Many of the games played were new to us. Ayumi especially enjoyed the footraces, and Geoff loved feeding the dogs.

Moving on, we continued to make good progress despite the broken road. Every few days we would find a lodge where we could purchase food, mostly hamburgers. Fruits and veg- etables, our real hunger, were simply unavailable outside two or three stores in our Yukon journey.

With the increase in latitude, trees became more stunted and the mosquito hordes hiding in the muskeg bogs even more alarming. June 10 brought with it, amazingly, a blizzard.

Alaska

Alaska! The very name had been connected with me for so long: *El hombre inglés hasta Alaska, caminando,* I had been called in Latin America, the Englishman headed for Alaska, walking. And now I was actually in the promised land, near the end of seven years of struggle and of wonder.

June 1983—I must be into my thirty millionth step by now. My years of labor had been directed toward getting me exactly here during the summer. I now wore shorts, and my neck warmly appreciated the sun overhead in the clear blue sky, for the tales of winter in Alaska were so extreme as to rival black comedy. Sixty degrees below zero didn't exist in the "real world." What could it mean? It meant that the slightly inebriate driver who dropped his keys in the snow and picked them up suffered immediate frostbite and had to have two fingers amputated. It meant that the soldier from Fort Greely who took a swig of brandy while on guard duty dropped dead— lungs frozen. Out here even a breath of fresh winter air can frost the lungs, with the same consequences. At Mile 1260, Jim Shock poured me a drink and introduced me to his "friend"—a skull. "We found him out in the backcountry. Figure he was a gold stampeder . . . probably froze to death." There was no doubt about my objective; to cross Alaska before these deadly conditons were even a remote possibility.

The international border—the point where the Alaskan Highway actually reached Alaska—was immediately recognizable even without the signs: It was where the mud strip instantly gave way to smooth blacktop. And whereas during my last days in the Yukon I had been surrounded by stunted, poverty-stricken trees, for some reason this part of Alaska was a world of sturdy evergreens.

No sooner did I begin admiring the Americans' road-building enthusiasm, however, than I became embroiled in eighteen solid miles of massive road reconstruction: They were straightening the road. I had mixed feelings about this. On the plus side I was thankful for the resulting blacktop; on the negative side, negotiating through the machines and barriers and rubble was a time-consuming nuisance, sometimes hazardous.

But that wasn't even the real reason I objected to the road-straightening. The bend in the road, the curve in the highway, something road engineers abhor and avoid at all costs, is something I cherish. So much interest is added to walking when every corner might hide a welcome surprise (so long as it isn't a bear). It's such a delight to be confronted with something sudden, new, and bold, so much more pleasant than struggling for hours to reach that abandoned hut or shuttered store straight ahead on the horizon.

The net effect was a psychological paradox. As with the entire walk, I had to have a goal, but the goal itself wasn't the important thing—getting there was the important thing. Yet I would never start, never have the motivation to keep going, if I didn't have the goal in the first place.

A little past the construction, hearing the buzz of an engine behind me, I casually swung my head around to check for danger. *Christ!* With a gasp I threw myself onto the highway.

The wing of a small airplane careered barely ten feet overhead, blowing my hat off. The machine, flashing red lights all the way, a wisp of smoke trailing behind, bounced to a landing on the blacktop thirty yards down the road. From beneath the wing a fat, bubbly Indian woman freed herself from the aircraft like a pea from a pod. She reached back inside the cockpit and retrieved from the pilot a great bundle of washing and some plastic bags—she had been out shopping!

Moments later, the Cessna banked into the air, the fat squaw disappeared into the bush, and I was once again alone with my thoughts and the Alaskan hinterland.

In this land of great opportunity and few roads (in most regions the Alaskan Highway is the only real road), the immense distances can only be reasonably handled by air; in fact, half of all the private aircraft in the world are registered in Alaska. Near any urban center, such as they were, I couldn't look up without seeing at least one fixed wing clawing itself into the sky.

I reached Northway, which had been named long ago after the local Athabascan chief. That same man, Chief Walter Northway, was still very much alive, and Yosh, the children, and I got to meet him. Glowing with a beauty both spiritual and physical, Chief Walter was believed to be 107 years old. How could I tell? He was obviously an old man, yet there wasn't a line in his face. With his thick, coarse hair and humorous eyes he could have been fifty—or a hundred and fifty.

Chief Walter told me a story of long ago—long before the turn of the century, he said—when he was just a boy and had gone hunting with his uncle. Stopping to rest, they glanced into the distance—and the future. Terror-stricken, the boy bolted at the bizarre sight of two men, while his uncle stood firm. Neither had imagined such strangeness—white men.

Chief Walter invited our family to an Athabascan wake, which in this case was also the occasion for a traditional potlatch—a monumental giveaway ceremony arranged and conducted by the family of the deceased for the purpose of enhancing their prestige. When we entered the large, darkened meeting lodge the drums were already beating out a monotonous dirge and several chanters wailing in vigorous unison.

Through the window a single beam of sunlight illuminated the rising dust. The whole assembly sat on chairs in a great circle. At least two hundred Indians were present, plus a couple of whites and my Japanese family. The conversational hum was all in Athabascan, a strange-sounding tongue that, I later learned, is linguistically related to Aztecan and other central Mexican languages—but not to any language nearby! It was great fortune to be there; someone sitting nearby told me that Athabascans and others from hundreds of miles around had descended on Northway just for the occasion.

Eventually food was served, including salmon and cornbread. The key item in the feast was a long-simmering moose stew that was nearly overflowing a stupendous cooking pot. After the food, Chief Walter, decked out in beads and buckskin, gave a powerful (though unintelligible to us) speech to the family who had suffered the loss. Tears were shed, and then a more lighthearted dance began.

Hours slipped into yet more hours. The time for the gift-giving was at last at hand. Piled high in the center of the meeting hut rose a great heap of presents. According to the grieving family's accounting, there were four hundred seventy blankets, mostly the Hudson's Bay Company issue, thirty-nine Winchester repeating rifles, seventeen elaborate ornamental feathers, and some small beadwork. Everyone received something; even Yoshiko and I were given a blanket each. (The Indians of these parts save for much of their lives to pay out the several thousand dollars needed for their final potlatch. Expensive, yes, but at that still cheaper than the standard American funeral—and a lot more beneficial.)

Throughout the proceedings another grand old man sat in the shadows. Andrew Titus Isaacs wore the heavy neck pendant of Paramount Chief of All the Athabascans of the North. Many years before, Chief Andrew, along with several others, stood around the tribe's previous leader, his uncle, as he lay on his deathbed. The doomed man's finger pointed at Andrew, and thus was the office passed on. Sometime in the future Chief Andrew would repeat the ceremony.

"Perhaps you could point at me," I breezily suggested.

The Paramount Chief burst into peals of laughter at the very idea of a paleface—and an Englishman at that—leading his august people.

Yoshiko literally cheered: After 348 miles she had finally found a store selling a carrot. In fact, this was not to be the longest gap in our search for fresh vegetables. North of Fairbanks there would be nothing of this sort for five hundred miles.

Camping was still the mainstay of our existence, but with our indefatigable gain in latitude and the sun near the summer solstice we had a problem. The children simply could not believe that bedtime was bedtime. How could they, when the sun was shining brightly through the orange nylon of the tent hours after lights-out? It was like living in a lightbulb.

In all the world, Alaska has the loveliest roadsides. There is none of the litter and junk of more populous ares, but rather endless flowers, both wild and planted. I would sometimes find myself compelled to stop just in order to sniff the pungent aroma of the sky-blue forget-me-nots. And everywhere I would see fireweed, with its reds and purples. (Its name, by the way, has nothing to do with these brilliant colors, but arises from the fact that this hardy plant is always the first to return after a forest fire.) Red and yellow poppies abounded, helped on their way by the environmentally conscientious Highways Department, who mix in poppy with their grass seed.

Near Delta Junction, goats wandered among the trees, nibbling at the leaves and even the trunks, which gave them the appearance of being partially shredded. Geoffrey, like most boys his age a great lover of animals, was lightly bucked by one fierce billy—and came up laughing. Every day was an adventure and experience for our children, indeed for us, and we constantly expressed the hope that in the years to come they might remember some of these grand days.

The Alaska Highway officially ended at Delta Junction, Mile 1422 from Dawson Creek, B.C., although nobody took much notice of this. Fairbanks, the hub of Alaska, was taken generally as the terminus.

At some forgotten spot on the road, a truck selling fireworks was parked, its back open. They had been at it for six weeks, the men said. The Fourth of July was just around the corner, and business was "booming." This was intoxicating stuff that even we could not resist, and so we bought a skyrocket and two "death spinners." "How sad," Yoshiko observed. "Fireworks—but no darkness!"

From Delta Junction onward we encountered more people on the road and would usually have neighbors at our campsite. The journey now included a social life. Moreover, food was no longer a problem. At the Fort Greely commissary, a sympathetic soldier let us buy provisions, and so we happily munched on salami and radishes for a full day. A bottle of wine thrown our way by fellow campers did no harm, either.

I rolled into camp one evening after having been soaked by rainshowers for the better part of the day. A couple of swigs out of Yoshiko's bottle of sherry left me totally unconcerned. Perhaps I should have tried this six years ago, I thought. On this sort of venture, however, one must be on guard against the danger of descending into alcoholism. Luckily I had always been too limited by money to get involved, and I much prefer a Coke anyway.

This same day, Yoshiko, with her excellent eye for such things, had situated the tent on a cliff overlooking a broad expanse of muddy delta and built a fire there. Ordinarily the wind strikes here at a wrenching sixty miles an hour, but in this tranquil, perpetual twilight the smoke curled straight up into the sky from our three sizzling steaks. Now this, I thought, was the way to travel.

I was within sight of mile 18,500, the milestone that, once passed, would make the walk the longest in history. At distance 18,499 miles from Ushuaia, I halted. The spot was marked by a suitably preposterous twenty-foot-high plaster replica of Santa Claus that towered over a campground, where we set up the family tent. We had arrived in North Pole, Alaska.

The giant Santa wasn't the only thing pointing to heaven. The campground was also in the shadow of the transmitting tower of KJNP, the most powerful radio station in Alaska. This multimillion-dollar enterprise was the brainchild of Don ("Hallelujah Jesus") Nelson. A ball-turret gunner and pris- oner-of-war in World War II, Nelson had returned home a changed man and gradually descended into the hellish life of a bitter, foul-mouthed alcoholic. Then, seized by the reform- ing spirit, he became a fundamentalist Christian and entered a seminary, only to flunk out. The spirit finally moved him up the Alaska Highway to the Far North, where he launched his evangelical career by sweeping church floors. With a min- imum of funds, he began broadcasting his message of salva- tion and eventually extended it throughout the Far North, including the Scandinavian countries and the USSR. His zeal for "air missionary" work was such that he once loaded tons of Bibles and chewing gum into an airplane and dropped the lot off the coast of the Soviet Union (a risky business, as Ko- rean Airlines Flight 007 testifies).

Before completion of the record-tying and record-break- ing 18,500th and 18,501st miles, the family and I drove on ahead into Fairbanks, where, I thought, the publicity poten- tial for such an event must be enormous. Although I had grown to detest the process of drawing media attention to the jour- ney, I now needed publicity, if only to help the family get back to Britain, where we planned to settle down at least for awhile.

In the dust-tinged half-light, silhouetted against a smudge of red on the southwestern horizon, Fairbanks looked ro- guish. On the verge of our small triumph, Yosh and I and the children drove into town, convinced that some hotel would grant us a room for the duration at the very least, but eleven straight managers said no before one of them finally said OK—

for a night. It was clear that no Fairbanks hotel was going to do us long-term honors, and so the next day we headed back to North Pole and pitched the tent under the giant Santa.

Now began weeks of trying to alert a somewhat reluctant media to our fast-approaching attempt to reach the Arctic Ocean, and I began by contacting—or trying to contact—the several journalists who in the past couple of years had expressed interest in covering the end of the walk. Handling public relations out of a tent has to be experienced to be understood. The nearest telephone was a quarter of a mile away, wedged next to the door of the men's room inside a log-cabin gas station. Over the next few weeks I spent dozens of hours there, staring at the walls while waiting for a line connection to Toronto, New York, or London. The decor of that cubicle permanently etched itself into my memory—especially one item, the framed portrait hanging over my head, a ghastly rendition on black velvet of "Elvis the King."

The day finally came, and the Big Moment was, as it usually is for ordinary folk, a mixture of pride, embarrassment, and anarchy.

"Congratulations, George!"

"Congratulations!"

"Well done!"

The family and I were engulfed by reporters, microphones, and TV crews. Only twenty minutes before we had set out like a Turkish army retreat from the three-story Santa Claus, which of course lent its own unfortunate "dignity" to the occasion.

Newsman Alex Epstein placed me in front of his TV camera. "George Meegan, you have strived, it seems, forever, and now you have made the longest unbroken foot journey in history." Faint applause. I nodded.

Having knocked off the symbolic two miles (for this one occasion I used miles instead of kilometers), I followed up the next day by finally taking the walk into Fairbanks. Yoshiko accompanied me for the entire 11 miles. While the experience did her feet in quite badly, she was delighted because she could now recall the physical misery of her Patagonian adventure with the knowledge that she didn't have to repeat it. Whereas in Tierra del Fuego she had limped in frustration, she now limped into Fairbanks in exaltation.

North of Fairbanks, the Steese Highway eventually leads to the Dalton, originally known as the Haul Road, which pierces the Arctic Circle and continues on to the North Slope oilfields at Prudhoe Bay—the end. Along the entire length of the Haul Road, 416 miles, there are exactly two gas pumps, and nothing else. Tens of thousands of tons of stores are annually trucked up the Dalton by specially licensed drivers, and while the general public are not allowed up the road without signed permission from the director of state transport, which is rarely granted, I imagined in my case that his signature would be a mere formality. It wasn't.

"No, Mr. Meegan" was the bureaucrat's pronouncement. "How can I possibly say yes?" I was staggered and immediately began to pedal furiously, presenting for his inspection my ever-present sheaf of clippings and the Jimmy Carter photo. He perused the ensemble for a few moments in noncommittal silence, and then relented. The governing factor in the end may have been his soft spot for the English and England, since he had spent two years at school there. If this man, John D. Horn, had so willed it, my journey could have come to an inglorious halt right there in his office.

But there was yet another, more formidable obstacle. The oil companies controlled the Arctic Ocean end of the road, and as far as I could determine they had never allowed anyone else to cross their land. I was put in touch with the Sohio corporate representative in Fairbanks. The rep, a cautious "company man," a breed I hadn't had to deal with on the walk, obtained a provisional go-ahead—revocable if corporate Big Brother Arco disagreed.

I spent most of the next few days under "Elvis the King" trying to correlate and rationalize the schedules of my various friends in the media. I began to sound like a bureaucrat myself. Events were seldom earthshaking, except perhaps the morning of Tuesday, July 12, when Elvis, along with the rest of us, began to sway alarmingly—it was a small earthquake. (A larger one came later.)

Fairbanks to Prudhoe Bay measures 501 miles. I could at least whittle some of that down before taking on the Dalton Highway, I thought, using Fairbanks as a base. One empty weekend, I officially moved my walk out of Fairbanks and north over the large hills on the Steese Highway. The four lanes soon reduced to a single file. Glad to be walking again, by the time I reached Fox I felt so strong that, after a Coke and cake from the Mexican-run store, I swung onto another connecting highway, the Elliot. It was past midnight, the sky was tinged with daylight still, and nothing moved whatsoever save I and my creaking Yoshikart. I could have been ten thousand miles from anywhere, and yet the town was only a twenty-minute drive away.

Back in Fairbanks, preparations for the final leg took on the flavor of packing for an ocean voyage. A thousand and one things had to be done, and all of them pretty well without money. Don McIntyre, a former USAF colonel, provided us with flares. An airhorn for bear protection was found, and film bummed. Dot Simpson produced a Coleman stove, and the legendary dog sledder Mary Shields gave us four Snowy Owl feathers from the coast of the Bering Sea for good luck. A couple of sacks of provisions had to be loaded and so forth, ad infinitum.

As for a rifle, after all my exhaustive inquiries the decision had come down on the side of "no gun"—the head of the Alaska Fish and Game Department was the deciding opinion. (I now felt most "un-Alaskan": One of my first impressions on entering Fairbanks had been a pickup screaming by bearing the large insignia, emblazoned on the door, of the National Rifle Association, the group whose lobbying efforts have been crucial in blocking federal legislation that could curb America's gun mayhem. Some places the NRA may keep a low profile, but not in Fairbanks.)

The afternoon ticked by under sheets of chilly rain. With some trepidation we all clambered aboard the grossly overladen subcompact. Against our better judgment, the kids would have to accompany us, for we had nowhere to leave them. Amid all the gear there was barely room for them to turn. I didn't envy them their weeks, nor Yoshiko's task.

It was hardly encouraging when we all had to bounce together and not breathe too deeply just to get up the first hill out of Fairbanks. Our reservations about even reaching the infamous Dalton would have been graver still had we known our spare tire was the wrong size. And of course no one for thousands of miles around had ever seen the Mazda's unique rotary engine.

At five miles an hour, we eventually crested the first hill. Thank goodness it was cool rain—the engine always ran better out of the sun. We found our way back to my mark on the Elliot Highway, where I was left off.

Here the story again becomes Yoshiko's as well as mine— as it always was. Her view of the events leading up to the end of the journey appears in the following long journal-letter that she sent home to Japan (and which she later translated):

Father, Mother,
9 *Aug.* '83 We are now approximately 400 km south of Prudhoe Bay. George would go alone, but problem of carrying food and attracting bears in night is true. It was a serious decision on us to have George alone with greater danger or lesser risk on whole family.

As long as we keep being near car (though a fragile one compared to wildest grizzly bear), we can rush into the car when something happened. This already trained to children on the way to Fairbanks from British Columbia. So we decided, OK, let's go all together.

If you drive ten minutes from Fairbanks . . . you will find yourself surrounded by famous Alaskan mother nature.

We left Fairbanks on 31 July and I drove ahead of George to organize the place to sleep, meal for night, etc. and utter accidentally I drove the Mazda onto the land of family which was almost hidden from the road by tall trees. Most all of Alaska seems tall trees. Nancy and Joe Carlson have fifteen children, sometimes take care of more. No electricity, and twenty miles away from the nearest water. The big log house was built by the couple with the great help of all children.

After a few hours talking with Nancy in the dark, warm house, somehow I found a courage in myself to ask if they could look after our children for three weeks. Nancy's face was covered with surprise and shock. I could understand this, as it was such a huge responsibility to request of anyone. But she was almost to tears and said, "Really? *Could* we?"

"Pardon?" was my amazed response. Yes, really she wished to care for our children, besides their already fifteen. This was one of greatest gestures of my journey, such a happy accident too.

On the next day George took a day off walking to see the children's new home.

Joe is such a good father of all children and Nancy is a great mother. Joe had already given jobs to our children, so important, I think. Ayumi is to collect eggs under chickens every morning and Geoff to pick tomatoes. Where are our children? Chasing a duck and admiring two beautiful ponies. Oh my goodness, I almost bring my heart in mouth to see my little daughter on back of a motorcycle with her new boyfriend. Around here nobody seems to care on driving license, even though this boy is same age as Ayumi—five years old!

Without kids we are able to sleep in car, so much safer than tent. Three mornings ago I woke up suddenly with George's shout, "Yosh, bear!" I opened my eyes and immediately saw the bear, inches away, watching at me. He turned his eyes to check all inside very slowly, and then he put his big front back onto the ground and off our glass window. He then slowly moved into the bush, showing us his big furry bottom. I really appreciate Joe and Nancy for taking our kids, for without them we would be all the family sleeping in the tent and this Mr. Bear could damage us.

Anyway, I went back to sleep, leaving my husband still with eyes wide open. It was 4:15 A.M. and the morning sun had already arrived. Later, we examined our campsite and found many heavy footprints and clean teeth marks in our only soap.

Next morning we had a visit from a friendly silver fox and also some gray unknown birds will actually take food from our hands. This north world is so special.

The other day we saw a mother moose and calf eating grass

and roots so peacefully in a marsh. They didn't rush away, instead they kept looking back at us, checking. We were sorry to give this happy mother and child concern. They, like us, were frightened of possibly hungry bears. It is especially easy to be surprised when picking berries. In Alaska you can find many kinds of berries everywhere. I picked a full cooking pot of blueberries, so delicious, without need to pay $1.99 per pound!

Poor car makes it to five thousand feet of Atigan Pass, highest of Brooks Mountain Range. Here strong wind of ice and snow. George became cold, but manage OK.

Yesterday we passed the Arctic Circle. The view is just magnificent. So far, far away you can see the wet green horizon and by looking the other way, mountains with tops of snow. Thousands of ponds reflect the blue round sky.

Have given up to try to take photos as it is impossible to catch this beauty in a snap picture.

As standing on top of one of these hills that we'd conquered weeks before, I suddenly got anxious and wondered after we go back to Japan, which is such a small set of islands with so many people, if I could live in that sort of society with contentment. Would I not miss this far horizon terribly? Also I think of our children's education. Sitting at a desk and studying so hard just to pass examination, which in Japan is so constantly and gives terrible pressure, which I once felt. Or finding an egg under a chicken and learn how to live with true nature. Which is better?

12 Aug. '83 Here there are many grizzly bear that grow two or even four times larger than black bear. We heard that somebody in Alaska left his camper door open and Mr. Grizzly Bear smashed it off with one hit. Somebody told us that one smack from any bear would damage our poor car.

However, there is not only bear seen here but many other beautiful animals too. Caribou, elk, fox, moose, as well as bear have such freedom in this great Alaska nature world, indeed a sort of perfection. Even at the campsite in Fairbanks we met so many squirrels, birds, rabbits, and beaver that build dam of stick—more animals than people even.

13 Aug. '83 George tell me he was approached by a big

387

red grizzly bear. It appear Mr. Grizzly let George pass—he doesn't see—and the bear came out on the road and followed George behind. (Mr. Grizzly like to attack from behind.) George so very, very lucky, for truck come and make frantic siren noise. George turn, he tell me, and see with big eyes big bear running with long red hair like so fast across road behind him and into trees.

This is one of today's adventures. Not to worry, because George is fine, but why this happen just after the fish and game warden said to him, "You will have no trouble with bears!"

Every day now I see the Alaska pipeline like a streaking-away silver rope on orange posts all the way to the horizon. It is the reason for this road from the beginning. Do not think the pipeline is straight, but it makes a snake trail across the ground in case it is so frozen or so warm that it won't break open.

The oil is warm to help it move in pipe, but this would melt the permafrost and hurt the nature land. So for this reason the pipeline is lifted off ground for most its length. However, animals must migrate crossing, and to allow this they have sunk a section in the permafrost even for four whole miles with refrigeration on outside and heating inside. Amazing!

14 Aug. '83 As everything is depending on this tiny poor second-hand car, I'm driving sometimes as giving her a whip, or at other time giving her a soft stroke. When she goes uphill my underarms begin to sweat. It is barely enough to say that this car is going ahead. And of course you find at each of these times the disgusting traffic sign "LIMIT 40 MPH." Bucca yaro!

I'm writing this in the car parked near a small pond. Suddenly a noise of engine, but where from? No, it was not a truck, but a small airplane. Such a narrow path wide enough only for two cars and I was blocking one side totally. Yet somehow this pilot with such confidence passed beside my car. And his right wing was almost touching my roof—and he even waved his hand at me!

16 Aug. '83 It is sixty miles to reach the Arctic Ocean. We will enter Prudhoe Bay the day after tomorrow. It's very cold, even it's still summer. I feel we have come to the end of the earth.

Winter temperatures reach the dreadful level of −80° F. This is far beyond any kind of instantaneous freezing machine. I once heard if you drop a mass of iron, it will be reduced to a mass of pieces. If you sprinkle warm water into the air it will immediately disguise itself to ice, like a firework, before crashing to the ground.

18 Aug. '83 This is the last day of the long, long walking journey, except the last ten miles. Almost every day the Mazda has broken down with something, but anyway the tiny rotary engine had got up us to the end. Many truckers had looked at us in amazement, to see such a tiny car with B.C. registration so far north, and even lower than their wheel.

We will return with news people in September to finish the last yards of the journey publicly.

Since we entered the tundra two days ago the view changed dramatically, to just unchanging green flatlands. Front, back, and sides, it's the same everywhere. Caribou can be seen on the soaked grassy tundra, feeding and showing off their beautiful horns so proudly.

This morning George started his journey as usual. I cleaned inside the car. A few minutes passed before I noticed that George was not on the road. Strange. I looked for him around the car for he might be fixing his gear or something. But after all what I found was a man walking with his head down looking at the surface of his road—but that road was going back to Ushuaia, on Tierra del Fuego! Never happened before in his journey of many years, to walk back down the road he marched up. Moreover this happened on *the* very last day.

It is likely to mistake the direction on this empty land, but even so I cannot to think that this accident must be showing something which is in his heart. So far George was asked by many people, "Mr. Meegan, how do you feel after so nearly finishing your long trail? You must be happy." After a while of thinking he always answered, "Sad."

I shouted at George: "Not *that* way, *this* way!" I pointed the correct way. He still didn't notice the way was wrong and looked confused. Then his mistake hit him. While passing the car a second time he waved me away to hide his redfaced embarrassment. I was sorry to shame my husband.

Where I stand now is one dot. One mere dot that is surrounded by an utter perfect circle of horizon. If it is possible I would like to stay on this dot, just like now, until I myself melt into the ground completely. The feeling of tension and relief at the same time extends to the maximum in my body.

The wind is getting stronger, like when we both started together at the bottom of South America. Pampas in Argentina, tundra in Alaska. Without our children, we are alone again. Once again there is no wood for fire and therefore as before our food must be cold. The very taste of meat and raw onion rolls back the years to our far-off origin.

The journey itself seems to be going back to its beginning.

19 Aug. '83 We have arrived at Prudhoe Bay, our last community.

How many cities, towns, and villages have we passed so far? Even if it was a poor stick shack, until we got there, it was our destination. And like this we have passed one thousand many destinations. Prudhoe Bay *was* the last destination but one—the bitter end. No more keep-walking-forever as holding a map and dream.

Father, Mother, I will post this long letter from the end of the earth. Thank you for supporting our journey for all our married life and even before. We have all grown old while studying the great map of George's great walk. After all, he really did it. Now we must think of our future life. Father, Mother, we can pay you back nothing except the information that this our road life has ended safely. Its success is our tribute to you both. Thank you very much.

Yoshiko

As Yoshiko was writing this, my long walk was drawing to a close. The last few miles were primarily for the public finish that was expected.

Actually, it was only in recent weeks that I had even decided to finish at all. Did I really need to go to the very limit, to the edge of my journey? Surely I had proved, against all the odds, despite the predictions of the naysayers, that I could do it. Would not finishing utterly kill forever my dream, like signing the death certificate of a soldier missing in action? As

390

for the additional world's records awaiting me, did I really need them? Did I really have to pick up these nuggets of fool's gold? They were mine anyway; why not leave them where they lay, in the tundra mud?

My final decision to go ahead with the finish was for the most inglorious of reasons. Having spent half my life trying to answer the dreaded question "Why?" I was now so very close to providing an answer of sorts, if only a phony one—that not to bring the journey to completion would condemn me to spending the rest of my life coming to grips with the hideous question, "Why not?" I had better finish, and finish soon.

First, however, I had to travel south to Anchorage to tilt at the bureaucratic windmills of Arco (Atlantic Richfield Company), which controlled the land leading to Prudhoe Bay on the Beaufort Sea. After I had walked nineteen thousand miles, and now within hours of the end of this seven-year odyssey, Arco representatives were arbitrarily withholding permission to cross this land. In the words of one of them, I would be allowed there only over their "dead bodies." The American media seemed to be egging me on in this David-and-Goliath situation, eager to see me rip into Big Oil. And although I could have exploited the company's shortsightedness by reaping a publicity bonanza, I decided to soft-pedal the matter. And sure enough, they eventually changed their minds.

The few miles to the end were with Yoshiko, the same girl who was there at the very beginning. A bus loaded with media representatives followed slowly behind us, the entire event under the total (if reluctant) control of Arco.

At one point one of the wheels of the Yoshikart came off its axle and rolled to the road's edge, and everything came to a standstill until my friend from Pittsburgh, Jim Willis, appeared, pulled a large paper clip from the pages of his notebook, and helped us rewire the wheel to the cart. The Yoshikart and I had been holding each other together for years now, and after more than nineteen thousand miles of rolling after me it didn't want the journey to end either.

Our equilibrium restored, and thankfully alone again, Yosh and I resumed this oddest of marches.

"Hey, Yosh, remember Ushuaia, the haunted house, and the one-legged gaucho? Good fun, eh?" Yoshiko smiled and nodded.

"George, could you imagine this?" she said, pointing at the aircraft circling overhead on polar bear lookout for our protection.

"I don't know, love. Don't know *anything* anymore. The future's scary . . . What do you say we go back to Patagonia!"

Yosh just smiled. And so we moved on, hand in mittened hand, our only real possessions the memories of who we once were.

Soon Yosh and I rounded a bend of the gravel road and came within sight of the others. Our children, who had been in the care of baby-sitters all morning, now broke loose from their nannies and came running toward us. Geoffrey clambered his way onto my shoulders for a better view of the proceedings, while for the last few yards Ayumi straddled the Yoshikart. We were all together, at last, at the end.

Each step now brought me excruciatingly closer to that end. The brilliant colors of the flags assembled for the occasion—the colors of my life—whipped in the wind, in stark contrast with the bleak landscape; their very intensity in the midst of all this grayness was painful to behold. Here, symbolically laid out before me, was my dream. I felt not an inkling of the glow of victory, only sad, sad loss.

"All gone, Yosh. All gone. Finished, all gone."

Yosh touched my shoulder. "Don't be sad," she said. "It's not the end, but a new beginning!"

All choked up, I was handed the Union Jack. I unfurled it, releasing the glorious blue, red, and white flag, which exploded to life in the wind, tossing and struggling like a porpoise in a fishnet. Striding across the snowy hillock, I plunged it into the ground at the head of the line of banners. I then turned to the ocean. Stumbling down the slope of black sand, I crouched and slipped my hand into the silty gray water. I

looked across the Beaufort Sea; there was nothing now between me and the North Pole. In fact, there was now nothing
between me and what others call reality. I had run out of
land. My constant companion, the road, was no more. Sitting
in the muck, I sank my head into my mittens and sobbed.
Then I cried out: "It's over!"

The remainder of that day is a blur. I needed solitude,
but this was going to prove impossible. Arco had made preparations for a celebration at its base camp, where an enormous chocolate sheet cake, complete with their company logo,
served as a centerpiece. The gesture was understandable, but
all wrong. The journey was dead, and not yet even buried,
and at the gathering I was forced into making small talk with
people I didn't know, feeling absolutely terrible, all the while
screaming inside, "Awful! Awful! Let me be alone! Can't you
see that something inside me has just died!"

No, this was not the way to end. I had already had my
personal end, thank God, a little farther back on the road the
previous month (just before setting out south to overturn the
oil veto). There, on the final slope of the last hill of the final
road which I had so loved and now had lost, there, utterly
alone, I had my personal terminus, my own way of saying
good-bye to the road.

The fog had robbed me of my horizon—I could smell but
could not see the ocean. A few miles back an animal, half
she-wolf, half husky, had felt the soul of a wondrous walk and
had upped and followed me; now she was gone. I paced
northward, unseeing, unseen, alone in the total gray vapor.
But a cloud thicker than the surrounding mist had settled on
me. I had survived the consequences of seven years of . . .
what? Humble pilgrimage? Massive ambition?

How dreadfully the fear of *consequences* can stifle so many
valiant potential deeds, I thought, a fear threatening like a
black hole to annihilate the star of one's soul, sucking the
very matter out of an idea until it collapses and disappears,
leaving but a memory, a dream unfulfilled.

Now, at this terminus, I gave thanks to the Universal

Presence for having granted me the inner gravity to resist the fear of consequences.

I gave thanks for the incalculable privilege of life and the freedom to live it as I saw fit, and for the love of a girl named Yoshiko, who had both shared and sacrificed.

I gave thanks for the opportunity to share my fellow human beings' laughter as well as their sadness, their love as well as their misery, and for learning to love this frail, endangered, yet still magnificent planet that had borne me safely and in harmony with my road.

I had found the essential, if flawed, goodness that resides in everyone, everywhere.

I had come to understand the need for hope, which requires oneness with the universe.

Here, at the top of the continent, I felt that the Americas "belonged" to me in a way that they belonged to no one else who has ever lived. Throughout the journey I had never been alone, for I always carried the hearts of the multitudes, from the Latin American peasant to the suburban schoolboy struggling with his homework while looking out the window and wondering, "If . . ." This was their journey, too; the walk belongs to the world's dreamers.

The fog's opaque curtain slowly lifted. Off to the northeast I could now see that the tundra starting at the foot of my last hill streaked almost to the horizon, broken only by the Sagwon Bluffs fifty miles away. With the Yoshikart cradled over my left shoulder, I fell to my knees in the dark red dirt.

This *was* the end. Great sobs shook my frame, and my tears mingled with the frozen dust. No more hills—forever.

Appendixes

Appendix I

Honors

George Meegan holds the following official world records:

The first and only crossing of South and Central America on foot

The first and only traverse of all Latin America on foot

The first and only walk from the Tropic of Capricorn, through the equator, to the Tropic of Cancer

The first and only march between the equator and the Arctic Circle

The first and only connection on foot between the Atlantic, Pacific, Southern, and Arctic oceans

The most degrees of latitude ever covered on foot (125°08′)

The first and only crossing on foot of the entire western hemisphere

The longest unbroken march of all time (19,019 miles)

Meegan is a Fellow of the Royal Geographical Society as well as honorary and sole holder of the Guiness Champion Legs of Great Britain trophy.

Appendix II

North American Hotels and Motels

I owe a very special thanks to the people at the following hotels and motels who shared in this weary traveler's dream. I apologize in advance to those not mentioned—my notetaking and memory are not of the best. The establishment's name is followed by location; when the two are the same, only the name is given.

TEXAS RAMADA—Brownsville, Corpus Christi, Victoria, and Baytown. TWILIGHT—Angleton; JEAN LaFITTE—Galveston; CASTLE—Beaumont; HOLIDAY INN—Orange.

LOUISIANA HOLIDAY INN—Sulphur; IMPERIAL 400—Lake Charles; RAMADA WEST and EAST—Baton Rouge (the manager, Mr. C. Triptow, had to answer the question on TV of "Why do you put up bums?"); a motel on I-12 near Denham Springs; RAMADA—Hammond; DOWNTOWN HOWARD JOHNSON—New Orleans. Mississippi—SCOTTISH—Pascaguola.

ALABAMA A motel near Irvington; RAMADA and HOLIDAY INN—Mobile; HEART OF DOTHAN.

FLORIDA RODEWAY—North of Pensacola on I-10; THRIFT—Milton; SCOTTISH and another—Crestview; ADAMS—DeFuniak Springs.

GEORGIA QUAIL—Blakely; 8 INN—Americus; ESQUIRE—Hazelhurst; SCANDIA—south of JESUP (the owner,

Mrs. Mandelin, did me the honor when the big motels around would not. Her concern extended to breakfast and some dollars despite the crushing personal pressure on her that day of finding out whether the rest of her life would be in a wheelchair—what grace, what courage!); RAMADA—Richmond Hill; TRAVEL LODGE—Savannah.

SOUTH CAROLINA RAMADA—Hardeeville; FOREST—Ridgelands; the motel at Garden Corner; TOOMER'S—Jacksonboro; a motel near Rantowies; BROOKGREEN—Mt. Pleasant.

NORTH CAROLINA ONSLOW—Jacksonville; CRAVEN and RAMADA—New Bern; WASHINGTON; HOWARD JOHNSON's—Roanoke Rapids.

VIRGINIA BEST WESTERN—Petersburg; PATRICK HENRY—Chester (Frank Vogenberger saw me sitting exhausted on my Yoshikart and said, "Do you want a room?" It remains the only time without an introduction that I never had to ask.); AMERICA HOUSE and H. J.—Richmond, RAMADA—Carmel Church.

WASHINGTON, D.C. HOLIDAY INN—Thomas Circle and Rhode Island Avenue

MARYLAND HOLIDAY INN—Baltimore.

PENNSYLVANIA BRUNSWICK—Lancaster; AKRON; WASHINGTON—Allentown.

NEW JERSEY HOWARD JOHNSON'S near Plainfield; RAMADA—Clifton.

NEW YORK STATE Poughkeepsie.

VERMONT TRAVEL LODGE.

QUEBEC NOYAN; S&S—St. Jean sur Richelieu; FLORENCE—Taschereau; CHEZ NOUS LETEÉ—Chomeday.

ONTARIO LA SALLE and MONTEREY—Ottawa; PERTH PLAZA; a motel in Kaladar; MOONLIGHT—Havelock; ROCK HAVEN—Peterborough; DIANA—Orono; MOODY'S—Pickering; EMERALD ISLE—Thornhill; BAYSHORE—Barrie; EDEN ROC—Pointe Au Baril; ELLAS—Britt; Motel at crossroads 69 and 64; ESTAIRE (despite owner Bob Segfried's huge debt); SHERATON—Sudbury; TRADE-

WINDS—Sudbury; WAYSIDE—Massey; McIVER's near Blind River; SOMERSET—Echo Bay; CANADIAN and BELAIR—The 500; TORONTO AIRPORT HOLIDAY INN.

MICHIGAN STRONGS; FOX RIVER—Seney; TERRACE—Munsing; WONDERLAND—Ispeming; MAPLE RIDGE—Michigamme; OTTAWA near Trent Creek; PLAZA—Ewen; NELSON'S—Bergland.

WISCONSIN L. GENE and BEST WESTERN—Ashland; RED—Iron River

MINNESOTA CROSSROADS—routes 21 and 33 cross; STARDUST—Floodwood; WARBA; HOLIDAY INN—Grand Rapids; BAHR's—Deer River; a big motel at Cass Lake; CARRIAGE—Bagley; DAISY'S—Fosston (Alvin Hagen—Daisy—upon discovering my next motel didn't see the dream, paid himself!) WIN.E.MAC—Erskine; COUNTRY CLUB—Crookston

NORTH DAKOTA VERMAR—Larimore; a motel in Lakota; 8—Devil's Lake; BLUE MOON—Leeds; CENTER—Rugby; ECONO, EMPIRE, and SANDMAN—Minot; SAN WAYVE—Kenmare; BOWBELLS HOTEL.

SASKATCHEWAN CANADA FAI—Estevan; MIDALE; ROYAL—Weyburn; YELLOW STRAW (this couple gave me sandwiches with a hidden twenty-dollar note inside!) MILE-STONE: SANDMAN & IMPERIAL 400—Regina; MID-LAND—Mortlach; MORESE; CENTER—Swift Current; LAZY DEE—Gull Lake; TOMPKINS—Piapot; PRAIRIE PRIDE—Trans-Can/Maple Creek Cross

ALBERTA IMPERIAL, WESTLAND, and PAL—The Hat; Y.M.C.A. and VILLAGE PARK—Calgary; TELSTAE—Irvine; PIDGEON MT.; SIDING 29 and Y.M.C.A.—Banff; a Danish-run motel—Lake Louise.

BRITISH COLUMBIA PONDEROSA—Golden; NORTH-LANDER—Rodger's Pass; REVELSTOKE; 3 VALLEY GAP; One in Sicamous; PARK—Enderby; VILLAGE GREEN—Vernon; TEDDY BEAR—Oyama; LODGE—Kelowna; TOTEM—Peachland; TUMBLEWEED—Summerland; OKANOGAN FALLS; PRINCETON; FLAMINGO—Hope; HOTEL VANCOUVER; EXECUTIVE—Victoria; COUN-

TRY—Chilliwack, one in Boston Bar; one in Lytton; SPORTSMAN & 4 CIRCLE—Spence Bridge; one in Cache Creek; one in Clinton; 100 Mile House and Exeter, PARK-LA-LA HACHE SANDMAN—Williams Lake; VALHALLA and GOLD PAN (where lives Robyn Hart, Order of Canada, who at age eight saved the life of a fellow boy in the river—Robyn doesn't swim!)—Quesnel; INN OF THE NORTH, PRINCE GEORGE, and two others—Prince George; SILVER SANDS—Chetwynd; ALASKA HIGHWAY G. DAWSON, CENTRAL TRAVELLERS—Dawson Creek; STAGE COACH—and TRAVEL LODGE—Fort St. John; PINK MT.; BUCKING HORSE; TRUTCH, PROPNET RIVER; BLUE BELL & STAGE COACH—Fort Nelson; STEAMBOAT; SUMMIT; R&J's; TOAD RIVER; MUNCHO LAKE, HIGHLAND GLEN.

YUKON WATSON LAKE; Yukon and North Lake—Teslin; JAKE's CORNER; LAKEVIEW MARINA—Marsh Lake; BEN ELLE—Whitehorse (a suite for eight nights, one of the most helpful in North America); KLUANE & GATEWAY—Haines Junction; PARK LODGE—Kluane; BURWASH LANDING; KLUANE WILDERNESS VILLAGE and WHITE RIVER; IDA'S—Beaver Creek; DOWNTOWN, TRIPLE J. & WHITEHORSE ROOMS—Dawson City.

ALASKA NORTHWAY; TUNDRA—Tok; DOT LAKE; KELLY'S—Delta Junction; GREATLAND—Fairbanks; COLD FOOT; SAG RIVER CAMP—Prudhoe Bay.